Sunset
Wine Country
CALIFORNIA

By the Editors of Sunset Books and Sunset Magazine

Good wine *begins in a vineyard, ends in a glass.*

Lane Publishing Co.
Menlo Park, California

A resource & a reader. . .

For nearly two decades, California's *Wine Country* has been valued by wine-loving explorers and armchair travelers alike as both a working resource and a fireside reader.

In the preface to the original 1968 edition, we observed that California's wine industry seemed poised on the brink of phenomenal growth, and we vowed to keep up with new developments. It hasn't been easy, but we've done it. Three new editions and numerous interim updates later, we're still keeping pace—while the wine industry, to our delight, continues to lead us by about half a step. We're already looking forward to picking up new wineries the next time around.

Research & Text: Rod Smith
(this edition)

Bob Thompson
(previous editions)

Developmental Editor: Helen Sweetland

Coordinating Editor: Deborah Thomas Kramer

Special Consultant: Margaret Smith,
Sunset Magazine

Design: Cynthia Hanson
Lea Damiano Phelps

Maps & Illustrations: Rik Olson

Picker's job *is to be ready at the time when grapes are in perfect balance for wine.*

Cover: Indian summer sunset burnishes Napa Valley vineyards. View is southeast from benchland near Oakville. Photographed by Ed Cooper.

Editor, Sunset Books: Elizabeth L. Hogan

Second printing May 1989

Photographers: Andrée Abecassis: 6 bottom, 13 bottom. **DavidBartruff:** 25 top. **Morton Beebe:** 2. **Ron Botier:** 10 top, 16 top, 23. **Scott Clemens:** 14 bottom, 25 bottom, 26 top, 27 top. **Gene Dekovic:** 17 top. **Faith Echtermeyer:** 20 bottom, 21 top. **Lee Foster:** 30 bottom right. **Peter Fronk:** 28 top, 30 bottom left. **Richard Gillette:** 16 bottom. **Hal Lauritzen:** 18, 20 top, 31 bottom. **Luther Linkhart:** 11 top. **Fred Lyon:** 1, 31 top. **Jack McDowell:** 17 bottom, 19 top right, 26 bottom, 27 bottom, 30 top. **Ted Streshinsky:** 4, 5, 6 top, 7, 8, 9, 10 bottom, 11 bottom, 14 top, 15, 19 top left & bottom, 21 bottom, 22, 24 top, 28 bottom. **Bob Thompson:** 3, 12. **Dick Warton:** 24 bottom. **Darrow M. Watt:** 29. **Ronn Wiegand:** 13 top.

Contents

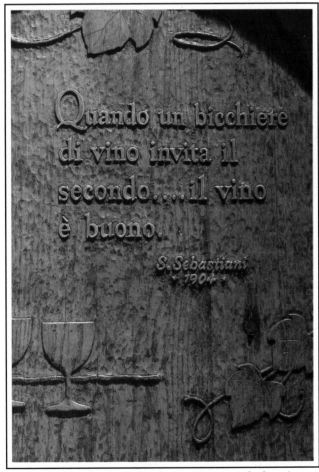

"When one glass *of wine invites the second, the wine is good."—Samuele Sebastiani*

The Vintage Year

By dawn's early light, *harvest pickers in Napa Valley race to take advantage of cool morning air.*

It's growing time *in the gentle hills near Paicines. Vines soak up last warmth of spring evening.*

For most wine buffs, thoughts of the calendar revolve around the vintage. But the annual winegrowing cycle has crucial moments all through the year.

Spring. In an important sense, a vintage begins in March, when a pale fringe of new leaf begins to cover the bare bones of the winter vines. Wildflowers glow in the winter cover crops. After these are disked under at the end of the rains in April, luminous new grape leaves contrast with fresh-turned earth, the canes still short enough to make each row stand out separately.

Summer. Little happens in this season, but what does happen is important. The vines have made their growth; the cellars tend to be as idle as they get. By June, the fruit buds look very much like clusters of miniature grapes. In the middle third of the month, these buds unfold into one of the most insignificant floral displays in all of botany, but this flowering marks a critical stage. To set a full crop, vines must now have 10 to 14 days of dry, moderately warm weather. Rain is a disaster; extreme heat is not much better.

Autumn. The vintage moves to a peak as September moves to a close. A few grape varieties ripen early in

the month and a few straggle into November and even December. But most California grapes ripen in the last three weeks of September and the first three of October. The business of crushing hundreds and thousands of tons of grapes is hectic and messy, but as soon as fermentations get going, matters begin not only to look better, but to smell just fine. A fermentation that smells sweet is sure to yield good wine for drinking regardless of how it looks at the time.

The harvest is enormously photogenic. Pickers, crushers, and presses are all in hurried motion from before sunup until well after nightfall. Demands upon winemakers at this time are incredible.

Winter. After Thanksgiving comes the quiet season. Pruners shear away last year's canes. New wines are racked clear; the fresh wines of the past harvest begin going to bottle for release in early spring. Crowds of summer and fall visitors dwindle, leaving winery hosts more time to answer questions. There is a price: December through February is the rainy season. However, with luck, visitors can catch the tail end of a storm and be treated to showy weather, with just enough warmth to promise spring.

Sheep mow *winter cover crop for independent vineyardist near Plymouth.*

Spring—a season for photographers

Balmy days *bring flowers and tiny new grapes to the Anderson Valley in Mendocino County. Many wineries offer inviting spots, such as this one at Navarro Vineyards, where visitors can bask in the sun while sipping wine at its source.*

Spring's soft light *adds glow to picturesque wineries in Sierra foothills. The barrel aging cellar (above) is at Monteviña. Tiny cellar (right) belongs to StoneRidge.*

Sparse spring rains *mean irrigation is a way of life in counties from Monterey south.*

Change of color *means harvest is about 45 days away.*

Summer—
a time for getting ready

Getting ready, *cellar worker at Lost Hills Winery in Lodi washes down 30,000-gallon redwood tank.*

Workers at Paul Masson *vineyard near Soledad inspect trellised vines in rows spaced extra wide, to allow mechanical harvesting.*

Autumn foliage *lends a fiery light to venerable vineyard in western Sonoma County.*

Autumn—the busy harvest season

Picker hoists *lug-sized container for trek to gondola. To beat the sun, harvesters get into vineyards about dawn, end days around 4 P.M.*

Hectic pace *of vintage can be seen, almost felt. At wineries, grapes go into crushers tons at a time.*

To beat midday heat, *mechanical harvesters pick throughout cool night hours.*

Winter—a period to pause

Toward end of winter, *pruners begin work in Lodi Tokays as storm gives way to clearing skies.*

Winter is the season *to taste newly fermented white wines for the first time. . .*

. . .and to begin assessing the development and potential of last year's reds. This winemaker has drawn samples of Cabernet Sauvignon from several barrels to evaluate their blending potential.

Sampling the Wineries

Diversity *is the byword in California's wine country. Tiny Hanzell (left) is modeled after rustic Burgundian cellars, while wine sleeps in spacious, modern quarters at Fetzer (below). Scale may vary, but winemakers' goals are the same.*

A quarter-century of progress *has filled the Alexander Valley with more vines and more than twice as many wineries as in the 1960s.*

California's wine districts extend as far south as San Diego and as far north as Mendocino. Vines crown ridges looking out to the Pacific Ocean, carpet a score of coastal valleys, sprawl across the great Central Valley, and march up the slopes of the Sierra foothills.

California's first wineries, adjuncts to the Franciscan missions, were spaced a hard day's ride apart, from San Diego to Sonoma. Nearly all of their wine went to sacramental use, but some was also used to welcome neighbors, and some to settle the dusty thirst of summer travelers or drive the chill from winter visitors.

When the Franciscans abandoned their California winemaking in the 1830s, others were there to pick up the reins, not only in the original districts, but in areas farther north, and, above all, farther east in the Central Valley. In essence, winemaking in California had its present geographic shape by the late 1880s. Prohibition dimmed the outline from 1918 to 1934 but did not erase it.

From the viewpoint of visitors, however, there has been a tremendous revolution in the state's wineries since 1968, when the first edition of this book appeared. For example, the original edition described 18 wineries in the Napa Valley and the same number in Sonoma County. The current edition shows 131 for Napa and 109 for Sonoma. Even more striking: Monterey County had but one winery in 1968, and Santa Barbara County had none, while between the two of them, the total vineyard acreage ranged around 30. In this edition, Monterey shows 10 and Santa Barbara 17 wineries open to visitors, while Monterey's grape acreage reaches 31,000 acres and Santa Barbara's exceeds 9,000.

In the search for space, the Mother Lode area, the Sacramento Valley, Mendocino, Lake, and Ventura counties, and Temecula and Escondido areas add to the total winery count. Future expansion will be limited only by the world's thirst for fine wines.

The following pages are a guide to the rewarding diversity of the state's wineries, some large and many small. Napa and Sonoma have the greatest numbers of cellars of all sorts, but other districts challenge them in all respects, including colorful history.

Wine *is made ofttimes in grand buildings such as The Christian Brothers Greystone Cellars, built in 1888.*

An architectural array

Distinctive hop kilns, *the North Coast's nineteenth century architectural legacy, reveal an earlier preoccupation with another type of fermentation. Hop Kiln Winery's magnificent triple-crowned specimen is a California historical landmark.*

Redwood siding *and shake roof of Lambert Bridge blend easily into oak-studded hill in background.*

Typical *of several area wineries, Geyser Peak complex combines old and new. Original 1880 building now contains aging cellar.*

Some old favorites

Beringer's Rhine House, *1876 replica of the founders'*
Rhenish home, serves as tasting room and hospitality center.
Winery tour includes a peek into century-old aging tunnels.

A remnant *of the past, Inglenook's original cellar is particularly appealing in fall when draped by flaming ivy.*

Buena Vista's *historical plaque credits Agoston Haraszthy as being the father of California's modern wine history. Restored winery recaptures tranquility of another era.*

BUENA VISTA WINERY
AND VINEYARDS

BIRTHPLACE OF CALIFORNIA WINE, FOUNDED IN 1857 BY
COLONEL AGOSTON HARASZTHY FATHER OF THE STATE'S
WINE INDUSTRY. LIMESTONE TUNNELS WERE DUG INTO
THE HILLSIDE AND VINEYARDS WERE ALSO ESTABLISHED.
HARASZTHY TOURED EUROPE IN 1861 TO GATHER THE
CUTTINGS THAT DEVELOPED CALIFORNIA'S WINE IN-
DUSTRY.

CALIFORNIA REGISTERED HISTORICAL LANDMARK NO 392

PLAQUE PLACED BY THE STATE DEPARTMENT OF PARKS
AND RECREATION IN COOPERATION WITH BUENA VISTA
WINERY AND VINEYARDS, DECEMBER 1, 1960.

Classic *stone building at Charles Krug represents traditional old Napa winery estate.*

From vineyards below, *Sterling's hilltop architecture resembles rambling Grecian church. Tasting room offers incomparable valley views.*

. . . and some bold new statements

Combining traditions, *the oak barrels and elegant lighting in this aging cellar are French, but the redwood paneling is purely Californian.*

Dramatic design *by architect Michael Graves, combining classical and postmodern elements, makes Clos Pegase one of Napa Valley's most visually distinctive new wineries.*

Robert Mondavi's *architecture may hark back to Franciscan mission days, but inside it's one of the more modernly equipped cellars in the state.*

Touring & Tasting

Currier & Ives *could not have printed a better Central Coast vineyard scene than this one near Paicines. Following California ranch tradition, vines share the range peacefully with cattle.*

Most of state's *sizable cellars offer formal visitor facilities with scheduled tours and tasting rooms. Visits to smaller wineries are informal, may require appointments.*

Touring the wine country is not a new idea. Visitors have been crossing thresholds into California wine cellars for more than two centuries, 1969 having been the official bicentennial. But if the paths are well worn, they are more inviting than ever because of the presence of many new wineries and more complicated because of the resulting diversity.

The old-line cellars, the ones that were around for the first edition of this book in 1968, were, in a great majority of cases, of a size to run formal visitor facilities, including tour guides and special tasting rooms. Some of the new names have followed their model, but a great many newcomers are too small to have either guides or tasting rooms; so, they welcome visitors by appointment as personal guests, and offer tasting only when there is a bit of wine to spare.

One logical visitor approach to this situation is to use the cellars with developed tour programs as sources of primary information, saving the appointment-only places for a time when an hour's talk about the fine points of winemaking does not require a taste to be worthwhile. The other logical approach is to choose the sources of wines that are personal favorites, no matter what size or shape the cellar.

Whatever approach is taken to the state's wineries, they are rewarding for their diversity. Over the course of two centuries, California has acquired winemakers from every corner of the globe. They have contributed differing notions about how grapes should be grown, how wine should be made, how buildings should be designed, and even what kind of dog should stand sentry.

Someone bent on record-setting could visit as many as 20 cellars a day in some districts . . . but should not. Such a visitor would miss all the details, and details are what wine is all about. Experienced travelers in the vineyards limit themselves to three, or at most four, stops a day.

To many visitors, the words "touring and tasting" are synonymous. We offer some tips on tasting for serious bibbers in our special feature on page 142. Professional tasters judge wines by sight (wine's appearance), smell (aroma and bouquet), and taste. But in the end, judgment is a purely personal exercise.

Any visit to California's wine country can be rewarding. The seasons may govern timing of a trip: spring is the most picturesque, autumn the most dramatic. In winter, vintners may have more time to explain the winemaking process. Though summer can be hot in many wine districts, this is the season when some cellars offer accompanying entertainment (see page 97).

Bed-and-breakfast inns abound in the Napa and Sonoma valleys, the Mother Lode regions, and along the South Coast. Hotels and motels throughout the state make it possible to extend wine forays.

Many veteran wine country visitors assemble picnic lunches using local cheese shops, delis, and bakeries. Many wineries offer picnic sites; a few have dining rooms. Virtually all have wine for sale.

Different lessons *come at different places. At Estrella River Winery, visitors are guided through big fermenting room full of stainless steel tanks.*

A peek behind the scenes

Tours *at Beaulieu Vineyards offer close look at its famed Cabernet Sauvignon and other reds.*

Guides at Beaulieu *need a sense of direction to keep up with expansions, but visitors get good look at winemaking from crushing station to bottling line.*

Riddling *is the traditional method of moving yeast sediment down toward bottle necks for removal; each bottle of new sparkling wine is given a quarter-turn daily. Riddler at Domaine Chandon wears safety glasses while handling highly pressurized bottles.*

It takes concentration *and an experienced palate to judge the progress of a wine straight from the barrel. Winemaker draws sample with the traditional glass tube called a "thief."*

Sipping and swirling —the final test

Tasters *take different poses at different places. At Mirassou, the job is done standing at a bar. In any case, the nose is a taster's most important asset.*

Casual outdoor tasting *is a convival and educational way to end informal group tours at Sequoia Grove.*

Informal atmosphere *reigns at Thomas Kruse and other small cellars where people often gather around an upturned barrel.*

From picnics to performances

Wineries *may offer more than a tour and a taste. Many cellars, such as Rodney Strong Vineyards (below), provide picnic tables; others present concerts. Paul Masson's old mountain winery (right) is the setting for summer series.*

Tree-shaded picnic *between vines and winery is a relaxing interlude for Livermore visitors.*

Sterling's showmanship *starts at the parking lot. Visitors pay moderate fee to be whisked up to hilltop winery on aerial tramway.*

Fun among the vines

Festivals *crowd winery calendars. In May, Healdsburg's town plaza (left) draws tasters. At Soledad (below), footpower crushes a bit of ceremonial wine each October.*

A few wineries *maintain restaurants for luncheon or dinner; this one is at Chateau Souverain near Geyserville.*

For bird's-eye view *of Napa Valley vineyards, take a ride in a bright balloon.*

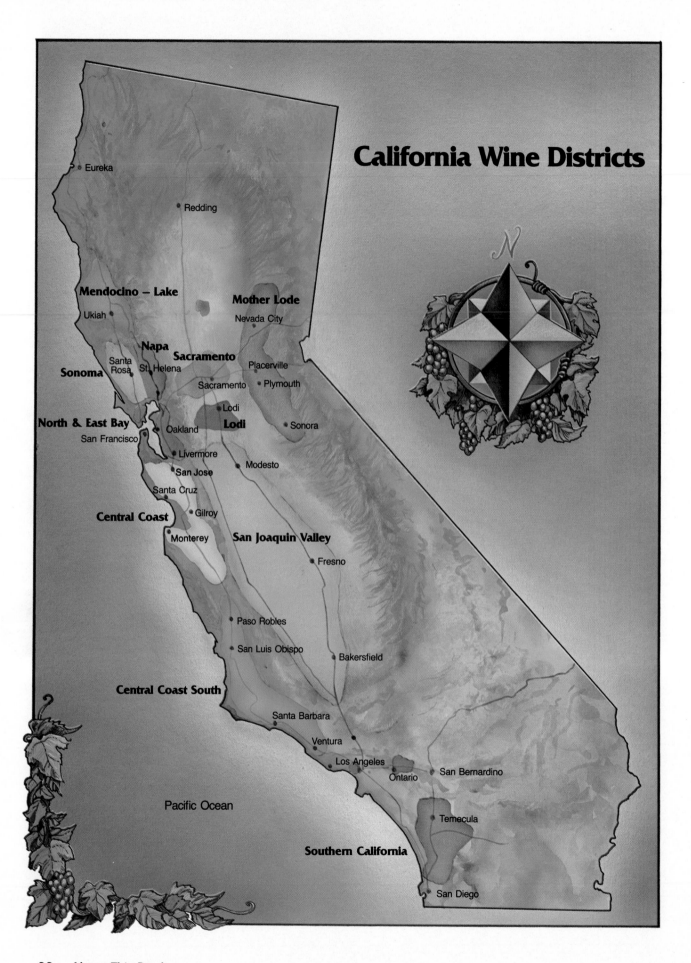

California Wine Districts

Eureka

Redding

Mendocino – Lake

Ukiah

Mother Lode

Nevada City

Napa

Santa Rosa

St. Helena

Sacramento

Placerville

Sonoma

Sacramento

Plymouth

Lodi

Lodi

Sonora

North & East Bay

Oakland

San Francisco

Livermore

San Jose

Modesto

Santa Cruz

Gilroy

Central Coast

Monterey

San Joaquin Valley

Fresno

Paso Robles

San Luis Obispo

Bakersfield

Central Coast South

Santa Barbara

Ventura

Los Angeles

San Bernardino

Ontario

Pacific Ocean

Temecula

Southern California

San Diego

About This Book

The following explanations will help make *California's Wine Country* a more useful and reliable guide.

The basic organization alphabetically lists wineries within a small region that can be covered easily by car on a day (or longer) of touring. Only the Napa Valley among the chapters takes all of its wineries in one chunk. Other, larger counties or districts have subdivisions focused, usually, on a single town. The purpose is to group all the wineries within reach, allowing a potential tourist the fullest range of choice in planning a visit.

The system is best suited to newcomers to the pleasures of winery touring. Veteran hands often will wish to skip from district to district, singling out cellars of particular interest. Newcomers may wish to take similar tacks. There is a complete alphabetical listing of wineries in the index to assist in such planning.

Highway or Byway

Anyone slightly familiar with California geography knows that Napa, Sonoma, and Mendocino form a tight circle crowded with well over one-half of the state's wineries. As the map on the facing page hints, it is possible to visit selected places in any two of the three counties in a single day's outing from San Francisco. But even many well-informed Californians are less aware that San Luis Obispo and Santa Barbara counties now have enough cellars in a small radius to keep a studious visitor busy for almost a week, and are within weekend range of either Los Angeles or San Francisco.

Some districts lend themselves to byway visits. The Mother Lode, for example, is an easy detour between San Francisco and Lake Tahoe, or San Francisco and Yosemite National Park. In Southern California, Temecula is an equally easy detour for travelers between Los Angeles and San Diego.

Using the Maps

Within each chapter or subchapter is a useful locator map. Each map has accompanying tour information for wineries located within this area. Although the maps are reasonably accurate and complete, their scale often makes winery locations a bit uncertain. Road directions in the accompanying winery listings supplement the maps. It is also wise to use detailed road maps, especially for urban areas, such as the Santa Clara Valley in the Central Coast and Cucamonga in Southern California, where maps in the book show only a few key roads.

In addition to road directions, the tour information lists the hours and days each winery is open to visitors. It must be recognized that these specifics may change without notice, even at large wineries. At small family-owned cellars where the proprietor is also the winemaker and tour guide, hours may change from day to day because of business pressures.

Also in the tour information blocks are abbreviated notations on the winery's tour facilities. These should be translated as follows:

IT (informal tour) almost always means that visitors are free to poke about a small winery without a guide, usually with some advice from the host about any areas that might be off limits. This notation also is used in the cases of a few larger wineries that have developed sign-guided tours for visitors.

GT (guided tour), in the case of larger wineries, almost always means trained guides shepherd groups of visitors through a set route as often as enough people gather. These tours can be particularly useful for getting a handle on the basics of winemaking. Most of the time, such tours cover every aspect of wine production from the arrival of grapes for crushing through to the bottling line.

With the rapid increase in numbers of small wineries, many guided tours now are offered by the proprietor or winemaker. Such cellars offer tours only by appointment for the obvious reason: the winemaker has another, more timely job to do. These tours are of greatest value to connoisseurs and would-be connoisseurs trying to learn the fine points of production.

Ta (tasting) means the winery will provide samples of one or more of its wines at no charge. In the early days of this book, this was almost automatic; now, with the wineries often swamped with visitors and with many tiny cellars in operation, tasting is no sure bet. At many large wineries, visitors are offered only two or three set wines each day. At many small ones, they may be offered no tasting at all, either for lack of wine or because of governmental restrictions on a winery's use permit. The absence of a "Ta" notation does not mean there is no chance at all for tasting, but it does mean the proprietor at least has discretionary powers. If the notation is not there, it is wisest not to anticipate a sampling of the winery's wares.

At a minimum, wineries listed as welcoming visitors offer wines at retail prices. Usually, there is no minimum purchase; however, in a few instances (usually because of use-permit restrictions), wineries sell in case-lot minimums. Most of these details are noted in the main description. Fledgling wineries, and those which discourage visits or play host infrequently due to size and staff limitations or remote location, are noted separately in sections headed "More Wineries."

In & Around Sonoma

Rich in California history as well as in vines

Vallejo Home

Few districts have more of the character of old California than Sonoma County. The town of Sonoma sprang up around the last of the Franciscan missions in the 1830s. Already the Russians had founded and abandoned their fur-trading outpost on the coast at Fort Ross. After Sonoma's mission days, the town served as headquarters for Mariano Vallejo during his term as governor of Mexico. The Bear Flag Revolt, a triggering incident in the union of California with the United States, unfolded on Vallejo's doorstep.

Later, horticulturist Luther Burbank did much of his work in and around Santa Rosa, proving incidentally that this region is a veritable garden spot. One of Burbank's friends, Jack London, labored at his home in the hills above Glen Ellen to prove that even paradise can be customized.

Grapes and wine have been companions through all these historic episodes, a part of Sonoma from the beginning. The mission had vineyards in the 1830s. Vallejo took them over along with the rest of the property and ran a lively competition with Agoston Haraszthy to see who was the better winemaker. In the judgment of history, Vallejo's fame is mostly political, whereas Har-

aszthy is remembered for his long reign as the father of California winemaking.

Today the historical heart of Sonoma winemaking in the Sonoma Valley is but a small statistical part of the county's vineyards. By far the greatest acreage of vines and by far the greatest number of wineries are dotted along either side of U.S. Highway 101 from Santa Rosa north to the Sonoma-Mendocino county line near Cloverdale. Healdsburg is the hub of this larger district, nearly all of it within the watershed of the Russian River. All told, the county had a shade more than 32,000 acres of vines in 1987 and over 100 wineries.

Sonoma Valley

In a world often indifferent to yesterday, the town of Sonoma clings to much of its past. The town plaza was the heart of things after Fra Jose Altimira founded the mission in 1832. It remained the heart when the secular government of Mariano Vallejo supplanted the mission, and again when the Bear Flaggers did away with the Mexican regime. It remains the heart of town.

Time has changed the details of the plaza but not its essence. A good many of the adjacent buildings had weathered before California gained statehood in 1850. Most of the rest have had a chance to weather since. The square itself remained a patch of bare ground only until 1910, when the sizable city hall was built in its center using a buff-colored local sandstone. Sheltering trees have grown up since to shade the benches on which townsfolk and visitors take their ease in summer's heat.

West and north, a string of resort towns reaches back to the turn of the century, surviving in spite of losing their original purpose. The hot springs that made the district a favored spa for fog-chilled San Franciscans of the Gay Nineties cooled after the earthquake of 1906, never to heat up again.

Encircling the town of Sonoma and stretching away to the north beyond the resorts, vineyards and wineries were and are integral parts of the Sonoma Valley.

The Wineries

Winegrowing north of San Francisco had its beginnings at Sonoma. Today the wineries, like the rest of the valley, reflect old times and new in their architecture— sometimes even in their equipment.

In the spring of 1987, the valley had more than a score of cellars. One is among the oldest in the state. More than half of them have plenty of time to plan tenth-vintage celebrations.

Adler Fels twice earns its name, which translates from German as Eagle Rock. Visitors drive up a steep hill to get to the winery gate, then up a steeper one to the aerie-high winery and its commanding views down the valley and up to landmark Eagle Rock, with its resident herd of mountain goats.

Having given a German name to a California property, proprietors David Coleman, Ayn Ryan, and Lila Burford built a winery that mixes lines and materials from both places to appealing effect. The gambrel rooflines seem pure Californian. A tower nestled into an angle of the building has a Rhenish air. Redwood siding is local, but the patterns of its application borrow from Alpine half-timbering.

Within, the cellar is the typical California blend of new and old, from float-top tanks to European oak barrels. It was first used for the harvest of 1980. Older reds were made elsewhere. The list of wines produced in it includes Chardonnay, Gewürztraminer, late-harvest Riesling, and Cabernet Sauvignon. There also is a tiny lot of sparkling wine sold only on the premises.

Buena Vista Winery has endured various fortunes since Agoston Haraszthy founded the firm in 1857.

Haraszthy, the now-a-colonel, now-a-count Hungarian who is widely credited as being the father of the modern California wine industry, set a tone. He brought the first really sizable importations of European grape varieties to northern California, but, because he had unacceptable political affiliations, he never received payment from the state for his effort in its behalf. The hapless Haraszthy disappeared in Nicaragua just a few

years before phylloxera began to play havoc with his vines.

Haraszthy's sons, Attila and Arpad, and other partners carried on after his departure until the 1906 earthquake severely damaged the winery buildings. Finally, the sons went looking for greener fields, and Buena Vista closed its doors. The old stone buildings were abandoned until 1943 when newspaperman Frank Bartholomew bought the property and started reconditioning the place.

The long of memory might have crossed their fingers when they saw the first new vines in very crooked rows. (They were planted by World War II submarine crews on rehabilitation leaves, presumably without their navigation officers.) It was not a bad omen, however. Buena Vista has prospered since its reopening.

Bartholomew retained control until 1968, when he sold the winery to Young's Market Company of Los Angeles. Young's added a large new vineyard and a fermenting winery on a back road in the Carneros district before selling in turn to a German firm, A. Racke, in 1979. Throughout these changes, the old property has retained much of the appearance and all of the tranquility of 1860.

The larger, uphill building, built as the main cellar, now houses wines aging in a variety of cooperage. The stone barn and three tunnels carved into the hill behind it have a self-guiding tour with photographs and other memorabilia to illuminate past as well as present. Tasting takes place in the smaller, downhill building, originally the press house.

Outside are two picnic grounds, one directly in front of the main cellar, the other between it and the press house. In summer, this is the place to picnic on French bread from the bakery on the town plaza, fresh fruit from the market next door, cheeses from the factory diagonally across from them, and local wine.

Buena Vista wines include the full varietal range, plus sherries and proprietary variations called Spiceling, Steelhead Run, and Pinot Jolie.

Carmenet Vineyard is as much like a Bordeaux cellar as it's possible to be among the sunbaked volcanic crags of the Mayacamas Mountains—that is, not a whole lot on the surface. Step into the cool subterranean aging caves, however, and California recedes to a distant rumor. The French oak barrels all contain Bordeaux-style blends of the grape varieties that the Bordelaise loosely designate "carmenet": Cabernet Sauvignon, Merlot, Cabernet Franc, Sauvignon Blanc, and Semillon. These are appropriately combined into Carmenet Red and Carmenet White.

Just outside the wooden cave doors, set into the white tufa hillside like a hobbit's front gate, is an engineering marvel called a pneumatic foot, which rides a circular rail above a ring of steel fermenting tanks. During red wine fermentation the foot is positioned over each vat in turn, to "punch down" the cap of grapeskins for increased color extraction and flavor concentration.

The vineyards make a lovely sight in that harsh environment. Some of the steep terraces go back to the nineteenth century, but most of the contours were re-engineered by Chalone, Inc., when they took over the

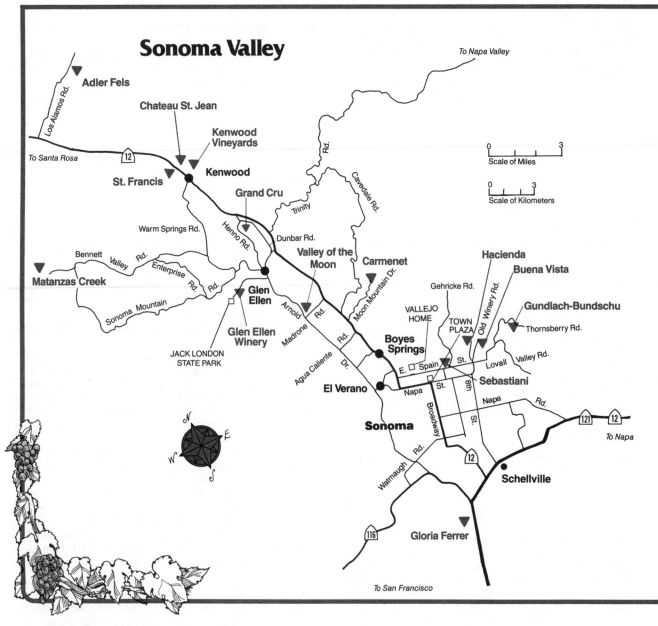

Sonoma Valley

property to found Carmenet in 1981. Visits have been extremely limited, but visitor facilities were scheduled to be built in 1987.

Chateau St. Jean set out to look as romantically French as any property could, given the fact that Sugarloaf Ridge, which looms up just behind the winery, is a quintessential California coastal hill.

A mock medieval tower is the architectural signature of the building. More than mere ornament, its secondary purpose is to provide a central vantage from which visitors on the self-guided tour can look down to see the entire winemaking process. At Chateau St. Jean this means state-of-the-art equipment designed to handle many small lots of wine. This winery has dedicated itself particularly to offering many wines of a single type, each from a specified vineyard; hence the great numbers of small fermentors rather than a fewer number of larger ones. The principal types are Chardonnay, Sauvignon Blanc, Gewürztraminer, and Riesling. The

latter two vary not only by vineyard, but also in degree of sweetness, late-harvest styles being another specialty (see the special feature,"*Botrytis cinerea*, the noble mold," on page 113).

In 1979 an ambitious *méthode champenoise* program began in converted apple-shipping warehouses at Graton, in western Sonoma County. The wines are Brut and Blanc de Blanc; tours are by appointment.

Even before the new winery was built, the property had a romantic air about it. An old country estate house now used for the offices and tasting room dates back to the Roaring Twenties. From all accounts it helped the era earn its name.

Chateau St. Jean dates from 1974. New construction was completed in 1981. Not incidentally, the "Jean" is pronounced as in blue jeans rather than in the French fashion. The cellar was named to honor one of the original founders. In 1983 it was purchased by its present owners, Suntory International, Ltd.

Adler Fels. From Kenwood, N on State 12 to Los Alamos Rd., then E 2.2 mi. to winery drive, Corrick Ln. (5325 Corrick Ln., Santa Rosa, CA 95405) Tel (707) 539-3123. By appt. only.

Buena Vista Winery. From SE corner of Sonoma Plaza, E on E. Napa St. across RR tracks at 8th St., E. to Old Winery Rd., then NE to winery (P.O. Box 182, Sonoma, CA 95476) Tel (707) 938-8504. Picnic. Daily 10-5. IT/Ta.

Carmenet Vineyard. From Sonoma, 3 mi. N on State 12, E 3.5 mi. on Moon Mountain Dr. to winery gate (1700 Moon Mountain Dr., Sonoma, CA 95476) Tel (707) 996-5870. By appt. only.

Chateau St. Jean. From State 12 at N side of Kenwood, E on private winery drive, Goff Rd. (P.O. Box 293, Kenwood, CA 95452) Tel (707) 833-4134. Daily 10-4:30. IT/Ta. GT by appt.

Gloria Ferrer Champagne Caves. From Sonoma, S .8 mi. on State 12 to State 12/121 intersection, SW 1.4 mi. on State 121 to winery at 23555 (P.O. Box 1427, Sonoma, CA 95476) Tel (707) 996-7256. Daily 10:30-5:30. Ta. fee. GT daily 10:30-4:30.

Glen Ellen Winery. From Glen Ellen, W .8 mi. on London Ranch Rd. to winery gate (1883 London Ranch Rd., Glen Ellen, CA 95442) Tel (707) 996-1066. Picnic. Daily 10-4. IT/Ta.

Grand Cru Vineyards. From State 12 at Glen Ellen, W 100 ft. on Arnold Dr. to Dunbar Rd., N .3 to Henno Rd., then double back on Vintage Ln. to winery (P.O. Box 789, Glen Ellen, CA 95442) Tel (707) 996-8100. Picnic. Daily 10-5. IT/Ta.

Gundlach-Bundschu. From SE corner of Sonoma Plaza, E on E. Napa St. to Old Winery Rd., N 4 blocks to Lovall Valley Rd., E 5 blocks to Thornsberry Rd., then continue E .8 mi. to winery at 3775 (P.O. Box 1, Vineburg, CA 95487) Tel (707) 938-5277. Sa-Su 12-4:30 or by appt. IT/Ta.

Hacienda Wine Cellars. From SE corner of Sonoma Plaza, E on E. Napa St., N on 7th St. E./Castle Rd. to winery gate (P.O. Box 416, Sonoma, CA 95476) Tel (707) 938-3220. Picnic. Daily 9-5. Ta. GT by appt.

Kenwood Vineyards. On E side of State 12 opposite Warm Springs Rd. in Kenwood (P.O. Box 447, Kenwood, CA 95452) Tel (707) 833-5891. Picnic; groups must reserve. Daily 10-4:30. Ta. GT by appt.

Matanzas Creek Winery. From State 12, 6.9 mi. N of Sonoma, W .8 on Arnold Dr., NW 2.3 mi. on Warm Springs Rd., W 5.1 mi. on Bennett Valley Rd. to winery on E side (6097 Bennett Valley Rd., Santa Rosa, CA 95404) Tel (707) 542-8242. By appt. only.

St. Francis Winery. On W side of State 12 at N edge of Kenwood (8450 Sonoma Hwy., Kenwood, CA 95452) Tel (707) 833-4666. Daily 10-4:30. IT/Ta.

Sebastiani Vineyards. From NE corner of Sonoma Plaza, E 3 blocks on E. Spain St. to 4th St. E. (389 Fourth St. East, Sonoma, CA 95476) Tel (707) 938-5532. Daily 10-5. GT/Ta.

Valley of the Moon Winery. From Sonoma, N 4 mi. on State 12 to Madrone Rd., W .75 mi. to winery (777 Madrone Rd., Glen Ellen, CA 95442) Tel (707) 996-6941. Daily except Th. 10-5. Ta.

Wineries Not on Map— Restricted or No Visitor Facilities

Arrowood Winery. (P.O. Box 987, Glen Ellen, CA 95442) Tel (707) 938-5170. No visitors.

B. R. Cohn Winery. (P.O. Box 878, Sonoma, CA 95476) Tel (707) 938-1212. By appt. only.

H. Coturri & Sons. (P.O. Box 396, Glen Ellen, CA 95442) Tel (707) 996-6247. By appt. only.

Hanzell Vineyards. (18596 Lomita Ave., Sonoma, CA 95476) Tel (707) 996-3860. By appt. only.

Haywood Winery. (18701 Gehricke Rd., Sonoma, CA 95476) Tel (707) 996-4298. By appt. only.

Kistler Vineyards. (997 Madrone Rd., Glen Ellen, CA 95442) Tel (707) 833-4662. By appt. only.

Las Montañas. (4400 Cavedale Rd., Glen Ellen, CA 95442) Tel (707) 996-2448. By appt. only.

Laurel Glen Vineyard. (P.O. Box 548, Glen Ellen, CA 95442) Tel (707) 526-3914. No visitors.

Ravenswood. (21415 Broadway, Sonoma, CA 95476) Tel (707) 938-1960. By appt. only.

Richardson Vineyards. (2711 Knob Hill Rd., Sonoma, CA 95476) Tel (707) 938-2610. By appt. only.

Sky Vineyards. (1500 Lokoya Rd., Napa, CA 94558) No visitors.

Sonoma Hills Winery. (4850 Peracca Rd., Santa Rosa, CA 95404) Tel (707) 523-3415. By appt. only.

Key: GT (guided tour); IT (informal tour); Ta (tasting).

H. Coturri & Sons may well be the most innovative winery in California. What do they do that's so new and unusual? Absolutely nothing.

That is, the Coturri brothers begin with immaculate grapes and let nature proceed, which is considered heretical in some circles and heroic in others. Philip (the grower) provides healthy fruit, with wild yeast strains that are perfectly suited to fermenting those particular grapes, then Tony (the winemaker) treats the wine as wines have been treated for ages, stoutly refusing to add sulfites or adjusting agents, and to filter the wine following its natural fermentation—it's gently racked from barrel to barrel, the old way.

They've been doing that since 1965. The current roster is Cabernet Sauvignon and Zinfandel, with smaller lots of other varietals as desirable fruit becomes available. In 1987 the winery had suspended all visits to their remote corner of Sonoma Mountain, but plans were afoot to accommodate visitors.

Gloria Ferrer Champagne Caves is the second American venture by a Spanish family whose roots in the wine trade go seven centuries deep. The first, a 1930s New Jersey wine import firm, was doomed by the Spanish Revolution. More recently, the success of their Freixenet sparkling wines in this country encouraged the Ferrer family to build this splendid *méthode champenoise* production facility, complete with subterranean aging vaults, in the golden hills of Sonoma County's famous Carneros region. The wife of Freixenet's president lent her name to the winery, completed in 1986.

The Carneros is a gentle, often misty terrain where valley-warmed air meets cool, moist air from the northern arm of San Francisco Bay. Chardonnay and Pinot Noir (the traditional Champagne constituents) are considered to achieve something akin to perfection here, especially at that stage of scant ripeness required for the sparkling wine alchemy. Grapes are being purchased locally, pending maturation of the estate vines.

The winery itself gives an impression of having been airlifted intact from the hills west of Barcelona. Its jumble of red-tiled roofs, white walls, and radial arches suggests a little Catalonian village crowning the long slope above Highway 12.

The winery tour amounts to a crash course in the art of effervescence. The highlight, naturally, is a descent to the bubbly underworld of three interconnected tunnels where, in myriad bottles racked beneath 16-foot arched ceilings, the pressurized wines coalesce toward something finer.

Gloria Ferrer's version of stardust may be tasted after the tour in the elegant *Sala de Catadores* (Hall of the Tasters), accompanied by tapas and, weather permitting, a glimpse of distant San Francisco.

Glen Ellen Winery restores to life one of the Sonoma Valley's historic wine estates, one less touched by time than almost any other.

A fine old house is at the shady center of a grove of trees growing in the midst of a rolling vineyard not far from Jack London's old ranch. Built by the pioneer Wegner family in the 1860s, it is being restored by the Bruno Benziger family, new owners since 1980. The Benzigers have kept grounds in which a horse and buggy would not look out of place, adding only a curiously appropriate flock of peacocks.

Visitors taking the self-guided tour will find the white-painted winery just behind the house and downhill from it. It is not the original, which was beyond redemption, but as near the spit and image of it as modern winemaking equipment would allow. In the form of a classic California barn, complete with twin cupolas, it hides stainless steel fermentors and other processing gear outside and inside its rear wall, leaving the front elevation peaceful and timeless. The Benzigers, father and sons, built it themselves, finishing just in time for the vintage of 1981.

Their roster of wines includes Chardonnay, Sauvignon Blanc, Cabernet Sauvignon, and a pair of proprietary generics.

Grand Cru Vineyards exemplifies several aspects of wine in contemporary California.

It is one of several wineries located in old cellars restored to use after decades of vacancy. It is one of several organizations in which scientists have been involved, bringing with them extremely sophisticated notions about equipment and techniques. And it is a company that started almost as a weekend hobby, but quickly grew into a good-sized, full-time business.

Specifically, Grand Cru is located alongside and in the 1886 stone and concrete fermenting tanks of the Lemoine Winery. In 1970, the new proprietors erected a battery of stainless steel fermentors right next to the concrete originals, an instructive sight and, no doubt, a daily source of relief to the cellar workers who do not have to pitch pomace over the tops of the new models as their forebears did when concrete was all the style.

The mechanically minded will want to have a close look at Grand Cru. To give just one example, the crusher and Bucher tank press look conventional enough but are powered by variable-speed hydraulic systems rather than by standard direct-drive electric motors. Other touches visible on the self-guided tour are just as refined.

In addition to its tasting room, the winery has an oak-shaded picnic lawn with views of the fermenting area in one direction and of the vineyard in the opposite one. Sonoma Mountain looms benignly over the scene.

Grand Cru has been owned since 1981 by Walt and Bettina Dreyer. Wines produced here include Chenin Blanc, Sauvignon Blanc, Gewürztraminer, Cabernet Sauvignon, and Zinfandel. A particular specialty is a sweet "Induced Botrytis" Gewürztraminer (see the special feature, "*Botrytis cinerea,* the noble mold," on page 113).

Gundlach-Bundschu was a famous winery in Sonoma's early history. In 1976 its traditional label, still owned by the founding family, reentered the ranks of the modern-day Sonoma wine community.

Jacob Gundlach and son-in-law Charles Bundschu had a worldwide market for their wines from the 1850s until the 1906 earthquake (and ensuing fire in their San Francisco warehouse), followed by Prohibition, caused them to close their doors. Though the Bundschus went out of the wine business, they retained ownership of their vineyards and orchards in Sonoma.

In 1970 the fifth generation in the form of Jim Bundschu began rebuilding on one of three original winery sites. In the summer of 1976 he formally reopened the cellars to the public.

Behind an early-day quarried stone facade is a new building overflowing with equipment and cooperage.

A tasting room just inside the front door is framed by tall stacks of European oak barrels. Behind the barrels come a bottling line, stainless steel fermentors, the press, a centrifuge, and other processing gear. The rest of the barrel collection is at another of the old family winery sites nearby.

Many of the grapes used for Gundlach-Bundschu wines come from the original vineyards, first planted in 1858. Wines from the old vineyard and two newer plots nearby include Riesling, Gewürztraminer, and Chardonnay in whites. Cabernet Sauvignon, Merlot, and Zinfandel are primary reds. A particular specialty is a white called Kleinburger, from a little-known German grape variety.

Hacienda Wine Cellars looks more at home than any of its peers in Sonoma's old Spanish colonial setting because it is housed in a textbook example of Spanish colonial architecture.

The winery dates from 1973, when it was founded by the same Frank Bartholomew who restored Buena Vista to life in the 1940s. Though Bartholomew had a hand in the winery until 1985, the principal owner since 1976 has been veteran grape grower A. Crawford Cooley. The building goes back farther, to 1926, having formerly been the community hospital.

Tours of the well-appointed cellars are by appointment only, but the richly furnished tasting room is open daily. At one end of it, tasters can look through an iron grill to see the barrel-aging cellar. The crusher, press, and fermentors are outdoors at the rear. Oak tanks and the bottling department are in an added wing next to the fermenting tanks.

Hacienda maintains a spacious picnic lawn next to the winery. Some of its tables are in plain sun, some nestle in the shade of oaks, but all look downslope to the town of Sonoma and the valley floor.

The winery produces Chardonnay, Gewürztraminer, Sauvignon Blanc, Dry Chenin Blanc, Cabernet Sauvignon, Pinot Noir, Zinfandel, and a small quantity of vintage Port.

Hanzell Vineyards is the property of Barbara de Brye of London. With Bob Sessions as winemaker, Hanzell continues the revolution launched in the late 1950s by founder James D. Zellerbach.

The notion was and is that California can equal some of the great wines of Burgundy. The architectural statement of intent is a facade copied after that part of the Clos de Vougeot that comes into view at the end of the entrance tunnel. Inside the winery the effort becomes more concrete with a cellar full of barrels made from oak harvested in the forest of Limoges and coopered in Beaune.

But Hanzell is not mere copying. The production is so carefully planned that the crusher can handle exactly as many grapes per hour as required to fill one stainless steel fermentor with must, and so on through the whole sequence of winemaking.

A visit is both a learning experience about thoughtful winery design and a sort of pilgrimage to a place where California wine found a new impetus toward a distinctive style. Hanzell is so small that appointments are required and tasting is not possible. Students of vinous California make the journey gladly to see the place and to buy Chardonnay, Pinot Noir, or Cabernet Sauvignon when some of the small annual supply is available.

Haywood Winery occupies a bunkerish concrete cellar cut into a rocky hillside above Sonoma town.

On two levels, it has fermentors, press, and other working gear just inside the front door. A few steps up is a dim, cool parallel gallery given over to French oak barrels. The building had a short life as the winery of Views Land Company before it was purchased by Peter Haywood and rechristened with his family name. Haywood's first vintage was 1980.

Although a surprising amount of wine is made within a tight confines, the cellar is a one-man show; so, visits must be by appointment only. All from Haywood's vineyards higher up the hill behind the winery, the wines are Chardonnay, Riesling, Sauvignon Blanc, Gewürztraminer, Cabernet Sauvignon and Zinfandel. Spaghetti Red is a proprietary blend.

Kenwood Vineyards, just off State Highway 12 on the south side of Kenwood, has grown from a typical country winery into a modern, sophisticated one without losing the earthy charms of old-fashioned wood barns that are its main cellars.

The place was built in 1906 by the Pagani Brothers, John and Julius, who were more than typically thoughtful. One example: the big stemmer-crusher rests in a notch cut into a bank between two roads. The proprietors can dump grapes into the crusher without lifting them very high and let stems mound up below, out of the way of work. This is but one of several design fac-

Sonoma Mission

tors the current owners have left intact for lack of any way to improve on them.

However, the Martin Lee family has changed the interiors of two old buildings into a thoroughly modern winery. At the upper level of the larger cellar are two long galleries of stainless steel fermenting tanks, Willmes presses, and self-emptying dejuicing tanks designed by the Lees. Below, next to the tasting room and in a separate cellar building at one side, are galleries of French and American oak barrels. (The barrels adjoining the tasting room replaced the last of the old Pagani redwood tanks in 1982.) Bottling and cased-goods storage are in a new building designed and executed in 1982 to match the originals. Which building is which is instantly recognizable, but the unpainted board-and-batten exteriors form a pleasing whole.

In the tasting room, decorated with posters taken from Kenwood's artist series labels, Chardonnay, Chenin Blanc, Riesling, Sauvignon Blanc, Cabernet Sauvignon, Pinot Noir, and Zinfandel are available.

Matanzas Creek Winery occupies an interesting position in the current era of establishing legal boundaries for vineyard districts.

As a matter of hydrology, the winery and its surrounding vineyard are just barely in the Russian River watershed, a few score yards over the ridge that separates the Sonoma Creek drainage from that of the Russian River. However, the property is closer in space, climate, and soils to the Sonoma Valley than to any part of the larger Russian River area planted to vines; so, by government decision the vines are part of the Sonoma Valley.

Whatever the fine points of geography, Sandra Mac-Iver released her first wines in 1979, from facilities in a converted dairy barn on the property. By 1985 she and her husband, Bill, had moved operations into a technologically superior facility on another part of the property. The building resembles a buried spaceship, an impression that's confirmed by the hardware arrayed inside, from ranks of glycol-jacketed tanks to a central electronic control system that monitors fermentation.

Matanzas Creek concentrates on Chardonnay, Sauvignon Blanc, and Merlot. The winery is opened twice a year to mailing-list customers.

St. Francis Winery is the youngest of Kenwood's three wineries, but its vineyards date from 1910. Proprietor Joe Martin bought the property in 1973 and built his cellars in the classic form of a California barn in time for the 1979 vintage. Red-painted and neat as a pin, the winery has typical modern equipment.

The handsome oak tasting room, in a separate building, overlooks the historic vineyard from which St. Francis produces Chardonnay, Gewürztraminer, Riesling, white Pinot Noir, and Merlot.

Sebastiani Vineyards anchors the northeast corner of settled Sonoma, starting at Fourth Street East and Spain Street and fanning out in several directions, but mostly northward toward sharply rising hills.

The main wood aging cellars, with the tasting room in one corner, are on the east side of Fourth Street next to a railroad track. In a corner opposite the tasting room, the Sebastiani family has gathered a small crusher, a basket press, and a single 500-gallon oak cask. With this equipment Samuele Sebastiani made his first wine, a Zinfandel, circa 1895. Here is the place to set a perspective for the astonishing changes that have come since then.

From this vantage, orderly rows of varnished, red-hooped redwood tanks extend not quite to infinity, but for a long way. Behind the main wood aging cellar is an ultramodern fermenting room filled with stainless steel tanks for the white wines. Behind this building, in an open space, are the crushers. Behind them, in a separate building, are red wine fermentors. Still farther along is a long, low building filled with oak barrels in which are stored the Sebastiani's most prized reds. Across the railroad track from all this is the largest building of them all: the stainless steel storage cellar where wines that are ready await their turns for bottling.

Samuele no doubt bottled his early wines at any handy bench and table—when he bottled any at all. Today, bottling and case storage require yet a fifth building, across Fourth Street from the others.

The tour does not take in all of these points. It would tax a marathoner if it did. Rather, it focuses on some of the crucial elements. There is an elevated walkway around the outside of the white wine fermenting room that gives unobstructed views of the crushers and continuous presses as well as the fermentors. Visitors in harvest season may tarry as long as they wish to see how wine begins. Visitors also trek through the main aging cellar with its encyclopedic collection of cooperage. The fillip here is a collection of carved cask heads. Any number of wineries have the odd carved cask or barrel. The Sebastianis have scores of them, nearly all the work of a local man, Earle Brown, who turned a retirement hobby into the task of Sisyphus.

Samuele Sebastiani died in 1946, leaving a prosperous but generally anonymous business to his son August. Most of the wines had gone into the world under other labels. In the mid-1950s August started abandoning bulk winemaking in favor of having the family name on the family product. He made enormous strides in that direction before his death in 1980. His widow, Sylvia, and son, Sam, continued the course he set; Sam left the family business in 1985.

A full range of table, appetizer, and dessert wines is on hand in a tasting room handsomely crafted from old wine tanks. Of special interest are Barbera (practically a synonym for Sebastiani), Green Hungarian, and Gamay Beaujolais Nouveau.

Valley of the Moon Winery, an agreeable collection of sturdy wood-frame buildings, perches on the banks of Sonoma Creek.

Enrico Parducci bought the old vineyard property in 1941, and eventually turned over the reins to his son, Harry, whose son in turn is coming up through the business. The vineyards go back to the 1850s, and were for a time owned by Senator George Hearst.

There is no tour of the new-in-1978 cellar filled with stainless steel fermentors or of the wood aging cellar with its well-used assemblage of redwood uprights, oak ovals, and oak barrels. But there is tasting in a cool, dark room shaded by a huge California bay laurel that also serves as a sort of trademark for the Valley of the Moon label. This winery long has been a source of generic jug wines. It continues to be, but also has become a source of varietal table wines in fifths. Included in the roster: French Colombard, Semillon, Pinot Noir, and Zinfandel.

More Wineries. The Sonoma Valley has in addition to its regularly visitable wineries several other establishments that offer extremely limited welcomes to the public, the limiting factor mainly owing to lack of size.

Arrowood Winery is the solo venture of Richard Arrowood, Chateau St. Jean's founding winemaker and one of the younger winemakers who helped shape the development of California's wine industry in the 1970s. In 1987 he was building a winery at his own vineyard in the Sonoma Valley.

B. R. Cohn Winery is an outstanding example of someone financing the rather expensive winery startup with proceeds from a lucrative, and totally unrelated, primary career—in this case, rock'n'roll. Cohn bought the old Olive Hill Farm while managing a rock group to stardom and in 1987 was constructing a winery; initial wines already were being produced in temporary quarters.

Kistler Vineyards makes small lots of Chardonnay, Pinot Noir, and Cabernet Sauvignon in a cellar high in the hills east of Kenwood, almost on the Sonoma-Napa county line. The winery and a surrounding vineyard are owned by brothers Steven and John Kistler, who made their first wines in 1979.

Las Montañas is, of course, up in the mountains. Alita Olds is one of the few California winemakers to maintain a commitment to winemaking by wholly natural means. Her method includes natural yeast fermentation, which is absolutely appropriate to the full-flavored Zinfandel grapes that grow on her remote estate high in the Mayacamas.

Laurel Glen Vineyard, well up Sonoma Mountain, makes Cabernet Sauvignon as its primary wine. Pro-

Plan a picnic

Sonoma County is a pleasing example of California's capacity for contrast. Its coast, however beautiful, tends to be cool and foggy in summer; the valleys are warm and dry.

At the expense of 2 or 3 hours' driving in pastoral countryside, visitors can have a look at winemaking, cheesemaking, and oystering, crabbing, or clamming. At the expense of $8 or $10, they can assemble a picnic that combines all the joys of fermentation as an accompaniment to a main course of seafood.

A well-warmed valley dweller can scoot west from U.S. Highway 101 at Santa Rosa on the Bodega Highway or take a slightly longer route from Sonoma west on State Highway 116 to Petaluma, then west on the Petaluma-Point Reyes Station Road ('D' Street). The latter route has few peers. It is its own pastoral symphony.

In the morning, with the dew still on the grapes, the valleys offer a kind of stillness. Just west of Sonoma, State 116 follows a curving course through dry, spaciously arranged hills, little populated and beginning to warm.

Once Petaluma is behind and the 'D' Street extension begins to be Point Reyes Station Road, the grass is greener—here begins dairy country. In the midst of these spacious rolling hills, the Marin French Cheese headquarters come into view. Here, especially with a bottle of wine and a loaf of bread aboard, is the place to lay in a stock of cheese and have a look at how it is made. From the cheese company, it is but a short jump after the retreating morning fog to Marshall and one of the Tomales Bay oyster markets.

What to take? Small individual cutting boards, steak knives (to double as personal cheese knives), wine glasses, and a corkscrew are the only utensils required for this picnic. A large tray will come in handy.

---

prietors Patrick and Faith Campbell have their winery at the end of a shared private road, so cannot offer tours or retail sales. The first crush was 1980.

Ravenswood is the small winery of Joel Peterson and partners. Located behind a woodworking shop south of Sonoma town, it specializes in Cabernet Sauvignon and Zinfandel. The winery began elsewhere in 1976.

Richardson Vineyards, on the flats south of Sonoma town, began in 1980. Dennis Richardson produces small lots of Cabernet Sauvignon, Gamay Nouveau, and Zinfandel among reds. Sauvignon Blanc is the white. Because winery and home are together, the proprietor offers no tasting or retail sales.

Sky Vineyards is a tiny vineyard and winery producing only Zinfandel. Owned by Lore Olds, it is above Boyes Springs on a slope so remote that no electricity is available for the cellars. The proprietor made the first wine for his label in 1979.

Sonoma Hills Winery is a miniscule Bennett Valley winery owned and operated by Teresa Ferrari-Votrubas since 1983. She has room for only one varietal, Chardonnay, to the tune of 1,000 cases per annum at most. Some grapes are estate grown; the rest come from Sonoma Mountain.

Other Than Wineries

With all its history, the Sonoma Valley is a particularly easy place in which to find changes of pace from wine cellars. With all its people, it is not such an easy place in which to find uncrowded picnic parks.

On the old Sonoma Plaza and all around it, visitors cannot help but consort with the shades of history. Sonoma's mission, last in the Franciscan chain, stands on the northeast corner of the plaza, the most eye-arresting part of a complex State Historic Monument.

The chapel no longer serves a religious purpose but has been preserved in its original state, or nearly so. Other rooms in the lengthy adobe building house collections of mission appointments, pioneer memorabilia, civic documents, and Indian arrowheads and other tools of the times.

Across First Street East, the old Mexican army barracks have been restored to something like their original appearance. Other buildings on the plaza date from mission or Mexican times but are not open to tour as part of the state park. However, the stately home of General Mariano Vallejo, last Mexican governor of California, is open as a major element of the park. Its long entry drive is three blocks west along Spain Street from the barracks. The house is a museum of family life at the top in the mid-nineteenth century. Its name, Lachryma Montis, after a spring on the property, also went on the label of Vallejo's wines.

Not far down Broadway from the plaza is privately owned Train Town, a narrow-gauge steam train that rambles around a meadow full of old-fashioned buildings rather larger than doll houses. It is the most exciting relief in the area for children who have walked through more wineries than they cared to visit.

Sonoma Plaza has become a major tourist stop in recent years. Whenever the weather is mild or better, the little park at its center bustles with picnickers, children playing on swings and other equipment, and park-bench dozers. The ring of shops is just as crowded. But the average weekend horde pales in comparison to the throngs that show up for the oldest of the state's vintage festivals. It usually is scheduled for the last weekend in September.

The festival puts considerable emphasis on local history. Many Sonomans allow themselves to be conscripted for on-stage or backstage service in a historical pageant or in one of the parades that celebrate the careers of the mission fathers, the Vallejo family, and the Haraszthys.

The wineries themselves play a quiet role. They elaborate on their daily welcome to visitors but do not invade the serenity of history. The effect is startlingly uncommercial.

A few miles north of Sonoma at Glen Ellen, Jack London State Park is another major visitor attraction in the Sonoma Valley. London finished his days on a ranch in the hills west of Glen Ellen, leaving some considerable marks on the property. His wife's staunch stone house is now a museum of family memorabilia. His own grandiose home, Wolf House, remains the burnt-out shell of stone walls it became on the eve he planned to occupy it. Higher up the hill is the old working ranch, which the author built around several big brick buildings that earlier had been the Kohler and Froehling Winery. The turnoff from State Highway 12 to the park is marked clearly.

Plotting a Route

The town of Sonoma lies 45 miles north of San Francisco. U.S. Highway 101 across the Golden Gate Bridge is the most direct northward artery from the city. It connects with State Highway 37 just north of Hamilton Air Force Base. That road runs east to an intersection with State Highway 121, which leads north toward the town of Sonoma. There is one more turn, clearly marked, onto State Highway 12, which runs right into the plaza as Broadway. All but the State 121 and State 12 legs are divided highway.

The main approach from the north is winding, scenic, two-lane State 12, which cuts inland from U.S. 101 at Santa Rosa.

Coming from the East Bay, the direct approach is

Picnic at the Vineyards

Interstate Highway 80 to Vallejo, then west on State 37 to American Canyon, State 29 to Napa, and State 121 to the same intersection with State 12 that serves travelers on U.S. 101. For travelers coming from the Central Valley, substitute State 12 from Cordelia for the State 37 section of the route from the East Bay.

The Sonoma Valley is connected with other parts of the world by unhurried roads, too. These provide scenic if slightly slow access to the Pacific shore on one side and the Napa Valley on the other.

The dawdling route west toward the sea is State Highway 116 from Sonoma through Petaluma.

On any day of touring both Sonoma and Napa wineries, the back road from Sonoma through Vineburg to an intersection with State 121 trims a mile or two from the State 12/121 route. Another alternative is the Trinity-Oakville Grade road between State 12 near Glen Ellen and State 29 at Oakville on the Napa side. It crosses a steep-sided part of the Mayacamas Mountains. In either direction the climb is slow and grinding, the descent wearing on brakes. The rewards are superlative panoramas of both valleys and some pleasing smaller views in between. Yet another alternative is St. Helena Road–Petrified Forest Road, which connects with State 12 between Kenwood and Santa Rosa on the Sonoma side, and with State Highway 128 near Calistoga in the Napa Valley. This route is not quite as taxing as Trinity–Oakville, but doesn't fall far short of the mark. Part way along, Spring Mountain Road branches away to St. Helena. The latter is the steepest, curliest route of them all.

The Russian River Region

Between Geyserville and Forestville the Russian River suffers a period of extreme indecision before it turns west in a serious and successful bid to reach the Pacific Ocean.

Its meanderings create a whole maze of hillsides and benches favorable to the growing of fruit, especially apples and grapes. In a great crescent west and north of Santa Rosa, fruit growing remains the principal business of an agricultural district of diverse physical charms.

U.S. Highway 101 slices straight up the Russian River Valley, offering a surprisingly pleasant introduction to the region as it goes. But the truly joyous scenery is reserved for those who dawdle along the two-lane country roads flanking the freeway on either side. The differences of climate and soil reveal themselves at every turning. Redwood forests give way to grassy plains, which give way in turn to oak-covered knolls. The oak knolls look up to bare, steep hillsides.

Through all of this change grapes stay in the landscape, not in the unbroken carpet that marks the Napa Valley, but in steady abundance. For students of the fine points of wine, Sonoma is yielding to a long list of more specific names almost before it is recognizable for itself. In the drainage of the Russian River alone, winemakers and bibbers alike speak of Alexander Valley, Dry Creek, the West Side, Chalk Hill, Green Valley, and Cloverdale with easy familiarity.

The Wineries

The Russian River watershed supports wineries every bit as diverse as its climate and soils might suggest, from gigantic Colony to tiny A. Rafanelli. The diversity is new.

From the end of Prohibition until the end of the 1960s this was mainly a region of middle-sized family wineries that sold most or all of their production to large firms with well-advertised labels. During the late 1960s there began a two-pronged shift. One prong was the development of several sizable firms owned by corporations and attuned to the production and marketing of vintage-dated varietal wines at comparatively modest prices. The other was a sharp increase of small, mostly privately owned cellars dedicated to small-lot winemaking, often of single-vineyard wines selling toward the top end of the price scale. Their arrival caused many of the old-line firms to turn to vintage-dated varietal wines for sale under their own labels.

With the advent of the 1960s newcomers, this became a rewarding region to visit. With the flood of new entries from the 1970s and early 1980s, it rivals Napa for numbers of opportunities but does not have so many tourists crowded onto so few roads.

In the introduction to this section, one sentence suggests that the region does not need to be toured in subdistricts. True. But it can be. The wineries come in clusters closely paralleling the country's vineyard geography, with the added possibility of sticking close to U.S. 101 from end to end.

Alexander Valley Vineyards manages to bring several major historic themes in California winemaking together into one piece of architecture.

Set at the rear of its sizable block of home vineyard, the 1975 cellar building uses adobe block and weathered wood to evoke thoughts of colonial Spain, the Old West, and contemporary California.

As for the working winery, it offers to those who would take the appointment-only tour a mixture of typical and original ideas. The original ideas are embodied in a lower cellar that is kept cooler and more moist than one on the upper level. The lower one is full of French oak for Burgundian varieties, especially Chardonnay, while the upper one is full of American oak for the aging of Cabernet Sauvignon. The notion, as old European hands will recognize, is to duplicate the environment of a *cave* in Beaune on the one hand and a *chai* in the Medoc on the other.

The proprietary specialty is a rather devilish red called Sin Zin. Tasting of this and of Alexander Valley Vineyards' Chardonnay, Chenin Blanc, Gewürztraminer, Riesling, Cabernet Sauvignon, Merlot, and Pinot Noir goes on in a pleasant room, or, not infrequently, outdoors on a shaded porch. Picnickers may obtain permission to use the outdoor tables.

History buffs may wish to wander up a grassy knoll behind the winery to the gravesites of the Cyrus Alexander family, the pioneers after whom the valley is named and whose sprawling ranch had its homestead on what is now the winery property of Harry Wetzel, Jr., and Harry Wetzel III.

Balverne Winery and Vineyards is a model California wine estate embracing 710 acres (including the ruins of a one-time General Vallejo residence) in the pale, stony hills of the Chalk Hill viticultural area. Founder Bill J. Bird, a man of the land above all else, is dedicated to the proposition that winemaking is a year-round process that starts with winter pruning and culminates only at the conclusion of bottle aging, 2 to 5 years beyond the vintage. Throughout that time, from raindrops to release, Balverne wines never leave the property.

Bird began planting grapes in 1974 and eventually carved 35 separate vineyards out of the estate's rugged contours at varying elevations (from 200 to 1,000 feet). Four distinct vineyard areas, totaling over 250 acres, produce Chardonnay, Sauvignon Blanc-Semillon, Cabernet Sauvignon (field-blended with Cabernet Franc and Merlot), and the Balverne specialty, a dry Gewürztraminer in the classic Alsatian style.

The first winery building was completed for the 1980 crush; with the completion of a metal fermenting and aging facility in 1986, Bird's all-in-one vision was fully realized. Impressive as this modern equipment is, however, the real thrill for visitors lies in contemplating the contrast between wild terrain and the sculpted terraces of the Laurel, Deerfield, Pepperwood, and Stonecrest vineyards for which the winery is a functional hub.

As a rule, Balverne offers tours only to the trade and wine groups. However, with enough advance notice and a modicum of flexibility, it's possible to find accommodation in their schedule.

Bandiera Winery was founded just after Prohibition by Emil Bandiera. Over the years it evolved into the California Wine Company (CWC), an umbrella for several different brands that did well enough in the marketplace but never managed to establish a clear identity until 1980, when CWC president John B. Merritt, Jr. consolidated all operations under the Bandiera name. Now Bandiera wines are labeled with colorful illustrations of California wildflowers, which have nothing particular to say about the elixir in the bottle but can certainly brighten a meal.

The old-time winery near Cloverdale was retired from active duty except for storage and some fermenting. Major winemaking operations now take place in an industrial-scale facility close by, with a comfortable tasting room not far away on Cloverdale's main drag (next to the Chamber of Commerce).

Bandiera owns or leases substantial North Coast acreage, including some 200 acres in the Napa Valley. The winemaker's stylistic philosophy looks more toward pleasant consumption in gentle company than any bold display of varietal intensity or vineyard character. The roster includes Chenin Blanc, Chardonnay, Fumé Blanc, Zinfandel, and Cabernet Sauvignon.

Bellerose Vineyard is essentially French and quintessentially Californian.

The property at the mouth of Dry Creek Valley is an old-time winemaking estate in California. As far back as the 1870s it was a stage stop, which explains some of the buildings. Not long after, circa 1887, it became the vineyard and winery of Capt. Everett A. Wise. Following Prohibition it came back as a typical Sonoma County mixed farm, growing grapes and prunes among other crops. In 1979 it was returned to winemaking.

Charles and Nancy Richard (pronounced Ri-shard in tribute to French ancestors) have given the place a French name and set about making a red wine based in Cabernet Sauvignon but including all the major grapes of Bordeaux (Cabernet Franc, Malbec, Merlot, and Petit Verdot). Other wines are Merlot and a barrel-fermented Sauvignon Blanc. The name of a second Cabernet Sauvignon, Workhorse Red, refers to Charles Richard's use of Belgian draft horses for most of the vineyard work.

Again after a French fashion, the winery comes in two separate buildings. Fermenting and bottling take place in a new wood-frame building that faces an imposingly large, solid, nineteenth-century barn, both set in a grove of trees part way up a long slope. Barrel aging goes on in the second cellar built up from surviving stone walls of the Wise winery.

Belvedere Winery represents a departure from the usual winery-vineyard relationship. Instead of issuing wines from one or more vineyards under a single brand, as is usually done, founder Peter S. Friedman has elevated the concept of vineyard designation to a new high with his Grapemaker Series: individual wines from special vineyards, with a unique label design for each grower. Belvedere/Grapemaker wines have included Robert Young Vineyards Cabernet Sauvignon, York Creek Vineyards Cabernet Sauvignon, and Chardonnay and Pinot Noir from Bacigalupi Vineyards.

A second program relies on Friedman's considerable expertise to offer the cream of each vintage's bulk wine market under the Discovery Series label. In any given year these are likely to include Sauvignon Blanc, Gewürztraminer, and white Zinfandel.

Both of these innovative programs are accommodated in a well-equipped 22,000-square-foot facility well up in the Russian River benchland. The two large ranch-style buildings almost qualify as *trompe l'oeil*, being fitted so deftly into the landscape that the space they contain takes visitors by surprise, as do sudden apparitions of well-placed equipment. The towering stainless steel tanks by the crush pad behind the foremost building are all but invisible to casual passersby.

The tasting room deck affords a grand view of neighboring vineyards and the upper Russian River Valley. Tours must be set up in advance, but the effort is well worthwhile for anyone desiring to see a particularly satisfying resolution of formal and functional concerns.

Davis Bynum Winery has evolved a good deal in getting to its present location on the site of a one-time hop barn above a sharp bend in the Russian River west of Healdsburg.

The property of a former San Francisco newspaperman after whom it is named, the firm started in 1965 in an ordinary storefront on a busy commercial street in the East Bay town of Albany, feinted once in the direction of the Napa Valley, then moved to its current wooded, hilly location in time for the vintage of 1974.

The main working winery is in a big, unadorned masonry block building of two offset sections. The rearward one holds stainless steel fermentors and other large cooperage. The section nearer the entry drive has cased goods and a tasting area on its upper level and barrel aging cellars below grade. Crusher and press sit on a pad at one end. At the opposite side of the main building, an old barn left over from an earlier proprietorship contains the bottling line and empty bottles awaiting use. Both buildings are well back from West Side Road, behind a cluster of wood-frame office buildings, equipment barns, and residences.

Visitors are mildly discouraged from taking tours because the buildings are crowded with working gear, but are warmly welcomed at the tasting bar, which sits as a sort of clearing amid stacks of cases.

Wines under the Bynum label come mainly from local grapes but include some from as far away as San Luis Obispo County. The roster of varietals includes Chardonnay, Sauvignon Blanc, Gewürztraminer, Cabernet Sauvignon, Pinot Noir, and Zinfandel. Bellfleur is a proprietary blend (red and white).

Chalk Hill Winery is a sleek establishment on a beautiful, and wild, piece of land. Only about 150 acres of the 540-acre Frederick P. Furth estate are planted to vines, and that's probably pushing the vineyard workers' luck slightly. The rugged terrain has its advantages, however. Frigid air tends to roll off, rather than sitting on the vines and freezing them, and the gradual dissipation of mist with altitude makes for naturally defined growing strata, with each grape variety thriving in its own optimum climate zone. The white soil for which the appellation is named, incidentally, is not the calcium-carbonate limestone called chalk in Europe (as in the cliffs at Dover), but rather is a mineral-rich volcanic ash, deposited eons ago, which magically amplifies the varietal intensity of grapes such as Chardonnay and Sauvignon Blanc.

The graceful wooden winery was designed to have grapes crushed and tanked no longer than 20 minutes from the vine. Varieties produced include Chardonnay, Sauvignon Blanc, Cabernet Sauvignon, and a rare late-harvest Semillon.

Chateau Souverain is patterned on the old hop barns that still dot the Sonoma countryside. The stark profiles of its twin towers and its sheer size make the building highly visible from U.S. 101 even though it sits deep in a fold in the western hills between Healdsburg and Geyserville.

By design this winery lends itself to tours. Elevated walkways run throughout it, allowing clear views of every department from crushers to bottling lines. It is a very substantial winery to see. The stainless steel fermenting tanks outside at the rear of the building are both sizable and numerous. So are the stainless steel storage tanks inside. However, the most impressive perspectives are from walkways above long, unerringly straight rows of Slovenian oak tanks and both French and American oak barrels.

Tours end in a handsome tasting room on the upper level, with views out to rolling vineyard or up through heavy beams of the east tower.

Souverain Cellars has packed a great deal of history into its brief existence, an exemplary demonstration of the speed with which life moves in these modern times.

The winery was built in 1972 by Pillsbury Company as a younger sister to the original Souverain Cellars in the Napa Valley. It was first known as Ville Fontaine, while construction had not progressed enough to allow crushing on the current site. By 1973, when the Sonoma cellar was ready for wine to be made there, the name had changed to Chateau Souverain. By the 1974 harvest the cellar was complete, but, shortly after the vintage, Pillsbury again changed the name, this time to Souverain of Alexander Valley. By 1976 the Pillsbury Company had sold both wineries. There is no Souverain at all in the Napa Valley now (its two homes there are now Burgess Cellars and Rutherford Hill Winery), and the Sonoma winery has become Chateau Souverain again under its new owners, Wine World, Inc.

Throughout all of the name changes, the focus at Souverain has remained on vintage-dated varietals.

Clos du Bois makes its wines twice, first in the vineyard and again in the winery. Founder Frank M. Woods was primarily a grower who spared no expense to make sure that the promise of each spring's budbreak was fulfilled in a wine glass some years later. In 1986, Woods sold his interest to Hiram Walker, Inc.

The winery, occupying most of a block in a south Healdsburg residential neighborhood, displays much of the technological arsenal with which science has armed modern winemakers. Some of it is impressively obvious—towering stainless steel settling tanks, for instance, that loom over the outdoor crush pad like NASA rocket engines—and some of it, such as the sophisticated system controlling fermentation temperatures, is all the more impressive for being virtually invisible. (Note: the increasing use of such high-tech toys in California wineries is aimed at maintaining the wine's integrity, not changing it.)

The roster of wines, most with euphonious vineyard designations, such as Marlstone, Calcaire, and Briarcrest, includes Gewürztraminer, Riesling, Chardonnay, Pinot Noir, Merlot, and Cabernet Sauvignon. These can be sampled in a tasting room that came with a 1986 winery expansion.

Colony is the new label for a cooperative winery that was known as Italian Swiss Colony for almost a century; when Allied Grape Growers purchased it from Heublein, Inc., in 1982, the name was streamlined to ISC wines. The winery has been operating continuously at Asti, near Cloverdale, for 100 years.

Andrea Sbarbaro founded Asti in the early 1880s as a communal refuge for Italian Swiss who were out of work and out of money in San Francisco. The communal idea did not work out, but Sbarbaro reorganized the winery into a private company and persevered.

It must have been hard to get visitors to Asti in Sbarbaro's time. An inveterate practical joker, he rigged the grounds of his mansion with all kinds of gadgets modeled after the ones at Hellbrunn Castle in Austria, which is to say most of them sprinkled or sprayed their victims with abundant water.

The mansion still is there but defused and, what is more, safely off the tour routes just in case some of the old booby traps escaped demolition. The winery, meanwhile, is one of the prime tourist attractions in all the California wine industry.

Jack London's Wolf House Ruins

Tours depart from a chalet-style reception building for close-up looks at a modern crushing station, an impressive array of big stainless steel fermentors, and an even more impressive collection of big redwood tanks. Included among the latter is the largest one known, an 80,000-gallon piece with enough room inside to sleep a platoon of infantry. Back in the tasting room, hosts offer the wide range of wines labeled as Colony, made entirely from grapes produced by cooperative growers.

De Loach Vineyards belongs firmly in the new wave of small family-owned and -operated wineries in Sonoma County. Cecil De Loach is his own winemaker, son John manages the vineyards, and son Michael runs the sales side of the business.

Winery and vineyards are out at the west edge of the Santa Rosa plain, where the first low rolls lead to genuine hill country within a mile. At the middle of one block of family vines, the cellars are well-proportioned, sturdily made, impeccably maintained wood-frame buildings patterned on local barns. The original was built in time for the winery's first vintage in 1979. By 1982 it was so full of fermentors and French oak barrels that the proprietor had to go outdoors to get from one end of the place to the other, in his view reason enough to add a second structure so that barrels and fermentors could be separated and spaced out a bit.

The roster of wines, all from family vineyards, includes Chardonnay, Gewürztraminer (dry and late-harvest), Sauvignon Blanc (in two styles), Cabernet Sauvignon, Pinot Noir, and Zinfandel (red and white).

Diamond Oaks Vineyard was founded in 1981 on the ruins of the noble but doomed Rege Winery (more recently, for a short time, Le Bay Cellars). In 1987, owner Dinesh Maniar was preparing to replace the old Rege barn-cum-winery with an ultramodern facility on the low hilltop off 101 south of Cloverdale.

In the meantime, Diamond Oaks continues to produce Cabernet Sauvignon, Chardonnay, and Sauvignon Blanc from Maniar's several hundred acres of vineyard in Sonoma and Napa counties. The tasting room occupies its own little building alongside the winery.

Domaine Laurier's vineyards stretch, long and narrow, between Green Valley Creek and steep, wooded

(Continued on page 49)

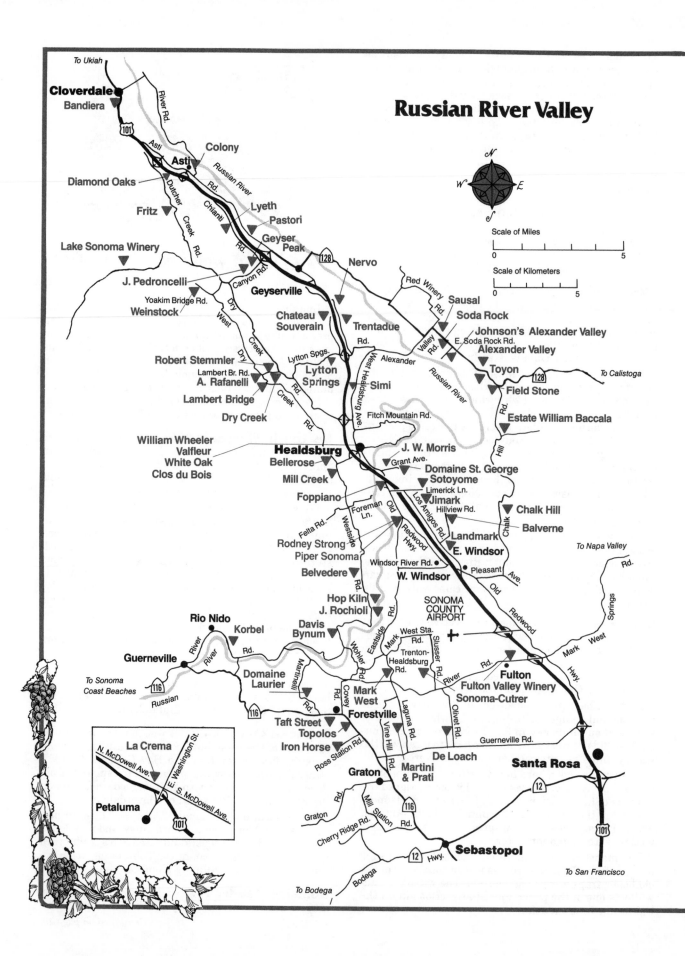

Russian River Valley

To Ukiah

Cloverdale
Bandiera

Colony

Asti

Diamond Oaks

River Rd.

Russian River Rd.

Fritz

Lyeth
Pastori

Geyser Peak

Lake Sonoma Winery

Nervo

J. Pedroncelli

Geyserville

Yoakim Bridge Rd.
Weinstock

Chateau Souverain

Trentadue

Red Winery Rd.

Sausal
Soda Rock

Johnson's Alexander Valley

Robert Stemmler

Lytton Spgs.

Lambert Br. Rd.
A. Rafanelli

Lytton Springs

Simi

E. Soda Rock Rd.
Alexander Valley

Toyon

Lambert Bridge

Alexander

To Calistoga

Dry Creek

Field Stone

Fitch Mountain Rd.

William Wheeler
Valfleur
White Oak
Clos du Bois

Estate William Baccala

Healdsburg

J. W. Morris

Bellerose

Grant Ave.

Domaine St. George

Mill Creek

Sotoyome

Foppiano

Limerick Ln.
Jimark

Hillview Rd.

Chalk Hill

Balverne

Rodney Strong
Piper Sonoma

Landmark
E. Windsor

To Napa Valley

Belvedere

Windsor River Rd.

W. Windsor

Pleasant Ave.

Hop Kiln
J. Rochioli

SONOMA COUNTY AIRPORT

Rio Nido

Korbel

Davis Bynum

West Sta. Rd.

Trenton-Healdsburg Rd.

Slusser Rd.

River

Fulton

Fulton Valley Winery
Sonoma-Cutrer

Guerneville

Domaine Laurier

To Sonoma Coast Beaches

Russian

Mark West

Forestville

Taft Street
Topolos
Iron Horse

Ross Station Rd.

De Loach

Santa Rosa

Graton

Martini & Prati

La Crema

N. McDowell Ave.
E. Washington St.
S. McDowell Ave.

Petaluma

Graton Rd.

Mill Station Rd.

Cherry Ridge Rd.

Sebastopol

To Bodega

Bodega

To San Francisco

Alexander Valley Vineyards. From intersection of Alexander Valley Rd. with State 128, E then S 2 mi. to winery drive at 8644 (P.O. Box 175, Healdsburg, CA 95448) Tel (707) 433-7209. Ltd. picnic. M-F 10-5, Sa-Su 12-5. Ta. GT by appt.

Balverne Winery and Vineyards. From U.S. 101 E. Windsor exit, N 1 mi. on Old Redwood Hwy., E .4 mi. on Arata Ln., N 1.7 mi. to 10810 Hillview Rd. (P.O. Box 70, Windsor, CA 95492) Tel (707) 433-6913. By appt. only.

Bandiera Winery. (155 Cherry Creek Rd., Cloverdale, CA 95425) Tel (707) 894-4295. Tasting room at S city limit of Cloverdale at 555 S. Cloverdale Blvd. Daily 10-5. Ta.

Bellerose Vineyard. From Healdsburg Ave., W on Mill St./Westside Rd., to intersection with W. Dry Creek Rd., then N .2 mi. to winery drive (435 W. Dry Creek Rd., Healdsburg, CA 95448) Tel (707) 433-1637. By appt. only.

Belvedere Winery. From junction of U.S. 101 and Westside Rd., SW 3.6 mi. to winery. (4035 Westside Rd., Healdsburg, CA 95448) Tel (707) 433-8236. Daily 10-4:30. Ta. GT by appt.

Davis Bynum Winery. From junction of U.S. 101 and Westside Rd., SW 8 mi. to winery (8075 Westside Rd., Healdsburg, CA 95448) Tel (707) 433-5852. Daily 10-5 in summer, weekends 10-5 remainder of year. Ta. GT by appt.

Chalk Hill Winery. From Old Redwood Hwy. in E. Windsor, E .8 mi. on Pleasant Ave. to Chalk Hill Rd., NE 1.5 mi. to winery drive. (10300 Chalk Hill Rd., Healdsburg, CA 95448) Tel (707) 838-4306. By appt. only.

Chateau Souverain. From U.S. 101, Independence Ln. exit, W .4 mi. on Independence Ln. (P.O. Box 528, Geyserville, CA 95441) Tel (707) 433-8281. Restaurant. Daily 10-4. Ta.

Clos du Bois. From Healdsburg Ave. at Healdsburg town square, E 3 blks. to Fitch St., S 2.5 blks. (P.O. Box 339, Healdsburg, CA 95448) Tel (707) 433-5576. Daily 10-5. Ta. GT by appt.

Colony. From U.S. 101, Asti exit, E .25 mi. to winery (P.O. Box 1, Asti, CA 95413) Tel (707) 433-2333 or 894-2541. Picnic; groups by appt. Daily 10-5. GT/Ta.

De Loach Vineyards. From U.S. 101, W on Guerneville Rd. 7.4 mi. to Olivet Rd., N .3 mi. to winery (1791 Olivet Rd., Santa Rosa, CA 95401) Tel (707) 526-9111. Daily 10-4:30. GT by appt.

Diamond Oaks Vineyard. From U.S. 101, Dutcher Creek Rd. exit, .6 mi. on Dutcher Creek Rd. to winery drive (26700 Dutcher Creek Rd., Cloverdale, CA 95425) Tel (707) 894-3191. Sa-Su 10-5, M-F by appt. Ta.

Domaine Laurier. From Forestville, W on State 116 .8 mi. to Martinelli Rd., N 1 mi. to winery drive at 8075 (P.O. Box 550, Forestville, CA 95436) Tel (707) 887-2176. By appt. only.

Domaine St. George. From U.S. 101, Healdsburg Ave./Old Redwood Hwy. exit, E .2 mi. to Grant Ave., then E to winery drive at end of Grant (P.O. Box 548, Healdsburg, CA 95448) Tel (707) 433-5508. IT by appt.

Dry Creek Vineyard. From U.S. 101, Dry Creek Rd. exit, W 2.5 mi. to Lambert Bridge Rd., S .1 mi. to winery (P.O. Box T, Healdsburg, CA 95448) Tel (707) 433-1000. Picnic. Daily 10:30-4:30. IT/Ta. GT by appt.

Estate William Baccala. From Healdsburg, N 2.9 mi. on Healdsburg Ave., E & S 6.8 mi. on Alexander Valley Rd./State 128, S 1.9 mi. on Chalk Hill Rd., E .1 mi. on Thomas Rd. (4611 Thomas Rd., Healdsburg, CA 95448) Tel (707) 433-9463. Daily 9-5. Ta. GT by appt.

Field Stone Winery. On W side of State 128, .2 mi. N of Chalk Hill Rd. (10075 Hwy. 128, Healdsburg, CA 95448) Tel (707) 433-7266. Picnic. Daily 10-4. Ta. GT by appt.

L. Foppiano Wine Co. From U.S. 101, Old Redwood Hwy. exit, SW .5 mi. to winery at 12707 (P.O. Box 606, Healdsburg, CA 95448) Tel (707) 433-7272. Picnic. Daily 10-4:30. Ta. GT by appt.

Fritz Cellars. From U.S. 101, Dutcher Creek Rd. exit, SW 3 mi. to winery drive on W side of rd. (24691 Dutcher Creek Rd., Cloverdale, CA 95425) Tel (707) 894-3389. Picnic. W-Su 12-5. Ta. GT by appt.

Fulton Valley Winery. From U.S. 101, River Rd. exit, W .5 mi. to winery (875 River Rd., Fulton, CA 95439) Tel (707) 578-1744. Picnic, deli. Daily 10-5. GT/Ta.

Geyser Peak Winery. From U.S. 101, Canyon Rd. exit, W to Chianti Rd., .1 mi. to winery drive (P.O. Box 25, Geyserville, CA 95441) Tel (707) 433-6585. Picnic. Daily 10-5. Ta. GT by appt., groups only.

Hop Kiln Winery. From junction of U.S. 101 and Westside Rd., SW 6 mi. to winery (6050 Westside Rd., Healdsburg, CA 95448) Tel (707) 433-6491. Picnic. Daily 10-5. IT/Ta.

Iron Horse Vineyards. From Forestville, S 1.4 mi. on State 116 to Ross Station Rd., W to winery drive at end (9786 Ross Station Rd., Sebastopol, CA 95472) Tel (707) 887-1507. By appt. only.

Jimark Winery. From U.S. 101, Old Redwood Hwy./Healdsburg Ave. exit, S .5 mi. on Old Redwood Hwy., E .6 mi. on Limerick Ln. (602 Limerick Ln., Healdsburg, CA 95448) Tel (707) 433-3118. W-Sa 10-4. Ta.

Johnson's Alexander Valley Winery. From intersection of Alexander Valley Rd. with State 128, E then S 1.75 mi. to winery drive (8333 Hwy. 128, Healdsburg, CA 95448) Tel (707) 433-2319. Picnic. Daily 10-5. IT/Ta.

F. Korbel and Bros. From U.S. 101, River Rd. exit, W 14 mi. to winery (13250 River Rd., Guerneville, CA 95446) Tel (707) 887-2294. May-Sept Ta 9-5, GT 9:45-3:45. Oct-Apr Ta 9-4:30, GT 9:45-3:30.

La Crema. From U.S. 101, Washington St. exit, E .1 mi. to McDowell Ave., N .25 mi. to winery at 971 Transport Wy. (P.O. Box 976, Petaluma, CA 94952) Tel (707) 762-0393. GT by appt. only.

Lake Sonoma Winery. From U.S. 101, Canyon Rd. exit, W 2 mi. on Canyon Rd., N 3 mi. on Dry Creek Rd. to winery drive (9990 Dry Creek Rd., Geyserville, CA 95441) Tel (707) 433-8534. Picnic. Daily 10-7 in summer, 10-4 remainder of year. IT/Ta.

Lambert Bridge. From U.S. 101, Dry Creek Rd. exit, W 3 mi. to Lambert Bridge Rd., S 1 mi. to West Dry Creek Rd. (4085 W. Dry Creek Rd., Healdsburg, CA 95448) Tel (707) 433-5855. Daily 10-5 May-Oct, 10-4 Nov-Apr. IT/Ta.

Landmark Vineyards. From U.S. 101, E. Windsor exit, N along Los Amigos (frontage road) .3 mi. to winery (9150 Los Amigos Rd., Windsor, CA 95492) Tel (707) 838-9708. Picnic. W & F 1-5, Sa-Su 10-5 or by appt. GT/Ta.

Lyeth Vineyard and Winery. From U.S. 101, Canyon Rd. exit W, N 3 mi. on Chianti Rd. to winery (P.O. Box 558, Geyserville, CA 95441) Tel (707) 857-3562. M-F 11-4. Ta. GT by appt.

Lytton Springs Winery. From U.S. 101, Lytton Springs Rd. exit, W .7 mi. to winery (650 Lytton Springs Rd., Healdsburg, CA 95448) Tel (707) 433-7721. Daily 10-4:30. IT/Ta.

Mark West Vineyards. From U.S. 101, River Rd. exit, W 5.5 miles to Trenton-Healdsburg Rd., N .1 mi. to winery (7000 Trenton-Healdsburg Rd., Forestville, CA 95436) Tel (707) 544-4813. Picnic. Daily 9-5. IT by appt.

Martini & Prati. From Santa Rosa, W on Guerneville Rd. 7 mi. to Laguna Rd., N 1.1 mi. to winery (2191 Laguna Rd., Santa Rosa, CA 95401) Tel (707) 823-2404. M-F 9-4. Ta. GT by appt.

Mill Creek Vineyards. From U.S. 101, Healdsburg Ave. exit, W on Mill St./Westside Rd. to winery at 1401 (P.O. Box 758, Healdsburg, CA 95448) Tel (707) 433-5098. Picnic. Daily 10-4:30. Ta. GT by appt.

J. W. Morris Winery. From U.S. 101, Healdsburg Ave./Old Redwood Hwy. exit, E .2 to Grant Ave., E .1 to winery (101 Grant Ave., Healdsburg, CA 95448) Tel (707) 431-7015. Daily 10-4. Ta.

Key: GT (guided tour); IT (informal tour); Ta (tasting).

(Winery listings continued on page 48)

. . . *Continued from page 47*

Nervo Winery. From U.S. 101, Independence Ln. exit, N .5 mi. on frontage road to winery at 19585 (P.O. Box 25, Geyserville, CA 95441) Tel (707) 857-3417. Picnic. Daily 10-5. Ta.

Pastori Winery. From U.S. 101, Canyon Rd. exit, N 1.5 mi. on frontage rd. to winery (23189 Geyserville Ave., Cloverdale, CA 95425) Tel (707) 857-3418. Daily 9-4. Ta.

J. Pedroncelli Winery. From U.S. 101, Canyon Rd. exit, W 1 mi. to winery (1220 Canyon Rd., Geyserville, CA 95441) Tel (707) 857-3619. Daily 10-5. IT/Ta.

Piper Sonoma Cellars. From U.S. 101, Windsor exit, W to Old Red-wood Hwy., N 3 mi. to winery (11447 Old Redwood Hwy., Healdsburg, CA 95448) Tel (707) 433-8843. Daily 10-5 except Jan-Mar, Fri-Su 10-5. GT/Ta fee.

A. Rafanelli Winery. From U.S. 101, Dry Creek Rd. exit, W 3 mi. to Lambert Bridge Rd., W 1 mi. to West Dry Creek Rd. (4685 W. Dry Creek Rd., Healdsburg, CA 95448) Tel (707) 433-1385. Case sales by appt. only.

J. Rochioli Vineyards. From junction of U.S. 101 and Westside Rd., SW 6 mi. to winery (6192 Westside Rd., Healdsburg, CA 95448) Tel (707) 433-2305. Daily 10-5. Ta.

Sausal Winery. From intersection of Alexander Valley Rd. with State 128, E then S .7 mi. to winery drive (7370 Hwy. 128, Healdsburg, CA 95448) Tel (707) 433-2285. Daily 10-4. Ta. GT by appt.

Simi Winery. From U.S. 101, Dry Creek Rd. exit, E to West Healdsburg Ave., N 1 mi. to winery (P.O. Box 698, Healdsburg, CA 95448) Tel (707) 433-6981. Picnic. Daily 10-5. GT/Ta.

Soda Rock Winery. From intersection of Alexander Valley Rd. with State 128, E then S .8 mi. to winery (8015 Hwy. 128, Healdsburg, CA 95448) Tel (707) 433-1830. Picnic. Daily 10-5. Ta. GT by appt.

Sonoma-Cutrer. From U.S. 101, River Rd. exit, W 3.1 mi. on River Road, N .9 mi. on Slusser Rd. to winery drive (4401 Slusser Rd., Windsor, CA 95492) Tel (707) 528-1181. By appt. only.

Sotoyome Winery. From U.S. 101, Old Redwood Hwy./Healdsburg Ave. exit, S .5 mi. on Old Redwood Hwy. to Limerick Ln., E .5 mi. to winery drive (641 Limerick Ln., Healdsburg, CA 95448) Tel (707) 433-2001. Picnic. Fri-Su 11-5 or by appt. GT/Ta.

Robert Stemmler Winery. From U.S. 101, Dry Creek Rd. exit, W 2.5 mi. to Lambert Bridge Rd., W on Lambert Bridge Rd. to winery (3805 Lambert Bridge Rd., Healdsburg, CA 95448) Tel (707) 433-6334. Picnic with reservation. Daily 10:30-4:30. Ta.

Rodney Strong Vineyards. From U.S. 101, Windsor exit, W to Old Redwood Hwy., N 3 mi. to winery (11455 Old Redwood Hwy., Healdsburg, CA 95448) Tel (707) 433-6511. Picnic. Daily 10-5. GT/Ta.

Taft Street. From State 116 at Forestville, S one blk. on First Street to 6450 (P.O. Box 878, Forestville, CA 95436) Tel (707) 887-2801. By appt. only.

Topolos at Russian River Vineyard. On State 116 at S limit of Forestville (5700 Gravenstein Hwy. N., Forestville, CA 95436) Tel (707) 526-0550. Restaurant. W-Su 11-5. Ta. GT by appt.

Toyon Vineyards. From Healdsburg, N 2.9 mi. on West Healdsburg Ave., E & S 6.2 mi. on Alexander Valley Rd./State 128 to winery (P.O. Box 271, Ross, CA 94957) Tel (707) 433-6847. By appt. only.

Trentadue Winery. From U.S. 101, Independence Ln. exit, N .5 mi. on frontage road to winery drive (19170 Redwood Hwy., Geyserville, CA 95441) Tel (707) 433-3104. Daily 10-5. Ta.

Valfleur Winery. From Healdsburg Ave. at Healdsburg town square, E 1 blk. to Center St. (312 Center St., Healdsburg, CA 95448) Tel (707) 433-2016. Daily 10-5. Ta. GT by appt.

Weinstock Cellars. From U.S. 101, Canyon Rd. exit, W 2 mi. on Canyon Rd., N .2 on Dry Creek Rd., SW .8 mi. on Yoakim Bridge Rd., N 1.3 mi. on West Dry Creek Rd. to winery drive at end of paved road (10101 W. Dry Creek Rd., Healdsburg, CA 95448) Tel (707) 433-3186. By appt. only.

William Wheeler Vineyards. From Healdsburg Ave. at Healdsburg town square, E on Plaza St. 1.2 blocks to 130 (P.O. Box 881, Healdsburg, CA 95448) Tel (707) 433-8786. M-F 9-5 or by appt. IT/Ta.

White Oak Vineyards. From Healdsburg Ave. at Healdsburg town square, E 2 blks. to East St., S 2 blks. to Haydon St. (208 Haydon St., Healdsburg, CA 95448) Tel (707) 433-8429. By appt. only.

Wineries Not on Map—Restricted or No Visitor Facilities

Caswell Vineyards. (13207 Dupont Rd., Sebastopol, CA 95472) Tel (707) 874-2517. By appt. only.

Dehlinger Vineyard. (6300 Guerneville Rd., Sebastopol, CA 95472) Tel (707) 823-2378. By appt. only.

Duxoup Wine Works. (Healdsburg, CA 95448) No visitors.

Fisher Vineyards. (6200 St. Helena Rd., Santa Rosa, CA 95404) Tel (707) 539-7511. By appt. only.

Hafner Vineyard. (P.O. Box 1038, Healdsburg, CA 95448) Tel (707) 433-4675. By appt. only.

Hanna Winery. (5345 Occidental Rd., Santa Rosa, CA 95401) Tel (707) 575-3330.

Horizon Winery. (P.O. Box 191, Santa Rosa, CA 95402) Tel (707) 544-2961. By appt. only.

Hultgren & Samperton Winery. (2201 Westside Rd., Healdsburg, CA 95448) Tel (707) 433-5102. By appt. only.

Jordan Vineyard and Winery. (P.O. Box 878, Healdsburg, CA 95448) Tel (707) 433-6955.

Marietta Cellars. (P.O. Box 1260, Healdsburg, CA 95448) Tel (707) 433-2747. No visitors.

The Merry Vintners. (3339 Hartman Rd., Santa Rosa, CA 95401) Tel (707) 526-4441. By invitation only.

Murphy-Goode. (3740 Hwy. 128, Geyserville, CA 95441) Tel (707) 579-9272. No visitors.

Nalle Winery. (P.O. Box 454, Healdsburg, CA 95448) Tel (707) 433-1040. By appt. only.

Pat Paulsen Vineyards. (P.O. Box 565, Cloverdale, CA 95425) Tel (707) 894-3197. Tasting room at 26155 Asti Store Rd., Asti, CA. Daily 10-6. Ta.

Pommeraie Vineyards. (10541 Cherry Ridge Rd., Sebastopol, CA 95472) Tel (707) 823-9463. By appt. only.

Porter Creek Vineyards. (8735 Westside Rd., Healdsburg, CA 95448) Tel (707) 887-1150. Th-Su 10-4:30. Ta.

Preston Vineyards. (9282 W. Dry Creek Rd., Healdsburg, CA 95448) Tel (707) 433-3372. By appt. only.

Quivira Winery. (P.O. Box 1029, Healdsburg, CA 95448) Tel (707) 431-8333. By appt. only.

River Road Vineyards. (6109 Anderson Rd., Forestville, CA 95436) Tel (707) 887-1819.

Sea Ridge Winery. (P.O. Box 287, Cazadero, CA 95421) Tel (707) 847-3469. Tasting room at 935 Hwy. 1, Bodega Bay. Tel (707) 875-3329. Dec-Mar Th-Su 12-5, Apr-Nov daily 11-7. Ta.

Seghesio Winery. (14730 Grove St., Healdsburg, CA 95448) Tel (707) 433-3579. By appt. only.

Thomas Sellards Winery. (6400 Sequoia Cir., Sebastopol, CA 95472) Tel (707) 823-8273.

Joseph Swan Vineyards. (2916 Laguna Rd., Forestville, CA 95436) Tel (707) 546-7711.

Viña Vista Vineyards. (P.O. Box 47, Geyserville, CA 95441) Tel (707) 857-3722.

Williams-Selyem Winery. (P.O. Box 195, Fulton, CA 95439) Tel (707) 887-7480. By appt. only.

Key: GT (guided tour); IT (informal tour); Ta (tasting).

. . . Continued from page 45

hills northwest of Forestville, in the Green Valley sub-appellation of Sonoma County.

Proprietors Jacob and Barbara Shilo (pronounced shee-lo) are committed to the prominent grape varieties—and traditional methods—of Burgundy and Bordeaux. Chardonnay and Sauvignon Blanc are largely barrel-fermented; Pinot Noir and Cabernet Sauvignon are fermented slowly in open-topped wooden vats.

Domaine Laurier was founded in 1978 (the grapes were planted a decade earlier). An understated Tudor-style winery that the Shilos built in 1983 is gently humbled by the 150-year-old California laurel tree for which the estate was named.

Domaine St. George

is the new name for an old, established winery that was known for years as Cambiaso Vineyards. It is owned by the international Four Seas Corp.

The winery, which sits near the top of a round hill south of Healdsburg, was founded in a wooden barn by Giovanni and Maria Cambiaso in 1934.

Today, Domaine St. George has a big, ultramodern cellar full of stainless steel fermentors and storage tanks and an equally modern structure for its bottling line and cased-goods warehouse. The old cellar now holds redwood tanks, a growing collection of oak tanks and barrels, and a retail sales desk.

The production roster includes excellent generic jug wines and the following varietals: Chardonnay, Chenin Blanc, Sauvignon Blanc, Cabernet Sauvignon, Petite Sirah, and, of course (this is Sonoma County!), Zinfandel.

Dry Creek Vineyard

is a rather ironic name for a winery that is owned by an avid sailor and nautical historian and that depicts sailing ships on all of its various labels. It is located in Dry Creek Valley, west of Healdsburg.

The winery was founded in 1972. Proprietor David Stare completed the first stage of his masonry-block building, designed after a small Loire Valley winery, in time for the harvest of 1973. In 1978 a new wing set perpendicular to the original one doubled the size of the cellars. Visitors are welcome to picnic at tables set on a lawn in the angle formed by the two wings.

Within, it is possible to see all steps in wine production from a point where the two wings join, although the walls require a couple of steps one way or another to get the views clearly. Vineyards are but another few steps away. Dry Creek wines include Chardonnay, Chenin Blanc, Sauvignon Blanc, Cabernet Sauvignon, Zinfandel, Merlot, and Petite Sirah, with late-harvest Gewürztraminer most years.

Estate William Baccala

belongs to a new species of California winery that is able to move itself intact from shell to shell until it finds an environment that suits it.

William Baccala founded his first winery in Mendocino County in 1982, operated it successfully for several years, and then sold it, moving almost immediately into the recently vacated Stephen Zellerbach Vineyard in Alexander Valley. From the standpoint of the consumer scanning a retail shelf, little changed except the fine print on his stylish watercolor label.

The Zellerbach winery was built in 1981. Its handsome exterior does ample justice to the dramatic setting in 74 acres of vineyard. The well-equipped interior, with its California-style arsenal of jacketed stainless steel, large wood cooperage, and many oak barrels of diverse origin, does equal justice for the grapes that Stephen Zellerbach planted in 1978: Cabernet Sauvignon, Merlot, and Cabernet Franc, which offer greater proof with each passing vintage that they are the varieties of choice in that neck of the valley. Chardonnay and Sauvignon Blanc are purchased from other vineyards in the area.

Wine nomads will find Baccala's tasting room an entirely pleasing stop, especially late in the afternoon when cooler air begins flowing down from the hills laden with aromas headier than any wine.

Field Stone Winery

is dedicated to efficiency in several ways.

First, it was built underground to keep the cellars naturally stable in temperature. The building is not a cave. Rather, founder Wallace Johnson carved a trench into a soft knoll in the Alexander Valley, built the cellars in it, then covered the whole structure with earth from the excavation. The facade is field stone turned up during cultivation of the family vineyards, hence the name and the unobtrusive appearance of the winery in the landscape.

Second, the place is a veritable study in using every inch of space. For example, the stainless steel fermentors do not stand in rows, but are clustered so tightly together that a cat would have a hard time getting between them. However, gates and valves are turned in just such a way that a cellar worker can reach five tanks without moving a step.

Finally, the working winery was designed to handle mechanically harvested, field-crushed must. Nothing is surprising about this, for the late Wallace Johnson was a pioneer developer of the mechanical harvester, and was experimenting with field crushers and field presses at Field Stone until his death in 1979. The winery continues in family hands, and the mechanical experiments continue, though such balky varieties as Gewürztraminer and Johannisberg Riesling are harvested by hand.

Amid all the steel and other modern gear, the tasting room is a comfortably old-fashioned, woody place. Wines available there include dry Chenin Blanc, Gewürztraminer, Johannisberg Riesling, a proprietary rosé called Spring-Cabernet, Cabernet Sauvignon, and Petite Sirah.

L. Foppiano Wine Co.

perches directly alongside Old Redwood Highway not far south of its exit from U.S. 101 at Healdsburg.

Not least among the modern touches in the large old winery is a fermenting room full of stainless steel tanks, which the family moved into place by the simple expedient of removing the roof and lowering them into position with cranes. Among the traditional touches are some well-used redwood tanks, and a couple of long lines of unbreakable concrete aging tanks, which also form exterior walls. (Since they cannot be destroyed, the Foppianos still use them as giant bottles, an easy trick after the invention of glasslike coatings.) The old cellar building acquired a new facade in the early 1980s.

The Foppianos are a more durable presence in California winemaking than the brief existence of their label would suggest. The original Foppiano, John, bought the property in 1896. The first Louis Foppiano took over in 1910. His son, also Louis, reestablished the business in 1934 and still directs it with help from his son, Louis.

They began bottling vintage-dated varietals in the late 1960s after a long career in the bulk and jug wine business. Production shifted sharply to varietal wines in the 1970s. The roster now includes Chardonnay, Sauvignon Blanc, Cabernet Sauvignon, and Petite Sirah. Riverside Farm is a second label. There are no regular guided tours, but visitors with an appointment may have a look around the sturdy old cellars.

Fritz Cellars stands out as individual in an era of distinctive winery architecture.

Buried in a steep hillside well above Dry Creek Valley, the winery is an extended round arch bent at the middle of its long axis at about the same angle as a boomerang. The main entrance announces the arch with tall, round-topped doors trimmed in the art deco style. The arch disappears for a moment in the tasting room, but reappears in a fermenting cellar painted pale blue for cheer and ribbed every few feet for support. Beneath rows of stainless steel fermentors—slanted at the top to fit the curving wall—is another cellar filled with upright oak tanks and fat, Burgundian barrels. This one is rectangular.

The roster of wines produced in this well-rounded environment includes Chardonnay, Sauvignon Blanc, Pinot Noir Rosé, Gamay Beaujolais, and Petit Sirah.

Tasters can stay inside or, in fair weather, can examine the wines outdoors at umbrella-shaded tables in the

Oak Casks

entry court. Fritz also has tree-shaded picnic tables downhill from the winery along the bank of a sizable pond.

Fulton Valley Winery is a good place to punctuate a wine tour with a bite to eat and a breath of fresh air—perhaps from the basket of a hot-air balloon tethered over the vineyard. The gourmet deli alone is worth a stop.

The winery is a substantial presence just off the freeway at the head of the Russian River Valley. The outside says barn, but the inside says modern enology; tours are more intimate here than they are at some larger wineries in the district, providing a good chance to question the knowledgeable guides.

The wine roster here includes Sauvignon Blanc, Chardonnay, Gewürztraminer, Cabernet Sauvignon, Pinot Noir and, when the vintage warrants, late-harvest Riesling.

Geyser Peak Winery is one of several Sonoma County wineries that are both old and new. It has been owned by the Trione family since 1982.

As an old cellar it made both bulk wine and wine vinegar under the ownership of the family Bagnani. Long-time drivers of U.S. 101 through Geyserville still lament the disappearance of the old sign advising that no Geyser Peak wine was available for sale because the proprietors drank it all. However, it had to go. All of the Bagnanis in the world would have a hard time keeping up with current supplies.

Under the subsequent ownership of the Jos. Schlitz Brewing Co., Geyser Peak was a great deal more than it had been, and a little bit less. To get rid of the little bit less part, the firm no longer made or sold vinegar. As for the great deal more: Two large concrete-walled buildings, flanking the stone-and-wood barn that was the original winery, were joined in 1982 by a third, which partially hides the old-timer from the freeway. The old cellar now holds redwood and oak cooperage and a complex of packaging lines. The two flanking cellars contain presses, stainless steel fermenting tanks, and stainless steel storage tanks. Yet another building on the opposite side of U.S. 101 has much of the wood cooperage.

Tours of all this are limited to groups with appointments. However, all comers are welcome to taste Geyser Peak wines in a handsomely appointed room in the steel aging cellar next to the original building. The roster includes just about every varietal, plus dessert and sparkling wines.

Geyser Peak also offers picnic tables under shading trees on the opposite side of the original winery, and more tables in a grove of trees east of the highway and next to a vineyard. A pair of hiking trails round out the public welcome. One runs along the river from the picnic ground there. The other courses through hills behind the winery.

Hop Kiln Winery occupies the most outrageously dramatic building of any cellar in the whole of Sonoma County. As the name forthrightly states, it was a hop kiln, which is a guarantee of one tower, but not necessarily three. Neither is it a guarantee that all three will soar above the general roof line. However, at Hop Kiln, there are three, each soaring to the same point of improbability. Kiln and barn are registered California Historical Landmarks.

Hop Kiln belongs to Martin Griffin, hence the full name, Hop Kiln Winery at Griffin Vineyard. He uses the ground floor as his winery and a sort of mezzanine as the tasting room.

The view from the tasting room windows is of vineyards on a long bench above the Russian River southwest of Healdsburg. The interior view at tasting level is of antique woodworking—cabinets, bar, and more. The view below the rail is of the working winery.

The winery itself is very small. A crusher and press are outside the back wall. Inside are a few small stainless steel tanks and several racks of oak barrels. To lean on the mezzanine railing is to see all, but the proprietors will take people downstairs so they can see the works up close, and also so they can have a look at the old hop-drying equipment. One of the stone kilns has recently been converted into a sparkling wine cellar.

The surprisingly extensive roster includes Chardonnay, Gewürztraminer, Sauvignon Blanc, Riesling, Petite Sirah, Zinfandel (also bottled as Primitivo), Pinot Noir, and Cabernet Sauvignon. A proprietary white is called A Thousand Flowers; the counterpart red is known as Marty's Big Red. Verveux, the house sparkling wine, is a Brut-style Riesling.

Iron Horse Vineyards is a new winery on a middle-aged vineyard planted on a pioneer property in the Green Valley hills near Forestville.

In 1982, the winery expanded into its third new building. The original, largest of the three, holds stainless steel fermentors and other processing equipment, plus some oak cooperage. The newest building, adjacent to the original, became the barrel aging cellar on completion. Both offer splendid views of the rolling vineyard and hills beyond it. The third building, downslope from the others, evolved into a separate cellar for sparkling wine after initial service as the main barrel aging cellar. All three are wood-frame structures with board-and-batten siding in the classic style of California barns.

Founded in 1978 by Audrey and Barry Sterling and Forrest Tancer, Iron Horse concentrates on producing three sparkling wines from previously planted vineyards at the winery: Blanc de Blanc, Brut, and Blanc de Noir. Still wines include Chardonnay, Fumé Blanc, Pinot Noir, and Cabernet Sauvignon. Tin Pony is an occasional proprietary label.

The winery name, incidentally, comes from a former owner of the property who had a predilection for railroadiana and who had a zoo-sized rail line on the place.

Jimark Winery markets wine under two labels: Limerick Lane Cellars and Michtom Vineyards. The big old winery, which takes its name from owners Jim Wolner and Mark Michtom, is a stolid elephantine presence by Limerick Lane in the rolling hills south of Healdsburg, covered with ivy and surrounded by gnarly head-pruned vines. These belong to other growers—the grapes that meet their destiny at Jimark are grown on the proprietors' 130-acre Alexander Valley ranch.

The Limerick Lane Cellars roster includes nonvintage Cabernet Sauvignon and Eirish Gold, a proprietary blend of French Colombard and Chardonnay. Michtom Vineyards offers Chardonnay and Cabernet Sauvignon.

Visitors are generally welcome at the winery on weekends, and during the week by appointment, but the schedule varies throughout the year, so it's best to call beforehand.

Johnson's Alexander Valley Winery looks like a good many of the wooden barns that dot the countryside in northern Sonoma County. Vertical wooden siding and a sharply peaked metal roof mark the structure. However, this is another book not to be judged by its cover.

The winemaking equipment is modern from stemmer-crusher to temperature-controlled stainless steel fermentors, and the oak cooperage is of the same sort to be found in wineries that just started operations this year.

More surprising, the building is also a sort of unofficial museum and repair shop for pipe organs, parts of which line the cellar walls.

Several times a year, the cellar doubles as a concert hall for a guest organist playing a vintage 1924 theater pipe organ. During the warm season, monthly concerts are held outdoors on a small stage next to a picnic lawn.

The tasting room is amidships, between the fermentors at one end and the wood aging cellar at the other. In it, visitors may sample Johnson varietal wines daily, the roster including Chardonnay, Chenin Blanc, Riesling, Gewürztraminer, Cabernet Sauvignon, Pinot Noir, and Zinfandel.

The winery and surrounding vineyards are owned by the Johnson family. Ellen makes the wine. Jay is the business manager and organ buff.

F. Korbel and Bros. is most famous for sparkling wine. The winery was founded in 1882 by Francis, Joseph, and Anton Korbel, a trio of diligent brothers from Bohemia. The three settled first in San Francisco, then moved to the Russian River area to mount a large-scale redwood logging operation. When the trees were gone, they decided to plant grapes on newly bared hillsides above the Russian River.

A few of the stumps were too much for them, and remained implacable in the midst of vine rows for decades. Finally, time and larger machinery overcame them, but surviving trees ring Korbel vineyard blocks near Guerneville, giving some hint of the labor required to clear these lands.

Since 1954 the winery has belonged to the Heck family. Alsatian by origin, the Hecks have mixed tradition and progress in the making of sparkling wine.

The process here is *méthode champenoise*. Much of the basic method used at the winery is little changed from the earliest days of sparkling wine. What has changed has changed slightly and slowly. The well-organized tour includes a collection of ancient machines to be compared to contemporary counterparts, plus a video and slide presentation explaining the process.

Tours start near the parking lot at a former Northwestern Pacific Railroad depot, acquired in 1935 for $5 in one of the best deals anyone ever made with a railroad. They end at Korbel's tasting room in an elegantly refurbished one-time brandy barrel warehouse. The Hecks also offer tours of their extensive rose garden, which includes older shrub varieties.

The list of regular sparkling wines includes—in ascending order of sweetness—Natural, Brut, Extra Dry, Rosé, and Sec. Two special wines are Blanc de Blanc, from Chardonnay, and Blanc de Noir, from Pinot Noir. Varietal still wines also are produced.

La Crema is one of many recent starts in California winemaking that has foregone fancy architecture in favor of getting started with good equipment.

The winery occupies half of a warehouse east of the freeway, U.S. 101, in Petaluma. Within the plain walls, Chardonnay is fermented in barrels, and Pinot Noir in custom-designed, open-topped stainless steel vessels resembling giant buckets. Both wines age in French barrels. There are several individual vineyard Chardonnays and Pinot Noirs each year.

Proprietor Jason T. Korman welcomes visitors by appointment.

Lake Sonoma Winery was founded in a different county far to the southeast as Diablo Vista Winery. Owner Robert Polson first made wine from purchased grapes in Benicia, Solano County, in 1977. Eight years later the operation migrated to the Polson family vineyard site at the northernmost end of Dry Creek Valley, just on the dry side of Warm Springs Dam. The body of water created by the dam, in addition to providing the winery's name, inspired one of winedom's more engaging label illustrations: an autumnal grape leaf adrift in rippling pastel waters.

The tidy little 6,000-case winery has its own tasting room and gift shop and offers a choice picnic spot commanding the upper Dry Creek Valley. Although Lake Sonoma wines are shipped throughout the country, in California they are available only at the winery.

Grapes from the 20-acre estate are supplemented with fruit purchased locally. The roster includes Chardonnay, Sauvignon Blanc, Cabernet Sauvignon, Merlot, Zinfandel (red and white), and a blend of estate-grown Chenin Blanc, Sauvignon Blanc, and Semillon called Hillside White.

Lambert Bridge is one of several new California wineries housed in a gracefully proportioned wooden building, but it is surely the only one with a huge fireplace at one end of the main aging cellar.

Unstained redwood siding and a shake roof on the building cause it to blend easily into a site between vines in the foreground and an oak-studded hill in the background. The interior of the barrel cellar is finished in wood as well, except for the stone fireplace. Overhead illumination comes from chandeliers high in the rafters. These cause cellar workers to curse now and again when they overfill one of the oak puncheons in the soft shadows, but the effect for visitors is one of fine romance.

Owner Gerard Lambert crushed his first vintage in 1975. The main cellar was completed in 1976. An expansion housing the stainless steel fermentors, press,

and other working gear followed in 1979. The tasting room was a 1986 addition.

On the west side of Dry Creek Valley, the winery concentrates on producing Chardonnay, Cabernet Sauvignon, and Merlot from its own vineyards, planted between 1970 and 1973. When conditions warrant, a small amount of late-harvest Riesling is produced as well.

Landmark Vineyards draws its name from a long double row of old cypress trees lining the entry drive. The winery buildings draw their architectural style from the two-story Spanish colonial house at the head of that drive.

The owning William Mabry family launched the label from leased space in 1974, completed the first winery building at what is now the Home Ranch in Windsor in 1976, and made a substantial addition to it in 1979. The original wing holds stainless steel fermentors and part of the oak cooperage. The newer structure has the rest of the cooperage, a bottling room, and cased goods storage.

Tasting goes on in the old house, which has had its former living room turned into a retail sales area, and the erstwhile dining room into a gracious spot for tasting. Visitors also may picnic in the old gardens.

Landmark produces only Chardonnay from family-owned vines at the winery and in the Alexander and Sonoma valleys.

Lytton Springs Winery was founded in 1975 to focus on one wine, Zinfandel, from grapes grown in an old vineyard long known as Lytton Springs but now renamed Valley Vista. In recent years the proprietors have supplemented their own grapes with small lots from similar vineyards nearby as a matter of practical necessity, but the basic plan remains unchanged.

In classic coastal hills north and west of Healdsburg, the cellar is typical in equipment (stainless steel fermentors, oak barrels) and plain in architecture (prefabricated metal). For students of Zinfandel, the combination of old vineyard and new cellar make an altogether appropriate place to look at the techniques of making California's inimitable red. The winery is open daily for informal tours. A new tasting room and picnic area were being built in 1987.

Mark West Vineyards perches on the crest of a round knoll just where the Santa Rosa plain gives way to the westernmost hills of the Coast Ranges. It has that happy facility, easily found in Sonoma County, of seeming remote from the rest of humanity without being very far off a major road.

The winery is an L-shaped building with re-sawn redwood siding and a shake roof, appropriate materials for the lightly wooded countryside all around. Vineyards form a skirt around the knoll.

Owners Bob and Joan Ellis offer bountiful hospitality, including facilities for group tours, private dinners, weddings, and so on. Picnickers can show up with appetites only—there is a deli on the premises.

Wines include Chardonnay, Gewürztraminer, and Riesling in dry and late-harvest styles; Pinot Noir and Zinfandel; and a sparkling Blanc de Noir.

How to read a California wine label

The first new regulations since 1933 governing what California wine labels may or must say were adopted in 1983. Most winemakers had been following these rules for some time.

Estate Bottled. Vines and winery must be within the geographic appellation shown, and the winery must control the grapegrowing.

1984. A vintage date can appear only if 95 percent or more of the grapes were harvested and crushed in the year stated. The margin simplifies topping up of wines aging in cask.

Sonoma County. Some statement of geographic origin is required. To be labeled California, 100 percent of the grapes must be grown in the state. For "Sonoma County," at least 75 percent must be grown in the named county. As many as three counties may be used in a multi-county appellation if corresponding percentages are shown.

Chalk Hill. As wine producers gain a better understanding of the ways in which soil and climate affect the quality of wine grapes, distinctive regions are defined as U.S. Viticultural Areas. For "Chalk Hill" or another Viticultural Area, 85 percent of the grapes must be grown in the named appellation.

Sauvignon Blanc. Varietal labeling requires that 75 percent of the wine be from the grape named. If used with an appellation, the minimum required percentage of the named grape must come from the appellation area. Generics (named for colors or after ancestral regions in Europe) have no requirements as to grape varieties used.

Designated Vineyard. At least 95 percent of the grapes were grown in the named vineyard.

Produced and bottled by. At least 75 percent of the grapes were fermented by the bottling winery. **Made and bottled by** requires at least 10 percent of the grapes to be fermented by the bottling winery. **Cellared and bottled by, vinted and bottled by,** and other phrases do not require the bottler to have fermented any of the wine.

Alcohol 12.5 percent by volume. The law allows a 1.5 percent variation on either side of the stated amount. Some labels also give, voluntarily, residual sugar (unfermented grape sugar), total acid, and other specifics. Sometimes the term **Table Wine** is substituted for numerals; it means simply that the wine contains between 7 and 14 percent alcohol.

Martini & Prati is a winery of few exterior charms. Wooden and concrete-block buildings ramble in all directions across a small knoll planted to grapes. The major physical distinction is a high water tower.

Indoors, however, the firm has a vast array of aged redwood tanks, oak oval casks, and other sorts of cooperage. These cellars are pleasant to see.

The winery dates to the 1880s, including a previous proprietorship, and to 1902 under the Martini side of its present ownership. Its age explains both its external homeliness and its interior attractions.

In Sonoma County this winery was for years second in size only to Italian Swiss Colony (see Colony, page 45), though a very distant second. Recently, newcomers have dropped it several notches down the list even as it has continued to grow.

Most of the wine made here goes elsewhere in bulk, but wines sold in jug or bottle under the Martini & Prati label cover a range of types. The Zinfandel and Burgundy are much prized by the proprietors. The company also maintains the Fountain Grove label from a once-famous winery near Santa Rosa. It now is reserved for the most prestigious varietals made at Martini & Prati. The tasting room is open daily, but tours require advance notice.

The Merry Vintners is an easy winner in the triple-entendre category: Merry Edwards is the founder and winemaker, and she and her affable husband, Bill, are indeed the merriest of vintners. The real Merry Vintners, however, as depicted on the winery's inaugural label, are the microscopic *saccharomyces cereviseae* (wine yeast) who have been Edwards' partners in an illustrious winemaking career that began at Mt. Eden Vineyards in the early 1970s, gained further luster at Matanzas Creek Winery, and now goes boldly forth in proprietary quarters near Santa Rosa.

Edwards is a Chardonnay specialist; thus The Merry Vintners is a Chardonnay winery producing two wines from each vintage: a tank-fermented Vintage Preview Chardonnay, released the summer following harvest, and a barrel-fermented, bottle-aged Reserve. Grape sources represent a range of Sonoma County microclimates.

The small, energy-efficient cellar was largely built by Merry, Bill, and Merry's parents. It houses the lab and French oak cooperage; crush pad and tanks are just outside. Visits to this family-run operation are, necessarily, by appointment only.

Mill Creek Vineyards, just west of Healdsburg, is the property of the Charles Kreck family.

Kreck and his two sons, Bill and Bob, planted their first vineyards in 1965 and began making wine in leased space in 1974. Their own winery saw its first crush in 1976.

The small cellars, hidden away well uphill from the tasting and sales room, are open to tour only by appointment because the family is virtually the entire work force. Those who persist in getting to the concrete-block building will find a winery typical of California in all its equipment, but more crowded than most.

The tasting room is, meanwhile, open to all daily. The two-story building looms out of vineyards just where they turn from flat to hilly. Patterned after a traditional mill house, it even has a sizable overshot waterwheel that works, although to no greater purpose than symbolizing the name of the winery. The Krecks cut their own timbers from family-owned property and built their two-story visitor building themselves. An adjoining picnic area is available on a first-come, first-served basis.

Harvest Time

The varietal roster includes Chardonnay, Sauvignon Blanc, Gewürztraminer, red and white Cabernet Sauvignon, Merlot, Pinot Noir, and Gamay Beaujolais.

J. W. Morris Winery has demonstrated that reincarnation, in the wine business at least, need involve no loss of identity. Originally based in the East Bay industrial community of Emeryville, the label established a reputation in the 1970s that persisted even after its demise during one of those rocky periods to which agricultural industries are particularly prone.

Winegrowers Ken and Tricia Toth purchased the label and all that went with it in 1983. They moved it, lock, stock, and fermentors, to spacious quarters just south of Healdsburg.

From the outside it doesn't look much different than it did in Emeryville, just bigger. The telltale pallet stacks, a big tank press, and some idle gondolas are the only clues to what's inside the huge concrete structure (there is also, of course, a sign). Inside, the enormous steel tanks and mountains of cooperage say everything that needs to be said about modern winemaking in the Golden State.

J. W. Morris produces a long roster of wines, including Sauvignon Blanc, Chardonnay, Cabernet Sauvignon, generic red and white table blends, and small quantities of special reserve wines from the Toth's own Black Mountain Vineyard in the Alexander Valley. The original J. W. Morris essence is preserved with a line of vintage and nonvintage ports.

Nervo Winery is a fine stone barn alongside a frontage road to U.S. 101 not far south of Geyserville. A landmark for years, it lasted two generations as a family enterprise. In 1974, manager Frank Nervo and his family sold the business to the Geyser Peak Winery a short distance to the north. Since then, Nervo has been maintained as a separate label, and the winery has been kept as an aging cellar and tasting room.

Pastori Winery came into being in 1975 as a full-grown business, partly because wine is a tradition in the Pastori family and partly because the proprietor brought with him stocks he had made in earlier vintages as the winemaster of another cellar.

Frank Pastori's father, Constante, launched a winery near Geyserville in 1914. After Prohibition, Frank grew grapes on the family ranch but did not restart the winery. (He did, however, revive the old bond number, 2960, for his new start.) For some years before launching out on his own, he had served as winemaker at the nearby Nervo winery.

The old Nervo stocks were part of Pastori's initial inventory in his wood-frame and concrete-block cellar north of Geyserville.

With both old and new wines at Pastori, the emphasis is on varietal types. Reds, including Cabernet Sauvignon and Zinfandel, head the list. They are available for tasting in a no-frills tasting and sales room in a front corner of the cellar.

J. Pedroncelli Winery is located a mile into the rolling hills west of Geyserville, on the ridge that separates the Russian River Valley from Dry Creek Valley.

The wood-frame main winery building, behind a finely crafted facade of redwood, dates from 1904, with seven separate additions made in later years. It is flanked on one side by a masonry building, erected all of a piece, and on the other by a concrete-block building that arose in three distinct phases. Because the episodic additions have made the winery a bit difficult to walk through, the Pedroncellis do not offer tours.

The tasting room is separated from stacked cases of aging wine by a sturdily wrought frame full of French oak barrels. These were brought from Europe in 1967 in time to hold a prized lot of Pinot Noir. Their arrival signaled the Pedroncellis' shift from bulk wine and generics to a focus on vintage-dated varietals.

The Pedroncelli family has owned the property since 1927. They sold grapes until 1934, made wine in that year, and have made it annually since. The founder was John Pedroncelli, Sr. The present proprietors are his sons, John, Jr., and Jim.

Grapes for Pedroncelli wines come primarily from hilly vineyards adjacent to the winery and a mile or so to the west, though the family had to give up one block of vines because they couldn't cultivate it after a particularly sure-footed horse died in 1965. The only livestock on the premises now are dogs that have been reduced to barking at tractors for a living.

Pedroncelli varietals include Chardonnay, French Colombard, and Gewürztraminer among whites, Cabernet Sauvignon and Zinfandel among reds, and a dry Zinfandel Rosé. The generics are cheerfully identified as Sonoma White, Rosé, and Red.

Piper Sonoma Cellars combines an extreme commitment to the Champagne ideal with the theatricality appropriate to such a festive and cost-intensive wine. It operates separately from—but is schematically part of—the Rodney Strong Vineyards complex near Windsor.

The initial notion behind the 1980 partnership between the Champagne giant Piper-Heidsieck and Strong's New York-based distributor was to link the French firm's two centuries of bubble technology with the viticultural resources available in the Russian River Valley, which is climatically similar to Champagne. Piper-Heidsieck became sole owner in 1987.

Architect Craig Roland designed a sleek, minimalist structure that, by sleight of glass and concrete, contains substantially more space than it appears to from the lawn. It was completed in 1982. In 1986 the company was owned briefly by Schenley, Inc.

Visitors symbolically leave the real world behind by crossing a bridge to the hospitality center. The razzle-dazzle within includes a multimedia *méthode champenoise* primer in a 28-seat theater, a contemporary art gallery, and a stylish cafe-tasting salon with panoramic views.

After being acclimated and enlightened, visitors are exposed to the full glory of a winemaking process so expensively painstaking that its only justification is the miracle it produces.

The tour goes step by step from the little wooden boxes in which the hand-picked grapes arrive to the final disgorging in a tiled, glassed-enclosed room that would not seem out of place in an aerospace lab.

Computer enthusiasts will delight in the interface of circuits and senses here. Although the winemaster's palate is the final arbiter, computers make it possible to act on sensory decisions with superhuman delicacy. The clumsy-looking gyropalettes are computer-driven machines that can riddle thousands of bottles simultaneously, moving more slowly and surely than any human hand; the big Vaslin press can exert the pressure of a butterfly's kiss on 8 tons of grapes at once. And so on.

Piper Sonoma produces 100,000 cases per year of vintage-dated Brut and Blanc de Noir and a limited quantity of Tête de Cuvée and Brut Reserve, made from special lots of Pinot Noir and Chardonnay and aged slightly longer on its yeast. Tasting is not complimentary.

Pommeraie Vineyards hides its trim, barn-style winery building west of Sebastopol, between a steep bank on one side and a row of thick, tall trees on the other.

The 2,000-case production makes a visitor facility impractical, but there are tours by appointment for anyone with an interest in their small lots of Cabernet Sauvignon, Chardonnay, Muscat Canelli, and Traminer. Pilgrims are rewarded with looks at a conventional contemporary California winery: stainless steel fermentors under a roof overhang at one end of the building, and a mixture of American and French oak barrels in the main cellar.

Pommeraie was founded by the Ken Dalton and Robert Wiltermood families in 1979. They sold it in 1985. The name comes from an archaic French word for apple orchard, fair tribute to the immediate neighborhood; the current owners, Judith Johnson and Curtis Younts, can't resist making apple wine in small quantity.

A. Rafanelli Winery comes as close as any spot is likely to get to a perfect vision of the family cellar. A gentle fold in a hillside above West Dry Creek Road cradles a trim red barn. A pasture full of sheep is visible on one side of the barn, a hillside covered in oaks is on the other, and a comfortable white frame house screens out the road on the remaining side. Inside the barn there is wood paneling in all three of its major rooms—one for fermenting, one for oak aging, and, above stairs, one for bottling and cased goods storage.

Americo Rafanelli built this quiet place for himself and his wife in 1972. Americo's son, Dave, has been the proprietor since 1986. He makes Zinfandel (and a little Cabernet Sauvignon) more to please himself than to be in business, and for this reason sells only in case lots and only by appointment.

J. Rochioli Vineyards has been owned and operated by the Rochioli family since shortly after Repeal. Like all grape growers (and most winemakers), Joe and Tom Rochioli believe that fine wines are made in the vineyard and are merely finished, at most enhanced, in the winery proper.

That consists here of a beautifully crafted redwood building alongside a hulking old Sonoma County barn that, along with some houses, occupies a shaded bluff overlooking the 70-acre benchland vineyard and the Russian River Valley beyond. The sign and gravel drive appear suddenly on a writhing stretch of Westside Road, but can be easily anticipated by keeping an eye out for the distinctive triple-crown profile of Hop Kiln Winery, which is right next door.

J. Rochioli's estate-grown Chardonnay, Sauvignon Blanc, Pinot Noir, and Cabernet Sauvignon provide good examples of the intense varietal flavor that grapes develop where a cooling marine influence extends inland to sheltered, well-drained spots such as this one. The tasting room patio, well-shaded and framed by roses, is a fine place to link a view with a palate impression in one's tasting memory.

Sausal Winery started out purely in the bulk-wine business, but, in 1978, began a slow turn toward offering its wines under its own label.

Set on a gentle slope in the Alexander Valley, the cellars are housed in an attractive wood-frame building with redwood siding. The main section is two long rows of good-sized stainless steel fermentors, similar rows of stainless steel storage tanks, and a comparative handful of oak tanks and barrels, all in neat order.

Though the winery dates only from 1973, the owners are long-time grape growers and winery proprietors in the Alexander Valley. Leo Demostene was a partner in the old Soda Rock Winery. His two sons and two daughters built Sausal as a tribute to him. They own and operate the winery and family vineyards today.

Sausal established its reputation with estate-grown Zinfandel. Chardonnay and Cabernet Sauvignon followed. The wines may be tasted daily, but tours are by appointment only.

Sea Ridge Winery seems to ride the mist on a Sonoma County coastal ridge as if it were a ship on the Pacific Ocean, just three miles west. Founding partners Tim Schmidt and Dan Wickham make only Chardonnay and Pinot Noir from what must be the westernmost vineyards in the continental United States. Naturally air-conditioned by sea fog but elevated enough to bask in sunshine most days, these extreme coastal vineyards experience a long, remarkably temperate growing season that brings out everything in the way of flavor that fine grapes have to offer. An extra snap of intensity comes from decomposing chunks of ancient pelagic limestone that are liberally distributed in the soil.

The little winery is a model of Burgundian efficiency. Crushing and Pinot Noir fermentation occur outside the 3,000-square-foot cellar; Chardonnay is barrel-fermented, and all wines are aged in French oak barrels within.

Visitors would do well to make Sea Ridge their gateway to the wine country, driving up the coast to Jenner and then flowing inland with the marine influence that makes Sonoma and Napa counties so hospitable to *vitis vinifera* grapes. Alternatively, make Sea Ridge's tasting room in Bodega Bay the last stop before riding into the sunset. Note that visiting the winery itself requires an appointment.

Simi Winery more than any other in Sonoma County reflects the ups and downs of wine in California. It has grown to its present size in an epic series of lurches.

The founders, Giuseppe and Pietro Simi, built the sturdy stone building that now houses wines aging in barrel in 1890, after a start in San Francisco and an interim stay in a since-disappeared cellar in downtown Healdsburg. The place prospered even after both brothers died in 1904, continuing until Prohibition under the management of Giuseppe's daughter Isobel. The national dry spell just failed to bankrupt her and husband Fred Haigh. At Repeal, Simi flowered again for a short time for the Haighs, then fell into a long, slow decline mirroring a general condition in the county's winemaking community.

At about the time the market for wine began awakening in the late 1960s, after 66 years in control, Isobel sold Simi to the Russell Green family. The Greens revitalized the place during a five-year proprietorship, then sold in 1974 to a British brewery firm, Scottish & Newcastle, which continued the refurbishing until it sold in turn to Schieffelin & Company of New York in 1976. Schieffelin held the reins until 1980, when the French firm of Moët Hennessy acquired the property as a running mate to its Domaine Chandon sparkling wine cellars in the Napa Valley.

Between them, the latter two owners literally tore the lid off the old Simi from 1979 through 1981. First was added a state-of-the-art fermenting facility in a new building uphill from the stone original. Then the roof was removed from the old building, and a new aging cellar built inside the reinforced shell. Matching roofs tie the structures together aesthetically, but enough differences remain to symbolize two eras.

Since Simi has its tasting room in a separate building on the opposite side of a Southern Pacific rail line, it has the only tour that crosses a fully signaled, grade-level railroad crossing. Consequently it also has the only tours that wait for the afternoon freight to roll through.

The roster of vintage-dated varietal wines includes Chardonnay, Chenin Blanc, Sauvignon Blanc, Rosé of Cabernet, and Cabernet Sauvignon.

Soda Rock Winery, under the ownership of Charles Tomka, Jr., has, as one of its subsidiary goals, a desire to prove that good wine can be made using the museum pieces left as equipment by former owner Abele Ferrari.

Tomka bought the long-idle winery in 1979. Rather than throwing away decades' worth of equipment and material accumulated by a legendary pack rat, he sorted it all out, reconditioning the salvageable and putting the rest out of the way in case a new use develops. He has had to buy very little, for Ferrari designed and built things to last when he directed the long-time winery equipment supplier called Healdsburg Machine. Here, then, is where to see how winemakers lived in the years immediately after Prohibition.

The crusher sits in front of a handsome stone facade scavenged by Ferrari from a defunct schoolhouse. On the other side of the wall is a hydraulically operated basket press complete with tracks to roll the baskets to and fro. Some of the fermentors are open-topped redwood. Most of the tanks are redwood, too, with 3-inch staves milled from virgin heartwood. The biggest pump in the place is a masterwork of durability.

Amid all of this, in gleaming contrast, are a couple of stainless steel dairy tanks for fermenting youthful

Caves: Touring under the wine country

Some of the most fascinating places in the wine country are underneath it. California has its share of visitable caves, though not as large a share as Europe, where winemaking predates air-conditioning by several centuries. The traditional use of subterranean chambers for wine storage arose because wine must be kept at a cool, constant temperature (ideally about 55° F) to age properly, and solid rock has no peer among insulating materials for both energy and cost efficiency. Thus practicality, and not romance, explains the proliferation of caves in the world's wine regions.

There would undoubtedly be more caves than there are if not for the fact that many rock formations are unsuitable for tunneling. The classic wine caves of Champagne were carved out of limestone. There is precious little limestone in California, but there is, in certain areas, something just as good. Its phonetically appropriate name is "tuff."

Tuff is the primary reason that most of the state's winery caves are concentrated along the Mayacamas Mountains, the ancient volcanic spine dividing Napa and Sonoma counties. The same mineral-rich volcanic ash that makes such good soil for grapevines is homogenous and tight-packed tuff under the surface, which makes for excellent tunneling. Tuff is initially soft and easy to dig, but it hardens like concrete upon exposure to air.

The hard labor that created the nineteenth-century caves was performed largely by Chinese coolies recruited from railroad and mining gangs. They worked in near darkness, progressing as little as a foot per day under dangerous conditions, with several men attacking the head wall with pickaxes while those behind formed a human chain to remove debris. Following the expulsion of Chinese laborers by the Exclusion Act of 1882, the tunneling was done by Irish and Italian diggers.

In sharp contrast, modern caves are most often dug by small crews using big machines. The most efficient is a Welsh coal mining machine, called a road-header, which was designed to excavate wide seams of anthracite in a hurry.

A road-header resembles a backhoe, except that the business end is a long hydraulic boom with a bit-studded head revolving at high speed on the end. By moving the head evenly over the stone wall, the operator advances steadily through solid rock, creating an arched tunnel of nearly uniform dimensions while the debris is conveyed mechanically to dump trucks outside the entrance. Thus, a road-header can accomplish in days what might have taken men with picks and shovels a year to do in a previous era.

The Napa and Sonoma valleys offer examples of both old and new winery caves. Some of the former can be seen at Buena Vista, Beringer, Inglenook, Spring Mountain, and Storybook Mountain. Recently dug caves include those at Carmenet, Far Niente, Rutherford Hill, and S. Anderson. The old and the new can be seen side by side at Schramsberg.

Where the walls are exposed (some are coated with Gunite, for safety), the age of each tunnel can be read from marks in the stone. The coolies signed their handiwork with the tips of pickaxes, backed by muscle; modern engineers sign theirs with diamond-carbide teeth.

Existing caves are noted in individual winery descriptions, but be aware that they are not automatically accessible to visitors. If seeing a cave is the object of a winery visit, be sure to call ahead and determine whether it is permitted. And don't forget to pack a sweater.

whites, and several rows of new French oak puncheons for fermenting and aging the Chardonnay.

In an appropriately dark, cool tasting room, the proprietors offer Sauvignon Blanc, Cabernet Sauvignon, Pinot Noir, and Zinfandel, in addition to Charlie's Private Blend (red and white). These and the other Soda Rock wines (under a label that, in character, recycles the original design) are sold only here.

Out front, long-time landscape designer and gardener Charles Tomka, Sr., has developed a splendid country garden. Tree-shaded picnic tables provide close views of Tomka's handiwork and more distant views of grassy, oak-dotted slopes looming above the Alexander Valley.

Sonoma-Cutrer is a one-varietal winery dedicated to producing three distinctive Chardonnays per vintage from its own vineyards in the Russian River Valley, Chalk Hill, and the slightly cooler Carneros region farther south.

In founder Brice Jones' extraordinary winery, built in 1981 after years of contemplative research, nature and technology team up like seasoned pros who take up each other's slack without missing a beat. Visitors (with appointments made in advance) will see a blend of agricultural and industrial design so well balanced that the building itself gives an uncanny impression of living and breathing, a kind of bionic entity that consumes ripe grapes and, some time later, gives birth to Sonoma-Cutrer Chardonnay.

The three wines (designated Les Pierres Vineyard, Cutrer Vineyard, and Russian River Ranches) begin with hand-picked grapes that are brought to the winery in ventilated wooden lug boxes. The bunches are chilled in an ingeniously air-cooled tunnel, then sorted and culled on oscillating inspection tables before gentle

Cordon-trained Vine

anaerobic pressing, barrel fermentation, and aging in a deep cellar. The earth and gravel cellar floor was designed to breathe, the theory being that this enhances the subtle respiration of the Limousin oak barrels and, hence, the wine's development.

The property is further distinguished by its lofty stature in the world of croquet—the Wine Country International Croquet Championship convenes here annually.

Sotoyome Winery,

Sotoyome Winery, nestled among vines on a steep slope just south of Healdsburg, is one of a few California cellars that actively defy gravity.

In pre-electric days, most wineries were built so fresh fruit arrived at the high side of a building and bottled wine left by the low side, gravity having done most of the moving in between. The habit persists in most hillside cellars. But here the outdoor crushing and fermenting deck is downhill from the metal building that holds the miscellany of redwood tanks and oak barrels in which proprietor Bill Chaikin's estate-grown Petite Sirah and Syrah (similar but different varietals) age. Pale Syrah is a proprietary rosé.

People interested in small-scale winemaking will find much to engross them in weekend tours of this well-organized and impeccably kept cellar dating from 1974.

The name, Sotoyome, comes from a huge Mexican land grant that one-time historian Chaikin is trying to establish as an appellation of origin.

Robert Stemmler Winery

Robert Stemmler Winery is the patiently achieved end product of a long winemaking career. The neat, sober, brown building next to the proprietor-winemaker's home in Dry Creek Valley is not large. Even so, it has been built and equipped in stages.

Stemmler, born and trained in Germany, made wine for several major firms in Napa and Sonoma counties from the fifties into the seventies before launching his own small cellar. Through the seventies he divided time between consulting work for others and his own growing business. Only in the eighties did he strike out entirely on his own.

The impeccably clean and orderly cellar is open daily. The list of wines include Chardonnay, Sauvignon Blanc (dry and late-harvest), Pinot Noir, and Cabernet Sauvignon.

Rodney Strong Vineyards

Rodney Strong Vineyards is a case study in California's modern viticultural development. It's no coincidence that the major points of evolution are well-represented here; many of them originated with proprietor Rodney Strong.

This is a winery of some importance to both students and afficionados of California wine. As a local saying has it, "Scratch a Sonoma County vintner, and you'll find a former Rod Strong assistant." Though that may be stretching things, it makes the point. Not only are Strong's individual contributions to the refinement and promotion of Sonoma County wines inestimable, but his rather awesome winery complex is an ideal place to get a handle on such seemingly arcane matters as appellations, clonal selection, the intricacies of fermentation and aging—in short, the whole bunch of grapes.

The company started way back when as a small tasting room and mail-order business under the name of Tiburon Vintners. Headquarters was an old frame house in the Marin County town of Tiburon. A few successful years later, the company acquired an old winery in the Sonoma County town of Windsor, adding the Windsor Vineyards label to the earlier one. The business still was essentially mail order. Another few successful years later, in 1973, the corporation changed its name to Sonoma Vineyards and built a substantial winery a few miles north of the first Windsor premises. It became Rodney Strong Vineyards in 1984.

The headquarters winery, a pyramid set into one of the company's vineyards alongside Old Redwood Highway near Windsor, looks like something Edgar Rice Burroughs might have dreamed up.

Architect Craig Roland's notion was to establish separate work areas radiating from a central processing core. For a time things worked that way. Fermentors were in one wing, barrels in another, and so on. Several California wineries are descended from this prototype, but it grew too far out of its framework to keep the form. Consistent expansion has added a big battery of temperature-controlled fermentors to the rear of the original building, and a huge aging cellar to one side. The latter is now largely hidden by Piper Sonoma, another Rodney Strong project with a life of its own.

The tasting room is suspended high up among the roof beams. Visitors may taste at tables, then stroll out to a ring of balconies overlooking the cellar action. A full tour of the facility is offered—and is worthwhile; picnic tables are available on the greensward outside, also the site of summer concerts.

Rodney Strong vineyard-designated wines include Chardonnay, Riesling, Sauvignon Blanc, Zinfandel, Pinot Noir, and the legendary Alexander's Crown Cabernet Sauvignon.

Taft Street

Taft Street occupies the venerable premises of the old American Wine Company, which prospered from Repeal to about 1952. Thirty years later six general partners, led by Anderson G. Bartlett, acquired and renovated one of the two concrete-block winery buildings in metropolitan Forestville. (The other one houses an eclectic mix of shops and light industry.)

The winery isn't pretty, but the old crushers out front and the rusty traces of a railroad spur that once serviced the American Wine Company lend it a certain sepia charm. Inside, Taft Street is just another clean, well-equipped California winery.

The flagship varietals are Cabernet Sauvignon (Napa Valley appellation) and Chardonnay (Russian River Valley), the latter assembled from up to 14 separate vineyard lots, partially barrel-fermented and aged in French oak. A second line of wines, marketed as good values, includes Chardonnay, Sauvignon Blanc, and nonvintage Cabernet Sauvignon. These are carefully selected bulk wines augmented with leftover lots from the premium assemblage.

Visitors are welcome at Taft Street, but an appointment is required.

Topolos at Russian River Vineyard is housed in a building just zany enough to look right in spite of its being on the southern outskirt of architecturally staid Forestville. Wooden towers in a Russian style soar above a concrete main cellar. Another tower alongside, equally Russian, has an office on the ground floor and a lab up under the eaves. The grounds are planted with largely native Californian flora.

The structure preceded proprietors Jerry and Michael Topolos, who have installed a conventional small winery in it. The tasting room is in a bottom corner of a separate, less overstated building housing a charming indoor-outdoor restaurant. The list of Topolos wines includes Chardonnay, Sauvignon Blanc, Riesling, Cabernet Sauvignon, Petite Sirah, Alicante Bouchet, Pinot Noir, and Zinfandel.

Toyon Vineyards demonstrates a studied de-evolution that is a refreshing change from the humdrum escalation of most winery operations.

The Don Holm family began growing Cabernet Sauvignon in the Alexander Valley in 1972. They were soon tempted, as so many growers are, into the production end of the wine trade. Starting in 1979 they made their own wine in a Healdsburg industrial bay. The romance paled after a few years, however, and they began having Toyon grapes custom-crushed at other wineries starting with the 1983 vintage.

In 1987 the Holms were still debating whether to build a winery on their Alexander Valley ranch. The label does well in the meantime, with estate-grown Cabernet Sauvignon in addition to Sauvignon Blanc, Semillon, and Gewürztraminer purchased from neighboring vineyards.

Visitors are welcome at the ranch with sufficient advance notice, both to purchase Toyon wines and to enjoy them with a picnic in the lovely vineyard on a knoll overlooking the valley.

Trentadue Winery nestles in the middle of its capacious vineyards at the end of a half-mile private lane leading east from the U.S. 101 frontage road between Healdsburg and Geyserville.

Owner Leo Trentadue crushed his first vintage in 1969 and has been expanding steadily since then. By 1972 he had enlarged the business enough to build a substantial masonry-block building as his main fermenting and aging cellar. He put a large tasting room on the second floor from which visitors can look down into the working parts of the cellar. The room also houses a miniature department store of wine-related merchandise.

Trentadue sells most of his wine on the spot. Principal on his list are Chardonnay, Chenin Blanc, white Zinfandel, Cabernet Sauvignon, Carignane, and Merlot, in addition to occasional sherry and late-harvest wines. The fruit from Leo's old Zinfandel vines goes to Ridge Vineyards under a long-term contract.

Valfleur Winery makes a good case for growers as wine producers. Proprietor Sandra Jones and her family planted their Jimtown Ranch vineyards in the heart of Alexander Valley in 1974. Virtually from the start the Jimtown grapes, particularly Chardonnay, were the object of fierce competition among North Coast wineries.

In 1982, Sandra and her brother Derek founded Valfleur and began taking the lion's share of Jimtown Ranch Chardonnay for themselves, although for contractual reasons the celebrated vineyard name couldn't appear on the label until the 1984 vintage. Sandra purchases fruit from neighboring Alexander Valley growers for Valfleur Sauvignon Blanc and Cabernet Sauvignon.

In 1987 the wines were being made in temporary quarters in Geyserville, pending the completion of Valfleur's permanent winery. The wines may be tasted at a comfortable hospitality center in downtown Healdsburg. The tasting staff can direct those visitors wishing to get a road's-eye view of Jimtown Ranch.

Weinstock Cellars restores the ring of credibility to the phrase "kosher varietal wine," long thought to be self-contradictory. As it happens, modern winemaking standards jibe closely with those of Kashruth, the ancient Jewish dietary laws. Kosher wines must be produced under rabbinical auspices, in compliance with conditions of purity specified by Kashruth. Excepting the former requirement, the description would fit any premium winery worth its bond.

Robert Weinstock was building a new winery in 1987 to produce varietals from his family's vineyards. The Weinstocks have grown grapes in the Dry Creek Valley (Zinfandel, Petite Sirah) and Alexander Valley (Chardonnay, Sauvignon Blanc, Riesling) since 1972. Inaugural 1985 releases were custom-crushed elsewhere.

William Wheeler Vineyards ferments its wines in an inaccessible part of Dry Creek Valley, but ages them in downtown Healdsburg.

Proprietors William and Ingrid Wheeler have a modern fermenting facility in a bare-bones building at their remote "Norse" vineyard. Having decided it was easier to take wines out than to bring supplies in, they acquired a one-time pool hall four doors off Healdsburg Plaza and transformed it into an elegant aging cellar and reception room for visitors.

On one side of a central wall, wines age in French oak barrels. One the other, the finely furnished reception area fronts a cellar full of stainless steel and upright oak tanks. The mezzanine extends as a little platform into the two cellars; so, a complete tour requires opening three doors and taking 10 steps.

The winery made its first wines in 1979. The roster includes Chardonnay, Sauvignon Blanc, white Zinfandel, and Cabernet Sauvignon.

White Oak Vineyards stoutly defends the notion that small is beautiful, a position that starts with the winery itself being nestled in the lee of a far larger outfit on Healdsburg's south fringe. Look for the butt of an old puncheon mounted outside a raked wooden building at the corner of Fitch and Haydon. That's the tasting room and office; the winery is right behind it—small, clean, precisely equipped, professional in every way. Owner Bill Myers designed and built the winery, and scoured the surrounding districts for special hillside vineyards from which to purchase fruit for Sauvignon Blanc, Chenin Blanc, Riesling, barrel-fermented Chardonnay, and Zinfandel. The first vintage was 1981.

More Wineries. In addition to all those listed above, the Russian River watershed supports another score of cellars. A few are bulk producers without any reason to court visitors, but most sell bottled wine, or are about to begin doing so. They shrink from public attention in some cases because they are so new that they have no wine ready to sell, in others because use-permit restrictions do not allow them to offer tasting or to sell at retail. In several instances the privacy is simply a point of preference.

Caswell Vineyards was founded by Dwight and Helen Caswell in 1983, on the site of the century-old Pieronne winery. Cabernet Sauvignon and Zinfandel are made in a two-story garage pending construction of a winery in 1989.

Dehlinger Vineyard, established in 1975 and located in its attractive permanent cellar since 1976, produces Chardonnay, Cabernet Sauvignon, and Zinfandel, primarily from its own rolling vineyards near Forestville. There are neither tastings nor retail sales, but winemaker Tom Dehlinger does give tours to friends of his wines by appointment.

Duxoup Wine Works is a tiny Dry Creek Valley winery where prodigous feats of enology are performed by proprietor Andy Carver and his wife, with a little help from their friends, who are sometimes thanked by having their names emblazoned on oak barrels in the cellar.

Fisher Vineyards, in the hills between Santa Rosa and St. Helena, produces only Chardonnay and Cabernet Sauvignon from winery-owned vineyards. Proprietor Fred Fisher sometimes extends invitations to visit his small, handsome redwood cellars.

Hafner Vineyard is a tiny Alexander Valley cellar founded by Richard and Mary Hafner in 1982. Their son, Parke, is the winemaker; Chardonnay and Cabernet Sauvignon are from the family vineyards.

Hanna Winery, near Santa Rosa, is the property of Dr. Elias Hanna. The first vintage was 1985. Varietals include Sauvignon Blanc, Chardonnay, and Cabernet Sauvignon.

Healdsburg Winegrowers may show up as a name in some lists of wineries. The label is Bacigalupi. Chardonnay and Pinot Noir are the only varieties. Owner Charles Bacigalupi offers no tours, tasting, or sales at the small aging cellar behind his home southwest of Healdsburg. For those who insist on getting close to the source, these wines are fermented and bottled at nearby Belvedere Wine Company.

Horizon Winery specializes in Zinfandel. The cellar, near Martini & Prati, is part of owner Paul Gardner's residence. Gardner made his first vintage in 1977. Although production is too small to permit general tours and tasting, Gardner does sell wine by appointment.

Hultgren & Samperton Winery made its first wines at a hillside site southwest of Healdsburg in 1979. The list begins with Cabernet Sauvignon and ends with Chardonnay. The proprietors of the small cellar offer no tasting and no retail sales.

Jordan Vineyard and Winery produces Cabernet Sauvignon and Chardonnay at a baronial building northeast of Healdsburg. It offers tours by appointment.

Lyeth Vineyard and Winery is the small but lavish project of a Swiss financier. Fashioned on the Bordeaux estate model, the establishment is located near Geyserville. Two wines are produced: a red from Cabernet Sauvignon, Merlot, and Cabernet Franc, and a white Sauvignon Blanc-Semillon blend.

Marietta Cellars is the label of C. Bilbro Winery, which is hidden in the hills west of Healdsburg. It produces Cabernet Sauvignon and Zinfandel.

Murphy-Goode began in 1979 as a partnership between long-time Alexander Valley grape growers Dale Goode and Tim Murphy. Publicist Rick Theis and marketing whiz Dave Reddy joined the team in 1985 to produce the first Murphy-Goode Fumé Blanc, which they had custom-crushed.

Nalle Winery produces Zinfandel, Zinfandel, and Zinfandel, in that order. The winery is in Dry Creek Valley and so are the grapes it crushes. Owner Doug Nalle moonlights as a winemaker at another winery.

Pat Paulsen Vineyards, tucked away at the end of a shared private lane southeast of Cloverdale, produces from its own vines Cabernet Sauvignon, Sauvignon Blanc, and a dry Muscat. Its location prohibits on-site tours or retail sales, but Paulsen maintains a tasting room at Asti. The first vintage was 1980.

Porter Creek Vineyards is a small cellar set on 20 acres of vineyard in the rising Russian River Valley benchland along Westside Road; George R. Davis is the proprietor.

Preston Vineyards is a family-owned and operated winery well up the Dry Creek Valley from Healdsburg. The principal wines are Sauvignon Blanc and Zinfandel. Begun in the late seventies, the winery was expanded in 1982, but remains small enough that the proprietors do not offer tasting or retail sales.

Quivira was the tag Spanish explorers gave to the mythical heaven-on-earth we call California—sort of a suburb to El Dorado. Quivira Winery Sauvignon Blanc appeared in 1985, and a Zinfandel one year later. A winery was under construction near Healdsburg in 1987.

River Road Vineyards makes Chardonnay, Johannisberg Riesling, Sauvignon Blanc, and Zinfandel in leased space pending construction of a permanent cellar between Forestville and Guerneville. Proprietor Gary Mills plans to accommodate visitors.

Seghesio Winery was founded in 1902 by Eduardo and Angelina Seghesio, who survived Prohibition by selling their grapes and then produced bulk wine for half a century. The third and fourth generation Seghesios began bottling varietals under their own label in 1981. Zinfandel heads a short list.

Thomas Sellards Winery near Sebastopol was founded in 1980. The first small lots of Cabernet Sauvignon, Petite Sirah, and Zinfandel were bottled in 1983. The proprietor receives visitors by appointment.

Joseph Swan Vineyards, near the intersection of Laguna Road with River Road, is the old-timer of this lot of wineries. Since the late 1960s, Swan has sold all of a very limited production of Chardonnay, Pinot Noir, and Zinfandel via a mailing list.

Viña Vista Vineyards has been growing at a steady but slow pace since the mid-1960s as a mail-order winery. The cellars on a hill near Asti usually are not open to visitors because the proprietor keeps an unpredictable schedule, but tours sometimes can be arranged.

Williams-Selyem Winery was known as Hacienda del Rio until 1986. Partners Bert Williams and Ed Selyem produce small amounts of hand-crafted Pinot Noir and Zinfandel near Fulton; wines are fermented in stainless steel dairy tanks using wild yeast.

In addition to these wineries Sonoma County still has several producers dealing only in bulk. Some are prominent enough in the landscape to attract attention. These include the Chris Fredson Winery, on Dry Creek Road west of Healdsburg; the Frei Brothers Winery (owned by E & J Gallo), a short distance farther west along the same road and somewhat secluded from view; and the Sonoma Cooperative, in the village of Windsor. The old Sonoma County Cellars, a gloomily handsome brick building on Healdsburg Avenue not far from Dry Creek Road in Healdsburg, is used only for storage.

Other Than Wineries

The Russian River, in its endless tacking back and forth, is a diverse source of entertainment when wine has had its turn.

In winter the Russian River is a big, muddy, fast-flowing stream, its banks populated by steelhead anglers. In dry summers it becomes a miles-long series of pools connected only by the merest of trickles. Between these extremes of its cycle, but especially in spring, the river is popular with canoeists and paddle boaters. For people who do not own boats, several rental firms have canoes at Healdsburg.

A county park at Healdsburg, Veterans Memorial, is near the bridge at the south edge of town. It has sandy bathing beaches and shady picnic sites. The next-nearest parks are in Santa Rosa. Howarth Park is particularly handy for anyone headed into or out of the Sonoma Valley.

The town of Healdsburg pays wine a direct tribute each year on a weekend in mid-May. At that time the town square comes alive with a friendly, increasingly crowded wine festival.

Santa Rosa is the commercial hub of the region, offering the widest range of hotels and restaurants; both Healdsburg and Cloverdale have modest motels. They and Geyserville add restaurants to the entertainment possibilities. For lists, write: Cloverdale Chamber of Commerce, P.O. Box 476, Cloverdale, CA 95425; Healdsburg Chamber of Commerce, 217 Healdsburg Avenue, Healdsburg, CA 95448; or Santa Rosa Chamber of Commerce, 637-1st Street, Santa Rosa, CA 95404.

Plotting a Route

U.S. Highway 101 is the nearly inevitable means of heading into the Russian River area from either north or south, and it is an efficient route through the wine district. However, confirmed shunpikers can find local routes running alongside it on either side.

State Highway 128 is a particularly engaging road from end to end, one in persistent contact with wineries. It starts at a junction with State Highway 1 on the Pacific shore in Mendocino County, rambles through the Anderson Valley (see page 67), joins U.S. 101 from Cloverdale to Geyserville, then slides away into the Alexander Valley. South of there it slips through Knights Valley and over a shoulder of Mt. St. Helena on its way into the Napa Valley.

State Highway 12 is another road that passes through several wine districts. First it connects the town of Sonoma, in the Sonoma Valley, with Santa Rosa; then it continues through vineyards as far as Sebastopol, in what Sonomans call the West Side. There it connects with State Highway 116, which continues through Forestville and Guerneville.

Within the district a whole network of local roads ambles around the West Side. Some of the most useful and scenic of these are the Dutcher Creek, Dry Creek, West Dry Creek, Westside, Eastside, and River roads.

Wine Cave

Mendocino & Lake Counties

Quiet charm in the northernmost vineyards

Mendocino Hop Barn

Of all the effects of the boom in California wine, one of the most mentioned in literature on the subject is the fragmenting of the North Coast counties into smaller districts. Nowhere is the shift more visible than in neighboring Mendocino and Lake counties. Mendocino hardly had a name of its own not long ago. Now wine fanciers recognize Ukiah and Anderson valleys readily, and are beginning to know about McDowell, Potter, and Redwood valleys as well. Lake County was once recognized only as a source of a few extra tons of red grapes for Mendocino, if it was recognized at all. Now it, too, has at least one named subdistrict, Guenoc, easing into the memories of wine bibbers.

The reasons behind all of this awareness are new wineries scattered throughout these sprawling, colorful precincts. They have added hundreds of miles of new territory and at least two dozen new cellars.

Here more than in most California wine districts are grand diversions: the Mendocino coast is an anchor point on the west; Clear Lake is a warmer, easterly alternative.

Mendocino County

Northernmost of California's coastal winegrowing counties, Mendocino is the pick of the lot for winery visitors who want a little pioneering as part of the experience.

All along the north coast, terrain alternates persistently between hill and valley, but, in Mendocino, steeper hills separate smaller valleys than in Napa and Sonoma counties. Settlements are fewer, the countryside between them wilder. Given these facts, local winemakers have scattered their small numbers across a remarkable amount of territory.

Like the rest of California, Mendocino has blossomed as a wine district since 1970, and especially since 1978. From the end of Prohibition until the end of the 1960s, Parducci Wine Cellars at Ukiah carried the Mendocino flag almost unaided. All but a handful of the county's grapes flanked U.S. Highway 101 within a few miles. Now the county has a few more than a score of wineries and substantial vineyards in no fewer than five distinct valleys stretching well beyond U.S. 101 to both west and east.

The hub, and most logical headquarters for visitors bent on seeing most or all of Mendocino's wineries, is the agreeable town of Ukiah. Another approach, better suited to vacationers, is to stay at one of the scenic, old-timey coastal villages, visiting wineries near Philo as a day trip and those nearer Ukiah on the way to or fro.

Ukiah-Hopland Wineries

For crows, 18 of Mendocino's wineries are close to Ukiah or Hopland. Visitors with only casual interest do not have much more distance to cover than the crows do. Several major wineries with well-developed visitor programs are within a few hundred yards of U.S. 101. However, for diligent seekers after particular cellars, the tumbled terrain here may add a good many miles to a day. To give the clearest example, Redwood and Potter valleys adjoin each other northeast of Ukiah, but are not connected directly by road.

Braren Pauley Winery made its first wines in 1980 in an archetypal California barn refitted as a small winery inside, but untouched outside save for the little sign over the door that announces the firm as a member of the Wine Institute.

The site, next to young vineyards north and west of Potter Valley, puts the cellar farthest off the main routes in Mendocino County by some miles, but not in the least settled neighborhood. Visits start two doors north at the residence of partner and winemaker William Pauley, then repair to the working cellar.

Wines made here include Chardonnay, Sauvignon Blanc, and Zinfandel.

Cresta Blanca Winery holds forth in two solid, square-cut buildings in the northeast quarter of Ukiah.

The one that has a barn roof goes back a ways, to the days when it was a fermenting winery for Guild Wineries and Distilleries and known as Mendocino Winery. The other, with exposed aggregate walls, was built after Guild turned the property into Cresta Blanca. In an eye-appealing switch, the older building is filled with stainless steel fermentors and other sleek new processing gear, whereas the new structure contains long rows of timeless oak casks and barrels along with the bottling line. A tour here is informative.

Both buildings sit behind a pleasingly cool, spacious tasting room and gift shop, an arbor-shaded picnic patio, and a green lawn with bordering gardens.

Chardonnay, Chenin Blanc, Gewürztraminer, Riesling, white and red Zinfandel, Colombard, Gamay Rosé, and Cabernet Sauvignon are offered in the tasting room. The firm also produces sparkling and dessert wines.

Readers of old books about wine may wonder how Cresta Blanca comes to be at the north edge of Ukiah. As a name, Cresta Blanca dates to 1882, when Charles Wetmore founded a winery and made famous wines in the Livermore Valley, east of San Francisco Bay. After Prohibition, his property was bought by Schenley Dis-

tillers, which later caused Cresta Blanca to move to several locations before finally settling into the old Roma Winery at Fresno. After Guild bought that facility, it reestablished Cresta Blanca as an independent winery in its present home.

Dolan Vineyards is well hidden on a steep slope in Redwood Valley. The proprietors, Paul and Lynne Dolan, make only Chardonnay and Cabernet Sauvignon, and those only in small lots. Paul gets his fill of other varietals as the winemaker for a major winery nearby.

The small, wood-sided cellar building, retrieved from an existing barn, is an impeccably orderly example of a two-person operation. A pair of stainless steel fermentors, the crusher, and the press sit on a pad outside the front door. Inside, two rooms full of French oak barrels hold the aging wines. Appointment-only tours are informal. Tasting is subject to the Dolans having any wine on hand.

Fetzer Vineyards maintains its public face in what used to be Hopland High School on the west side of U.S. 101 in downtown Hopland.

One-time classrooms now serve as gift shops offering wine-related trinkets, picnic items, and several sorts of made-in-Mendocino crafts. However, wine tasting is the main event, and goes on in what must have been the assembly hall. The long list of Fetzer table wines includes Chardonnay, Sauvignon Blanc, Cabernet Sauvignon, Petite Sirah, Pinot Noir, and Zinfandel, as well as Premium Red and Premium White. Bel Arbres is a second label.

The winery is some miles north of Ukiah in an attractive, hidden part of Redwood Valley west of U.S. 101. It is a remarkable story of growth. The company was founded by the late Bernard Fetzer in 1968. His background in forest products led to a small, handsome redwood winery building that since has been remodeled into offices. His business acumen led the family firm to far larger cellars, built on a flatter spot a hundred yards or so downhill from the hill-ringed original. Nine Fetzer children continue to manage the enterprise their father built.

Appointment-only weekday visits reveal an attractive, well-organized winery that is now the largest in the county. Family-owned vineyards provide both fore- and background scenery for the long, angular series of fermenting and aging cellars.

Frey Vineyards is an original. The winery building is both a classic expression of the wood butcher's art and a piece of history. Owned by a father and eight children, it was built in a Nordic style over a span of years, using timbers salvaged from the old Garrett winery at Ukiah. Well up in the Redwood Valley, it sits at the center of a sort of family compound containing a main residence in much the same style as the winery, other houses, a part of a school bus that might have appealed to Ken Kesey, and several piles of materials waiting for a use. A menagerie of amiable dogs and cats and more aloof chickens, ducks, and peacocks wander in and around certifiedly organic gardens and vineyard.

The small cellar is crowded with stainless steel dairy tanks converted to fermentors, barrels, and stacks of

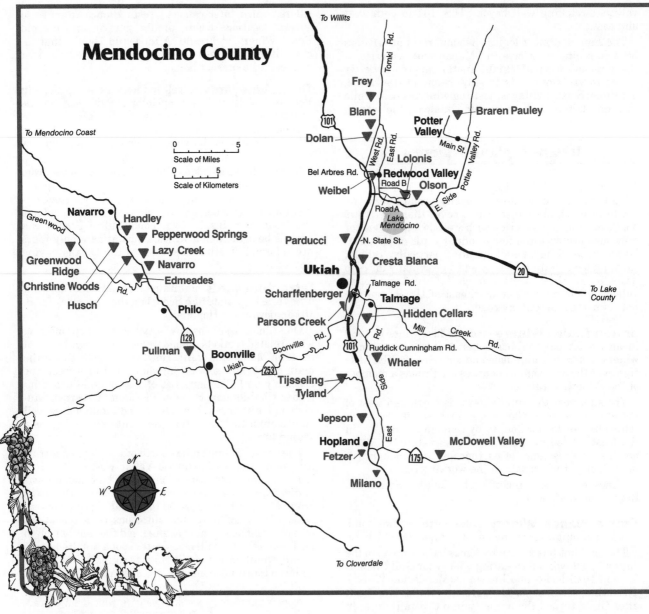

Mendocino County

To Willits

Frey

Blanc

Dolan

Potter Valley

Braren Pauley

Main St.

Lolonis

Bel Arbres Rd.

Redwood Valley

Weibel

Road B

Olson

Road A

Lake Mendocino

To Mendocino Coast

Scale of Miles

0   5

Scale of Kilometers

0   5

Navarro

Handley

Pepperwood Springs

Greenwood

Lazy Creek

Greenwood Ridge

Navarro

Christine Woods

Edmeades

Rd.

Husch

Parducci

N. State St.

Ukiah

Cresta Blanca

To Lake County

Scharffenberger

Talmage Rd.

Talmage

Philo

Parsons Creek

Hidden Cellars

Pullman

Mill

Creek

Rd.

Boonville

Boonville

Rd.

Ukiah

Ruddick Cunningham Rd.

Whaler

Tijsseling

Tyland

Jepson

Side

East

Hopland

McDowell Valley

Fetzer

Milano

To Cloverdale

wines in cases. The Freys regularly make small lots of Gewürztraminer, Grey Riesling, Chardonnay, and three different Cabernet Sauvignons. Sauvignon Blanc, Syrah, and Zinfandel joined the roster in 1981.

Hidden Cellars came out of hiding in 1983, after years of greeting the public with a sign reading, "Welcome. Please be careful not to scare the bears and wild bulls nor trample the poison oak." From primitive quarters in the Mendocino County outback, proprietor Dennis Patton moved operations to the historic Hildreth Ranch in time for the 1983 crush. The new winery is surrounded by orchards and vineyards, and welcomes visitors.

At first glance the winery looks like more of the same, but there are things of uncommon interest going on here. Patton has evolved specialized techniques for dealing with the soupy must of botrytised fruit for his late-harvest whites (see the special feature, "*Botrytis*

cinerea, the noble mold," on page 113). He also experiments with barrel fermentation, using different strains of yeast in different types of French and American oak.

The wines include Chardonnay, Sauvignon Blanc, Riesling (dry and late-harvest), and one red, Zinfandel. Chevrignon D'Or is a blend of botrytised Semillon and Sauvignon Blanc.

Jepson Vineyards came into being under most favorable circumstances. When Chicago businessman Robert S. Jepson, Jr. purchased the former Villa Baccala winery shortly after its completion, it was like getting a used auto that's only been driven to church.

Jepson immediately began improving the already excellent vineyard and winery facilities off Highway 101 north of Hopland. The landmark century-old farmhouse was expanded for luncheon and conference duty, new equipment was fitted in the ranch-style winery, and several blocks in the 108-acre vineyard were

Blanc Vineyards. From U.S. 101, .5 mi. E on School Way (Redwood Valley exit), N 1.7 mi. on West Rd. (10200 West Rd., Redwood Valley, CA 95470) Tel (707) 485-7352. By appt. only.

Braren Pauley Winery. From Potter Valley, W on Main St. to end, then N .2 mi. to winery at 12507 Hawn Creek Rd. (1611 Spring Hill Rd., Petaluma, CA 94952) Tel (707) 778-0721. By appt. only.

Christine Woods Winery. Directions given with appt. (P.O. Box 3112, Philo, CA 95466) Tel (707) 895-2115. By appt. only.

Cresta Blanca Winery. From U.S. 101, Lake Mendocino Dr. exit, E to State St., then S 1 mi. to winery (2399 N. State St., Ukiah, CA 95482) Tel (707) 462-2987. Picnic. Daily 10-5. GT/Ta.

Dolan Vineyards. 1.6 mi. N of Redwood Valley via West Rd. to Inez Wy. (1482 Inez Wy., Redwood Valley, CA 95470) Tel (707) 485-7250. By appt. only.

Edmeades Vineyards. 3.5 mi. N of Philo on State 128 (5500 State 128, Philo, CA 95466) Tel (707) 895-3232. Daily 10-6 Jun-Sept. 11-5 Oct-May. Ta. GT by appt.

Fetzer Vineyards. Winery: From U.S. 101, Uva Rd. exit, N 1 mi. on Uva to Bel Arbres Rd., then W .5 mi. to winery (P.O. Box 227, Redwood Valley, CA 95470) Tel (707) 485-7634. By appt. only. Tasting room: on U.S. 101 at Hopland. Picnic. Daily 9-5.

Frey Vineyards. From Redwood Valley, N 3.8 mi. on East Rd./Tomki Rd. (14000 Tomki Rd., Redwood Valley, CA 95470) Tel (707) 485-7525. By appt. only.

Greenwood Ridge Vineyards. From Philo, N on State 128 to Greenwood Ridge Rd. [county], then W 7.8 mi. to winery (24555 Greenwood Rd., Philo, CA 95466) Tel (707) 877-3262. By appt. only.

Handley Cellars. E side State 128, 5.7 mi. N of Philo (P.O. Box 66, Hwy. 128, Philo, CA 95466) Tel (707) 895-3876. By appt. only.

Hidden Cellars. From U.S. 101, E 1.3 mi. on Talmage Rd., S .5 on Ruddick-Cunningham Rd. (1500 Ruddick-Cunningham Rd., Talmage, CA 95481) Tel (707) 462-0301. Daily 12-4 or by appt. IT/Ta.

Husch Vineyards. 5 mi. N of Philo on State 128 (4400 Hwy. 128, Philo, CA 95466) Tel (707) 895-3216. Picnic. Daily 10-6 Summer. 10-5 Winter. Ta. GT by appt.

Jepson Vineyards. W side U.S. 101, 2.9 mi. N of Hopland (10400 So. Hwy. 101, Ukiah 95482) Tel (707) 468-8936. Daily 10-4. GT/Ta.

Lazy Creek Winery. N of Philo on State 128 (4610 Hwy. 128, Philo, CA 95466) Tel (707) 895-3623. By appt. only.

Lolonis Vineyards. Directions given with appt. (2901 Road B, Redwood Valley, CA 95470) Tel (707) 485-8027. By appt. only.

McDowell Valley Vineyards. From U.S. 101 at Hopland, E 3.8 mi. on State 175 to winery (3811 Hwy. 175, Hopland, CA 95449) Tel (707) 744-1053. Picnic. T-Su 10-6 Jun 24-Oct 1. Ta. GT by appt.

Milano Winery. On U.S. 101 1 mi. S of Hopland (14594 S. Hwy. 101, Hopland, CA 95449) Tel (707) 744-1396. T-Su 10-5. Ta. GT by appt.

Mountain House Winery. On State 128 directly W of intersection with Mountain House Rd. (38999 Hwy. 128, Cloverdale, CA 95425) Tel (707) 894-3074. By appt. only. (Outside map area).

Navarro Vineyards. 3.5 mi. N of Philo on State 128 (5601 Hwy. 128, Philo, CA 95466) Tel (707) 895-3686. Picnic. Daily 10-5. Ta. GT by appt.

Olson Vineyards. From U.S. 101, 6 mi. N of Ukiah, E 1.5 mi. on Hwy. 20, NE .2 mi. on Road A, E .25 mi. on Road B to winery (3620 Road B, Redwood Valley, CA 95470) Tel (707) 485-7523. Picnic. Daily 10-5. IT/Ta. Additional tasting room on E side of Hwy. 128, 10 mi. S of Boonville (4791 Hwy. 128, Yorkville) Picnic. Daily 10-5.

Parducci Wine Cellars. From U.S. 101, Lake Mendocino Dr. exit, E to N. State St., N .5 mi. to Parducci Rd., then W to winery (501 Parducci Rd., Ukiah, CA 95482) Tel (707) 462-3828. Picnic (summer only). Daily 9-6 summer, 9-5 remainder of year. GT/Ta.

Parsons Creek Winery. From U.S. 101, Talmage Rd. exit, W to S. State St., then .2 mi. S (3001 S. State St., Ukiah, CA 95482) Tel (707) 462-8900. By appt. only.

Pepperwood Springs Winery. 5.5 mi. N of Philo on State 128, E 2 mi. on Holmes Ranch Rd. to winery (P.O. Box 11, Philo, CA 95466) Tel (707) 895-2250. Call for information.

Pullman Vineyards. W side State 128, 2.4 mi. N of Boonville (10500 Hwy. 128, Boonville, CA 95415) Tel (707) 895-3565. By appt. only.

Scharffenberger Cellars. From U.S. 101, Talmage Rd. exit, W .2 mi. to winery (307 Talmage Rd., Ukiah, CA 95482) Tel (707) 462-8996. By appt. only.

Tijsseling Winery and **Tyland Vineyards.** From U.S. 101 6 mi. S of Ukiah, McNab Ranch Rd. W 2.5 mi. to wineries (2200 McNab Ranch Rd., Ukiah, CA 95482) Tel (707) 462-1810. Picnic. W-Su 10-5 or by appt. IT/Ta.

Weibel Vineyards. On U.S. 101 6 mi. N of Ukiah, and .1 mi. N of intersection with State 20 (7051 N. State St., Redwood Valley, CA 95470) Tel (707) 485-0321. Daily 9-6. Ta.

Whaler Vineyard. 5 mi. S of Talmage on East Side Rd. (6200 East Side Rd., Ukiah, CA 95482) Tel (707) 462-6355. By appt. only.

Key: GT (guided tour); IT (informal tour); Ta (tasting).

budded over from Chenin Blanc and Colombard to Chardonnay.

And just to show that he wasn't kidding around, Jepson brought in a rare alambic pot still from Cognac, France, to indulge a passion for distilled spirits.

Visitors thus will see a model California wine estate with a mixture of architectural elements and some charming eccentricities. Jepson Vineyards wines are Chardonnay, Sauvignon Blanc, and sparkling Chardonnay. The brandy is distilled from French Colombard.

Lolonis Vineyards is a mecca for enthusiasts of notable vineyards, who will recognize in the Lolonis name a frequently designated grape source for several North Coast wineries. Tryfon Lolonis came here from Greece in 1915 and planted his vineyards five years later; now they are managed by his grandson, Ulysses.

Visitors (with appointments) will see a great vineyard in its prime, including some of Tryfon's original Zinfandel vines, with textbook examples of several different pruning styles. Among the remarkable viticultural practices at Lolonis are the use of ladybugs to combat pests, and biseasonal handpicking of leaves to intensify northern exposure (and flavor intensity).

In 1987 the Lolonis family was making wine in leased space, pending completion of a Greek-style winery on the ranch.

McDowell Valley Vineyards offers one of those staggered surprises of which California is almost routinely capable.

On winding, Model T-sized State Highway 175 east of Hopland, in a little valley all its own, is a sleek, low building instantly recognizable for a battery of solar panels integrated into the striking design of its front elevation. It looks lower than it is. In addition to being solar-powered, it has 10- to 14-foot earthen berms to help conserve energy.

Inside, a good-sized winery is equipped to the minute, from Willmes membrane press to stainless steel fermentors to millipore filter and sterile bottling room. The old note is a huge gallery of European oak barrels. All of this—down to the computer program controlling the solar units—was designed by Richard Keehn, who, with wife Karen, owns both winery and vineyards.

In pleasing contrast to the straight-edged modernity, a huge tasting room at the upper level is all native oak and redwood worked into the sinuous forms of art deco. It is, if memory serves, the only tasting room in the state with its own baby grand piano and a big floor for dancing. (In a place designed for parties, there is a kitchen big enough for a cooking school directly behind the tasting bar.)

For those who prefer to taste outdoors, a pair of wooden decks flanking the tasting room hold picnic tables, and offer fine panoramas of the vines or focused looks into the working winery.

The list of McDowell Valley Vineyards wines—all from the property—includes Sauvignon Blanc, Chardonnay, Cabernet Sauvignon, and Syrah. Domaine du Soleil is the second label. Not incidentally, the Keehns have established McDowell Valley as an appellation.

Milano Winery occupies one of the most picturesque of several old kilns left from the days when the nearby village of Hopland was earning its name growing and curing hops.

Winemaker James Milone cofounded the winery in 1977 in a building his father and grandfather built. Father and son now are partners in the winery. The weathered wood structure has been refitted completely on one side of a central partition to make an all-purpose fermenting and aging cellar. The other side, beneath the kiln tower, is to be remodeled as the small winery grows to fit its large building.

Cased goods and a tasting room are at the upper level, over the cellar. In the tasting room, a quiet nook with natural redwood walls, one of the Milones pours wines from a short list that includes Chardonnay, Cabernet Sauvignon, and, most prominent, Zinfandel.

Mountain House Winery occupies a small, plain building behind a large house—sober as Victorians go, but hardly plain—on the site of a nineteenth-century stage stop near the southern boundary of the county.

The winery is open from March through November; it's best to call ahead because hours vary. The label covers Chardonnay from Mendocino and Sonoma counties, Cabernet Sauvignon, and a late-harvest-style Zinfandel from Sonoma and Amador county grapes. Mendocino Gold is a proprietary blend of Chardonnay and Chenin Blanc.

Olson Vineyards has more to offer than two incredible vistas, but that fact generally escapes visitors for the first few minutes they spend on this vineyard plateau overlooking Lake Mendocino on one side and Redwood Valley on the other. It's a popular wedding spot.

Black oaks frame the handsome wooden winery and the matching house where Donald Olson, a retired electronics engineer, and his wife Nancy have lived since 1971. The 24-acre vineyard was planted shortly before their arrival. For a decade they sold their Petite Sirah and Napa Gamay grapes to other wineries; the first Olson Vineyards wines came with the 1982 vintage.

The production roster is surprisingly long for a 7,000-case winery. The wines include Chardonnay, Sauvignon Blanc, Riesling, and a rare Napa Gamay Blanc. Glacier is a proprietary blend of Riesling, Chenin Blanc, and French Colombard. The Olson reds are Zinfandel, Cabernet Sauvignon, Petite Sirah, and Viking Zin, made to be more readily accessible than the primary version of that variety.

Parducci Wine Cellars, just on the north side of Ukiah, is the patriarch winery in Mendocino County. Founder Adolph Parducci came to Ukiah in 1931, having launched his first winery in Cloverdale, Sonoma County, in 1916.

Three generations of the Parducci family have had a hand in the steady evolution from country winery to the present one, which concerns itself mostly with varietal table wines.

The progress can be measured by the steady expansion of family vineyard holdings. In the early 1960s they owned about 100 acres; in the mid-1960s they doubled that figure. By 1987 they owned approximately 500 acres, comprising four separate spreads embracing virtually every terrain and microclimate the Ukiah district has to offer. The core is Sun Valley Ranch, 100-odd acres first planted to vines by Adolph Parducci during Prohibition, which he survived by making wine for the Catholic Church.

A white masonry building of graceful proportions comes into view first for visitors to Parducci. Built in 1974, it is the bottling and case-wine storage cellar. The older buildings of the producing winery nestle into a narrow draw a hundred yards or so west, on the first gentle slopes of a small hill. This is one of few small wineries in California that insists on aging wines in large redwood or oak tanks, completely excluding small cooperage. The fermentors in the spick-and-span cellar are all stainless steel. Tours leave every hour.

The Parduccis' large, comfortable tasting room, gift shop, and art gallery occupies a well-made Spanish-style building near one end of the big bottling cellar. Out back is an arbor-shaded, summer-only picnic area with several tables set on an adobe patio.

Parsons Creek Winery occupies five bays in a rent-a-warehouse complex toward the south limit of Ukiah. The only outward evidence of the winery is a rolling must tank (for field-crushing) with the company name painted on the side. It sits in a little fenced yard at one end of a long, prefabricated metal building full of miscellaneous businesses.

Behind the anonymous facade is a well-designed and impeccably orderly winery. One bay holds two rows of stainless steel fermentors. The next one is filled with French-coopered American oak barrels. The last space has the bottling line and wine in cases.

Parsons Creek brings no whole grapes to the winery, but field-crushes instead, leaving stalks in the vineyard. The semiurban location imposes this bit of streamlining, which, in turn, thus far has limited the winery to white wines. Partner-winemaker Jesse Tidwell produces two Chardonnays (Mendocino and Sonoma) and a Riesling.

Scharffenberger Cellars divides substantial sparkling and still wine operations between two separate locations. Fermenting and related activities occur in three industrial bays in Ukiah. Cold storage, offices, disgorging (see page 90), and bottling take up a large, specially insulated warehouse building in another part of town. Visitors with appointments are shown around both premises and then directed to a third location—the tasting room on Highway 128 in Philo.

The Scharffenbergers are long-time grape growers. Their Eagle Point Ranch vineyards supply fruit for the still wines: Eagle Point Chardonnay and Sauvignon Blanc. Pinot Noir for Eagle Point Vin Rouge and Blanc de Noir (a still rosé) is purchased.

Scharffenberger sparkling wines are faithful to Champagne in their genesis (as visitors will see), but they say California with a sunburst in every bubble. Scharffenberger Brut is a traditional 70/30 percent marriage of Pinot Noir and Chardonnay; the Blanc de Blancs is all Chardonnay; and the Brut Rosé is entirely Pinot Noir, which acquires its Mendocino sunset flush the old-fashioned way.

Tijsseling Winery and **Tyland Vineyards** are near neighbors, but inextricably linked.

Tyland came first. Founded in 1977 by Dick and Judy Tijsseling, it is snugged away toward the head of a surprisingly long, narrow valley of vines running west from U.S. 101. A stemmer-crusher and press separate two tidy buildings of unpainted redwood, each with a battery of stainless steel fermentors sheltered under the connecting roof. The remainder of the uphill building is given over to a bottling room and cased wine in storage. The downhill structure holds a mixed collection of American oak tanks and barrels and French oak barrels, used to age Cabernet Sauvignon, Zinfandel, Chardonnay, and Sauvignon Blanc. These can be tasted at picnic tables overlooking the vineyards.

The larger Tijsseling Winery is managed by Dick but owned by his father, Herman. A few hundred yards closer to the highway than Tyland, the sizable concrete building is divided into three parts: a cavernous room filled in part with stainless steel fermentors and in part with sparkling wine on *tirage* at one end, a bigger room sized to hold 5,000 French oak barrels at the center, and a third section with cased goods and bottling. This winery is designed to produce Cabernet Sauvignon, Chardonnay, Sauvignon Blanc, and a pair of *méthode champenoise* sparkling wines, all from surrounding family vineyard the two wineries share. Tijsseling has its own tasting room, as well as a quiet picnic site.

Weibel Vineyards, the long-time producer of sparkling and other wines at Mission San Jose in Alameda County (see page 139), established a producing winery and attractive tasting room north of Ukiah in 1973.

In time the Weibels plan to add aging cellars to their several banks of stainless steel fermentors. At that point, the Mendocino winery will make their wines.

While sparkling wines will continue to be made at Mission San Jose, the Mendocino tasting room will be a

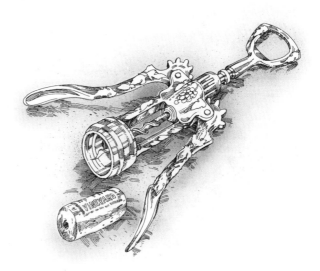

reminder of them. It resembles an upside-down Champagne glass of the shallow style known as a coupé.

More Wineries. Since 1982, several formerly small wineries in the vicinity of Ukiah have moved onto the fast track with bigger cellars and visitor facilities. In Spring 1987, a whole new crop of start-up wineries was on the brink of having wine with which to welcome visitors. Two are already established.

Blanc Vineyards was founded by Robert and Marlys Blanc, and their family, in 1983. The view from the California barn-style winery across the Redwood Valley is well worth a visit, which requires an appointment.

Whaler Vineyard belongs to the first Scandinavian sea captain to come into California winemaking since Gustave Niebaum launched Inglenook in the 1880s. Russ and Annie Nyborg made a small first lot of Zinfandel from their vineyard five miles south of Talmage in 1981. The original winery was a spruce little barn painted a dusty blue, except for bright yellow doors. The family added a second, larger building in the same style directly behind the first, for the harvest of 1982. With the expansion came several styles of wine, all Zinfandel and all from the property.

Anderson Valley Wineries

In this old-time apple-growing district near the Mendocino coast, vines and wineries are beginning to be as important in the landscape as orchards. The first two wineries opened in 1971. By 1987 the number had grown to ten, most small and family-owned. Prospects are for still more of the same sort of friendly places.

Edmeades Vineyards dates from 1971 as a winery, although its vines were among the first post-Prohibition ones planted in Anderson Valley, in 1963.

The property of Deron Edmeades, the winery proper is a tale of gentle growth. The original structure houses some of the aging cooperage. It perches on stilts on a steep bank just above the highway. A newer oak aging cellar is up on the crest of the same wooded hillock, overshadowed now by a more recent prefabricated metal building that houses the stainless steel fermentors and bottled wines. The tasting room is not in

Whale Watching

any of these buildings. Rather it is in a comfortable room of rustic wood next to the proprietor's house. The entry is instantly recognizable by the basketball hoop over the doorway.

The roster of Edmeades whites includes Chardonnay, Gewürztraminer, a blend called Cabernet-Fumé, and a proprietary white called Rain Wine. The reds include Cabernet Sauvignon and Zinfandel.

Greenwood Ridge Vineyards is among the most remote of western Mendocino's wineries and vineyards, and the most dramatically set in a neighborhood of handsome scenery.

The drive up Greenwood Ridge Road, marked as the turn to Elk where it leaves State 128, is one panorama after another of Anderson Valley. The drive from the county road into the winery does not offer any far views, but its curving path along the face of a steep hill does not lack for drama anyway. At the end of the drive, the scenery regains a spectacular scope. Proprietor Allan Green's vineyards run along the crest of the sharp ridge that gave them their name. Two connected, wood-sided winery buildings are cut into a slope just below the vines and just above a small pond, a quiet respite from the general grandeur of the place. Tours are by appointment only.

The winery also operates a tasting room on Highway 128 in Philo, offering samples of its Riesling, Merlot, and Cabernet Sauvignon.

Handley Cellars was dreamed up and executed practically single-handedly by its dynamic proprietor, Milla Handley. After learning the ropes at several prominent North Coast wineries, Handley made wine in a 20- by 30-foot basement for several years before building her own winery in 1987, on an old hillside farm southeast of Navarro.

The modest wooden building supplants a barn. It has a ridge vent along the top and a shed roof extending over the crush pad. Small stainless steel tanks line the fermenting room; another room accommodates cooperage. The lab and offices are to one side, with the tasting room facing Highway 128.

Handley's primary focus is barrel-fermented Chardonnay, along with some Sauvignon Blanc, but sparkling wines are steadily gaining priority. Handley Cel-

lars Brut is two parts Pinot Noir to one of Chardonnay (the usual). In 1984 she made her first Brut Rosé, a less chaste version of the Brut that blushes perpetually after one brief, wild moment of skin contact.

Handley Cellars is the northernmost winery in the Anderson Valley. The tower-cum-farmhouse beside the winery can be easily spotted from the road.

Husch Vineyards made an early start in Anderson Valley when Tony and Gretchen Husch launched it in 1971. The property now belongs to a family of veteran Mendocino vineyardists named Oswald, who have a large vineyard near Ukiah as well as the trim winery and rolling vineyard begun by their predecessors in Anderson Valley.

The L-shaped, wood-frame winery building, with its conventional array of stainless steel fermentors, oak upright tanks, and oak barrels, may be toured by appointment. The Oswalds offer all of their wines for tasting and sale from a refurbished one-time granary next to the winery, and provide several picnic tables shaded either by tall conifers or by a robust grapevine trained onto an arbor.

Wines include Chardonnay, Chenin Blanc, Gewürztraminer, Sauvignon Blanc (dry and late-harvest), Pinot Noir, and Cabernet Sauvignon.

Navarro Vineyards joined the roster of Anderson Valley wineries in 1975. Visitors are welcomed in an architecturally distinctive tasting room some hundreds of yards from the winery buildings, but right next to the highway.

A look around the weathered wood buildings of the winery requires an appointment. Proprietors Ted Bennett and Deborah Cahn built their small cellars to match an existing barn that they had earlier converted to a family residence. The winery also was built to spare some old oaks, which explains its irregular shape. The net effect is a visual pleasure, a cluster of tree-shaded, casual buildings on an impeccably orderly but not groomed knoll.

The sense of order extends into the winery; one cellar is devoted to reds (Pinot Noir and a bit of Cabernet Sauvignon), the other to whites (the specialty—Gewürztraminer, Chardonnay, Riesling and the popular Edelzwicker Vin Gris). The cooperage is European oak, divided about equally between puncheons and barrels. Stainless steel fermentors, a Howard basket press, and other modern processing equipment are on a deck at the rear.

Pepperwood Springs Winery is a handsome redwood version of the ubiquitous California barn, trimmed to a more current aesthetic. The setting is pristine oak woodland dressed with vine rows. Larry and Nicki Parsons founded the winery in 1981.

The label had just been established when the untimely death of one of the owners in 1986 suspended all operations. The property was subsequently sold. In spring 1987 the winery closed, but it reopened in 1988. Would-be visitors are advised to call for information when touring the area.

More Wineries. Anderson Valley is currently hosting a miniature wine boom. There were three established small cellars in 1987, with one large new one and several more emerging from the wings.

Christine Woods Winery commemorates the vanished township of Christine, a former North Coast tanbark and railroad-tie capital long since obscured by dense woods. Proprietor Vernon Rose found many relics while clearing land for his vineyards and winery; he plans to exhibit them in a new tasting room on Highway 128, scheduled for 1988 completion. Rose makes Zinfandel and Cabernet Sauvignon, among other wines.

Lazy Creek Winery remains the valley's original, and smallest, cellar. Hans and Teresa Kobler make about 500 cases of wine each year.

Pullman Vineyards is grower John Pullman's private label, established in 1983. He uses whatever grapes he doesn't sell to major wineries each year to make small lots of Boonville White and Boonville Red in a bare-bones winery near his house.

Roederer U.S., a subsidiary of the French Champagne firm Louis Roederer, became the Anderson Valley's largest winery in 1987 with the completion of a 44,000 square-foot facility amid 350 acres of Pinot Noir and Chardonnay vines about 4 miles west of Philo. The first release of non-vintage Brut sparkling wine appeared in early 1989, at which time the winery opened to visitors. Call the winery for visitor information.

Other Than Wineries

Most of the diversions in Mendocino County, other than wineries, are outdoorsy and, above all, watery.

In the Ukiah region, man-made Lake Mendocino fills a sizable bowl in the hills northeast of town. The lake has three recreation areas, two accessible from State Highway 20—the road to Lake County—and the third by way of Lake Mendocino Drive from U.S. Highway 101. All routes are signed clearly. The shoreside parks have boat launches, swimming beaches, and picnic areas. The lake is stocked with fish. The Russian River above the lake also has trout.

In Ukiah a fine municipal park just west of the main business district amplifies the potential for picnics. Scott Street leads to it from the main business street.

For a list of accommodations and restaurants in the Ukiah area, write to the Chamber of Commerce, 495-E East Perkins Street, Ukiah, CA 95482.

In the Anderson Valley north of Philo, Hendy Woods State Park has picnic tables and campsites in the shade of redwoods. Entrance to the park is a mile west of State Highway 128 on the Greenwood Ridge Road to Elk. Indian Creek, a quieter, less known picnic park, adjoins State 128 on the opposite side of Philo.

The headlands between Mendocino and Fort Bragg offer the best seats on the coast for whale-watching in late fall and again in spring. Look for both Humpbacks and California Greys.

Plotting a Route

U.S. Highway 101 burrows straight and fast through the Ukiah Valley, the upstream end of the Russian River watershed. The highway is partly two-lane but primarily freeway. No other direct route leads into the region from either north or south.

State Highway 128 runs the length of the Anderson Valley. It connects with U.S. 101 at Cloverdale in northern Sonoma County, and with State Highway 1 on the coast near Albion.

State Highway 20 is a winding way to get into the Ukiah Valley from the Sacramento Valley, and also connects Ukiah with the northern tip of Lake County's winegrowing area. In spring it has a glorious profusion of redbud as a scenic bonus. The other connector between Mendocino and Lake counties is State Highway 175 from Hopland to a point between Lakeport and Kelseyville. In a lot of spots it would keep a Model T well below peak speed.

One other connecting road to know about is State Highway 253, which runs a high, curving course across the Coast Ranges from Ukiah to Boonville, on State Highway 128. It is the shortest route between the Ukiah and Anderson Valleys, but its scenery discourages haste even more than do its twisting, climbing turns.

Lake County

Of all the North Coast counties of California, Lake is the most bucolic. It never has had a railroad. It has no city of substantial size. Lakeport (population 5,000) is its county seat and largest town. The whole county has but 49,000 residents—and therein lies its charm.

Kelseyville, Middletown, and the other towns and villages of Lake County bring to mind scenes of Penrod and other Booth Tarkington characters of an era that pretty well has disappeared from more populous parts of the state. Businesses are small and local. There is a good deal of waving and talking among familiars along Main Street. A three-piece suit would be an oddity on almost anybody, even the banker. This is not to say Lake County is out of touch with the world. Its great geographic feature, Clear Lake, draws tourists by the hundreds on cool days and by the thousands on warm ones, and its resort owners and farmers know all the new tricks of their trades.

The county's recent spate of new vineyards and wineries fits into this picture well.

When California winemaking began to stagger back to life after Prohibition, it quickly became a truism that Sonoma fell into the shadow of Napa, that Mendocino struggled along behind Sonoma, and that Lake trailed in the wake of Mendocino. In a short time, Lake ran out of wineries altogether, and had only a scattered handful of surviving vineyards. Lake still is last in line in numbers of wineries and acres of vines among these four counties, but its reawakening is well advanced.

The Wineries

In Spring 1987, Lake County had six wineries, divided about half and half between the Lakeport-Kelseyville area alongside Clear Lake, and the Middletown district to the south of it. One, Guenoc Winery, has a whole appellation all to itself.

Cobb Mountain Winery is a converted barn in the lee of its namesake, the highest peak in Lake County. San Francisco lawyer James Downing makes Zinfandel and Chenin Blanc from a 20-acre vineyard surrounded by deep pine woods, pasture, and Miwok Indian ghosts.

The land was scrutinized by California State archaeologists prior to planting, to make sure the development wouldn't destroy any historical sites such as the Miwok burial ground a half-mile up the road. They didn't find so much as an arrowhead on Downing's ranch, so he proceeded to plant his vineyard in 1980.

Guenoc Winery revives winemaking in a storied place. The property once belonged to the British actress Lily Langtry, who imported a winemaker from Bordeaux and gave him instructions to do something a long cut above ordinary. Alas for history, her timing was off. Prohibition ended the attempt before it could make a fair start.

The current owners, a Hawaiian family named Magoon, have set about a plan that puts Lily's in the shade. Their winery, completed during the spring of 1982, perches atop a hill that was substantially reshaped for the purpose. It is a plain rectangle, if anything 180 by 300 feet and covered with clear, heart-grade redwood could be called plain. From one end, the view is across a small lake. From the other, the scene is mostly vines, although Lily's old house—now a family residence—can be seen in the middle distance.

The winery proper is impressive for its modern gear as well as for its size. The westerly end is a huge room containing a Willmes membrane press and a still-growing collection of stainless steel fermentors. A middle section of almost equal size houses a small number of upright oak tanks and what appears to be half an acre of French barrels. The easterly portion, facing Lily's house, is devoted to storing bottled wines, all made from grapes grown on the property.

The Guenoc label covers Chardonnay, Chenin Blanc, Sauvignon Blanc, Cabernet Sauvignon, Petite Sirah, and Zinfandel. Victorian Red and Lily's White are proprietary bottlings.

Kendall-Jackson Winery's picturesque vineyards are situated, one might say, atop a volcano. That is, during Mt. Konocti's last active period some millennia past, a major chunk of the mountain's upper crust is said to have been blown sky-high and then thundered to earth near present-day Lakeport, forming the deep, mineral-rich soil in which Kendall-Jackson's perfectly manicured vines now grow.

More recently, the region was home to Miwok and Pomo Indians, whose obsidian spearheads are still recovered frequently by vineyard hands.

Kendall-Jackson is a lovely winery estate that somehow evokes a dreamier, more tranquil era than ours. This despite the antibucolic presence of two modern winery buildings—one of cement block, the other a metal pole barn, with a crush pad between them. The tasting room sports a long wooden bar and overlooks shaded picnic tables and the vineyard beyond, its rows punctuated with purple Japanese plum trees.

Kendall-Jackson wines include two separate barrel-fermented Chardonnays, and three vineyard-designated Zinfandels from very old, mountain vineyards. There are also Cabernet Sauvignon, Riesling, and Sauvignon Blanc. The owners have recently purchased another winery—Edmeades, in Anderson Valley—as well as substantial new acreage in Santa Barbara County.

The Konocti Winery hides among the last few trees of an old walnut orchard not far north of Kelseyville. The prefabricated metal building belongs to several partners, including a cooperative of more than 20 growers with nearby vineyards ranging in size from 2.5 to 40 acres. They make visitors more than mildly welcome.

A tasting room-gift shop occupies most of a small wood-frame building attached to the front of the winery. Outside, a number of picnic tables sit on a lawn well shaded by old walnut trees. On summer Sundays, the proprietors have local musicians on hand to complete Omar's famous triumvirate of treasures. On the second weekend in October, they stage a harvest festival with barbecue, art show, grape stomp, and, for those who would rather make distance than gallonage, a vineyard run.

Konocti will provide guided tours of its crowded cellars by appointment, but drop-in guests are allowed to stroll through on their own. The interior holds a diverse collection of stainless steel fermentors and storage tanks, redwood tanks, and American and French oak barrels. Out back, the roof extends to overhang more stainless steel fermentors.

The winery produces Chardonnay, Sauvignon Blanc, late-harvest Riesling, and Cabernet Sauvignon (white and red).

Channing Rudd Cellars began as a Bay Area portworks in 1977. Five years later, the Rudd family moved to a 60-acre ranch near Middletown and began planting what eventually became 25 acres of grapes to be used in estate table wines. As their own grapes approached maturity in 1987 the Rudds were purchasing grapes to make Petite Sirah and Zinfandel in a temporary winery on the property, and were contemplating major construction.

Stuermer Winery perches jauntily on the first rise of a small hill south of Lower Lake. Founded in 1977, it is the county's oldest winery in continuous production.

Two connected sections of a redwood-faced, steep-roofed building leave room for the owners, Harold Stuermer and his family, to enlarge their production a bit without new construction. Even when the buildings are filled with gear, this will be a small winery. In the rear, larger portion of the structure, stainless steel fermentors fill only part of the area set aside for them. Adjacent neat stacks of French and American oak barrels also leave room for more to come. The front section is set aside for stored wines in bottle, the tasting room, and offices.

Winemaker Daniel Stuermer makes only Cabernet Sauvignon under the primary label. Most bottlings are from single vineyards identified on the labels. All are from Lake County grapes. A wider varietal range is marketed under the Arcadia label.

Other Than Wineries

The principal activity around Clear Lake is visiting the shoreside resorts. In fact the short roster of widely spread wineries makes them an excellent adjunct to a lakeshore vacation.

Day-trippers or camping vacationers can stop at sizable Clear Lake State Park, not far north of Kelseyville via Soda Bay Road. Or continue east on the same road to reach county-owned Buckingham Park. The state park ranges from 1400 feet elevation down to lake level, and has camping and picnicking sites, swimming beaches, and boat launches. Buckingham, on a peninsula sticking into the lake, has similar amenities. For lists of accommodations, write to the Lake County Chamber of Commerce, 875 Lakeport Boulevard, Lakeport, CA 95453.

Lake County also boasts one of California's newest and most fascinating parks, both for spotting wildlife and for tracking human culture. At the southern end of Clear Lake, the water spreads into a swamp, pooling slowly through the tule grass under ancient oaks to where Cache Creek begins its long, rugged descent to the Sacramento River. The swamp is Anderson Marsh State Historic Park. Its 870 acres embrace more than 50 percent of Clear Lake's remaining wetland habitat; the dense population of fishes, birds, and animals includes numerous American Bald Eagles. From an archaeological perspective, Anderson Marsh has been occupied for more than 10,000 years, first by Pomo Indians and, more recently, by the pioneer family from Scotland who gave the new park its name. Evidence of both cultures is there in abundance.

In 1987 the California Department of Parks was just developing a long-range management plan. Trails and a visitors' center have been in place for some time, however. For information contact the Anderson Marsh Interpretive Association, P.O. Box 3217, Clearlake, CA 95422.

Plotting a Route

Lake County does not have a U.S. Highway or Interstate Freeway in it, which is part of its charm. The main road connecting the area with other parts of the world is State Highway 20, which intersects with U.S. Highway 101 near Ukiah, and with Interstate Highway 5 a little more than 50 miles north of Sacramento at Williams.

State Highway 175 runs, hilly and tightly winding, from U.S. 101 at Hopland to an intersection with State Highway 29 between Lakeport and Kelseyville.

The other routes into the county wind through Napa County. Both are slow and mountainous in spots. State 29 continues from the Napa Valley northward. The alternative route is Deer Park-Howell Mountain Road from the Napa Valley east to Pope Valley, then north on Pope Valley Road-Butts Canyon Road into Middletown.

One point of advice: State 175 between Clear Lake Park and Middletown appears to be a short cut compared to State 29. It is not.

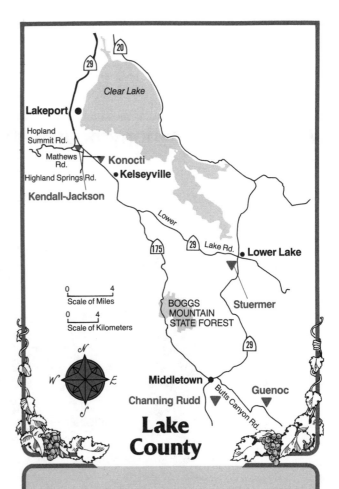

Lake County

Cobb Mountain Winery. (P.O. Box 263, Middletown, CA 95461) Tel (415) 934-1011. No visitors. (Not on map).

Guenoc Winery. From State 29 at N side of Middletown, SE 5.5 miles on Butts Canyon Rd. to winery drive at 21000 (P.O. Box 1146, Middletown, CA 95461) Tel (707) 987-2359. By appt. only.

Kendall-Jackson Winery. From State 29, 2.5 miles S of Lakeport, SW .8 mi. on Ackley Rd., E .3 mi. on Mathews Rd. (600 Mathews Rd., Lakeport, CA 95453) Tel (707) 263-9333. Picnic. Daily 11-5. Ta.

The Konocti Winery. From Kelseyville, N 1 mi. on State 29 to Thomas Dr. (P.O. Box 890, Kelseyville, CA 95451) Tel (707) 279-8861. Picnic. Daily 11-5. IT/Ta. GT by appt.

Channing Rudd Cellars. From State 29, NE of Middletown at jct. of Butts Canyon Rd. and St. Helena Creek Rd., take St. Helena Creek Rd. S 3.5 mi. to winery (P.O. Box 426, Middletown, CA 95461) Tel (707) 987-2209. By appt. only.

Stuermer Winery. W side State 29, 1.2 mi. S of Lower Lake (P.O. Box 950, Hwy. 29, Lower Lake, CA 95457) Tel (707) 994-4069. Th-Su 10-5 or by appt. IT/Ta.

Key: GT (guided tour); IT (informal tour); Ta (tasting).

The Napa Valley

A small place synonymous with Wine Country

Old Bale Mill-Napa

"**N**apa Valley" often is used interchangeably with "Wine Country," and not without reason. About 150 wineries, most of them handsomely traditional but some handsomely contemporary, are spaced at close intervals all the way from the Carneros district near San Pablo Bay to the skirts of Mt. St. Helena, 25 miles northwest. Many of their names reach far back into the nineteenth century, and far back in the memories of knowledgeable wine hobbyists. Napa further earns the title of Wine Country because the cellars in this valley are surrounded by seas of vineyards, some 30,000 acres of them.

Level and easy to negotiate as the floor of the valley is, it never becomes wide enough to lose the imminent sense of tall and consistently rugged hills on either side. Local roads burrow into the hearts of vineyarded land on flat and mountainside alike, offering visitors a whole gamut of views to admire.

The variable terrain that provides the views also makes the Napa Valley, in effect, several wine districts in one. The craggy ramparts enclosing the valley amount to a separate region superimposed on the valley bed. Howell and Spring mountains, for example, although included in the Napa Valley appellation, are viticultural worlds of their own. The valley floor, too,

has what Robert Louis Stevenson called "vinous bonanzas," where soil and climate combinations produce wines of uncommon character from one grape or another.

The near end of the valley is just a little over an hour from San Francisco; the far end is not quite two hours away if one hurries, nonstop. However, it is of the essence *not* to hurry.

The Wineries

An old rule of thumb among veteran visitors to California wineries is this: three cellars a day, no more. If there is any district in the state that tempts people to stretch the rule, Napa is it, because the wineries are so close together. It's wise to resist the temptation.

It is worth noting that, though the larger cellars are able to offer highly developed tour and tasting programs, the small cellars do not have enough hands to do that. More to the point, they cannot always give an appointment when someone calls for one, simply because the lone hand may have to spend the day delivering wine, or chasing after a replacement part for something that broke, or—the crux of it all—working on the winemaking itself. Patience and persistence are almost always rewarded in these cases.

There are no internal divisions in the alphabetical listing of Napa wineries because the cellars are so regularly spaced. However, they are so numerous that the map has been divided into three areas to fit them all in. Map entries are alphabetical within each area shown.

Alta Vineyard Cellar was an established winery without a home in Spring 1987. Rose and Benjamin Falk founded their winery in 1979, just downhill from Schramsberg, in a small stone building immortalized as M'Eckron's by Robert Louis Stevenson in *Silverado Squatters*. The Falks produced Chardonnay there until 1986, when they moved the operation to temporary quarters pending selection of a new site.

Beaulieu Vineyard in Rutherford is one of the Napa Valley's more telling demonstrations of the state of international winemaking in modern times.

The crushers are Garolla-types, made in Fresno after an Italian design. The presses are Willmes from Germany. The filters are both Italian and American. The cooperage includes American stainless steel for fermenting and California redwood, Kentucky oak, and French oak for aging the wines. This equipment was gathered for years by the former winemaker, Russian-born, French-trained Andre Tchelistcheff.

Touring Beaulieu (pronounced bowl-you, more or less) requires some sense of direction. The oldest part of the building dates (under another name) to 1885. Occasional expansion since then has not imposed any rigid order on the whereabouts of walls or working gear.

Beaulieu was founded as a company in 1900 by a newly arrived Frenchman named Georges de Latour. The winery was continued first by his widow, then by his daughter, who married the eminently Gallic Marquis de Pins. The de Pins' daughter, Héléne de Latour de Pins, ran the winery from 1951 to 1969, when she sold it to Heublein, Inc.

The buildings give some indication of their history. All the parts painted a cream color date from the original or the de Pins' years. The parts left unpainted are additions since Heublein acquired the winery.

The wines include Chardonnay, Sauvignon Blanc, Riesling, Cabernet Sauvignon in three separate styles, Gamay Beaujolais, and Pinot Noir. There are also sparkling wines, a pair of generics, and Muscat de Frontignan. Selected wines are available for tasting in a handsome building at one side of the winery. This building also is the beginning point for tours.

Beringer Vineyards dates from a modest migration of Germans into the Napa Valley in the mid-nineteenth century. Architecturally, it is German, but not modest.

The winery is fronted by Rhine House, built by Frederick Beringer as a replica of the Rhenish home he and brother Jacob left behind when they emigrated. Tours start at the front door and end in a tasting room handsomely turned out in period style.

Uphill from the stone and half-timbered house, about level with its steep slate roof, Beringer's original aging cellars include 1,000 feet of tunnels. The founding brothers employed Chinese laborers to dig the tunnels, starting in 1876, the winery's inaugural year. In some sections, pick marks still show plainly through a veil of dusty black lichen. After the caves developed a slight tendency to drop small chunks of rock on staff and visitors, the proprietors reinforced the weak spots with Gunite, giving some sections a newer look.

Beringer has long since outgrown the tunnels and the finely crafted stone building that fronts them. The third generation of Beringers had expanded beyond the original capacity before they sold their cellars in 1969 to Nestlé, Inc., which built a more efficient cellar across the Avenue of the Elms in 1975. Wine World, Inc., purchased the winery and vineyards in 1980.

Tasting at the Rhine House is of selected wines from a broad roster that includes Chardonnay, Sauvignon Blanc, Chenin Blanc, Cabernet Sauvignon, and a rare example of Cabernet Port.

Bouchaine Vineyards epitomizes the revitalization of a wine district that was well known a century ago but never quite recovered from Prohibition. Set on a rolling Carneros District hill overlooking San Pablo Bay, the winery building has been around for a good long time as a bulk cellar. Its current owners, a limited partnership, have transformed it from a weathered white barn into a striking redwood-sided building of impressive size. They also have made over parts of it from an obsolete winery into a modern cellar, but have kept some old gear for the firm's second purpose: making and storing wine for others under contract. The winery's name was changed from Chateau Bouchaine in 1986.

For visitors (by appointment), having a small, new winery inside a larger old one provides a chance to look at working examples of present and past side by side. The stainless steel fermentors have open-topped concrete ones as neighbors, for example, and a long, low room full of French oak barrels adjoins a long, tall room full of well-seasoned redwood tanks. Outside, 30 acres of Chardonnay vines bask in a mild climate that favors Burgundian grapes in particular.

The first substantial amounts of Bouchaine Chardonnay and Pinot Noir, along with some Sauvignon Blanc, were made from the vintage of 1982 but were not released until 1984. There also have been three vintages of Cabernet Sauvignon, from vineyards in the Rutherford area, sold by advance subscription.

Burgess Cellars is well above the Napa Valley floor on the lower slope of Howell Mountain.

The main building is one of the few classic stone and wood-frame wineries still in operation in the county. When such cellars were built into hillsides in the 1880s, the upper wooden story held the fermentors and other processing gear, while the cooler stone lower level held cooperage full of aging wines. Matters are still arranged somewhat along the original lines, although the premises now occupy three buildings rather than one.

The current name dates to 1972 when Tom and Linda Burgess bought the property. They offer Chardonnay, Cabernet Sauvignon, and Zinfandel.

Cain Cellars occupies a world of its own at the top of Sulphur Springs Canyon, above St. Helena. Owner Jerry Cain planted his vineyard at the canyon's apex to exploit a unique combination of soil, exposure, and natural air-conditioning. The winery, begun in 1982 and completed in 1986, overlooks most of the Napa and Sonoma valleys from its mountainside niche. On one side it looks southwest, across Sonoma County to the sea. The opposite view takes in most of the valley, Howell Mountain, and, occasionally, the Sierras.

The winery, built from local stone and more modern materials, is actually three structures tied into one another. The dramatic central tower provides a visual, but not architectural, center. The true story is told by three separate rooflines. On the left as one enters is the stone-faced tower, containing offices and hospitality facilities. The barrel cellar is a separate structure extending into the hillside to the right. Behind both, perpendicular to the barrel cellar, is a large fermentation wing, containing stainless steel tanks, storage, the lab, and a bottling line. Visits are by appointment only.

The roster of wines, all estate grown, includes Sauvignon Blanc, Chardonnay, Cabernet Sauvignon, and Merlot. As of 1987 the focus was on developing a formula by which to combine the two red varietals, plus Cabernet Franc and Malbec, into a proprietary red wine.

Cakebread Cellars occupies three distinctive wood-frame buildings. Part of their individual appearance comes from graceful proportion, part from impressive expanses of unornamented, unpainted redwood siding; but the unmistakable signature is a short, thick tower rising up at the intersection of the winery's two crossing wings. Another sure sign of the place, in season, is a long bed of brilliant flowers alongside the hospitality house.

This building, next to State Highway 29 north of Oakville, was completed in 1986. The winery began in 1974 in a smaller wood-frame building some hundreds of yards farther back in the vineyard, then moved to its present quarters in 1981. The original building now is used to make the barrel-fermented portion of the winery's Chardonnay.

The phased construction fairly typifies Napa's new wave of small, family-owned wineries. Owners Jack and Dolores Cakebread have complicated their own progress by sustaining other careers in professional photography and automotive mechanics, and have simplified it by installing their son Bruce as winemaker after sending him through the enology course at UC Davis.

Three varietals are made at Cakebread: Chardonnay, Sauvignon Blanc, and Cabernet Sauvignon.

Carneros Creek Winery, founded in 1971, nestles into a hidden fold of the Carneros district south of Napa city, in a small, pleasantly understated structure built in two phases—one wing at a time.

In these conventionally equipped cellars, stainless steel fermentors occupy a roofed shed at the rear, while French oak barrels take up the majority of floor space inside the masonry block walls.

When work does not demand undivided attention, someone—possibly partner-winemaker Francis Mahoney—may stop to talk shop with casual visitors, but the staff is small enough that an appointment is a surer way to make a visit instructive at a winery where discussion can dwell on separate lots of wines from individually identified vineyards. There is some emphasis on Chardonnay and Pinot Noir. Merlot and Cabernet Sauvignon complete the list.

Cassayre-Forni Cellars had joined, in spring 1987, that small but constant percentage of California wineries which are in transit from their initial sites to new quarters elsewhere. In this case, the former was south of Rutherford, but the latter had yet to be chosen.

Partners Paul Cassayre and Mike Forni established the cellars in 1977. As of the 1986 vintage, the roster included dry Chenin Blanc, Cabernet Sauvignon, and Zinfandel.

Caymus Vineyards straddles Conn Creek east of Rutherford, more or less at the heart of the huge nineteenth-century Spanish land grant from which it draws its name.

Proprietor Charles Wagner is an old hand in the Napa Valley, the second generation of his family to grow grapes on the property. He is also not a man for frills. As a result of both facts, he and his son Chuck have assembled their winery in a trio of plain buildings and equipped it in part with gear that goes back almost as far as the family does. For example, a stemmer-crusher dates from 1909, which makes new parts hard to come by. Similarly, the presses are a pair of baskets with the same kind of hydraulic lifts used for automobile hoists, a device once common but seldom seen in wineries these days.

This is not to say the Wagners turn a blind eye to the present. The fermentors are made of jacketed and insulated stainless steel. Two of the buildings house thoughtful collections of European and American oak in the forms of barrels, oval casks, and upright tanks. The third structure houses a modern bottling line.

As a winery, Caymus dates from 1972. It was one of the earliest to produce an *Oeil de Perdrix* ("partridge eye" in French) from Pinot Noir. That wine continues as part of the list along with Chardonnay, Sauvignon Blanc, Riesling, Cabernet Sauvignon, Pinot Noir, and Zinfandel.

Chateau Chevalier revives a flamboyant piece of nineteenth-century architecture.

An aggressive businessman named F. Chevalier erected a towered and turreted stone building on a steep hillside in 1891, which he named after himself.

After a long hiatus, the old building was purchased in 1973 by Greg Bissonette, and became a winery once again, although on a smaller scale than originally. Only the lowest level of three is used for winemaking.

The vineyard land on the skirts of Spring Mountain above St. Helena was cleared in 1969 and replanted in 1970. The current owner, Gil Nickel, bought it in 1986. The principal wines are Chardonnay and Cabernet Sauvignon. Even with grapes from other vineyards, production is so small that tasting is impractical.

Chateau Chevre got its name in whimsical tribute to a former use of the property. The translation from French is Goat Castle. The building in question is a small, indestructible, oddly shaped, white-painted concrete structure that now is a compact cellar, but used to be an all-purpose barn. Milk goats grazed where partners Gerald Hazen and Robert Mueller now grow vines, just south of Yountville.

Two-year-old wines in French barrels occupy one room. Year-old wines and the bottling line share the former milking room. Cased goods stack up in a narrow, tall wing that used to hold feed. A small crusher and press are outdoors on one side. Open-topped stainless steel tubs for fermenting sit outside the opposite wall. Hazen uses the tubs so that he can stay with the technique of punching down red wine caps by hand.

Sauvignon Blanc, Cabernet Franc, and Merlot are produced from the estate vineyard.

Chateau Montelena is both a relatively new winery and a Napa Valley old-timer.

The finely crafted stone building dates back to the 1880s, when Alfred L. Tubbs had it built on its hilly site north of Calistoga, just where the road to Lake County starts over one shoulder of Mt. St. Helena.

In its present form, dating from 1968, the winery has revived the primary label name from the pre-Prohibition Tubbs days, but otherwise is a modern, efficient example of a small, estatelike property. Within the old stone walls, one-half of the main cellar holds stainless steel fermentors; the other half is devoted to row upon row of oak barrels from a variety of sources. A flanking room contains the bottling line.

During the long interval between Tubb's proprietorship and the current one, an owner named Yort Frank began to make the property into a showcase Chinese garden. Tea houses on two islands in a small lake still survive as picturesque souvenirs of that effort.

Chateau Montelena has but four wines on its list. Chardonnay and Johannisberg Riesling are the whites; Cabernet Sauvignon and Zinfandel the reds. One or another is selected for tasting each day.

The Christian Brothers inaugurated their California winemaking in Martinez shortly before the turn of the century. A bas-relief in the winery office shows one of the brothers at Martinez crushing grapes in a horse trough with a wooden club.

By the time The Christian Brothers packed up to come to the Napa Valley in 1930, the equipment they barged across San Pablo Bay was much improved over the trough and club. Now their winery operations are a dazzling mixture of the traditional and the modern.

The monumental Greystone Cellars, at the northern edge of St. Helena, dates from 1888, when William Bowers Bourn (see Filoli, page 104) used a small part of his great fortune to construct the vast building as the largest stone cellar in the world. The Christian Brothers bought the property in 1950.

Crushing, fermenting, and sparkling winemaking all are done at the architecturally ordinary south St. Helena winery, its big, ultramodern fermenting installation visible from State 29 but not open to visitors.

There are tours of Greystone, which has, as a bonus attraction, some of Brother Timothy's seemingly limitless corkscrew collection.

At the tasting room, nearly all The Christian Broth-

Wine & Cheese

ers' long list of wines is available for sampling. The roster includes several estate bottlings from selected vineyards.

Clos du Val Wine Company, an altogether new winery at its founding in 1972, comes by its French name honestly, for both the principal owner and winemaker-manager Bernard Portet are French.

The winery building, elegantly proportioned and handsome in an understated, almost plain-faced way, occupies a square cut into one corner of the Chimney Rock Golf Course on the Silverado Trail north of Napa city, in the Stag's Leap viticultural area.

Inside, it once offered a rather clear example of a typical Bordeaux chateau. Two rows of stainless steel fermentors and the press occupied one end. Echoing rows of oak upright tanks adjoined the fermentors for initial racking of new wines. Two-high stacks of French barrels next to the uprights carried the wine the rest of the way to bottling. The recent addition of a rather vast auxiliary building has changed the picture somewhat, but this remains a good place to see how a Bordelais winemaker would arrange his working gear.

The roster of wines includes Chardonnay, Sauvignon Blanc, Semillon, Cabernet Sauvignon, Merlot, Pinot Noir, and Zinfandel. Wines under the main label often have a proportion of blended grapes for complexity. Those named Granval do not.

Conn Creek Winery plunges visitors into the core of things as soon as they step through glass doors at the front of a white stucco building that provides some refreshing turns on Mediterranean architectural themes other than Spanish mission.

A small entryway looks straight into a fermenting room with twin rows of stainless steel and a third row of oak upright tanks. The same entry looks obliquely into a gallerylike hall full of French oak barrels. Only the crusher and press (out back) and the bottling room of the working winery are not in instant view.

The reception area for visitors is at the top of a stairway immediately adjacent to the front doors. It consists

(Continued on page 82)

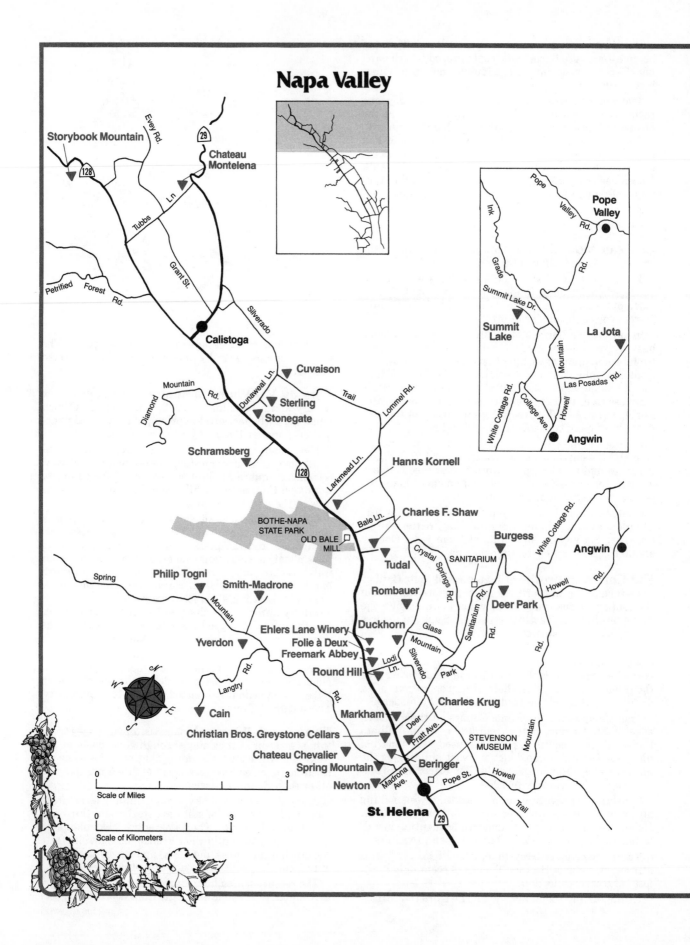

Napa Valley

Storybook Mountain

128

Evey Rd.

29

Chateau
Montelena

Ln

Tubbs

Grant St.

Petrified   Forest   Rd.

Silverado

Calistoga

Mountain   Rd.

Diamond

Dunaweal Ln.

Cuvaison

Sterling

Stonegate

Trail

Lommel Rd.

Schramsberg

128

Larkmead Ln.

Hanns Kornell

BOTHE-NAPA
STATE PARK

OLD BALE
MILL

Bale Ln.

Charles F. Shaw

Tudal

Crystal Springs Rd.

SANITARIUM

Burgess

White Cottage Rd.

Angwin

Spring

Philip Togni

Mountain

Smith-Madrone

Rombauer

Glass

Sanitarium Rd.

Deer Park

Howell   Rd.

Mountain

Yverdon

Rd.

Ehlers Lane Winery

Folie à Deux

Freemark Abbey

Duckhorn

Lodi
Ln.

Mountain

Silverado

Park

Rd.

Langtry   Rd.

Round Hill

Cain

Charles Krug

Mountain

Christian Bros. Greystone Cellars

Markham

Deer

Pratt Ave.

STEVENSON
MUSEUM

Howell

Chateau Chevalier

Spring Mountain

Newton

Madrona
Ave.

Beringer

Pope St.

Trail

St. Helena

29

0   3
Scale of Miles

0   3
Scale of Kilometers

Pope   Valley   Rd.

Ink

Grade

Summit Lake Dr.

Summit
Lake

Pope
Valley

La Jota

White Cottage Rd.

College Ave.

Mountain

Howell

Las Posadas Rd.

Angwin

Beringer Vineyards. W side State 29, N limit of St. Helena (2000 Main St., St. Helena, CA 94574) Tel (707) 963-7115. Daily 9:30-5:30 (last tour 4:00). GT/Ta.

Burgess Cellars. From State 29, N of St. Helena, E on Deer Park Rd. 3 mi. to winery drive at 1108 (P.O. Box 282, St. Helena, CA 94574) Tel (707) 963-4766. Daily 10-4. GT by appt.

Cain Cellars. From State 29 at St. Helena, W 3 blks. on Madrona Ave., NW on Spring Mountain Rd., S 2.3 mi. on Langtry Rd. to winery drive (3800 Langtry Rd., St. Helena, CA 94574) Tel (707) 963-1616. GT/Ta by appt.

Chateau Chevalier. From State 29 at St. Helena, W 3.3 mi. on Madrona Ave./Spring Mountain Rd. to winery drive at 3101 (P.O. Box 991, St. Helena, CA 94574) Tel (707) 963-2342. By appt. only.

Chateau Montelena. From State 29 N of Calistoga, W .2 mi. on Tubbs Ln. to winery drive (1429 Tubbs Ln., Calistoga, CA 94515) Tel (707) 942-5105. Daily 10-12, 1-4. Ta/GT by appt.

The Christian Brothers/Greystone. W side of State 29 at N limit of St. Helena (P.O. Box 391, St. Helena, CA 94574) Tel (707) 963-4480. Daily. GT/Ta.

Cuvaison. Just S of Dunaweal Ln., E side of Silverado Tr. at 4550 (P.O. Box 384, Calistoga, CA 94515) Tel (707) 942-6266. Picnic. GT/IT/Ta by appt.

Deer Park Winery. From State 29 N of St. Helena, E 2.5 mi. on Deer Park Rd. (1000 Deer Park Rd., Deer Park, CA 94576) Tel (707) 963-5411. GT/Ta by appt.

Duckhorn Vineyards. On Silverado Tr., .2 mi. N of Lodi Ln. (3027 Silverado Tr., St. Helena, CA 94574) Tel (707) 963-7108. M-F 9-4:30. GT by appt.

Ehlers Lane Winery. From State 29 N of St. Helena, E .2 mi. on Ehlers Ln. (3222 Ehlers Ln., St. Helena, CA 94574) Tel (707) 963-0144. GT/Ta by appt.

Folie à Deux Winery. E side State 29 N of St. Helena (3070 Hwy. 29, St. Helena, CA 94574) Tel (707) 963-1160. Tu-Su 11-5. Ta.

Freemark Abbey. E side State 29 N of St. Helena at Lodi Ln. (P.O. Box 410, St. Helena, CA 94574) Tel (707) 963-9694. Daily 10-4:30. Ta. GT daily at 2.

Hanns Kornell Champagne Cellars. From State 29 N of St. Helena, E .25 mi. on Larkmead Ln. (P.O. Box 249, St. Helena, CA 94574) Tel (707) 963-1237. Daily 10-4:30 GT/Ta.

Charles Krug Winery. E side State 29 at N limit of St. Helena (P.O. Box 191, St. Helena, CA 94574) Tel (707) 963-2761. Daily 10-5. GT/Ta.

La Jota Vineyard Co. From State 29 N of St. Helena, NE 6.1 mi. on Deer Park/Howell Mtn. Rd., E 2.2 mi. on Cold Springs/Las Posadas Rd. to pvt. winery road (1102 Las Posadas Rd., Angwin, CA 94508) Tel (707) 965-3020. GT/Ta by appt.

Markham Winery. E side State 29 N of St. Helena at Deer Park Rd. (P.O. Box 636, St. Helena, CA 94574) Tel (707) 963-5292. Daily 11-4. Ta.

Newton Vineyard. From State 29 at St. Helena, W on Madrona Ave. to pvt. drive at end (2555 Madrona Ave., St. Helena, CA 94574) Tel (707) 963-9000. GT by appt.

Rombauer Vineyards. NE of St. Helena, W side Silverado Trail 1.8 mi. N of Deer Park Rd. to winery drive (3522 Silverado Trail, St. Helena, CA 94574) Tel (707) 963-5170. GT by appt.

Round Hill Cellars. From State 29 N of St. Helena, E .3 mi. on Lodi Ln. (1097 Lodi Ln., St. Helena, CA 94574) Tel (707) 963-1841. Daily 9-5. GT/Ta.

Schramsberg Vineyards. From State 29 .5 mi. N of Larkmead Ln., W on Petersen Ln., N to winery at end of pvt. rd. (1400 Schramsberg Rd., Calistoga, CA 94515) Tel (707) 942-4558. M-Sa by appt. GT.

Charles F. Shaw Vineyards & Winery. From State 29 N of St. Helena, E .2 mi. on Big Tree Rd. to winery drive (1010 Big Tree Rd., St. Helena, CA 94574) Tel (707) 963-5459. Daily 11-5. Ta. IT by appt.

Smith-Madrone Vineyards. From State 29 at St. Helena, W 3 blks. on Madrona Ave., NW 5.5 mi. on Spring Mtn. Rd. to 4022 (P.O. Box 451, St. Helena, CA 94574) Tel (707) 963-2283 or 963-2291. GT/Ta by appt.

Spring Mountain Vineyards. From State 29 at St. Helena, W 3 blks. on Madrona Ave., NW 1.1 mi. on Spring Mountain Rd. to winery drive (2805 Spring Mountain Rd., St. Helena, CA 94574) Tel (707) 963-5233. Daily 10-4:30. GT/IT/Ta.

Sterling Vineyards. From State 29 N of St. Helena, E .5 mi. on Dunaweal Ln. to winery drive at 1111 (P.O. Box 365, Calistoga, CA 94515) Tel (707) 942-5151. Daily 10:30-4:30. IT/Ta.

Stonegate Winery. From State 29 N of St. Helena, E .1 mi. on Dunaweal Ln. (1183 Dunaweal Ln., Calistoga, CA 94515) Tel (707) 942-6500. Daily 10:30-4. Ta. GT by appt.

Storybook Mountain Vineyards. From Calistoga, N 4 mi. on State 128 to winery drive (3835 Hwy. 128, Calistoga, CA 94515) Tel (707) 942-5310. By appt. only, Sa preferred.

Summit Lake Vineyards. From State 29 N of St. Helena, NE 6.6 mi. on Deer Park/Howell Mtn. Rd., NW .8 mi. on College Ave., N 1 mi. on White Cottage Rd., NW 1.2 mi. on Summit Lake Dr. (2000 Summit Lake Dr., Angwin, CA 94508) Tel (707) 965-2488. GT/Ta by appt.

Philip Togni Vineyard. From State 29 at St. Helena, W 4.8 mi. on Madrona Ave./Spring Mtn. Rd. to winery drive (3780 Spring Mtn. Rd., St. Helena, CA 94574) Tel (707) 963-3731. GT/Ta by appt.

Tudal Winery. From State 29 .2 mi. N of St. Helena, E .2 mi. on Big Tree Rd. (1015 Big Tree Rd., St. Helena, CA 94574) Tel (707) 963-3947. By appt. only.

Yverdon Vineyards. From St. Helena, W 3 blks. on Madrona Ave., NW 4 mi. on Spring Mountain Rd. (3787 Spring Mountain Rd., St. Helena, CA 94574) Tel (707) 963-4270. M-F 8-3:30. GT by appt.

Wineries Not on Map— Restricted or No Visitor Facilities

Alta Vineyard Cellar. (P.O. Box 980, Calistoga, CA 94515) Tel (707) 942-6708. By appt. only.

Vincent Arroyo Winery. (2361 Greenwood Ave., Calistoga, CA 94515) Tel (707) 942-6995.

Casa Nuestra. (3473 Silverado Tr. N, St. Helena, CA 94574) Tel (707) 963-4684.

Chateau Boswell. (3468 Silverado Tr. N., St. Helena, CA 94574) Tel (707) 963-5472.

Clos Pegase. (1060 Dunaweal Ln., P.O. Box 305, Calistoga, CA 94515) Tel (707) 942-4981.

Diamond Creek Vineyards. (1500 Diamond Mountain Rd., Calistoga, CA 94515) Tel (707) 942-6926.

Dunn Vineyards. (805 White Cottage Rd., Angwin, CA 94508) Tel (707) 965-3642.

Frog's Leap Winery. (3358 St. Helena Hwy., St. Helena, CA 94574) Tel (707) 963-4704.

Robert Keenan Winery. (3660 Spring Mtn. Rd., St. Helena, CA 94574) Tel (707) 963-9177. By appt. only.

Lamborn Family Vineyards. (2075 Summit Lake Dr., Angwin, CA 94508) Tel (707) 965-2811.

La Vieille Montagne. (3851 Spring Mtn. Rd., St. Helena, CA 94574) Tel (707) 963-9059.

Robert Pecota Winery. (P.O. Box 303, Calistoga, CA 94515) Tel (707) 942-6625.

Ritchie Creek Vineyard. (4024 Spring Mountain Rd., St. Helena, CA 94574) Tel (707) 963-4661.

St. Clement Vineyards. (P.O. Box 261, St. Helena, CA 94574) Tel (707) 963-7221.

Spottswoode Winery. (1401 Hudson Ave., St. Helena, CA 94574) Tel (707) 963-0134.

Traulsen Vineyards. (2250 Lake County Hwy., Calistoga, CA 94515) Tel (707) 942-0283.

Key: GT (guided tour); IT (informal tour); Ta (tasting).

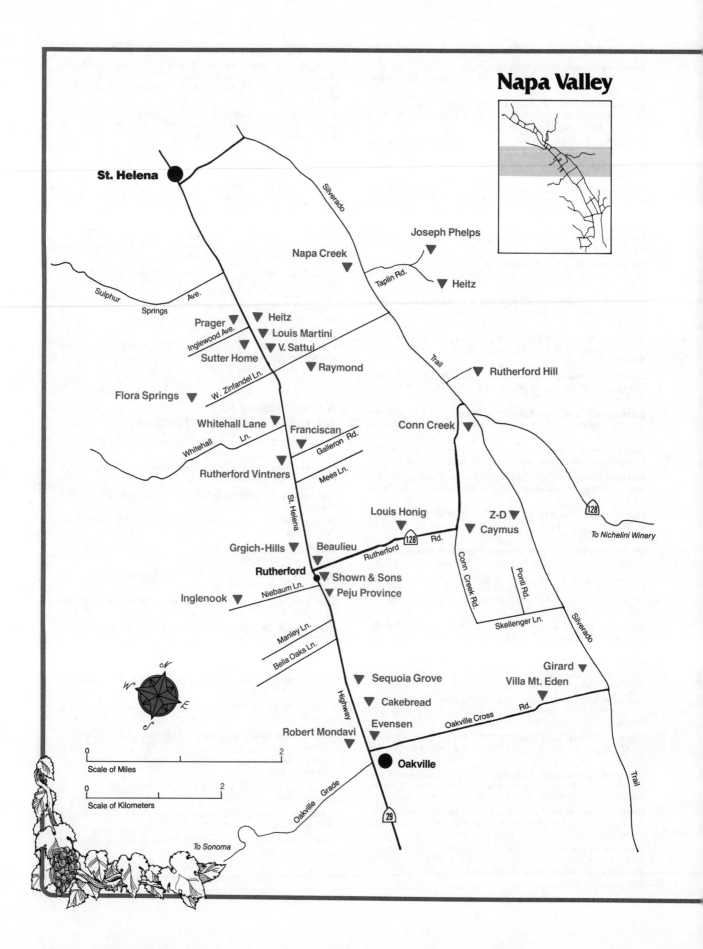

Napa Valley

St. Helena

Silverado

Joseph Phelps ▼

Napa Creek ▼

Taplin Rd.

Heitz ▼

Sulphur
Springs Ave.

Prager ▼   ▼ Heitz
Inglewood Ave.   ▼ Louis Martini
         ▼ V. Sattui
Sutter Home

Trail

▼ Raymond

▼ Rutherford Hill

W. Zinfandel Ln.

Flora Springs ▼

Whitehall Lane ▼

▼ Franciscan
Galleron Rd.

Conn Creek ▼

Whitehall   Ln.

Mees Ln.

Rutherford Vintners ▼

Louis Honig ▼

Z-D ▼
Caymus ▼

128

St. Helena

To Nichelini Winery

Grgich-Hills ▼   Beaulieu ▼
128
Rutherford   Rd.

Rutherford ●   ▼ Shown & Sons

Conn Creek Rd.

Ponti Rd.

Inglenook ▼   Niebaum Ln.   ▼ Peju Province

Skellenger Ln.

Silverado

Manley Ln.

Bella Oaks Ln.

Girard ▼
Villa Mt. Eden ▼

▼ Sequoia Grove

N
W   E
S

Highway

▼ Cakebread
Oakville Cross   Rd.

▼ Evensen

Robert Mondavi ▼

0   2
Scale of Miles

0   2
Scale of Kilometers

Oakville ●   Oakville

Oakville Grade

29

Trail

To Sonoma

Beaulieu Vineyard. E side of State 29 at Rutherford (P.O. Box 329, Rutherford, CA 94573) Tel (707) 963-1451. Daily 10-4 (last tour 3:15). GT/Ta.

Cakebread Cellars. On E side of State 29 midway between Oakville and Rutherford at 8300 (P.O. Box 216, Rutherford, CA 94573) Tel (707) 963-5221. Daily 10-4. Ta. GT by appt.

Caymus Vineyards. 1.5 mi. E of Rutherford at 8700 Conn Creek Rd., State 128 junction (P.O. Box 268, Rutherford, CA 94573) Tel (707) 963-4204. Daily 10-4. Ta. fee.

Conn Creek Winery. E of Rutherford at intersection of Silverado Tr. and State 128 (8711 Silverado Trail, St. Helena, CA 94574) Tel (707) 963-5133. GT/Ta by appt.

Evensen Winery and Vineyard. E side of State 29, N of Oakville at 8254 (P.O. Box 127, Oakville, CA 94562) Tel (707) 944-2396. By appt. only, weekends preferred. IT.

Flora Springs Wine Company. From State 29 at Zinfandel Ln., W on W. Zinfandel Ln. to winery drive (1978 W. Zinfandel Ln., St. Helena, CA 94574) Tel (707) 963-5711. GT/Ta by appt.

Franciscan Vineyards. E side State 29 S of St. Helena at 1178 Galleron Rd. (P.O. Box 407, Rutherford, CA 94573) Tel (707) 963-7111. Daily 10-5. IT/Ta.

Girard Winery. On W side of Silverado Tr. at 7717, .1 mi. N of Oakville Cross Rd. (P.O. Box 105, Oakville, CA 94562) Tel (707) 944-8577. GT/Ta by appt.

Grgich-Hills Cellar. W side State 29 .5 mi. N of Rutherford at 1829 St. Helena Hwy. (P.O. Box 450, Rutherford, CA 94573) Tel (707) 963-2784. Daily 9:30-4:30. Ta. GT by appt.

Heitz Cellars. (Winery: 500 Taplin Rd., St. Helena, CA 94574) Tel (707) 963-3542. GT by appt. Tasting room: E side State 29 S of St. Helena at 439 St. Helena Hwy. S. Daily 11-4:30. Ta.

Louis Honig Cellars. From State 29 at Rutherford, E 1.2 mi. on Hwy 128/Rutherford Rd. to winery road at 850 (P.O. Box 406, Rutherford, CA 94573) Tel (707) 963-5618. By appt. only.

Inglenook-Napa Valley. W from State 29 at Rutherford on pvt. lane (P.O. Box 402, Rutherford, CA 94573) Tel (707) 967-3355. Daily 10:30-4. GT/Ta.

Louis M. Martini. E side State 29 S of St. Helena at 254 (P.O. Box 112, St. Helena, CA 94574) Tel (707) 963-2736. Daily 10-4:30. GT/Ta.

Robert Mondavi Winery. W side of State 29 at 7801, N limit of Oakville (P.O. Box 106, Oakville, CA 94562) Tel (707) 963-9611. Daily 9-5 May-Oct, 10-4:30 Nov-Apr. GT/Ta.

Napa Creek Winery. E of St. Helena on Silverado Tr., .6 mi. S of Pope St. (1001 Silverado Tr., St. Helena, CA 94574) Tel (707) 963-9456. Daily 10-4:30. GT/Ta.

Nichelini Vineyard. From State 29 at Rutherford, E 11 mi. on State 128 (2950 Sage Canyon Rd., St. Helena, CA 94574) Tel (707) 963-3357. Picnic. Sa-Su, holidays 10-6. Ta. (Outside map area)

Peju Province. E side State 29 S of Rutherford Cross Road at 8466. (P.O. Box 478, Rutherford, CA 94573) Tel (707) 963-3600. Daily 10–6 May–Oct., 11–5 Nov.–Apr. Ta.

Joseph Phelps Vineyards. From Zinfandel Ln., N .5 mi. on Silverado Tr. to Taplin Rd., then E .2 mi. to winery at 200 (P.O. Box 1031, St. Helena, CA 94574) Tel (707) 963-2745. M-Sa 9-4 by appt. GT/Ta.

Prager Winery and Port Works. From State 29, .1 mi. S of Sulphur Springs Ave., W on private lane to winery (1281 Lewelling Ln., St. Helena, CA 94574) Tel (707) 963-3720. GT/Ta by appt.

Raymond Vineyards and Cellar. From State 29 S of St. Helena, E .5 mi. on Zinfandel Ln. to Wheeler Ln./winery drive (849 Zinfandel Ln., St. Helena, CA 94574) Tel (707) 963-3141. Daily 10-4. Ta. GT by appt.

Rutherford Hill Winery. From intersection with State 128, N on Silverado Tr. to 200 Rutherford Hill Rd. (P.O. Box 410, St. Helena, CA 94574) Tel (707) 963-9694 or 963-7194. Picnic. Daily 10:30-4:30. GT/Ta.

Rutherford Vintners. W side State 29 1 mi. N of Rutherford (P.O. Box 238, Rutherford, CA 94573) Tel (707) 963-4117. Daily 10-4:30. Ta. GT by appt.

V. Sattui Winery. E side State 29 S of St. Helena at White Ln. (111 White Ln., St. Helena, CA 94574) Tel (707) 963-7774. Picnic. Daily 9-6 Mar-Oct, 9-5 Nov-Feb. IT/Ta. GT by appt.

Sequoia Grove Vineyards. On E side of State 29 midway between Oakville and Rutherford (8338 St. Helena Hwy., Napa 94558) Tel (707) 944-2945. Daily 11-5. Ta.

Shown & Sons Vineyards. E side State 29 in Rutherford at 8514 (P.O. Box H, Rutherford, CA 94573) Tel (707) 963-9004. Daily 10-4.

Sutter Home Winery. W side State 29 S of St. Helena at 277 (P.O. Box 248, St. Helena, CA 94574) Tel (707) 963-3104. Daily 9-5. Ta.

Villa Mt. Eden. N side Oakville Cross Rd. at 620, near Silverado Tr. (P.O. Box 350, Oakville, CA 94562) Tel (707) 944-2414. Daily 10-4. Ta. GT by appt.

Whitehall Lane Winery. From Rutherford, N on State 29 to Whitehall Ln. (1563 St. Helena Hwy. S., St. Helena, CA 94574) Tel (707) 963-9454. Daily 11-5. Ta. GT by appt.

Z-D Wines. From intersection with State 128, S .7 mi. on Silverado Tr. (8383 Silverado Tr., Napa, CA 94558) Tel (707) 963-5188. GT/Ta by appt.

Wineries Not on Map— Restricted or No Visitor Facilities

Amizetta Vineyards. (1099 Greenfield Rd., St. Helena, CA 94574) Tel (707) 963-1053.

Buehler Vineyards. (820 Greenfield Rd., St. Helena, CA 94574) Tel (707) 963-2155.

Chappellet Winery. (1581 Sage Canyon Rd., St. Helena, CA 94574) Tel (707) 963-7136.

Far Niente Winery. (P.O. Box 327, Oakville, CA 94562) Tel (707) 944-2861.

Green & Red Vineyard. (3208 Chiles-Pope Valley Rd., St. Helena, CA 94574) Tel (707) 965-2346.

Johnson-Turnbull Vineyards. (P.O. Box 410, Oakville, CA 94562) Tel (707) 963-5839.

Long Vineyards. (P.O. Box 50, St. Helena, CA 94574) Tel (707) 963-2496. GT by appt.

Niebaum-Coppola Estate. (P.O. Box 208, Rutherford, CA 94573) Tel (707) 963-9435.

Piña Cellars. (P.O. Box 376, Rutherford, CA 94573) Tel (707) 944-2229.

Saddleback Cellars. (P.O. Box 661, 7802 Money Lane, Oakville, CA 94562) Tel (707) 963-4982.

Sage Canyon Winery. (35 Lopez Ave., San Francisco, CA 94116) Tel (415) 664-8721.

Schug Cellars. (P.O. Box 556, St. Helena, CA 94574) Tel (707) 963-3169. Ta by appt.

Shadow Brook Winery. (360 Zinfandel Ln., St. Helena, CA 94574) Tel (707) 963-2000.

Silver Oak Cellars. (P.O. Box 414, Oakville, CA 94562) Tel (707) 944-8866.

Stony Hill Vineyard. (P.O. Box 308, St. Helena, CA 94574) Tel (707) 963-2636. GT by appt.

Sullivan Vineyards and Winery. (P.O. Box G, Rutherford, CA 94573) Tel (707) 963-9646.

Villa Helena Winery. (1455 Inglewood Ave., St. Helena, CA 94574) Tel (707) 963-4334.

Woltner Estates. (154 Main St., St. Helena, CA 94574) Tel (707) 963-1744.

Key: GT (guided tour); IT (informal tour); Ta (tasting).

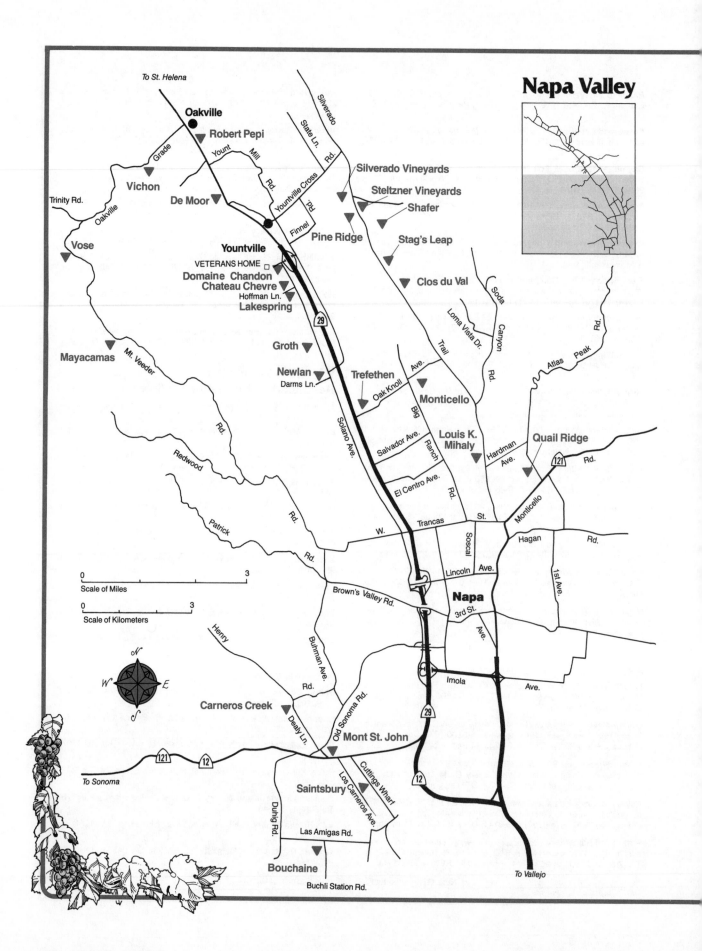

Napa Valley

To St. Helena

Oakville

Robert Pepi

Grade

Vichon

Trinity Rd.

Oakville

De Moor

Yount

Mill Rd.

State Ln.

Silverado

Yountville Cross Rd.

Finnel

Rd.

Silverado Vineyards

Steltzner Vineyards

Shafer

Pine Ridge

Stag's Leap

Vose

Yountville

VETERANS HOME

Domaine Chandon
Chateau Chevre
Hoffman Ln.
Lakespring

Clos du Val

Soda

Canyon

Rd.

Loma Vista Dr.

Atlas Peak Rd.

Mayacamas

Mt. Veeder

29

Groth

Newlan

Darms Ln.

Trefethen

Oak Knoll Ave.

Big

Monticello

Trail

Rd.

Redwood

Rd.

Solano Ave.

Salvador Ave.

Ranch

Louis K.
Mihaly

Hardman Ave.

Quail Ridge

121 Rd.

Patrick Rd.

Rd.

El Centro Ave.

Rd.

Trancas St.

W.

Soscal

Monticello Rd.

Hagan Rd.

1st Ave.

Brown's Valley Rd.

Lincoln Ave.

Napa

3rd St.

Ave.

0 Scale of Miles 3

0 Scale of Kilometers 3

Henry

Buhman Ave.

Rd.

Old Sonoma Rd.

Imola Ave.

29

N
W E
S

Carneros Creek

Dealy Ln.

Mont St. John

Cuttings Wharf

Los Carneros Ave.

121 12

To Sonoma

Saintsbury

Duhig Rd.

Las Amigas Rd.

12

Bouchaine

Buchli Station Rd.

To Vallejo

Carneros Creek Winery. From State 121 5 mi. S of Napa, N .1 mi. on Old Sonoma Rd., then W .4 mi on Dealy Ln. (1285 Dealy Ln., Napa, CA 94559) Tel (707) 253-9463. M-F 10-4. GT by appt.

Chateau Chevre. From State 29 .4 mi. S of Yountville, W .2 mi. on Hoffman Ln. (2030 Hoffman Ln., Yountville, CA 94599) Tel (707) 944-2184. IT/Ta by appt. only.

Clos du Val Wine Co. On E side of Silverado Tr., 3 mi. S of Yountville Cross Rd. (5330 Silverado Tr., Napa, CA 94558) Tel (707) 252-6711. Picnic. Daily 10-4. Ta. GT by appt.

DeMoor Winery. W side of State 29 at 7481, 2.2 mi. N of Yountville (P.O. Box 348, Oakville, CA 94562) Tel (707) 944-2565. Daily 10-5 winter, 10:30-5:30 summer. IT/Ta.

Domaine Chandon. From State 29 at Yountville, California Dr. exit W, S .1 mi. on Solano Ave. to winery dr. (P.O. Box 2470, Yountville, CA 94599) Tel (707) 944-2280. Restaurant, reservations advised. Tel (707) 944-2892. Daily 11-6 May-Oct, W-Su 11-6 Nov-Apr (last tour 5:00). GT/Ta fee.

Groth Vineyards & Winery. From State 29 frontage rd. at Darms Lane, N .3 mi. to 1225 Hillview Ln. (P.O. Box 412, Oakville, CA 94562) Tel (707) 255-7466. M-F. Ta by appt.

Lakespring Winery. From State 29 .4 mi. S of Yountville, W .2 mi. on Hoffman Ln. (2055 Hoffman Ln., Napa, CA 94558) Tel (707) 944-2475. GT by appt.

Mayacamas Vineyards. From State 29 at Napa, W and N on Redwood Rd./Mt. Veeder Rd. 8 mi. to Lokoya Rd., W .1 mi. to pvt. winery rd. (1155 Lokoya Rd., Napa, CA 94558) Tel (707) 224-4030. M-W at 10, F at 2. GT.

Louis K. Mihaly Vineyard. W side Silverado Trail at 3103, 1.6 mi. N of Napa. (P.O. Box 2840, Napa, CA 94558) Tel (707) 253-9306. By appt. only.

Monticello Cellars. From State 29 at N limit of Napa, E on Oak Knoll Rd. to Big Ranch Rd., then S .1 mi. to winery at 4242 (P.O. Box 2680, Yountville, CA 94599) Tel (707) 944-8863. Daily 10:30-4:30. Ta. GT at 10:30, 12:30, 2:30.

Mont St. John Cellars. At intersection of State 121 and Old Sonoma Rd. 5 mi. S of Napa (5400 Old Sonoma Rd., Napa, CA 94558) Tel (707) 255-8864. Daily 10-5. Ta.

Newlan Vineyards & Winery. On State 29 frontage rd. at Darms Ln. 3.5 mi. N of Napa at 5225 Solano Ave. (1305 Carrell Ln., Napa, CA 94558) Tel (707) 944-2914. GT/Ta by appt.

Robert Pepi Winery. E side of State 29 at 7585, 1 mi. S of Oakville Cross Rd. (P.O. Box 328, Oakville, CA 94562) Tel (707) 944-2807. Daily 10:30-4:30. Ta. GT by appt.

Pine Ridge Winery. W side Silverado Tr. at 5901, 6 mi. N of Napa (P.O. Box 2508, Yountville, CA 94599) Tel (707) 253-7500. Picnic. Tu-Su 11-4. IT/Ta. GT by appt.

Quail Ridge. On Atlas Peak Rd., .1 mi. N of State 121 (1055 Atlas Peak Rd., Napa, CA 94558) Tel (707) 257-1712. GT/Ta by appt.

Saintsbury. From State 29 5 mi. S of Napa, W 1.6 mi. on State 121, S .5 on Los Carneros Ave., E .1 mi. on Whithers Rd. to winery (1500 Los Carneros Ave., Napa, CA 94559) Tel (707) 252-0592. GT/Ta by appt.

Shafer Vineyards. On E side of Silverado Tr. 1.2 mi. S of Yountville Cross Rd. (6154 Silverado Tr., Napa, CA 94558) Tel (707) 944-2877. GT Tu-F 11:00 by appt. only.

Silverado Vineyards. W side Silverado Trail 6.9 mi. N of Napa to winery rd. (6121 Silverado Trail, Napa, CA 94558) Tel (707) 257-1770. Daily 11-4.

Stag's Leap Wine Cellars. On E side of Silverado Tr. 2.2 mi. S of Yountville Cross Rd. (5766 Silverado Tr., Napa, CA 94558) Tel (707) 944-2020. Daily 10-4. Ta fee. GT by appt.

Steltzner Vineyards. E side Silverado Trail 6.3 mi. N of Napa (5998 Silverado Trail, Napa, CA 94558) Tel (707) 252-7272. Ta by appt.

Trefethen Vineyards. From State 29, E on Oak Knoll Ave., .4 mi. to 1160 (P.O. Box 2460, Napa, CA 94558) Tel (707) 255-7700. GT/Ta by appt.

Vichon Winery. From State 29 at Oakville, W 1 mi. on Oakville Grade Rd. to 1595 (P.O. Box 363, Oakville, CA 94562) Tel (707) 944-2811. Daily 10-4:30. Ta. GT by appt.

Vose Vineyards. From Oakville, W 3.7 mi. on Oakville Grade to Mt. Veeder Rd., S 1.4 mi. to stone gate & sign (4035 Mt. Veeder Rd., Napa, CA 94558) Tel (707) 944-2254. Daily 10-4. Ta by appt.

Wineries Not on Map— Restricted or No Visitor Facilities

Acacia Winery. (2750 Las Amigas Rd., Napa, CA 94559) Tel (707) 226-9991.

Alatera Vineyards. (2170 Hoffman Ln., Napa, CA 94558) Tel (707) 944-2620.

S. Anderson Vineyard. (1473 Yountville Cross Rd., Yountville, CA 94558) Tel (707) 944-8642.

Artisan Wines. (5335 Redwood Rd., Napa, CA 94558) Tel (707) 252-6666.

Bouchaine. (1075 Buchli Station Rd., Napa, CA 94558) Tel (707) 252-9065

Cassayre-Forni Cellars. (20 Syar Dr., Napa, CA 94558) Tel (707) 255-0909.

Chimney Rock Winery. (5320 Silverado Tr., Napa, CA 94558) Tel (707) 257-2641.

William Hill Winery. (P.O. Box 3989, Napa, CA 94558) Tel (707) 224-6565.

Mt. Veeder Winery. (1999 Mt. Veeder Rd., Napa, CA 94558) Tel (707) 224-4039.

Napa Valley Wine Co. (P.O. Box 2502, Napa, CA 94558) Tel (707) 255-9463.

Plam Vineyards. (6200 St. Helena Hwy., Napa, CA 94558) Tel (707) 944-1102.

St. Andrews Winery. (P. O. Box 4107, Napa, CA 94558) Tel (707) 252-6748.

Stags' Leap Winery. (6150 Silverado Tr., Napa, CA 94558) Tel (707) 944-1303.

Tulocay Winery. (1426 Coombsville Rd., Napa, CA 94558) Tel (707) 255-4064.

Van der Heyden Vineyards & Winery. (4057 Silverado Tr., Napa, CA 94558) Tel (707) 257-0130.

Whitford Cellars. (4047 E. Third Ave., Napa, CA 94558) Tel (707) 257-7065.

Key: GT (guided tour); IT (informal tour); Ta (tasting).

. . . Continued from page 75

of a round tasting table in a spacious room with views onto the fermentors or out to a small patio and, beyond it, the hills east of Rutherford. The winery produces Chardonnay, Cabernet Sauvignon, Merlot, and Zinfandel, plus proprietary wines called Chateau Maja.

Cuvaison houses itself in a deft architectural tribute to the Spanish colonial heritage of California wine, its white-walled, red tile-roofed cellars distinguished by a long row of graceful arches facing onto the Silverado Trail not far down the valley from Calistoga.

The winery has grown steadily since its founding in 1970, when a since-departed partnership opened it in a building that looked suspiciously like a depression-era hunting camp. Interim owners erected the main cellar and remodeled the original building into the present tasting room, matching the two structures with style and taste.

The Swiss owner offers tours by appointment, revealing the archetypal small Napa winery: modern crusher and press, stainless steel fermentors, and French oak barrels. He provides for tasting all four of Cuvaison's wines: Chardonnay, Cabernet Sauvignon, Merlot, and Zinfandel. There are picnic facilities.

Deer Park Winery is one of several revivals of old Napa Valley properties that tucks a modern, efficient winery into a handsome old stone building. In this case, an energy-conscious proprietor is turning some inherited museum pieces to practical account.

The property first was the original Sutter Home location. After Prohibition, it was the John Ballentyne Winery until 1960. It became Deer Park when winemaker Dave Clark and partners bought it in 1979. For now, processing and aging both take place on the lower floor of a classic two-story, gravity-flow winery built into a hillside. In time the rehabilitated upper level will again hold the crusher, hydraulic press, and stainless steel fermenting tanks, leaving the lower story to hold ancient German oak casks, new French oak barrels and upright tanks, and the bottling line.

Cabernet Sauvignon

Sauvignon Blanc, Zinfandel, and Petite Sirah are the mainstays, sometimes joined by Chardonnay from the Clarks' San Diego vineyard.

DeMoor Winery has a playful architectural appeal from the outside. The front section of the building bears some resemblance to an igloo. Directly behind it another section has walls that taper inward, whereas the rear and largest segment is conventionally rectangular in all planes.

Within, the playfulness gives way to a serene beauty. The igloo is in fact a slightly modified geodesic dome, much of it finished in stained wood. A skylight of stained glass casts a churchly glow on upright oak tanks clustered under the peak, and on barrels lining the curved walls everywhere except for the short arc occupied by a tasting table.

The tapered center section allows for lofty stacks of oak barrels in which age Chardonnay, Sauvignon Blanc, Cabernet Sauvignon, and Zinfandel. The taller rear section holds stainless steel fermentors and still more barrels.

The winery was founded in 1975 as Napa Wine Cellars. The DeSchepper-DeMoor family of Belgium bought it in 1986. Other wines on the roster are Chenin Blanc and a late-harvest Sauvignon Blanc called Fié Doux.

Domaine Chandon was the first Napa Valley winery in the current era of heroic architecture to be built in a purely modern style. Barrel-vault roofs cover stone, concrete, and glass-walled buildings in a complex that flows across a gentle slope west of Yountville.

Within the buildings the story is more complicated, for this winery was built to make sparkling wines only according to the ancient verities of the *méthode champenoise*. There is no arguing the technical truths of this matter. Domaine Chandon is owned by Moët-Hennessy, the French proprietors of Moët et Chandon, and the winemaster in the Napa Valley is the same one as in Epernay. As a result, to see Domaine Chandon is to see sparkling wine made on a scale that the French tend to think of as right, using equipment and techniques favored there.

The main winemaking building has, on its curving upper story, twin rows of horizontal stainless steel fermentors and, on the underground lower story, row upon row of big, mechanized riddling racks. A glass-walled wing of this building holds the yeast-culturing room and all of the bottling and disgorging equipment.

As a counterpoint to the working winery, the parent firm has loaned ancient equipment, which is placed here and there about the premises, mainly in the separate building that houses the visitor center and an elegant French restaurant.

Well-conducted tours take in all of these details. There is a fee for tasting Chandon Napa Valley Brut or Blanc de Noir. The restaurant is popular enough that reservations are required for lunch or dinner.

Duckhorn Vineyards, on the Silverado Trail, has an air that would not be out of place in Bordeaux, appropriate enough since the winery makes only Sauvignon Blanc, Cabernet Sauvignon, and Merlot. Fermenting takes place in an open-walled building (*la* *cuverie,* if this were France); aging is next door in six rooms of a cool, dim building *(le chai).*

Limited in their ability to welcome visitors both by use-permit restrictions and the winery's small size, owners Margaret and Daniel Duckhorn nonetheless extend appointments to visitors who can take pleasure in discussing philosophical fine points of red wines modeled after traditional clarets.

The first wines released for sale were from the vintage of 1978. Three Palms Vineyard is the main red grape source.

Dunn Vineyards, located near the 2,200-foot summit of Howell Mountain in the Napa Valley's northeast corner, has the distinction of being the first commercial winery to operate on the mountain since Prohibition. The proprietors are Randall and Lori Dunn. After many years as the enologist at Caymus Vineyards, Randy Dunn began making his own wine on the mountain in the late 1970s, and officially founded the winery in 1982 with the avowed purpose of specializing in Howell Mountain Cabernet Sauvignon. There is precious little of it each year, and no other varietals are produced.

Dunn and his family make the wine in a modest cellar near the hacienda-style family home on the edge of a lake. Most of the grapes come from their own vineyard, planted on a pinnacle above the house, but they also purchase fruit in small quantities from neighboring growers.

As the de facto consulting enologist for the mountain's small, new viticultural community, Dunn has been instrumental in the revival of this once-famous wine region high above the valley. His own handmade wine, bottled, labeled, and wax sealed by the family, is generally spoken for well in advance of release, so there is no tasting offered. However, serious wine fans are sometimes allowed to visit by appointment.

Ehlers Lane Winery is the first permanent occupant, in modern times, of a fine stone building that has served well over the years as an incubator for fledgling Napa Valley wineries. Bernerd Ehlers built it in 1886. He produced wine until Prohibition, then sold the property to a local family named Murphy, who in their turn sold it to Alfred Domingues after Repeal. Until he ceased production in 1957, Domingues marketed wine simply by filling up the jugs and casks his customers brought around to the winery door.

Michael Casey bought the property from Domingues in 1968, then leased it to a series of start-up operations. Conn Creek Winery was first, followed in short order by Vichon and Saintsbury.

In 1983, Casey and his partner, John Jensen, hired Robert H. Moeckly to whip the 22-acre vineyard into shape and to renovate the winery. The first Ehlers Lane Winery vintage was 1983.

Ehlers Lane produces Sauvignon Blanc (blended with Semillon), Chardonnay, and Cabernet Sauvignon. A tour of the historic winery is well worth the effort of making the necessary appointment.

Evensen Winery and Vineyard looks slightly Alsatian more by chance than design, but the image fits. In an efficient cellar behind a half-timbered yellow house east of State 29 between Oakville and Rutherford, the owning Richard Evensen family makes only Gewürztraminer, the only variety grown in its vineyards adjacent to the cellar.

Flora Springs Wine Company occupies a fine old stone building set at the back edge of a vineyard, tight against a wooded hillside west of St. Helena.

Originally built in the 1880s by a pair of Scots as the Rennie Brothers winery and later used for many years by Louis M. Martini, the building gained an addition to its upper story in 1982. The twin purpose was to keep the hill behind from pushing it another inch eastward, and to allow the owning Komes and Garvey families to age their Cabernet Sauvignon and Merlot up top, along with a proprietary red blend called Trilogy. Chardonnay and Sauvignon Blanc inhabit the lower story.

However the aging wines are disposed, this is a flawless example of an ancient building turned into a modern cellar. The crusher, Willmes presses, and some stainless steel fermenting tanks stand on a pad at one end of the building. More stainless steel tanks and several lofty racks of French oak barrels fill much of the interior. Not incidentally, it is a good place to talk about the effects of stainless steel versus barrel fermentation, since the proprietors follow both practices.

Folie à Deux Winery borrows its name from clinical psychology. The term refers to a delusional state shared by two closely associated individuals. Stripped of all sinister aspects, it describes this venture of psychologists Larry and Evie Dismang perfectly.

The Dismangs' shared fantasy began in 1974, when they bought a defunct sheep ranch with an old house on it. They lived there while building a new solar-powered home next door, then set about converting the old house into a winery, which they completed in time for the 1981 crush. Now the processing facilities are located in a shed built onto the house. The lab is set up in the former kitchen, the executive offices are tucked into the attic, and barrels are packed into the cellar, as well as in a stone outbuilding and a chicken coop, refrigerated for the purpose.

Evidence of reality is provided by dry Chenin Blanc, Chardonnay, Cabernet Sauvignon, and a Muscat Canelli called à Deux, which is available only at the winery.

Franciscan Vineyards works on a scale that makes it highly informative to see. It is small enough that all of its departments fit together into a clear pattern, from freshly arrived grapes to finished wine. But it is big enough that much of the equipment is kindred to gear at much larger wineries, where patterns of production may not be so clearly visible.

In addition, the tour is sign-guided, allowing visitors to pursue learning at their individual paces. Hosts in the spacious tasting hall will amplify on any subjects the signs do not explain to satisfaction.

Franciscan has grown steadily through several ownerships but most spectacularly under the present proprietors, Peter Eckes and Agustin Huneeus. The original main cellar, built in 1973, was a plain box with concrete walls. A redwood-sided office and visitor area softened the front elevation. An addition in 1982 turned the redoubled cellars into an L, adding some niceties of design in the process. As originally, the stainless steel fermentors and other processing gear sit outside the north wall. Inside are stainless steel storage tanks and the bottling line. The new addition holds a much-enlarged collection of oak cooperage, most of it barrels from French and American coopers.

The tasting hall—too capacious to be called a room—offers the full range of Franciscan estate bottled wines, along with wines from Franciscan's vineyards in the Alexander Valley, which are bottled under their Estancia Vineyards label.

Freemark Abbey revived an old label and older winery building at its founding in 1967.

The original label dated from 1939 and endured into the early 1960s. (There was no particular religious affiliation. The name derived from those of the original partners: Free from Charles Freeman, Mark from Mark Foster, and Abbey from the nickname of Albert Ahern.) Seeing no way to improve on that ingenuity, the current partnership of seven owners applied it to a new generation of wines that includes Chardonnay, Riesling, and Cabernet Sauvignon. Some of the Riesling goes to make a late-harvest Edelwein when conditions favor *Botrytis cinerea*.

The current owners have been required to improve upon their winery building, or at least to enlarge upon the fine old stone cellars built in the 1880s as Lombarda Winery. After the demise of the original Freemark Abbey, that building was turned into a complex of specialty shops and a restaurant. The new Freemark Abbey for a time crowded itself into the lower story, less than half the original space. In 1973, weary of making wine sideways, the partners built a new structure alongside the old one to house bottling and cased wine storage. In 1982, a third building was added to house red wines aging in French oak.

Tours begin in the middle building in a room furnished to break an antique collector's heart. They lead first into the original cellars, where stainless steel fermentors and oak barrels still are so closely packed that visitors must go single file, then through the newer buildings, both shaped after Spanish colonial models.

Girard Winery perches on a knoll alongside the Silverado Trail, its textured block walls half hidden in the dappled light of a small oak grove. Like many family-sized wineries, this one is instructive to survey from a single vantage.

The hopper and crusher are on a concrete pad just outside the entrance to a small sales area. Stainless steel fermentors and the press occupy a separate room at the north end of the building. Oak upright tanks and racks of French oak barrels greet the eye directly inside the entry. Bottled wines in cases are at the opposite end of the building from the fermentors.

Chardonnay, Chenin Blanc, and Cabernet Sauvignon come from an adjoining vineyard set into the angle formed by the Silverado Trail and Oakville Cross Road.

Grgich-Hills Cellar, founded in 1977, is yet another of the small California wineries that demonstrate the internationality of winemaking.

Its proprietors are Miljenko (Mike) Grgich and Austin Hills. Grgich studied formal enology at the University of Zagreb in Yugoslavia before emigrating to the United States to begin a long career in the Napa Valley. (He worked for several wineries before launching his own.) Partner Austin Hills is pure Yankee, a vineyard owner for some years before joining forces with Grgich.

The architecture of their trim building nods to the Spanish colonial heritage of California with white plaster walls, red-tile roof, and arched entryways. The equipment includes, among other pieces, American stainless steel fermentors and French oak barrels.

Grgich-Hills offers tours by appointment. A walk across the parking lot reveals the fermentors and other processing gear under an overhanging roof at the rear. A talk with the host at the sales room in one front corner of the aging cellar covers the fine points.

Production is dominated by Chardonnay, Sauvignon Blanc, and Riesling. Zinfandel and Cabernet Sauvignon round out the roster.

Groth Vineyards & Winery consists of a modest tank farm and crushing equipment on a 121-acre vineyard along the Oakville Cross Road, at the heart of the valley. Groth wines are all made from that vineyard and from another one nearby. The grapes are converted to juice and fermented on the spot, within moments of picking; then the wine is transported to a leased, temperature-controlled space in a Napa industrial park for aging in Nevers and Limousin oak barrels.

Owners Dennis and Judy Groth chose their vineyard location primarily because of its soil. In that section of the valley, the alluvial soils of the Napa River bench begin to blend with mineral-rich volcanic soils that have worked their way down, over millennia, from the hills above the Silverado Trail. Several wineries are clustered there, amid dense vineyards. The Groths are among the newest arrivals, having made their first wines in 1982.

Their roster includes Sauvignon Blanc, Chardonnay, and Cabernet Sauvignon.

Heitz Cellars comes in two parts. The original winery building now is the tasting room and a supplementary aging cellar. It is a small, redwood-faced structure on the St. Helena Highway just south of town. The present producing winery is tucked away east of St. Helena and the Silverado Trail in a small pocket called Spring Valley.

The Heitz family bought the Spring Valley property in 1964, having outgrown the original winery in three years. When the Heitzes acquired the second ranch it had not changed a great deal since 1898, when Anton Rossi completed a stone cellar as the capstone of his development of the property.

Except for replanting abandoned vineyards and re-equipping the cellar with stainless steel fermentors and a veritable library of oak casks and barrels, the new owners did not change the appearance of the place they bought until 1972, when progress dictated more space for the making and aging of wine.

There are several ways to go about expanding a winery. An old building can be enlarged, torn down and replaced, or abandoned for a new site. The Heitzes elected to keep the fine old stone cellar intact and erect a whole new structure near it. The new building is an octagon of textured block.

The replanted vineyard, stretching away south to the end of the little valley, is devoted almost entirely to Grignolino for red and rosé.

Other Heitz varietal table wines come from selected—sometimes identified—vineyards throughout the Napa Valley. The roster is dominated by Chardonnay and Cabernet Sauvignons from several vineyards and includes Pinot Noir as well as the Grignolinos.

Regular tasting goes on only at the original winery on St. Helena Highway South, where all the wines also are available for retail sale. Because the Spring Valley winery buildings are behind the family home, visitors there must acquire an invitation beforehand.

Louis Honig Cellars began as a labor of love for the long-time California Superintendent of Schools, but quickly became known as a producer of estate-grown Sauvignon Blanc. No other wines are produced, but several different grape varieties are grown on the 60-acre ranch, which sits almost squarely at mid-valley, crosswise and lengthwise. Historically, the property was part of the Caymus Rancho land grant from the valley's Mexican period. The Honigs purchased it, already planted, from the proprietor of Caymus Vineyards (see page 74) in the late 1960s.

An old barn on the property was converted into the winery. There is a substantial tank farm out back, and a straightforward crush pad with a Fisher membrane press. Inside are many French oak barrels in which the Sauvignon Blanc is fermented and aged. The first vintage was 1980.

Inglenook-Napa Valley is located in several buildings, but for visitors all the action takes place in the stately original cellar at Rutherford.

Built in the 1880s, the stone-walled building looks much the way romantics think wineries should, though it was built by a Finnish sea captain and fur trader named Gustave Niebaum. The front wall has a long row of arched doors and another of arched windows. A cupola and several dormers serve as relief from the ordinariness of mere roof. Virginia creeper, which turns flame red in the fall, covers the exterior walls.

Inside, parallel tunnels contain ranks and ranks of 1,000-gallon oak oval casks. Most of these casks came from the Spesart Mountains in Germany in the last decades of the nineteenth century and show very nearly flawless craftsmanship. Ordinary cask heads begin to buckle after a time; these still follow the curves formed by their German coopers. The wood has blackened with age but has not bowed.

In its early days, all of Inglenook was under the one roof. Now a new aging cellar big enough to house a dirigible faces the original cellar across a courtyard. It is filled with towering racks of oak barrels. Fermenting and some aging takes place in a large new facility at the intersection of State 29 and Oakville Crossroad.

The evolutions have come in stages. The founding family revived Inglenook after Prohibition under the proprietorship of the late John Daniel. Daniel ran Inglenook until he sold it in 1964 to a grower-owned

Wine Press

marketing company called United Vintners. The latter expanded the business greatly before Heublein, Inc. acquired a controlling interest in United Vintners in 1969.

The tasting room, inside the original building, offers a broad sampling of selected wines each day. Tours start in the museum area at the entrance.

The Inglenook label, bearing a reproduction of Captain Niebaum's personal diamond-shaped crest, covers Chardonnay, Sauvignon Blanc, Cabernet Sauvignon, Merlot, Pinot Noir, Zinfandel, and a limited amount of Charbono that is always snapped up shortly after release by avid collectors of that rare, robust varietal. Special lots of Chardonnay and Cabernet Sauvignon, and a Semillon-Sauvignon Blanc blend, are bottled as Inglenook Reserve. Note: Inglenook Navalle jug wines are made by a separate San Joaquin Valley company, which has nothing but Heublein ownership in common with its Napa Valley cousin.

Robert Keenan Winery is a relatively new cellar within a set of old stone walls. The walls were put there in 1904 according to a keystone over one arched doorway. According to the keystone over the other arch, their builder was Pietro Conradi, who planted the original vineyard in about 1890.

Robert Keenan bought the long-idle property in 1974 and set about transforming it from a standard stone barn into an architecturally elegant modern winery. The revamped building has a centrally supported red-tile roof and some redwood gables as its most visible new elements. Several compatible touches are to be seen within. The equipment is typical of contemporary small cellars in this part of the world: a Howard basket press, stainless steel fermentors, and, for aging the wines, French oak barrels. All of this tucks into a serene fold on one flank of Spring Mountain.

There are three Keenan wines: Chardonnay, Cabernet Sauvignon, and Merlot. The winery offers tasting and tours by appointment only.

Hanns Kornell Champagne Cellars is devoted entirely to the production of traditional, bottle-fermented sparkling wines.

Vineyard

On Larkmead Lane toward the north end of the valley, the old two-story, tree-shaded stone building started as Larkmead Winery early in Napa's vinous history. Hanns Kornell bought the property in 1958 after getting a head start during six years in a leased cellar in Sonoma.

His is a remarkable one-man achievement. Kornell fled Germany in 1939 and followed a path set by earlier German liberals and political exiles (including winemaker Charles Krug several decades before). He landed in New York broke, worked his way west, in time got work as a maker of sparkling wine, and finally started producing his own champagne in 1952.

A guided tour of the Larkmead property provides a textbook picture of traditional Champagne making. The visitor can peer at yeast deposits in still fermenting bottles, observe wine as gravity brings it to perfect clarity in the riddling racks, watch the disgorgement and final corking, and, in general, stay within arm's length of the evolution of traditional, bottle-fermented sparkling wines.

There is a tasting room in the small wood-frame office building to the rear of the winery. Visitors are always welcome to taste some of Kornell's authentic *méthode champenoise* sparkling wines. The types include Sehr Trocken, Brut, Extra Dry, Demi-Sec, Rosé, Champagne Rouge, and sparkling Muscat Alexandria.

Charles Krug Winery,

in a shady grove of tall oaks amid vineyards, presents a classic picture of an old Napa estate winery.

Charles Krug, the man, founded his winery in 1861. He built one massive stone building to keep his wines and another to keep his horses, both at 59° F/15° C.

Krug died in 1892, leaving two daughters to carry on. With help from a cousin they continued until Prohibition, when the winery closed. It remained in the hands of a caretaker-owner until Cesare Mondavi bought the property in 1943. Since Mondavi's death in 1959, the winery has remained in his family's hands. His son, Peter, is now president.

Various aspects of the Krug ranch have changed over the years, but the two stone buildings remain and are the core of the present winery. The old main cellar continues in its original role. The one-time coach house now holds small cooperage for aging select wines. Over the years, the owners have erected three large buildings. The first holds the bottling operation, the second houses oak barrels. The newest, added in 1982, is a computer-driven fermenting and processing area replacing an ancient collection of open-topped redwood tanks. Small frame buildings alongside the original cellar house the winemaker's lab, the offices, and, most important to visitors, the tasting room. Tours of the sprawling premises are ably led and unusually complete.

The tasting room offers a selection of three or four wines to those visitors who complete the tour. They come from a complete range of varietal and generic table wines, including Chardonnay, Chenin Blanc, Gewürztraminer, Cabernet Sauvignon, Pinot Noir, and Zinfandel. The winery keeps special selections of older reds at the tasting room for sale to visitors. At the other end of the price scale are CK Mondavi generics.

La Jota Vineyard Company closed several historical gaps with the release of its first wines in 1984. By naming their Howell Mountain winery after the land grant on which it stands, Bill and Joan Smith restored Rancho de la Jota, perhaps the most remote of Mexico's one-time domains, to the "active" historical roster.

The Smiths' label also breathed new life into one of Napa County's few remaining "ghost" wineries, and one with a particularly lustrous past.

The winery was built in 1892 by Fredrick Hess, a San Francisco newspaperman, using thick stone blocks quarried on the property. Hess wines won medals at the Paris Exposition of 1900, but not even international renown could keep Hess from going out of business during Prohibition. The Smiths bought the property in 1974 and made wine for fun until 1978, when they planted 26 acres to red varieties and equipped the old winery for commercial service. The 1982 La Jota wines, Cabernet Sauvignon and Zinfandel, were among the first to issue from once-famous Howell Mountain in modern times. In 1986, Voignier joined the list.

Although it is one of Napa County's most remote wineries, La Jota is easily reached after a lovely drive through a California state experimental forest. However, visits are by appointment only.

Lakespring Winery, near Yountville, is a thoroughly California structure, and an imposing one in a quiet way. The red-tile roof has cupolas vented to help cool the interior, a classic touch all up and down the rural coast counties. Windowless walls have enough spare ornamentation to suggest the considerable size of the building, and enough insulation to make easy work for the coolers.

Inside is a thoughtfully designed, neat-as-a-pin cellar with stainless steel fermentors and storage tanks at the middle, fat Burgundian barrels and puncheons at one end, and bottled wines in cases at the other. Owned by a San Francisco family named Battat, Lakespring's roster includes Chardonnay, Chenin Blanc, Sauvignon Blanc, Cabernet Sauvignon, and Merlot.

Markham Winery is another of Napa's new starts in an old place. In this case the new start is by advertising executive Bruce Markham. He bought the first of his three vineyards in the valley in 1976. Then, in 1978, he bought a winery to have a home for his grapes.

The old place just north of St. Helena was founded in 1876 as the Laurent Winery, but for years had been known locally as The Little Co-op. Regular visitors to the valley may remember it as a plain building hidden by four steel tanks at State 29 and Deer Park Lane.

Markham's first moves included removal of those steel tanks to the rear of the cellars, which showed the stone-front building to be less plain than one might have thought. The subsequent addition of a tasting room enhanced an already appreciable front elevation.

The proprietor uses three of four long galleries in the main cellar for his own winemaking. The northernmost one holds the stainless steel fermentors and other processing gear. The next two hold French oak barrels and other wood cooperage, plus an ultramodern bottling room. The south cellar is leased to other wineries in need of temporary storage.

Selected wines from the roster of estate bottlings are available for tasting in a large, comfortable room. The list includes Chardonnay, Sauvignon Blanc, and Muscat de Frontignan in whites; Cabernet Sauvignon and Merlot in reds. There also is a Gamay Blanc.

Louis M. Martini

Louis M. Martini dates only from 1933 as a winery and yet is honored as one of the old-school labels in the Napa Valley. Family continuity is the key.

Its founder, the late Louis M. Martini, began his career as a California winemaker in 1906 in Guasti and owned his first winery as early as 1922. Those facts, along with his immediate post-Prohibition start in the Napa Valley, earned him a secure reign as dean of California winemakers. His son and successor, Louis P., continues the family ownership in the traditional vein and in the original cellars, now with help from daughter Carolyn and son Michael.

The original Louis built his winery without costly adornments, but he built it to last; so, it keeps some unusual old touches. Most of the Martini fermentors, for example, now are the familiar stainless steel tanks. Yet, for a while at least, the original open concrete fermentors for reds will be around and in use. (The proprietor recalls how well they were constructed, and he shudders at the prospect of demolishing the things.) Then, too, the Martinis cold-fermented white wines before refrigerated stainless steel tanks came into use; the huge, refrigerated room full of redwood tanks remains in the winery and in use because it does a couple of jobs very well.

The main aging cellar holds a diverse lot of redwood and oak cooperage as well as the bottling line. (The tour does not go to three flanking buildings that contain a majority of Martini's French and American oak barrels, nor does it go down into an underground cellar running most of the main building's length. In this latter room are ancient oak casks used to age particularly prized Special Selection wines purchased more readily at the winery than elsewhere.)

In the tasting room, in a building added to the main cellar in 1973, a daily selection of Martini wines is available for appraisal. The roster embraces seven white and seven red varietals, bottled in several tiers according to appellation, quality, and price. The supporting cast includes generic table wines and sherries.

Mayacamas Vineyards

Mayacamas Vineyards clings to the topmost ridges of the Mayacamas Mountains. Just getting to the winery taxes the suspension systems of most automobiles of ordinary manufacture. The road from the winery up to the highest vineyards is far more adventurous.

The owners are Bob and Nonie Travers, who acquired the site in 1968 from another family ownership.

The property centers upon an old stone winery erected by a man named J. H. Fisher in 1889, and operated as Mt. Veeder Vineyards until 1910 or so. Restoration proceedings began in 1941 when a couple named Jack and Mary Taylor bought the property and renamed it Mayacamas. They reconditioned the cellars by 1947 and ran them until the Traverses' arrival.

Mayacamas is cupped in the rocky rib of a long-extinct volcano, Mt. Veeder, and is surrounded by 45 acres of vineyard. In a couple of places, sheer rock walls stick up out of the earth to set firm limits on vineyard size. Several hundred feet higher than the winery, ridge-top terraces with views clear back to San Francisco carry the Chardonnay vines.

In addition to being a good example of traditional stonework, the original winery building provides a clear picture of how winemakers built on hillsides so gravity could move wine before the advent of electric pumps.

The primary wines of Mayacamas, not opened for tasting for lack of volume, are Chardonnay and Cabernet Sauvignon. Late-harvest Zinfandel, what little there is of it, is a house specialty.

Louis K. Mihaly Vineyard

Louis K. Mihaly Vineyard is just north of Napa, between the Silverado Trail and the Napa River. That was not a propitious location during the infamous Valentine's Day flood of 1986, when the vineyard briefly became part of the river bed. The vines were dormant, however, and the winery suffered only brief cosmetic damage. In laughing off the incident, Mihaly displayed the kind of élan that comes with seven centuries in the wine business.

Mihaly's family began growing grapes in his native Transylvania in the year 1241. Mihaly emigrated in the wake of the Hungarian Revolution of 1956, arriving in the Napa Valley in 1977 and planting his estate vineyard two years later. With the completion of a plain but technologically advanced winery complex in 1982, he officially opened the California chapter of his family's seven-century winegrowing history.

The roster includes Chardonnay, Sauvignon Blanc, and Pinot Noir, all estate grown and at least partially fermented in wood. Virtually all the annual production is sold to restaurants. Mihaly's unique perspective makes this a mandatory visit for all students of wine, but not without an appointment.

Robert Mondavi Winery

Robert Mondavi Winery in Oakville crushed its first wine in 1966 while carpenters still were struggling to get the roof on the building, an early instance of what is now a tradition in California.

The winery does not look that new, mainly because founder Robert Mondavi commissioned designer Cliff

May to pay strong architectural tribute to the role Franciscan missions had in developing California as a wine district. Appearance aside, most of the building is newer than 1966, steady growth having required Mondavi to expand thrice in one decade.

A faintly churchlike tower serves as the anchor point for two wings, one straight, one bent.

The south wing holds the tasting and sales rooms as well as other rooms designed for use in celebration of art, music, and dinners great and small. The sales room is furnished with early California pieces of interest. Also, one wall has an imposing demonstration for serious wine collectors. It is a stacked mass of agricultural tiles used as a wine rack.

To the north, the bent wing holds the offices and then a whole series of fermenting and aging cellars. Robert Mondavi, the man, is a ceaseless experimenter. As a result, his working winery is an everchanging one, full of wizard equipment for visitors to gaze upon and learn from. Up in the roof rafters, for one example, are several horizontal tanks powered so they can rotate continuously. The original purpose was to keep red wines mixing throughout fermentation for maximum color extraction. At this task the tanks were failures, but the ingenious Mondavis experimented until they learned other, successful ways to use them. Guides have able explanations of these machines, as well as of the French continuous presses and German centrifuges.

A spacious open arch separates the two wings of the winery, framing a view across long rows of vines to the steep flanks of the Mayacamas Mountains beyond. A plush lawn behind the arch is the site of summer concerts, art shows, and frequent special tastings.

The wine list at Mondavi includes vintage-dated Chardonnay, Chenin Blanc, and Sauvignon Blanc in whites; a Gamay Rosé; and Cabernet Sauvignon and Pinot Noir in reds. Opus One, a red table wine, is the product of a joint venture with Chateau Mouton-Rothschild of Bordeaux.

Monticello Cellars is, in this international era of California winemaking, a straight throwback to American roots. Proprietor Jay Corley grew up in agricultural Virginia with a profound admiration for Thomas Jefferson. His winery is designed as a direct tribute to Jefferson as an architect and as a connoisseur of wine.

Corley came to the Napa Valley during the first big wine boom in the early 1970s, but rather than rush into winemaking he planted vineyards and became a major supplier of Chardonnay and other grapes to the valley's new wineries.

The cellars themselves are in a tall, spare box of a building constructed in 1982. A single large room within is packed with the latest technology and traditional oak cooperage. The offices and hospitality center are placed opposite the winery's front doors in Jefferson House, the exterior of which is a copy of Jefferson's masterpiece of design, the home he called Monticello. Jefferson House was completed in 1984.

All wines come from Corley's vineyards, which surround the winery: Chardonnay, Gewürztraminer, Sauvignon Blanc, a Semillon-based Chevrier Blanc, and Cabernet Sauvignon. Late-harvest whites are produced as conditions warrant.

Mont St. John Cellars offers no tours of its small, well-equipped, conventional winery, but provides tasting of available wines in a Spanish colonial-style building at the front of the working winery in the Carneros district, at the southern tip of the Napa Valley.

The owners are a long-time Napa wine family. From the end of Prohibition until the mid-1970s, Louis Bartolucci owned the Oakville winery now used by Inglenook. He and his son, Andrea, dropped out of winemaking briefly, then dropped back in at the current location.

The wines, all from their own nearby vineyard, include Chardonnay, Riesling, Moscato di Canelli, Cabernet Sauvignon, Pinot Noir, and Zinfandel.

Mt. Veeder Winery is one of the genuine mountainside wineries of Napa.

Housed in a trim wood-framed building well up the peak of which it is a namesake, Mt. Veeder can be visited only by appointment. For wine buffs, the major fascination is a vineyard growing all the classic blending grapes used with Cabernet Sauvignon in Bordeaux, which is to say Cabernet Franc, Malbec, Merlot, and Petit Verdot. In addition, Mt. Veeder is of a scale to tempt newcomers with thoughts of joining the ranks of small, family-owned wineries.

The property was developed in 1973 by Michael and Arlene Bernstein, who sold it in 1979. Current owner Henry Matheson budded four acres to Chardonnay. Wine from those grapes and Cabernet Sauvignon comprise the roster.

Napa Creek Winery ranks among the most ingenious examples of an obsolete building recycled from other use to a winery. Amid all the converted dairies, it is the only reworked meat-packing plant.

Next to the Silverado Trail near St. Helena, the squat, solid old concrete and concrete-block shell was made to stay cool and clean. Proprietor Jack Schulze put some of his fermentors outdoors at the rear, but the ones he wanted to keep particularly cool went into the old refrigerator room, to one side of a cellar full of French and American oak barrels. Behind these, in a little spot toward the rear, a short roster of wines is available for tasting: Chardonnay, Gewürztraminer, Riesling, white Zinfandel, Cabernet Sauvignon, and Merlot.

Newlan Vineyards & Winery occupies—at least for a time—a small modular metal building adjacent to a green cottage at one side of a venerable vineyard near the city of Napa.

Within is a conventional small winery with stainless steel fermentors and oak barrels for aging.

The cellar started as Alatera (see page 98) in 1977, when Bruce Newlan was a partner in that firm. It became Newlan's exclusive property in 1982, but not his probable permanent site. He had tentative plans to build a newer, larger cellar on another of his vineyards nearby but has yet to do so. Whether he moves north a half mile or stays put, the roster of wines is expected to remain the same: Chardonnay, Cabernet Sauvignon, and Pinot Noir, plus an occasional late-harvest Riesling. Beau Nouveau is a Beaujolais-style Pinot Noir.

Newton Vineyard does not have many peers for sheer drama. Its vines occupy steep, terraced slopes on the skirts of Spring Mountain near St. Helena. The cellars, having been dug into the earth to help keep them cool, compensate with a dramatic cap—an observation tower that helps to hide a ring of stainless steel fermentors that might otherwise bring to mind some such astronomical measuring device as Stonehenge. A formal garden with boxwood hedges covers the rest of the roof, giving good views of other landscaping as well as the valley below.

New wines descend by gravity from the fermentors to age in French oak barrels in a recently excavated cave. After bottling, they descend by truck in low gear to storage space in town. The list includes Sauvignon Blanc, Cabernet Sauvignon, and Merlot, plus one non-Bordelais varietal, Chardonnay.

Nichelini Vineyard is way up in the hills east of St. Helena. East of Conn Dam and the reservoir called Lake Hennessy, State Highway 128 curls along bare-shouldered hills forming one side of a steep canyon. Just at the head of the canyon the road slips into a grove of oaks. There, amid the trees and set into the downslope, is Nichelini.

The winery, founded in the late nineteenth century and now in the hands of the third generation, makes a number of varietal table wines. Sauvignon Vert is the specialty in whites. Cabernet Sauvignon, Zinfandel, and Gamay share honors among the reds.

There are no formal tours, but poking around is encouraged when the family-owned winery is open. Tree-shaded picnic tables have room for as many as 40 people, if everybody is convivial.

Niebaum-Coppola Estate must rank as the most patient new winery in the valley. Its first wine, a Bordeaux-style blend called Rubicon from the 1978 vintage, wasn't released until 1985.

The name tells much of the history of the property. The vineyard is on part of what was Gustave Niebaum's land when he owned Inglenook. Motion picture maker Francis Ford Coppola now owns a substantial portion of the original property and has his winery in the stately, cream-colored building Niebaum used as his stables.

The winery location is permanent, but plans are under way to build a barrel house adjacent to it.

Peju Province was a handsome new addition to the Napa Valley landscape in 1983, its elegant stone chateau honoring time-proven values amid the area's rampant modernism. Owners Anthony and Herta Peju own 30 acres of vines around the winery.

The roster includes estate-grown Cabernet Sauvignon, white Cabernet, and French Colombard; Chardonnay and Sauvignon Blanc grapes are purchased.

Robert Pepi Winery crowns a steep knoll not far north of Oakville in fine style. One of several energy-conscious buildings added to the valley during the 1980s, it sacrifices no architectural drama to the point. Foam insulation hides as the sandwich layer between native stone outer walls and masonry block inner ones. These walls, and vents at the peak of a soaring slate roof, take care of most of the cooling needs.

Old Harvest Wagon

The working winery is well laid out: a crusher stands outside the north wall. A Bücher tank press is just inside, directly beneath stainless steel settling tanks and alongside stainless fermentors. Medium-sized French oak tanks fill the middle space. French barrels are at the opposite end of a rectangular building from the fermentors. All of this is in easy view from glass-walled offices and labs at the upper level. From a dormer at one end, views across the valley are outstanding.

Sauvignon Blanc is the great specialty. Its running mates are Chardonnay, Semillon, and Cabernet Sauvignon. The first crush was 1981.

Joseph Phelps Vineyards winery building is set against a vine-covered slope in the first row of hills on the east side of the Napa Valley. It was built in 1974 by a proprietor who came to wine as a builder of other cellars and was so attracted that he changed sides.

The wood building is in effect two pavilions joined by a closed bridge that holds offices and labs. On the uphill side, a Brobdingnagian wisteria arbor is made of timbers salvaged from a one-time trestle bridge. (Much of the handsome entry gate was recycled similarly by the proprietor, Joseph Phelps.)

The northerly pavilion holds the fermentors–stainless steel ones in a mostly woody environment—along with a considerable number of oval oak casks from Germany and a small number of upright oak tanks. This pavilion also has the reception area, entered from the central court.

The other part of the building holds lofty racks full of oak barrels from French and American forests. A bottling room adjoins the barrel racks.

For the most part, the walls at Phelps are of large-dimensioned, rough-sawn redwood in keeping with the hay barn-inspired shape of the building. But as a pleasant study in contrasts, the reception room and offices have walls and ceilings with fine paneling and richly detailed decorative trims.

Tasting of selected wines follows appointment-only tours. The list includes Chardonnay, Sauvignon Blanc, Gewürztraminer, Cabernet Sauvignon, Pinot Noir, and Zinfandel. The specialties of the house are a true Syrah and Riesling made in a variety of styles from early harvest to late harvest. Some of the latter are comparable in sweetness to German Trockenbeerenauslese. A proprietary Bordeaux-style blend is labeled Insignia.

Champagne: How the bubbles get there

Sparkling wine dates from the time of Dom Perignon, a Benedictine monk who made wine for l'Abbaye d'Hautvillers in the late 1600s. In a sense, effervescing wine had long since invented itself. Fermentation is the conversion of sugar by yeast into roughly equal parts of carbon dioxide (CO_2) and alcohol. Perignon invented only bottles and stoppers suitable for keeping the bubbles in.

His original method was chancy. It involved starting a secondary fermentation in the tightly corked bottle and hoping that the total accumulation of CO_2 would not explode the glass. Because Perignon and other early cellarkeepers took no notice of the interrelationship between sugar and eventual gas pressure, one scholar has it that the odds ran no better than 6 to 4 on any bottle in those pioneer years.

Now, with refined measurements, the same technique, called the *méthode champenoise,* still is used. The champagne master assembles a cuvée—a blend of still wines—to his taste, bottles it and adds a mixture of sugar and yeast before capping each bottle. The wine is then stored on *tirage* while this mixture produces the bubbles during the secondary fermentation. After the yeast has finished its work, it falls as sediment and is allowed to remain in the bottle for at least a few months, sometimes for several years.

After this period, the sediment is worked into the neck of the bottle in a process called "riddling." Then the neck of the bottle is frozen in brine (or another solution) so that the sediment can pop out as a plug of ice (aided by an average gas pressure of 100 pounds per square inch) when the bottle is uncapped. After this process, called "disgorging," a syrup called "dosage" is added. It governs the sweetness of the finished wine. Then the cork is driven into the bottle and wired in place.

Latterly, science added some variations. One is the German method called "Carstens transfer process." It starts out in the same way as the *méthode champenoise.* But when the time comes to remove the sediment, the bottles are emptied under pressure into a holding tank, the wine is filtered, and then the wine is returned to bottles with the desired dosage. Another method, French in origin, is called Charmat or "bulk process." In this case, the wine undergoes its secondary fermentation in a glass-lined tank, rather than in bottles. Then it is filtered on its way to the bottles.

A great many California wineries make sparkling wines; most have tours. Among the clearest demonstrations: Domaine Chandon, Gloria Ferrer, Korbel, Hanns Kornell, Mirassou, Piper Sonoma, Schramsberg, and Wente for *méthode champenoise;* Weibel and Guild for Charmat.

Pine Ridge Winery is one of several pleasing blends of the new and the nostalgic in the Napa Valley. Most of the working winery is housed in a solid box of a building but one of the aging cellars tucks under a frame building that used to be the Luigi Domeniconi winery and residence.

The new part of the winery is typical of its era: stainless steel fermentors and storage tanks for the new wine, oak puncheons and barrels for the maturing stocks. Wilt Chamberlain would not have any trouble getting around in there, but only a handful of NBA guards could enjoy the old cellar with its rows of fat, Burgundian barrels. Pine Ridge produces Chardonnay, Chenin Blanc, Cabernet Sauvignon, and Merlot. Not incidentally, this is a good place for serious students of wine to talk about the effects of wood on fermentation and aging. Proprietor-winemaker R. Gary Andrus has a ranging library of woods on hand to see which does what.

A more general attraction is a picnic ground in a shading grove of pines. Still another engaging prospect is a walking trail up onto the ridge that gives the winery its name.

Prager Winery and Port Works is a singular idea in the contemporary Napa Valley. While many wineries who have sold Port-types were dropping the idea, Jim Prager was starting a winery substantially devoted to locally grown Port-types. The small cellar has made half Port, half table wines since its founding in 1980.

Next to the proprietor's home south of St. Helena, the winery is one of few in the coast counties where visitors can talk about the details of dessert winemaking. As usual, all the gear looks like gear in any other winery. The differences are in the winemaker's head, and, in this case, in the addition of brandy to still-fermenting young wines.

Quail Ridge belongs to an elite corps of Napa wineries that have found homes in romantic buildings from the valley's era of growth in the 1880s.

The fine old stone building it occupies began in 1885 as Hedgeside Winery and Distillery, a firm owned by a California legislator named Morris M. Estee. In a mild irony, the government shut it down during national Prohibition, and the government reopened it to produce alcohol during World War II. No wine was fermented nor was brandy distilled in the building from 1950 until recently. Quail Ridge succeeded another proprietor, who was there only briefly, in time for the harvest of 1981; the company was founded at another site in 1978.

Proprietor Elaine Wellesley uses the north end of the building and a hand-hewn 300-foot tunnel—sharper than a dogleg, but not quite a right angle—to barrel-ferment and age Chardonnay. Cabernet Sauvignon and Merlot joined the roster beginning with the vintage of 1980.

Visitors are often invited to sit and talk around a table in the front part of the winery, in an atmosphere not unlike a French country inn save for the pleasing view of the cave stretching away in dim light, with the twin bottling tanks next to its mouth.

A real-estate office and a plastics fabricator use the southern end of the building. Their signs shout louder than Quail Ridge's does, but the ivy-covered stone facade is hard to miss.

Raymond Vineyards and Cellar

Raymond Vineyards and Cellar belongs to an old-line Napa Valley grape-growing and winemaking family. Roy Raymond and sons Roy, Jr., and Walter established their own vineyard in 1971, and made their first wines from the harvest of 1974 after substantial careers with other firms.

The olive green-painted permanent winery building went up between 1979 and 1981 in the midst of the family's vines just south of St. Helena and just east of State 29. Stone lower walls and wood-sided upper walls echo traditional Napa winery architecture. The working gear—stainless steel fermentors, Willmes presses, and French and American oak barrels—typifies the valley's modern era.

Tasting facilities were opened in 1985; a tour of the winery still requires an appointment. The list of wines from vines surrounding the winery includes Chardonnay, Sauvignon Blanc, Riesling (regular and late-harvest), and Cabernet Sauvignon.

Ritchie Creek Vineyard

Ritchie Creek Vineyard is the tiny winery of Richard Minor. Its only wines are Chardonnay and Cabernet Sauvignon from the steep vineyard near the Sonoma County line at the top of Spring Mountain.

The entry drive ends at the proprietor's house, at the top side of his forest-encircled vineyard. The winery tunnels into the slope just downhill from the bottom row of vines, the proprietor reasoning that it is easier to get boxes full of grapes downhill than it is to get them up.

Taking a look into the L-shaped tunnel with its double racks of French barrels requires an appointment. Tasting is at the discretion of the owner because production is so limited that a single bottle matters in the statistics.

Rombauer Vineyards

Rombauer Vineyards is a split-face block structure embedded in a tree-shrouded knoll off the Silverado Trail, north of St. Helena. The owners are Koerner Rombauer (the nephew of the author of *The Joy of Cooking*) and his wife, Joan. The Rombauers began as partners in Conn Creek Winery. They went on their own in 1980, custom-crushing their first two vintages at another winery while building their own. The Rombauer facility was completed in time to finish and bottle the red wines from the 1982 vintage; the first whites were produced there in 1983.

By a stroke of cosmic justice, the Rombauers' spacious, well-equipped winery has become a major custom-crushing house for other aspiring winery owners. For their own label, the Rombauers produce four wines, all from purchased grapes: a barrel-fermented Chardonnay in the Burgundy style, a stainless steel-fermented Chardonnay in the Chablis style, Cabernet Sauvignon, and a proprietary blend of Cabernet Sauvignon, Cabernet Franc, and Merlot, called Le Meilleur du Chai ("the best of the cellar"). Tours are by appointment only.

Round Hill Cellars

Round Hill Cellars shares a sturdy building and a fine old garden with an antique shop. The whole place was a winery early in Napa's wine history; now the stone front part of the premises has the antiques, while the working winery tucks behind a stucco-walled structure shaded somewhere between rose and salmon pink to go with the flowers.

Founding partner Charles Abela used to build boats, and it shows in the cellars where each bit of equipment stows neatly in less space than usual. The gear itself is typical of time and place: crusher behind the building, stainless steel fermentors close inside the rear door, and French and American oak barrels up toward the high-ceilinged, white, airy sales and visitor room. The latter is entered from the west side of the building, via a path through the most aromatic parts of the garden.

The Round Hill label covers a wide spectrum of table wines, with more or less parallel rosters of all the familiar varietals from both Napa and Sonoma counties plus generics from a broader range of sources. In 1987, the partners were constructing a new, larger winery on the Silverado Trail, near Rutherford.

Rutherford Hill Winery

Rutherford Hill Winery is situated high on a steep slope east of Rutherford, overlooking an old olive grove, an elegant French restaurant, and a checkerboard of vineyards on the valley floor below.

The cellar is architecturally distinctive and efficient. The shake-roofed, wood-sided structure echoes old Napa hay barns in form, though flying buttresses occurred to few or no farmers, and it is a great deal bigger than any barn that might have inspired it.

A dramatic reception and tasting hall is just inside a pair of towering doors at the lower level. Beyond the tasting hall is a long, dim cellar filled with stainless steel and oak storage tanks. French oak barrels and the bottling line fill the upper floor. Willmes presses, stainless steel fermentors and other processing gear are on a deck at the rear. The well-guided tour also takes in a half-mile of aging caves, bored into the hillside in 1985.

The roster includes Chardonnay, Gewürztraminer, Sauvignon Blanc, Cabernet Sauvignon, and Merlot.

There is reason other than wine for visiting Rutherford Hill. It is the California capital of *petanque*, the ancient Mediterranean game of bowls. All comers may play on the court, but betting against one of the cellar staff is a serious mistake.

Rutherford Vintners

Rutherford Vintners has a tasting and sales room open daily in a gray, wood-frame cottage next to State

29, a quarter-mile north of the Rutherford Cross Road.

To have a look at the workings of the trim winery in its grove of towering eucalyptus trees requires a group appointment since proprietor Bernard Skoda is the only tour guide as well as the winemaster.

Skoda has wedged a remarkable amount and variety of oak cooperage into his rectangular masonry block building. The back wall has German ovals for the Riesling. Both side walls have Slavonian oak ovals for mid-term aging of the reserve and regular Cabernet Sauvignons and Pinot Noirs. In the middle are a row of American oak upright tanks for initial aging, and separate racks of American and French oak barrels for final aging of the two reds. A separate rack of French oak barrels is for the Chardonnay. In one corner is a tall, refrigerated stainless steel tank for a specialty Muscat of Alexandria sold only at the winery.

The Willmes press and two rows of refrigerated stainless steel fermentors are under an overhanging red tile roof at the rear of the aging cellar.

St. Clement Vineyards occupies a fine old Victorian house near St. Helena. The native stone winery was carved out of the base of Spring Mountain to extend and cool the cellar, which is full of fat Burgundian barrels. Because the property is the residence of proprietor William Casey, and because production is so limited, no visitors are allowed save those who make appointments to purchase St. Clement wines in case lots. The wines are Chardonnay, Sauvignon Blanc, Cabernet Sauvignon, and Merlot.

Saintsbury is among a number of wineries that have been launched in a nineteenth-century stone winery building on Ehlers Lane (see page 83). Saintsbury's inaugural 1981 and 1982 vintages were produced there, while owning partners Richard Ward and David Graves constructed their permanent winery in the Carneros district. It was finished in time for the 1983 crush. The barnlike, cedar-sided structure, with its galvanized metal roof covering thick insulation, is a harmonious presence in the gentle Carneros landscape near Cuttings Wharf Road.

On one side of the building, a porched crusher and press give way to the interior fermentation room, which is filled with tall stainless steel tanks beneath a grid of metal catwalks. The separate barrel room contains several types of French oak cooperage.

The traditional eight-barrel locked stacks are only one indication that Graves and Ward are committed Burgundians. Naturally, the Saintsbury roster consists of Chardonnay and Pinot Noir, produced in Burgundian ways by California means. Garnet is a light, early drinking Pinot Noir. Grapes are purchased from established Carneros district vineyards.

Incidentally, the winery name is a tribute to the immortal nineteenth-century connoisseur George Saintsbury, whose classic *Notes on a Cellarbook* is recommended reading for all wine fans.

V. Sattui Winery, just south of St. Helena, opened its tasting room in 1976 and was discovered quickly by wine country visitors looking for a place to picnic.

In addition to the winery and tasting room, the at-

tractive building houses a gift, cheese, and deli shop. Flanking the white stucco, mission-style structure are many large, tree-shaded picnic tables. Beneath it are four small caves.

The label dates not from 1976 but from 1885, when Vittorio Sattui established it for his own wines. It disappeared during Prohibition, but has been revived at the new site by Vittorio's great-grandson, Daryl, and several partners.

Sattui wines include Chardonnay, dry and late-harvest Rieslings, Gamay Rosé, Cabernet Sauvignon, Zinfandel, and a Madeira blended from stocks going back 20 years. The wines are sold only at the winery.

Schramsberg Vineyards, having been founded by Jacob Schram in 1862, won quick immortality in the writings of Robert Louis Stevenson after the great Scots novelist visited the winery in 1880.

For a long time the immortality was more literary than practical. Stevenson's *Silverado Squatters* has gone on and on, but the winery began to fade as soon as Schram died. It closed altogether in 1921, experienced two ephemeral revivals in 1940 and 1951, then closed again.

The old property has lived up to Stevenson's hopes since 1965, when Jack and Jamie Davies launched Schramsberg anew, this time as a sparkling wine cellar. (Schram had made only still wines.)

It is a romantic place to visit for both its past and present. Stevenson's original description of the trail up from the main road remains fairly accurate, though the surface is a good deal better and the exact route has shifted somewhat. The original winery building still stands at the top of a large clearing next to the old Schram home. Several tunnels going back into the hill from the winery have been turned into modern fermenting rooms for production of the wines that become champagne a few hundred yards away.

A short lane leads to the champagne cellar itself, where a wood-faced building encloses more tunnels that hold the emergent champagne in bottles, thousands of them piled row on row in the *méthode champenoise* fashion.

Production is too limited to permit tasting of the five types of Schramsberg champagnes. Four are finished in the dry style called Brut: Reserve, the premier bottling; Blanc de Blancs from white grapes; Blanc de Noirs from black grapes; and Cuvée de Pinot, a rosé. The fifth wine, Cremant, is finished demi-sec.

Sequoia Grove Vineyards is a rarity in the Napa Valley's current era of sleek, sizable new wineries. The winery is a well-weathered, sturdy, unpainted board-and-batten barn of a classic size and shape for this part of California. It hides modestly in the cluster of young redwoods from which proprietor James Allen derived the name.

An appropriately casual air clings to all of the property. For example, a crushing and fermenting area at the rear overlooks several elderly cars in varying stages of rebuilding. Against these easygoing touches, the equipment is more typical of modern Napa: a stainless steel horizontal basket press, stainless steel fermentors, and French barrels in a building that looks like a typical barn but is well insulated and thoroughly air-conditioned.

There are but two wines, Cabernet Sauvignon and Chardonnay. The first vintage was 1979.

Shafer Vineyards occupies a striking corner of the district called Stag's Leap. Amid proprietor John Shafer's rolling vineyards is a modern, well-equipped, well-designed winery building that looks as if it has been around for decades, but that was begun only in 1979 and completed a year later.

The architectural secret is a front elevation made part of stone wall, part of stained redwood siding, after a fashion once common in Napa. A signature stone next to the entry announces the founding date. The first Shafer wines came a year earlier but were made in leased space nearby.

The working winery, along with conventional crusher, press, and fermentors, has an engaging library of wood cooperage ranging from stovepipe-thin American uprights to German oak ovals to fat, Burgundian barrels. The roster of wines produced here includes only Chardonnay, Cabernet Sauvignon, and Merlot from the property. Sales are made only to visitors with appointments.

Charles F. Shaw Vineyard & Winery looks more than a little like a French farm building for a purpose. The owner, whose name the label bears, has set out to make a wine in the Beaujolais Villages style from his property on the valley floor between St. Helena and Calistoga. The architecture is part of the announcement.

The building is almost jaunty with its gray walls, red trim, and steep roof. A visit to learn what sorts of equipment are required to make a fresh, light-hearted red wine will show that much of winemaking is in the winemaker's mind. The crusher, Willmes press, and stainless steel fermentors at the rear look much like those at other cellars; so do the tidy ranks of French oak barrels inside. The story is in the fine points of how they and Napa Gamay grapes are used to make a Napa Valley counterpart to such as Morgon or Fleurie. Chardonnay and Sauvignon Blanc also are produced.

Shown & Sons Vineyards pulled up roots and shifted from its original site along the Silverado Trail to its current west-side location in 1985, without missing a viticultural beat. Dick Shown founded the label in 1979, on property known since Napa's Mexican days as El Viñedo de los Aguacitas.

The new 25-acre vineyard near Rutherford, almost directly across the valley from the old one, also goes back to Mexican times as part of mountain-man George Yount's Caymus Rancho. The soil, too, is similar. Shown has budded pre-existing vines to the same varieties he left behind, and with his son, Chris, continues to produce estate-grown Chardonnay, Cabernet Sauvignon, and Zinfandel. There is one new twist. The old farmhouse, which became the present winery, has no crush facilities, so the fruit is crushed at a larger winery and brought back home for fermentation and aging, in French oak for the Chardonnay and American oak for the reds. A new proprietary blend is Ricardo's Robust.

Silverado Vineyards is practically a holy destination for wine-loving former Mouseketeers. The winery boasts a discreet stained-glass portrait of Mickey Mouse high in one transom, which is owner Lillian Disney's tribute to her late husband, Walt.

Along with partners Ron and Diane Miller, Mrs. Disney bought the former Harry See ranch along the Silverado Trail in the mid-1970s. In 1981 the trio built the winery, a handsome stone building in the early California style, on a knoll at the crest of a rise known historically as Parker Hill. Their 180 acres of vineyard slope away from the Stag's Leap area toward Yountville, traversing soil zones ranging from gravel to alluvial loam.

The cool, almost churchlike interior is fitted out with new stainless steel, French oak cooperage, up-to-date processing gear, and a well-equipped lab. No formal tours are offered, but there is a tasting-sales room at the winery, and one thing sometimes leads to another. The view from the tasting room is spectacular, especially in spring when the valley is carpeted with mustard and purple lupine.

The roster of wines from the estate includes Chardonnay, Sauvignon Blanc, Cabernet Sauvignon, and Merlot.

Smith-Madrone Vineyards belongs to brothers Charles and Stuart Smith and Stuart's wife, Susan, the three having built what may be the ultimate image of a California cellar to house their wines.

The building is set on a shelf at the midpoint of a long, steeply sloping vineyard looking out across the valley from an upper slope of Spring Mountain. The lower half is masonry, the upper half wood-framed and wood-walled after a model common to the 1880s. But this building has some contemporary turns. The roof of the fermenting and main aging cellar is sod-covered for energy-efficient insulation. A separate section of overhead has been designed to accommodate a residence

Howell Mountain Winery built in 1877

and offices, with steep roofs and offset walls that bring to mind contemporary seaside homes at such places as Sea Ranch.

As for the working winery, crusher and press rest on a pad outside. Inside, stainless steel fermentors occupy one end of the main level. French oak barrels occupy the other end and fill an underground cellar.

The Smiths make Chardonnay, Riesling, and Cabernet Sauvignon from vines they planted in 1972. Their first vintage was 1977.

Spring Mountain Vineyards evokes both of the great eras of building in the Napa Valley about as well as any single property can.

The first great era, the 1880s, gave rise to a splendid Victorian house, a less imposing but still fine barn, and a hand-hewn tunnel for storing wines in the cool earth. The original builder was Tiburcio Parrott, an enthusiastic participant in everything that made the late nineteenth century a golden age for most of humanity's tangible possessions.

In 1974 Michael Robbins bought the old property to house the winery he had founded in 1968 on another site. Parrott's legacy had fallen into considerable disrepair; so, the new owner set about restoring it before adding to the current era of fine architecture in the Napa Valley.

By 1976, he had the old buildings tuned up and was well advanced on the new construction. The new winery, built out from the face of the steep slope Parrott chose for his tunnel, reveals an eye every bit as romantic as Parrott's. To cite a single example, stained-glass windows in the front wall cast soft light onto rows of French oak barrels and are set so they can be seen sequentially as one walks toward the depths of the old tunnel. Cabernet Sauvignon ages in the new building. Chardonnay and Sauvignon Blanc age in the cooler tunnel. Due in part to the use of the winery as a set for a popular television series, the tasting room is nearly always crowded.

Balloon Tours

Stag's Leap Wine Cellars tucks neatly into its hillside amid a grove of oaks. The original 1972 building fit in so well that it was nearly invisible from the Silverado Trail, which is no more than a hundred yards away. A second building added in 1976 sits out in fuller view. A third, dating from 1981, peeks out from behind the first two. With the fourth addition, completed in 1984, the property began to resemble a Mediterranean village.

The original building is devoted to white wine aging. Outside, two rows of stainless steel fermentors run the length of the uphill wall. The 1976 building houses stainless steel storage tanks, the bottling line, and upright oak tanks. The third building, styled after a classic French country house, has the offices and more wine storage. Red wines age in the newest structure.

In all, Stag's Leap Wine Cellars is so thoughtfully designed as to offer a textbook example of how to put together a small, specialized winery. One example: Both crusher and press straddle a single channel cut into the concrete work pad. Stems, pomace, and washwater all course downhill, out of the way until the work is done, when they can be eliminated at leisure.

Warren and Barbara Winiarski own the winery and 121 acres of contiguous vineyard in the heart of the Stag's Leap viticultural area. Both winery and appellation are named for a red-rock crag that dominates the region from a nearby mountaintop.

The roster of wines includes Chardonnay, Sauvignon Blanc, Riesling, Cabernet Sauvignon, and Merlot. One or two are selected each day to offer for tasting in the 1976 building, among the oak uprights.

Incidentally, there is another, unrelated winery called Stags' Leap Winery (see page 100).

Steltzner Vineyards occupies its own miniature valley between the Silverado Trail and the towering red rock formation for which the Stag's Leap district is named. Dick Steltzner planted the vineyard in 1968. After years of tasting what other wineries were doing with his grapes, he decided in 1977 to introduce his own label. Initial wines were made at nearby wineries, but in 1983 Steltzner converted an old prune shed on the property into a winery. That was accomplished by coating the shed (a pre-Prohibition relic) with polyurethane and filling it with cooperage. He installed stainless steel tanks outside, along with a Demoisy crusher and a Bucher press.

It is not a flashy facility, but it does the job. Primary emphasis here is on the vineyard itself, which students of viticulture will find to be a comprehensive lesson in the dynamics of a microclimate. The single varietal is Cabernet Sauvignon.

Visits to the winery are by appointment only, but no appointment is required to purchase some of the other fruit grown on the property. The right turn off the Silverado Trail is sharp and comes up suddenly. Fortunately, it's easy to spot. Look for a sign that says, "Pick Your Own Blackberries."

Sterling Vineyards looks from the outside like a fair approximation of the sort of church crusaders left on similarly craggy hilltops on Greek isles.

From the inside, it looks like the modern winery it is. The main cellar runs downhill from the first step in winemaking. Crusher, German presses, and jacketed stainless steel fermentors are at the top. A series of oak aging cellars descend from that level to the lowest point in the main building. A separate two-story cellar near the crest of the hill holds two years' worth of reserve wines aging in small oak. A separate bottling building hides behind the first two.

There is more than working winery to interest visitors here. An aerial tramway transports them from parking lot to winery and back for a $3.50 fee. The sign-guided tour provides graphic and detailed information about grapes and wine, and also passes through a room full of excellent antique furnishings and decorations. As an audible extra, the bells of St. Dunstans ring out the quarter hours.

In a separate building adjacent to the reserve cellar, the tasting room is an elegantly airy place, with awesome views down the valley, plus tables and chairs for relaxed contemplation of the wines. In it the proprietors offer all their short list: Chardonnay, Sauvignon Blanc, Cabernet Sauvignon, Merlot, and a Cabernet Sauvignon Blanc.

Sterling was founded in 1969. In 1977 it was purchased by the Coca-Cola Company, which held it only briefly before selling to the present owner, Joseph E. Seagram & Sons, Inc.

Stonegate Winery, when it opened in 1973, was contained entirely within the small building at the rear of the present cluster of three. The original cellar now holds only white wines. Reds occupy the newer, larger structure directly alongside Dunaweal Lane, not far down the valley from Calistoga.

Founded and operated by the James Spaulding family, Stonegate remains a small winery, but not such a crowded one as in the days when the whole enterprise squeezed itself into what had been a tractor shed.

Most small wineries are instructive for start-to-finish demonstrations of what goes into making wine. Because the red and white cellars are separate, this one is unusually so. The stainless steel fermentors common to both cellars sit outside along with other harvest-season processing gear, the anchor point for separate lessons to follow about the hows and whys and whens of oak aging.

The stone gate pictured on the winery's label shows the way from parking lot to tasting room. The roster includes Chardonnay and Sauvignon Blanc in whites; Cabernet Sauvignon, Merlot, and Pinot Noir in reds. Some are special lots from identified vineyards.

Stony Hill Vineyard does not fit easily into a day of casual touring. An appointment is required to visit it, but that is only half the story. Stony Hill is at the top of a long, winding road, high in the west side hills. The drive up takes as long as a thorough look.

The cellar dates from 1951 when the late Fred McCrea and his wife, Eleanor, built it as a place to keep busy in retirement. The building, part stone, part plaster, nestles into a grove of trees at the foot of a sloping block of Riesling vines. A pair of handsome doors carved by the founder leads into a cellar containing European oak puncheons and barrels, and one of the last classic binning systems for bottled wines in the California wine country.

Stony Hill, under the direction of Eleanor McCrea and winemaker Mike Chelini, makes three vintage-dated wines, all white: Chardonnay, Gewürztraminer, and Riesling. They ferment in the puncheons, the carbon dioxide dispelled through bubbler hoses with their noses stuck into water-filled wine bottles. Then the wines age in either the puncheons or barrels. In propitious years there is also a minute quantity of late-harvest Semillon du Soleil.

A visit is pretty much in the way of a pilgrimage. Once a year the winery dispatches a letter to its mailing list, and all the wine sells out within a few weeks. Thus, there are neither tastings nor sales—only an opportunity to see a cellar legendary to its followers.

Storybook Mountain Vineyards came into its happy name and fabled label by a plausible set of literary word plays.

The winery was founded, and its three spacious tunnels dug, in the 1880s by a family named Grimm, which included a pair of brothers. With the brothers Grimm as a starting point, the name Storybook came easily. The label required a leap of imagination to get a picture of Aesop's fox and the grapes worked into the game, to compensate for the storytelling Grimms' failures to spin a tale on the subject.

Owner-winemaker Dr. J. Bernard Seps, a one-time professor, abandoned the study of history to make some. He restored the long-abandoned caves without harming their hand-hewn look and planted the steep amphitheater above them to Zinfandel, the only wine he produces. The first vintage was 1980.

Early visitors to Storybook Mountain found a second winery parallel to the main one. Seps shared the underground vaults with Schug Cellars, a specialist in Pinot Noir. A carved head on a new German oak oval announced that presence and also showed an old stone and concrete facade over the tunnels. That structure collapsed during the rainy winter of 1981-82, prompting Walter Schug to move his operation (see page 100).

Summit Lake Vineyards is a rustic Howell Mountain ranch that could almost pass (except for the tractor and pickup trucks) for a nineteenth-century homestead. Bob and Sue Brakesman's vineyard incorporates a block of pre-Prohibition Zinfandel vines, which give mute credence to fireside yarns about Howell Mountain's nineteenth century glory days as a winegrowing area.

Those days were long gone when the Brakesmans arrived to nurture the old vines, and the mountain's reputation, in the late 1970s. The past rejoined the present in 1983, however, when the Brakesmans and their colleagues (the Smiths of La Jota, Randy Dunn, Bob Lamborn, and growers Joice and Michael Beatty of Beatty Ranch) mounted a successful campaign to have Howell Mountain recognized as an official U.S. Viticultural Area (see page 53).

Meanwhile, the Brakesmans continued planting grapes on their property along Summit Lake Drive, and completed their tall, wood-frame winery in 1985.

Current production of Chardonnay and Zinfandel is too small to make regular tasting feasible, but it is worthwhile making an appointment to visit, if only for the view over spring-fed lakes to the far-off Napa Valley. One warning: A visit during crush may result in unexpected enrollment in the Tom Sawyer School of Winemaking. Bring boots.

Sutter Home Winery has dramatically charted the ups and downs of the California wine industry in its 100-year history.

The contrast is visible in its two facilities: one an historic cellar, the other an industrial-scale plant. The original winery is a handsomely proportioned structure originally built to house the cellars of J. Thomann, one of the major forces in the early history of Napa wine. The 1880s building proves the ageworthiness of properly assembled good wood.

The establishment got its name honestly. John Sutter and son Albert built their first winery in the east hills of the valley in 1890. Sutter's son-in-law transferred the winery lock, stock, and barrels to its present site on Highway 29 in 1906 and operated it until mid-Prohibition.

The Trinchero family bought Sutter Home in 1946. Over the years, they made its name a synonym for Zinfandel, primarily from Amador County grapes. Their outlook changed dramatically in 1984, with the growing demand for their white Zinfandel. They began buying vineyards and grafting over to Zinfandel, until in 1987 they owned some 1,700 acres in several counties. At the same time they constructed a large, modern facility south of St. Helena. Overnight, Sutter Home went from being one of the valley's smallest wineries to being one of its largest.

The current roster, available for tasting in the original winery, is largely white Zinfandel. There are also red Zinfandel and California's only sparkling white Zinfandel, along with several other varietals.

Trefethen Vineyards looks as though a good deal of history should surround it, and a good deal does. However, until the winery became Trefethen in 1968, that history was surprisingly quiet.

The vast, three-story, wooden building is the only survivor of its type in the valley. It is doubtful if it ever had a peer among wooden buildings in Napa. Its designer and builder was Captain Hamden McIntyre, who also designed the original Inglenook and Beaulieu wineries, and Greystone Cellars, now owned by The Christian Brothers. But while the other two cellars have had more or less famous labels attached to them down through the years, the Trefethen building was, until bought by the current owners, mainly a bulk winery, or leased as storage to a winery with its headquarters elsewhere. The Eugene Trefethen family has paid tribute to one of the winery's earlier careers with wines labeled Eshcol Red and Eshcol White, but rarely was there an Eshcol label when the winery went by that name.

This is a most agreeable and informative cellar to visit. The old cellar is filled with a mixture of American and French oak barrels used to age the Trefethen's estate-grown wines: Chardonnay, Riesling, Cabernet Sauvignon, Pinot Noir, and the two Eshcols.

Tudal Winery is a perfect example of the new wave of small, family-owned and -operated cellars in the Napa Valley.

Two generations of the Arnold Tudal family tend the vineyard and make the wine from crush through bottling in a handsome barn next to a tennis court. The cellar is so neatly organized that even casual visitors see at a glance how everything from French oak barrel to valve clamp is in use or precisely in its place.

Outside on a big L-shaped concrete pad are the temperature-controlled stainless steel tanks and other processing equipment.

There are only two wines: Cabernet Sauvignon from the property, and Chardonnay from grapes purchased locally. The first vintage was 1979.

Vichon Winery perches on a dramatic slope right next to a swooping curve a few hundred feet up Oakville Grade from the valley floor.

Though the winery began only in 1980, this is its second home. The first one was in a small stone barn at the end of Ehlers Lane north of St. Helena, a building that has become a sort of nursery for new wineries. Vichon was the second born there and has been followed by a third (see page 83).

The current structure contrasts with the first one. Vichon's permanent home restates some old Spanish colonial ideas—covered walkways, balustraded balconies—in modern ways with modern materials well suited to contemporary winemaking equipment. The label, also modern, shows an abstracted outline of the Mayacamas Mountain ridges above the cellars. It covers Chardonnay, Chevrier Blanc (a proprietary blend of Semillon and Sauvignon Blanc), and Cabernet Sauvignon. The winery is owned by the Robert Mondavi family.

Villa Mt. Eden began as a vineyard in 1881 and has endured as both vineyard and winery property through numerous ownerships.

The best known of its earlier proprietors was Nick Fagiani, who used the place to make Sherry-type wines just before Prohibition. The property now belongs to James and Anne McWilliams, who bought and named it in 1970 and installed sophisticated new equipment for a comeback as a table-wine cellar beginning in 1974.

Grapes for Villa Mt. Eden's estate-grown wines are field-crushed into rolling stainless steel tanks—a German system called the Mörtl—then fermented in stainless steel tanks before aging in either American or French oak barrels.

The one-story, white-stucco winery is one of several similar buildings grouped around an open courtyard in the classic fashion of a Mediterranean country villa. The surrounding vineyards are planted in a rare mixture of alluvial and volcanic soils.

Current wine production is small, and plans are to keep it that way. The roster is Chardonnay, Chenin Blanc, and Cabernet Sauvignon.

Whitehall Lane Winery advertises its location with its name. The jauntily designed building sits at the intersection of State 29 and Whitehall Lane, not far south of St. Helena.

Sampling wine & the arts

Music, art and fine wine are ingredients for festive occasions. Although spring and summer are the traditional visiting seasons in the wine country, music and art accompany the clinking of wine glasses all year long at a number of wineries. The events listed below are only a representative sample of the many diversions hosted by California vintners.

Call the individual wineries for more information. It's a good idea to plan well in advance for these popular attractions. Winery addresses can be found in the listings accompanying the maps in each chapter.

Buena Vista Winery offers an annual Shakespeare in the Courtyard and Midsummer Mozart Concert series, in addition to art shows and other events. For information, call (707) 938-1266 or (800) 338-9463.

Domaine Chandon hosts three separate evening programs during the year and two celebrations. The latter honor the Fourth of July and Bastille Day (July 14). "Oh Gosh It's Monday" features musical acts each Monday night in June. "Monday Night Madness" offers comedy on Monday nights during October and November, and a series of cabaret performances is offered on Sunday nights from January through March. For details, call (707) 944-2280.

Field Stone Winery features jazz, folk, and bluegrass in scheduled concerts throughout the summer. You'll need advance tickets for all but one free concert. For more details on tickets, dates, and times, call (707) 433-7266.

Greenwood Ridge Vineyards celebrates the fine art of wine tasting at its annual Wine Tasting Olympics, held on the last weekend of July. Music and refreshments enliven the festivities, but the focus is a contest to see who can identify various wines by variety, appellation and vintage. Novices and masters compete in separate categories, and prizes are awarded at the end. For information, call (707) 877-3262.

Johnson's Alexander Valley Winery, which incorporates the Johnson family's organ restoration works, offers occasional pipe organ concerts. In the summer season, concerts may take place on a small outdoor stage next to a picnic lawn. For performance details and times, call (707) 433-2319.

The Konocti Winery features musical talent on occasional Sunday afternoons from the Memorial Day weekend through September. A variety of music is performed, primarily country or bluegrass with an occasional string quartet thrown in.

Local artists display their works at Konocti's annual Harvest Festival on the second weekend in October. The annual Vineyard Run, included in the festival, has attracted so much attention that the runners may have to wear numbers! For more details, call the winery at (707) 279-8861.

Paul Masson Vineyards originated the tradition of performances of classical music among the vines in 1957 with their "Music at the Vineyards" series. More recently they started a companion series of jazz and folk music concerts called "Vintage Sounds." A comedy series was added in 1986. For ticket and program information, call (408) 741-5181 (April-Sept.).

Robert Mondavi Winery presents a summer music festival on consecutive Saturday evenings in July and August at 7 P.M. Ticketholders can picnic after 4:30 P.M.; wine and cheese tasting is offered during intermission. For more information, call (707) 963-9617, ext. 384.

Montevina Wines hosts two different types of activity at the winery in Plymouth, at the heart of the Gold Rush country. There are twice-yearly art shows in conjunction with a Sutter Creek art gallery, and irregularly scheduled dances. Wine tasting is complimentary at all events. For details, call (209) 245-6942.

Rodney Strong Vineyards offers a concert series as part of their summer Festival of the Performing Arts. Performances take place in the vineyard's outdoor Greek Theater. For schedule information and tickets, call (707) 433-6511.

Wente Bros. and the Livermore Art Association co-sponsor Art in the Vineyards in or about Memorial Day weekend. For information, call (415) 447-3603.

Wente also offers a summer concert series that varies with each year. For details and times, call (415) 447-3023.

The working winery is well designed and well equipped in the conventional way. Crusher, press, and stainless steel fermentors are in a semisheltered area at the rear. Barrels are located in one section of the main cellar; more barrels and larger cooperage are in the other. What is startling about the place is its secondary role as a sort of art gallery, or modest museum. Prints, posters, and other pieces of art crop up here, there, and even way up the walls. It takes an appointment to get around to all the art, though casual visitors are welcomed in a tiny retail sales room at the front.

Proprietors Dr. Alan Steen and Art Finkelstein produce Chardonnay, Sauvignon Blanc, Chenin Blanc, Blanc de Pinot Noir, Cabernet Sauvignon, Merlot, and Pinot Noir. The winery also offers proprietary wines including a Pinot Noir known simply as Fleur d'Hélène.

Yverdon Vineyards is a virtuoso one-man show of the building arts. Owner Fred Aves designed and built not only his two-story stone winery, but almost everything in it. He gathered and split local stone for the walls, designed and cast the flaring pillars that hold up the upper floor and gently sloping roof, designed and executed a series of quatrefoil stained-glass windows, designed a Gaudi-esque metal spiral staircase with grape-leaf motif, and even designed and cast concrete cradles for the oak casks he coopered himself.

About the only gear in the place which Aves did not build are the stainless steel fermentors, the Italian press, and some Swiss pumps and filters.

Tours are by appointment only. There is no tasting, but Yverdon Chenin Blanc, Riesling, Cabernet Sauvignon, and Napa Gamay are on sale weekdays. Finding the property is not easy; it is marked only by a plaque bearing the numbers 3787. The plaque is nailed to a tree next to a pipe and wire gate.

The name Yverdon commemorates the ancient Swiss town on Lake Neuchâtel, which is the ancestral home of the Aves family.

Z-D Wines is the first winery since Hanns Kornell to move from Sonoma to Napa. The purpose was to get into quarters larger than the original ones south of Sonoma town, selected when the enterprise was not much more than a hobby for founding partners Gino Zepponi and Norman de Leuze. Relief, as advertisements say, was only temporary. The business had become a full-time occupation by the day of the move in 1979 and has grown since. A good-sized prefabricated metal building on the Silverado Trail between Rutherford and Oakville is crowded not only from wall to wall, but also in spots from floor to ceiling, with stacks of barrels and bottled wine in cases.

Z-D's production historically has focused on Chardonnay and Pinot Noir. There is also Cabernet Sauvignon. Students of barrel-fermented white wines will be interested in the ones made here in American oak.

More Wineries. The Napa Valley has a substantial number of wineries with extremely restricted ability, or no ability at all, to welcome visitors. Their numbers are likely to grow because of recent ordinances prohibiting tasting and sales in several circumstances. These wineries are noted here to aid serious students of California wine who may have seen wines under their labels, and to explain their presence in the landscape.

Acacia Winery hides away on a back road in the Carneros district. The handsome cellars, built in 1982 by Mike Richmond and partners, are used to make only Chardonnay and Pinot Noir. Chalone, Inc., acquired Acacia in 1986. There are no public tours, tasting, or retail sales.

Alatera Vineyards is located on Hoffman Lane south of Yountville. Alatera produces several varietal table wines plus a proprietary Blanc de Noir (from Pinot Noir) called Paradis.

Amizetta Vineyards produces estate-grown wines from steep hillside vineyards in Conn Valley, east of the Silverado Trail. Spencer and Amizetta Clark planted their vineyard in 1979, and finished the gray stucco winery in 1984. The wines are Sauvignon Blanc and Cabernet Sauvignon, both blended with other varieties. Visits are limited but are not out of the question.

S. Anderson Vineyard belongs to a southern California family who commute weekends to their cellars near Yountville. The small winery produces Chardonnay from grapes grown on the property and a sparkling wine from Pinot Noir. Stanley and Carol Anderson have begun their permanent winery by digging an extensive cavern into a hillside, which will be its eventual site. Meanwhile, visitors are welcome to have a look around the cave and the temporary cellar, a prefabricated metal building set in their vineyard, on weekends and by appointment only.

Vincent Arroyo Winery was founded in 1984 by Vincent and Marjorie Arroyo at their vineyards near Calistoga. A new winery was in the planning stages in the spring of 1987. Their surprisingly varied roster tells something about the growing region: Chardonnay, Gamay Noir, Petite Sirah, and Cabernet Sauvignon.

Artisan Wines was founded in 1984 by winemaker Michael Fallow and marketing whiz Jefferey Caldeway to market three brands: Michael's is the signature label, Ultravino wines are purchased in bulk and finished at Artisan's Mt. Veeder facility, and Cru Artisan wines are imported. It's a sizable operation, but there are no visitor facilities.

Buehler Vineyards produces Sauvignon Blanc, Zinfandel, and other wines under the family label at an isolated location in Conn Valley. Proprietor John Buehler can offer neither tours nor sales. The private road leading to the winery and family home will not bear more traffic than residents already impose.

Casa Nuestra, a small, family-owned winery on the Silverado Trail north of St. Helena, is owned by the Eugene Kirkham family. They produce Chenin Blanc and Grey Riesling from their own vineyard. The proprietor accepts only written inquiries.

Chappellet Winery, east of Rutherford, is such an imposing hillside property that owner Donn Chappellet could afford to underplay the winery he had built in 1969. In the shape of a pyramid, it nestles into its slope at the bottom corner of a vineyard block. There are no visitor facilities here, and alas, for this is one of the most dramatic of California wine estates. Production focuses on Chardonnay and Cabernet Sauvignon.

Chateau Boswell is one of the most attention-getting

wineries along the Silverado Trail north of St. Helena. The building with its short, round, cone-roofed tower and mansarded front elevation stands but a few yards off the road. The winery was constructed during the summer of 1982, but owner Dr. Richard Boswell had begun making Cabernet Sauvignon for his label in leased space in 1979. Chardonnay joined the roster in the new cellar. The proprietors accept visitors by appointment only.

Chimney Rock Winery was constructing facilities above the Silverado Trail, south of Stag's Leap, in 1987. Owners Hack and Stella Wilson produced their first releases, 1984 Chardonnay and Sauvignon Blanc, at another winery.

Clos Pegase raises the ante for architectural statements in the Napa Valley. Owner Jan Shrem, an art collector, commissioned architect Michael Graves to design the complex, which combines ultra-modern and classical elements, including a barrel-aging cave beneath. The first wine, a 1985 Chardonnay, was made at another winery for 1987 release.

Diamond Creek Vineyards does not offer conventional tours of its cellars on the slopes of Diamond Mountain. But proprietor Al Brounstein does welcome groups of wine buffs during selected weekends in June, July, and August, when he hosts picnics around a little lake at the high side of his vineyard. Groups can petition for reservations by writing to Diamond Creek at the address on page 77. The only wines are three separate bottlings of Cabernet Sauvignon from three different blocks of vineyard.

Far Niente Winery is a solid old stone barn with all sorts of cupolas and other frills on its roof. The building, set well back from State 29 near Oakville Grade, is also the residence of the proprietor and is not open for tours, tasting, or sales. The Far Niente label is used for only two wines, Cabernet Sauvignon and Chardonnay, both from vineyards surrounding the property.

Frog's Leap Winery earns its whimsical name. The cellar of Dr. Larry Turley flanks a creek north of St. Helena that is much favored by frogs. The winery's first crush was 1981. The roster of wines is Sauvignon Blanc and Cabernet Sauvignon. Visiting is by invitation.

Green & Red Vineyard is located on the Chiles Valley-Pope Valley Road in Chiles Valley. Founded in 1977 to make Zinfandel and Chardonnay, it is so small that it has no room for visitors.

William Hill Winery is on the way to becoming a substantial winery with visitor facilities. Construction continued in 1987 on permanent cellars, at the end of Soda Canyon Road east of Yountville. Using leased space, the firm has been making Cabernet Sauvignon from its vineyards on Mt. Veeder since 1976.

Innisfree, an offshoot of Joseph Phelps Vineyards, was in the process of finding a separate, permanent home in 1987. The initial offering was a 1985 Chardonnay, produced at the Phelps winery.

Johnson-Turnbull Vineyards, near Oakville, produces only Cabernet Sauvignon from its own vineyard. The small winery, owned by a partnership of Reverdy Johnson and William Turnbull, does not offer tours or retail sales.

Lamborn Family Vineyards was shy a winery in

Harvest Gondola...

1987, but plans were under way by Bob Lamborn to bond and expand a serviceable shed beside his house. Until then, Zinfandel from his mature red-dirt vineyard on Howell Mountain is custom-crushed under his label at other wineries.

La Vieille Montagne, the winery and residence of John and Shawn Guilliams, is tucked between two larger wineries near the top of Spring Mountain Road. The winery is in the basement of a redwood octagon built into the steep hillside; the Guilliams live upstairs. Riesling and Cabernet Sauvignon come from 10 acres planted in 1978.

Long Vineyards is another small family winery. Founded in 1978 it belongs to Bob and Zelma Long. The property, on a remote corner of Pritchard Hill east of Rutherford, is restricted from offering tasting or retail sales. Long Vineyards wines include Chardonnay, Riesling, and Cabernet Sauvignon.

Napa Valley Wine Company operates from yet another of the rent-a-bay warehouse buildings that have sprung up all over California to the benefit of small, growing winery companies. Proprietor Donald Ross first crushed in 1978. The principal wine is Sauvignon Blanc; others on the list are Cabernet Sauvignon and Zinfandel. Ross also produces wines for the Inverness label.

Pannonia Winery takes its name from an ancient winegrowing province in Hungary. Visitors are welcome to taste or buy (case minimums) on weekends only. Pannonia offers Chardonnay, Riesling, and Sauvignon Blanc. The prefabricated metal winery buildings are on the west side of the Silverado Trail not far north of Napa City, between Hardman Lane and Soda Canyon Road.

Robert Pecota Winery, north of Calistoga, crushed its first wines in 1978. The mainstays of the house are Sauvignon Blanc and Cabernet Sauvignon. An added specialty is Flora, made from a UC Davis-developed hybrid based on Gewürztraminer. Because the winery is very small and is adjacent to the family home, it is not open to visitors.

Piña Cellars is housed in a very small wooden building on the Silverado Trail near Yountville. Proprietors are Davie Piña and his three brothers, members of a

grape-growing family that has been in the area since the 1850s. They make tiny amounts of Chardonnay.

Plam Vineyards is a family affair, owned and operated by Ken and Valerie Plam, on State Highway 29 north of Yountville. Their first release was a 1984 Chardonnay.

Saddleback Cellars is the personal project of Nils Venge, a well-known Napa Valley winemaker. Since 1983 he and his wife, Candy, have been making Chardonnay, Cabernet Sauvignon, and Pinot Blanc from 17 acres on the Oakville Cross Road. Candy's parents, Robert and Peggy Call, are senior partners.

Sage Canyon Winery was founded in 1981 by Gordon and Eugenia Millar. Its small size discourages visiting.

St. Andrews Winery, housed in a prefabricated metal building on the Silverado Trail near the city of Napa, makes only Chardonnay, and can sell it only by appointment in minimum lots of a case. The small staff will make tour appointments for bibbers who wish to discuss the fine points of making Chardonnay.

Schug Cellars began in a nineteenth-century cave at Storybook Mountain Vineyards in 1979, then moved to a modest facility near owner Walter Schug's St. Helena home in 1983. Schug produces Pinot Noir and Chardonnay but, alas, not much of either one.

Shadow Brook Winery began producing small amounts of Chardonnay and Cabernet Sauvignon in 1984, from 60 acres of vines planted in 1972 by owner and winemaker Emil Hoffman. The operation is housed in a converted turn-of-the-century wooden barn.

Silver Oak Cellars, which makes only Cabernet Sauvignon, occupies a handsome, almost Gothic masonry building set 200 yards back from Oakville Cross Road. Patterned somewhat after Greystone Cellars architecturally, the building was erected in 1982 to supplement a small cellar dating back to 1973. Owned by Raymond Duncan and winemaker Justin Meyer, Silver Oak offers no tours, tastings, or retail sales.

Spottswoode Winery is the proprietary label of long-time grape growers Harmon and Mary Brown. The limited production is dominated by Pinot Noir from their established vineyard in St. Helena, at the base of Spring Mountain. Visits are sometimes permitted, but only by appointment.

Stags' Leap Winery, owned by Carl Doumani and partners, dates from 1972. Its vineyards are at the old Stag's Leap Manor property in the southeastern quarter of the Napa Valley. There are no facilities to host visitors. (This is not Stag's Leap Wine Cellars, another company. For a description of that winery, see page 94.)

Sullivan Vineyards and Winery has taken shape on a site between Rutherford and St. Helena. Proprietor James O. Sullivan has planted vineyards, and has constructed a permanent winery building. The label was established in the marketplace with 1981 wines made in leased space nearby. The roster includes Chenin Blanc, Chardonnay, and Cabernet Sauvignon. The Sullivans see visitors by appointment only, at a site where residence and winery are side by side amid their vineyards.

Philip Togni Vineyard is the renowned winemaker's personal winery, 2,000 feet above St. Helena on Spring Mountain. The cellar, embedded in the mountainside to complement its modern equipage with the primitive energy efficiency of solid rock walls, was completed in time for the 1985 crush. Phillip and Birgitta Togni replanted the original 1883 vineyard in 1981 and make only estate-grown Sauvignon Blanc and Cabernet Sauvignon (blended with Cabernet Franc and Merlot).

Traulsen Vineyards is in an outbuilding styled after proprietor John Traulsen's handsome Mediterranean villa not far north of Calistoga on the highway to Lake County. The only wine produced at this tiny cellar is Zinfandel. The first vintage was 1980. There are no tours or tastings, but Traulsen does sell wine at retail prices by appointment.

Tulocay Winery is a tiny cellar adjacent to the home of its owners, William and Barbara Cadman, in the hills east of Napa city. The wines are Cabernet Sauvignon, Pinot Noir, and Zinfandel. There are no tours, tastings, or retail sales at the winery, which was founded in 1975.

Van der Heyden Vineyards & Winery is an example of how an innocent interest in wine can balloon into something serious. Andres and Sandra Van der Heyden were home winemakers in 1973, grape growers by 1977, and winery owners by 1984. They make Chardonnay from their 10-acre vineyard, located near Napa between the Silverado Trail and the river.

Villa Helena Winery was founded in 1984 by Donald and Lidia McGrath, who divide their time between St. Helena and southern California.

Vose Vineyards, up in the dramatic folds of the Mayacamas Mountains west of Oakville, opened their tasting room in 1985. Wines and a view are available daily. Proprietor Hamilton Vose III makes Chardonnay, Cabernet Sauvignon, and Zinfandel from grapes at the property, and also produces Sauvignon Blanc and a proprietary white wine from Zinfandel called Zinblanca.

Whitford Cellars is the tiny winery of long-time grape growers Duncan and Patricia Haynes. Having supplied grapes to other wineries since the 1960s, the Hayneses decided to make a little of their own Chardonnay and Pinot Noir for a family label, which they did starting in 1983.

Woltner Estates represents a major California foray by the family that owns La Mission Haut-Brion and other Bordeaux properties. In 1983 they cleared several hundred acres for Chardonnay on Howell Mountain and purchased a ghost winery there, and by 1987 had just begun making wine.

Other Than Wineries

The happy town of St. Helena is the hub of the Napa Valley, but attractions for visitors range from Yountville north beyond Calistoga.

A citizens' action committee called the Napa Valley Wine Library Association some years ago founded one of the valley's most enterprising allures for wine-oriented visitors. The association probably is best known for its summer weekend classes in wine appreciation, all taught by local winemakers and winery personnel, but it also earns its name with an excellent specialized library.

Wine courses begin in June and are scheduled intermittently through August. For information, write to Napa Valley Wine Appreciation Courses, P.O. Box 207, St. Helena, CA 94574.

The wine library, housed in St. Helena's public library two blocks east of Main Street via Adams Street, began largely with books from the shelves of then resident-writer M. F. K. Fisher and other local wine figures.

Another special possibility, located in a separate wing of the same building, is the Silverado Museum, a practical monument to the fine Scots writer Robert Louis Stevenson.

Stevenson followers have another, less formal opportunity at hand. The writer spent his honeymoon on the slopes of Mt. St. Helena, northeast of Calistoga. It was from a headquarters in an old miner's shack that he wrote *Silverado Squatters,* and also made the trips to Schramsberg chronicled in that cheerful little book. The cabin is long gone, burned in a forest fire, but the undeveloped Robert Louis Stevenson Park has a few markers commemorating the writer's presence. Reached by State Highway 29, connecting Calistoga and Middletown in Lake County, the park also offers scenic hiking trails.

Bothe-Napa State Park is the largest and most varied of several parks in the county. The gates are five miles north of St. Helena opposite the west end of Larkmead Lane.

An adjunct a few hundred yards to the south is the Old Bale Mill, a souvenir of the days when Napa County grew far more wheat than wine.

Three simple picnic parks are to be found in the valley. One is on Main Street toward the north end of downtown St. Helena. Lyman Park has a few picnic tables behind the lawn and an old-fashioned bandstand facing St. Helena's Post Office. A larger park, Crane, sits behind St. Helena High School's campus on the south side of town. Finally, Yountville has several picnic tables in a small park flanking Washington Street at the north side of town.

Wine valleys seldom are paradises for children; Napa is no exception, but it has a few enchantments for youngsters. Prime among them is the gliderport at the east end of Calistoga's main business street.

Last, but not least, the valley has a number of excellent restaurants and hostelries. These amenities are so heavily used that reservations are almost always necessary.

Plotting a Route

Napa County sandwiches neatly between U.S. Highway 101 to the west and Interstate Highway 80 to the east. State Highways 12, 29, 37, 121, and 128 connect the valley in various ways to the two great freeways.

Of all the possible combinations of access routes from San Francisco or Oakland, I-80, a short piece of State 37 north of Vallejo, then State 29 up the valley from Napa is the most direct, the flattest, and the least scenic. Driving at the speed limit, a typical lapsed time from the San Francisco-Oakland Bay Bridge toll plaza to St. Helena is about 1 hour 25 minutes. From Sacramento, the counterpart combination is I-80, State 12 from Cordelia, then State 29.

Another route from San Francisco that is slower (usually 1 hour 40 minutes), slightly hillier, and prettier goes across the Golden Gate and through Marin County on U.S. 101 to its intersection with State 37, then continues on the latter route, over State 121 through southern Sonoma County, and State 29 up the Napa Valley.

The slow, scenic way from Sacramento and points east is State 128 from Davis to Rutherford. This road follows Putah Creek for a time, then passes Monticello Dam and Lake Berryessa before climbing over the east hills and into the valley.

From the north, State 128 slips away from U.S. 101 at Geyserville, and runs through scenic vineyard country in Sonoma County before it crosses a shoulder of Mt. St. Helena into Calistoga.

As this latter route suggests, Sonoma and Napa combine well and easily. In addition to State 128 through Alexander and Knights valleys, other roads connect the two counties efficiently for wine tourists. From Santa Rosa, Petrified Forest Road crosses a scenic part of the Mayacamas Mountains on its way to Calistoga. Spring Mountain Road branches away from Petrified Forest Road on the Sonoma side of the mountains, ending in St. Helena. Trinity Road-Oakville Grade connects the Sonoma Valley with the Napa Valley from a point on State 12 near Glen Ellen. Of all the roads across the Mayacamas Mountains, this one is the most scenic, the steepest, and the most winding. Its cross-valley counterpart, Deer Park Road, is the gateway to Howell Mountain and the Pope Valley.

Once in the Napa Valley, motorists have two main north-south roads paralleling each other along the valley floor. State 29, the westerly one, has on it a majority of the wineries and all the towns. It cuts a wide swath a few hundred yards from the feet of the westerly hills. The eastern parallel is the Silverado Trail, which loops along a leisurely and almost purely noncommercial way on gentle slopes just a few feet above the valley floor. The slight elevation produces some striking vineyard panoramas. Once almost without wineries, it now has a considerable number on or near it.

Several crossroads tie the north-south routes together, making it easy for visitors to swap back and forth. The maps show the main ones. Several others may look promising on the spot, but—fair warning to the hurried—some east-west roads in the valley do not quite reach the other side.

The Central Coast

Santa Clara to Monterey—great vinous variety

Gilroy City Hall

The coastal counties south of San Francisco Bay are in a curiously unbalanced state at present. Though most of the vines grow in Monterey and San Benito counties, most of the visitable wineries are in Santa Clara and Santa Cruz counties.

The urban pressures that began to be inexorable on Santa Clara vineyards early in the 1950s will, no doubt, weigh ever more heavily on wineries through the 1990s. In the meantime, those who wish to see both vine and wine at the source have an enormous territory to consider when they go looking for the likes of San Martin, Mirassou, and others in this divided region.

The north side of Santa Clara County around San Jose, where commercial winegrowing got its start south of San Francisco Bay, has been urbanized heavily since the late 1950s. Though vines almost have disappeared, this area remains a focal point for sizable wineries. West of the populous Santa Clara Valley, the Santa Cruz Mountains have fully a score of small to tiny cellars divided between Santa Clara and Santa Cruz counties.

The part suburban, part rural southern half of Santa Clara also has a considerable number of wineries. Some

still have substantial vineyards around them, but housing tracts already have covered more acres than remain in vines around Gilroy.

Monterey County now supports a tremendous majority of the region's vineyards and continues to hatch wineries to go with its grapes. Neighboring San Benito County also has broad sweeps of the vine and a handful of wineries.

A serious student would need at least a week to cover all the ground between San Jose on the north and Greenfield on the south. More time would be better. Those with the advantage of living on the spot can carve the territory into several engaging two-day loops, but even they will need to be selective.

Santa Clara Valley

To remember the Santa Clara Valley as a beautiful bowl of cherries, plums, and grapes is almost impossible, even though it was dominated by orchards and vineyards well into the 1950s.

Now it is known as Silicon Valley after its prosperous electronics and space industries, and the roadsides are lined by manufacturing plants, car dealers, warehouses, and just plain houses.

Driving through the region to see its wineries is hardly a pastoral experience. Still, for all the gritty aspects of getting around, there are some pleasing moments to savor and some agreeable lessons to learn. Most surprising, the number of wineries is increasing.

The Wineries

The long-established firms are easy to visit. The proliferating small-to-tiny newcomers require appointments, which often are restricted to one or two days a week.

Domaine M. Marion has few peers for handsome setting, thanks to the novitiates of the California Society of Jesus, who established the cellar as Novitiate Winery back in 1888, when California was young and a 40-acre hilltop ranch could be had for $15,000. Present lessee M. Dennis Marion took over the historic premises when the Jesuits ceased wine production in 1986.

The winery building cuts into a narrow shelf halfway up a substantial hill near Los Gatos. Within, amid observable outlines of even older buildings, dim tunnels lead off in several directions. There is no telling which are the oldest of the oak casks lining the tunnels, although the newest (those brought in by Marion) are obvious and easily form a majority.

The thrust of Marion's program is what he calls "upblending," the fine art of buying bulk wines, then maturing and blending them to create finished wines that are greater than the sums of their parts.

Marion also crushes and ferments his own wines. To that end, he has upgraded much of the aged but still serviceable equipment used by the brothers, without compromising their venerable traditions. Getting around to see everything involves a considerable amount of climbing spidery iron stairways, and the tasting staff accommodate visitors at tour's end in the old friendly manner.

The roster runs an impressive gamut from sparkling Mendocino County Blanc de Noir, through Chardonnay, Sauvignon Blanc, white Zinfandel, and Cabernet Sauvignon to nonvintage Pacific Coast Red and White.

J. H. Gentili Wines is the first and only winery to operate within the Redwood City limits in this century. The name commemorates a familial genesis: "J" for owner and winemaker Jim Anderson and "H" for his father, Howard; "Gentili" is his mother's maiden name.

The winery occupies two wooden buildings near the family house in a residential district. One building was formerly the garage, but the gleaming metal inside now is not motorized. It's stainless steel, and the closest it gets to internal combustion is the annual fermentation. There are also American and French oak barrels here, some for fermenting and some for aging wines. The lab, offices, barrel storage, and secondary fermentation are housed in the other building.

Jim Anderson purchases fruit for his Chardonnay and Cabernet Sauvignon from the Napa Valley's Ruth-

erford district. Grapes for his red and white Zinfandel come from the Shenandoah Valley of Amador County. The situation and small scale discourage visits, but Anderson will conduct group tastings of his wines on request, provided all his barrel-racking is out of the way.

Kathryn Kennedy Winery, a tiny cellar on a residential road not far from downtown Saratoga, is Santa Clara Valley's ultimate specialist.

The single wine is Cabernet Sauvignon made entirely from a small block of vines surrounding the winery and reaching up a gentle slope to the owner's house.

The winery is a simple, gray-painted building with an adjacent concrete pad for crushing and pressing. The public is invited to visit once a year, during the President's Day weekend in February, for tasting, sales, demonstrations, and tours.

J. Lohr Winery, like several others in the district, has its winery in San Jose and its vineyards elsewhere. The brick-front winery just off The Alameda, founded by Jerry Lohr in 1975, occupies what was once the shop building of a brewery. Tours keep going in and out of little buildings inside a big one. Just inside the front door is a cool, spacious, redwood-paneled tasting room. The working cellar begins on the other side of an interior door, where temperature-controlled stainless steel tanks and other modern equipment are sheltered by a tall, airy, steel-framed building. To one side, an insulated substructure holds thousands of barrels of aging wine.

The last stop is the tasting room, where the roster includes table wines of virtually every prominent variety from grapes grown in Monterey, Napa, and Sacramento counties. Proprietary bottlings are Jade, a white blend of fruity, spicy varieties, and nonalcoholic Ariel.

Paul Masson Vineyards goes back to the turn of the century, when the flesh-and-blood Paul Masson ended his partnership with Charles Lefranc and built a handsome cellar of his own in the hills west of Saratoga. The original cellar was carved into a hillside in 1900, rebuilt after the earthquake in 1906, and rebuilt again after a gutting fire in 1941. The old man did not have to deal with the fire, at least. He had died a year earlier after 58 years of winemaking in California and 4 years of retirement.

The old cellar still holds small lots of dessert wines, but its interest (and only access) to visitors is on a stage out front. Paul Masson Vineyards presents several musical and dramatic programs each summer in an amphitheater facing a Romanesque church wall that serves as the building's facade (page 97).

No crushing or fermenting goes on at this site. Paul Masson wines are processed either at their Sherry Cellars in Madera (built in 1974) or at the Gonzales facility of the winery's current owners, International Vintners, Inc. Neither location is set up to handle visitors.

Although the roster of wines was substantially curtailed with the International Vintners purchase in 1987, Paul Masson still produces enough different wines, in sufficiently large quantity, to keep the label prominent from one end of a retail shop to the other. At the top of the line are vintage-dated Chardonnay, Chenin Blanc, French Colombard, Sauvignon Blanc, Cabernet Sauvignon, and Zinfandel. Most of these are from Monterey County grapes. There are also several rosés, generic wines in jugs, and proprietary blends such as Emerald Dry and Rhinecastle.

Dessert wines were favored by the winery's founder and still pull their weight in the lineup. There are several Sherries in varying degrees of sweetness, Ports, and Madeira. Sparkling wines range from brut-style to a fairly sweet rosé. The list is topped, appropriately, by brandy.

Mirassou Vineyards, now in the hands of its owning family's fifth generation, is one of the oldest wine companies in Santa Clara, but the family began marketing wines under its own label only in the mid-1960s.

A French vineyardist, Pierre Pellier, established the dynasty in 1854 in what is now downtown San Jose. (Following an exploratory visit in 1848, he returned to France to gather a wife and thousands of vine cuttings.) Subsequently another Frenchman, Pierre Mirassou, met and married a Pellier daughter. That was in 1881. The Mirassou family has figured in every California vintage since.

An old photo on the tasting room wall shows wooden tank trucks loading Mirassou bulk wines into railroad cars for the long voyage east in the era before World War I. After the enforced respite of Prohibition, the third and fourth generations resumed commercial winemaking, again anonymously. Only the diligent knew to go to the winery, which bottled tiny lots for sale to familiars. Now, with the fifth generation firmly embarked on the path of family identity with family vintages, Mirassou wines may be found all across the country.

The main winery building, with a richly appointed tasting room in one front corner, is a squarely built, solid masonry structure nestled into the beginnings of a steep slope southeast of San Jose. Once, not so many years ago, it was the whole winery. Now it holds only a small proportion of the aging cooperage and a bottling line. The bulk of storage and aging is accommodated in several bigger, modern buildings; sparkling wines expanded into their own leased quarters in 1987.

Outdoors, at the rear of the original cellar, is a complex assemblage of processing equipment. The usual stainless steel fermentors, a crusher, and two big Willmes-type presses are there. So are some specialized hoppers and dejuicers for handling the must of field-crushed grapes. Most Mirassou grapevines are in the Salinas Valley of Monterey County, which led the family to pioneer in mechanical harvesting and field-crushing of quality grapes for varietal wines.

As a result, this is one of Santa Clara's most instructive wineries to visit during the October-November harvest season if you wish to see both traditional and innovative approaches to winemaking. The main works are far enough out in the open to permit sidewalk superintending. Each scheduled tour concludes with a sparkling wine demonstration.

Still and sparkling wines may be tasted. The roster includes Chardonnay, Gewürztraminer, and a "light" specialty called Pastel among other whites, and Cabernet Sauvignon, Pinot Noir, and Zinfandel among the reds. Sparkling wines are Blanc de Noir, Brut, bone-dry Au Naturel, and Brut Rosé.

Pendleton Winery is quartered within a much larger winery south of San Jose. If the surroundings are not altogether romantic, the notion is eminently practical for small winery owners who own no grapes but buy from districts at every point of the compass in search of exactly what they want.

Owner R. Brian Pendleton has been one of this increasingly numerous breed only since 1979 but has had a winery since 1975. The business began as Arroyo Winery, acquiring its present name in time to use it on wines from the vintage of 1977.

The specialty is Chardonnay. It is supplemented by Cabernet Sauvignon and Pinot Noir.

More Wineries. One old-timer with limited visitor facilities is to be found in the region.

Gemello Winery dates from 1934, always with a member of the founding Gemello family (currently Sandy Gemello Obester) active in it. Located behind a bowling alley off El Camino Real in Mountain View, the red-wine specialist offers tours and tasting as announced in a newsletter; call Obester Winery (see map, page 110) for details.

Other Than Wineries

Urban distractions abound in the neighborhood. These notes cover three with historic ties to wine, some potential picnic sites, and a few attractions around San Jose, the area's largest city.

Leland Stanford in his day ranked as one of the state's most enthusiastic winegrowers, though histories suggest his skills did not come anywhere near matching his hopes. Skilled or not, he established three major wineries, one of them on the north side of the present Stanford University campus. The handsome brick building, on Quarry Road between the Stanford Shopping Center and the university's hospital, still stands. Today, it is filled with shops and restaurants.

Two other points of interest are just off Highway 280 near Woodside, in southern San Mateo County.

Filoli is a magnificent garden estate administered by the National Trust and open to public view. It was built in 1916 by William B. Bourn II (see Christian Bros., page 75). The name summarizes Bourn's credo: FIght, LOve, LIve. Architect Willis Polk designed the Filoli mansion, and Bruce Porter laid out the 16 acres of garden.

A modest fee for the docent-led tour (conducted by the Friends of Filoli) helps pay the gardeners. The tour begins in the house and rambles through a series of gardens that have been planted to afford year-round floral displays. The roses alone are worth a visit, but the most spectacular show is the wisteria's annual bloom in April and May (by happy coincidence, also the best time for winery visits).

For information and tour reservations, write Friends of Filoli Tours, Cañada Road, Woodside, CA 94062, or call (415) 364-2880.

California Wine Chart

Table wines

Varietals
Named for the grapes from which they are made.

White wines
Light, freshly fruity flavors. Most bottlings slightly sweet. Meant for early drinking.
Chenin Blanc
Emerald Riesling
French Colombard
Gewürztraminer
Green Hungarian
Grey Riesling
Sylvaner
White Riesling
  (Johannisberg Riesling)

Full-bodied, flavorful enough to withstand aging in oak. Dry. Many made to age well in bottle.
Chardonnay
  (Pinot Chardonnay)
Dry Chenin Blanc
Pinot Blanc
Dry Semillon
Sauvignon Blanc
  (Fumé Blanc)

Richly fruity. Sweet enough to serve with dessert rather than dinner.
Malvasia Bianca
Muscat of Alexandria
Moscato Canelli
Sweet Semillon
Late Harvest White Riesling

White wines from black grapes. Sometimes dry. Should be white to salmon color but usually pink, slightly sweet, more akin to rosé than to white.
Pinot Noir Blanc
Zinfandel Blanc
Cabernet Sauvignon Blanc
White Barbera

Rosé wines
Light, freshly fruity. Sometimes dry, more often slightly sweet. Meant for early drinking.
Rosé of Cabernet Sauvignon
Gamay Rosé
Grenache Rosé
Grignolino Rosé
Rosé of Pinot Noir
Zinfandel Rosé

Red wines
Fresh, fruity. Dry or just off-dry. Light-bodied, meant for early drinking.

Carnelian
Gamay
Gamay Beaujolais
Grignolino
Pinot St. George
Ruby Cabernet

Full-bodied, with distinctive flavors. Sturdy enough to require oak aging. Aging in bottle improves them.
Barbera
Cabernet Sauvignon
Charbono
Merlot
Petite Sirah
Pinot Noir
Zinfandel

Generics
Named—usually after European wine districts—to hint at style.

White wines
Light, relatively dry. Meant for early drinking.
Chablis
Dry Sauterne
Mountain White

Light, noticeably sweet, but suitable with meals.
Rhine

Medium-sweet to very sweet, meant for dessert rather than dinner.
Haut Sauterne
Light Muscat
Sweet Sauterne
Chateau _____
  (winery name)

Rosé wines
Fruity, slightly sweet to sweet.
Vin Rosé
Rosé

Red wines
Dry or just off-dry. Versatile with meals. Meant for early drinking.
Burgundy
Chianti
Claret
Mountain Red

Full-bodied, noticeably sweet, but suitable with meals.
Barberone
Vino Rosso

Appetizer wines
Made with higher alcohol content than table wines (17 to 20 percent compared to 12 to 13 percent), usually with deliberate oxidized flavors or with added herbal flavors.
Sherry (Cocktail, Dry, Medium-dry)
Vermouth (Dry, Sweet)

Special natural wines: These are appetizer wines flavored with fruit juices or natural essences. Citrus is especially popular as a flavoring. Also used: mint, coffee, chocolate, several herbs. Most carry proprietary names.

Dessert wines

Made with higher alcohol content than table wines, as in the case of appetizer wines, but markedly sweeter.
Angelica
Cream Sherry
Madeira
Marsala
Muscatel
Port (Ruby, Tawny, White)
Tokay

Sparkling wines

Made in a variety of styles, with a range of colors. Meant as versatile accompaniments to appetizers, entrées, desserts.

Champagne (white sparkling wine; subtitled by degree of sweetness)
  Natural—very dry
  Brut—dry
  Extra Dry—hint of sweetness
  Sec—noticeably sweet
  Demi-Sec—very sweet

Blanc de Noir (White champagne from black grapes, usually styled as Brut)

Cremant (Fewer bubbles than regular Champagne, usually sweet)

Sparkling Muscat, Sparkling Malvasia (From muscat grapes, usually sweet)

Pink Champagne (usually sweet)

Sparkling Burgundy, Champagne Rouge (Red sparkling wine, usually off-dry)

PROPRIETARIES: Some wines of each major type are labeled with special names coined by the proprietors of wineries. These proprietary names frequently echo generic place names; the wines parallel generics in range and use.

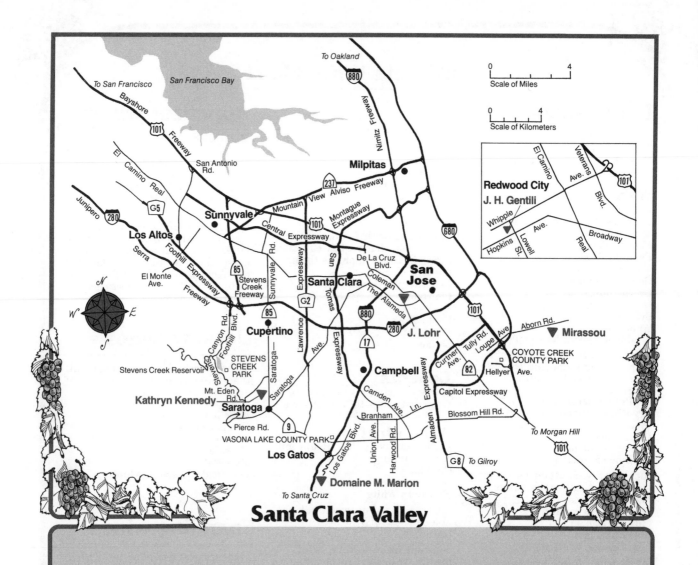

Santa Clara Valley

Domaine M. Marion. From Main St. in Los Gatos, S ¼ mi. on College Ave. to winery drive (P.O., Box 2389, Los Gatos, CA 95031) Tel (408) 395-7914. Daily 11–4:30. Ta. GT (daily 1 p.m. or by appt.).

J. H. Gentili Wines. From U.S. 101, W 1.5 mi. on Whipple, S .1 mi. on Lowell to winery (60 Lowell St., Redwood City, CA 94062) Tel (415) 368-4740. By appt. only.

Kathryn Kennedy Winery. On Pierce Rd., .5 mi. N of State 85/Saratoga-Sunnyvale Rd. (13180 Pierce Rd., Saratoga, CA 95070) Tel (408) 867-4170. GT by appt.

J. Lohr Winery. From I-880, SE 1 mi. on The Alameda, NE ½ blk. on Lenzen Ave. to winery (1000 Lenzen Ave., San Jose, CA 95126) Tel (408) 288-5057. Daily 10-5. Ta. GT (weekends or by appt.).

Mirassou Vineyards. From U.S. 101, Capitol Expwy. exit, E to Aborn Rd., then E on Aborn 2 mi. to winery (3000 Aborn Rd., San Jose, CA 95135) Tel (408) 274-4000. M-Sa 10-5, Su 12-4. GT/Ta.

Wineries Not on Map—
Restricted or No Visitor Facilities

Gemello Winery. (Rt. 1, Box 2Q, Half Moon Bay, CA 94019) Tel (415) 948-7723. Call for visitor information.

Paul Masson Vineyards. From Saratoga, 1.5 mi. W on Hwy. 9 to Pierce Rd., N 250 yards to entrance (P.O. Box 1852, Saratoga, CA 95070) Tel (408) 741-5182. Special event admission only; fee.

Pendleton Winery. Directions with appt. (499 Aldo Ave., Santa Clara, CA 95054) Tel (408) 980-9463. GT by appt.

Key: GT (guided tour); IT (informal tour); Ta (tasting).

Just north of Filoli on Cañada Road, the Pulgas Water Temple invites bicyclists and hikers to relax or picnic by a neoclassical temple and reflecting pool. (Motorists are effectively excluded by a strictly enforced parking ban for miles in both directions.) The temple's tiled well provides a last glimpse of Sierra Nevada water as it flows into Crystal Springs Reservoir.

Farther south, the Mission Santa Clara also has dim ties to the vine. Santa Clara is something of a curiosity piece because vines did not prosper there during the mission era. The failure mystified the mission fathers but has been cleared up since. Santa Clara is too cool for the Mission variety of grape to ripen properly. This was one of the earliest, if unheeded, hints at the complexity of microclimate zones in the coastal counties. The mission adjoins the campus of Santa Clara University on The Alameda, north of I-880.

For picnickers on the west side of the valley, Vasona Lake County Park straddles a creek and reservoir directly alongside State 17 at Los Gatos. It has abundant picnic and recreation facilities on well-kept lawns.

Other good possibilities are Lower and Upper Stevens Creek Parks. The former, a long strip along a narrow and shaded creek, offers picnic sites aplenty in March or April. But as spring wears into summer, the park begins to be crowded. The shallow creek is a fine playground for children, which accounts for a good part of the traffic. The sheltered and wooded nature of the place contributes the rest of the allure.

The more remote and tranquil upper park is off Skyline Road (Rt. 35), just north of the intersection with State 9.

Slightly west of Los Gatos, where the Coast Ranges begin to climb, Lexington Reservoir's shoreline is a developed picnic and water-sport park—but a less manicured one than Vasona.

Picnickers who prefer to be on the east side of the valley will find a county park alongside U.S. Highway 101, not far south of Mirassou. Long, narrow Coyote Creek County Park has a small lake as well as several tree-shaded picnic sites.

A potpourri of attractions in the greater San Jose area may appeal to families with children: Winchester Mystery House, Rosicrucian Egyptian Museum (with mummies), Kelley Park's petting zoo, and Great America. For information, write to the San Jose Chamber of Commerce (see address below).

Fuller descriptions of the Santa Clara Valley region may be found in the *Sunset Northern California Travel Guide.*

Plotting a Route

Getting around the Santa Clara Valley in the modern era is mainly a matter of picking the most efficient sequence of freeways and expressways.

U.S. Highway 101 (the Bayshore Freeway) steams straight and fast through an industrial corridor from San Francisco into San Jose. Interstate Highway 280 connects the same two cities almost as quickly, and has the advantage of coursing through unspoiled scenery.

On the industrialized east shore of San Francisco Bay, I-880/State 17 connects Oakland and San Jose, then continues westward to Santa Cruz. It intersects with both U.S. 101 and I-280.

Finally, Interstate Highway 680, the easterly equivalent to I-280, connects with U.S. 101 and I-280 at San Jose, providing an alternative to I-880 for anyone coming from Alameda County east of Oakland. For anyone coming from the south, U.S. 101 is the only quick approach.

The choice of expressways and major arterials within the region is almost limitless. The map on page 106 shows the most efficient ones for getting to wineries.

Accommodations and restaurants are as plentiful as the large population indicates. The quietest location is Los Gatos. For lists of visitor facilities, write to the San Jose Chamber of Commerce, P.O. Box 6178, San Jose, CA 95150; the Saratoga Chamber of Commerce, P.O. Box 161, Saratoga, CA 95070; or the Los Gatos Chamber of Commerce, P.O. Box 1820, Los Gatos, CA 95031.

The Santa Cruz Mountains

The Santa Cruz Mountains offer almost the perfect fantasy of specialized, hand-crafted winemaking.

Tumultuous slopes make every vineyard a scenic wonder and keep every vineyard small. Only here and there is the soil deep enough and the sun reliable enough for grapes to mature. So specialist winemakers fit themselves—one here, one there—into forests or onto mountaintops, or both at once.

This makes touring a demanding business. One must travel considerable distances on winding, narrow roads. With a few exceptions, the wineries are too small to have daily tastings and tours. Many are part-time enterprises of people with other jobs. But the rewards are singular for wine buffs who wish wine to be an enchanted product from enchanted places.

Even without wine these mountains are enchanted. Thick forests give way without warning to grassy meadows, which in turn give way to forests again. The enchantment is not undiscovered. The whole region is a vacationland for people who think rustic is better.

The Wineries

More than a score of wineries are in operation in the Santa Cruz Mountains or near them, from Half Moon Bay down to Soquel. An exact census is always hard to get in this region because the part-time cellars tend to start with little fanfare. Now and again one ends its career more quietly still.

Bargetto Winery, in the town of Soquel, is the largest and oldest winery in the area and still is small by general standards. It is housed in a trimly painted red barn that looks just as solid as it is.

The second generation of Bargettos owns it now. John Bargetto and a brother founded it in 1933, and John had a firm hand in the business until his death in 1964. His son Lawrence continues the operation.

Tours of the typical small cellar start at the crusher

out front and end in a creek-side tasting room and gift shop at the west end of the building. Bargetto offers a substantial range of varietal wines for tasting, including Cabernet Sauvignon, Pinot Noir, Chardonnay, Riesling, and Gewürztraminer. There are also fruit wines.

Bonny Doon Vineyard was set up, in part, to bottle the fantasies of its owner and winemaker, Randall Graham. As it turned out, some of the fantasies found their way to the labels, too. Le Cigare Volante, for instance, is a bottled pun involving UFOs (flying cigars) and a smoky, tobaccolike flavor that many connoisseurs associate with the blend's dominant variety, Syrah. Then there is Clos de Gilroy, which, to Graham's delight, some locals call "Close to Gilroy." The full benefit of Graham's wit can be appreciated by reading the winery newsletter (obtainable by writing the winery).

The winery itself is utterly serious. The original old barn on the redwood-shaded property was gradually converted to a two-story winery divided into thirds. One wing contains the bottling line and large oak tanks. The insulated center section holds French oak barrels, and the other outside third is the fermentation facility. Offices are upstairs.

The tasting room is an old wooden structure just off Pine Flat Road. Wines available for tasting in the open central courtyard reflect Graham's commitment to grape varieties of southeastern France, particularly the Rhone Valley. They are Syrah, Grenache, and Mourvedre (rosé). Chardonnay is the one concession to marketing reality. In addition, Graham produces ice wines (grape sugar is concentrated by freezing the grapes) from Muscat Canelli.

David Bruce Winery is up in the hills southwest of Los Gatos on Bear Creek Road. The building is plain, but some distinctive touches in the equipment make this an unusual winery to visit.

Outside are a French Demoisy crusher and a German Bucher membrane press. Both could be explained but are more believable if seen. Inside, the original number of oak barrels hang from the walls on cantilevered racks designed by the proprietor and still unique almost 20 years later. The first lot of barrels has been augmented by many more, stacked conventionally on the floor, and by a modern stainless steel fermenting room.

The other singular touch at David Bruce is a series of solar collectors on the roof of the fermenting room. They supply hot water to the winery.

Dr. David Bruce launched his winery in 1964, completed the sizable concrete-block aging cellar in 1968, and added the steel fermenting building in 1975.

A physician by profession and a winegrower by avocation, Bruce makes Chardonnay, Cabernet Sauvignon, and Pinot Noir.

Congress Springs Vineyards, new in 1971, is, in spite of the present winery's youth, an old property and one dedicated to preserving old vineyards and an old cellar.

Now the property of the Dan Gehrs and Vic Erickson families, Congress Springs was a winery as early as 1910 under the ownership of a Frenchman named Pierre Pourroy. Now, as then, the working winery is housed on the lower level of a sturdy concrete building; the upper level is home to the winemaker. And, as in the past, the principal vineyard sweeps east from the winery down a rolling slope. The view across Saratoga is worth the trip by itself.

The current proprietors also lease other old mountain vineyards in the region and buy small lots of grapes from local growers. The roster of Congress Springs wines includes Pinot Blanc, Semillon, Chardonnay, Cabernet Sauvignon, Pinot Noir, and Zinfandel.

Felton-Empire Vineyards somehow gives an impression of being away from it all, even though the winery and vineyards tuck in behind a row of houses just above the main business street in Felton.

This is a winery property with some history. It was the famous Hallcrest Winery of San Francisco lawyer Chaffee Hall until his death in the 1960s. In Hall's day the winemaking was organic, even primitive in some respects. It is no such thing now.

Owners John Pollard and James Beauregard brought in a microbiologist, Leo McCloskey, as their winemaker and partner. He transformed the cellars (seen via self-guided tour) into as technically impeccable a place as imagination can conjure.

On the upper level, along with a roomful of stainless steel fermentors and the tasting room, is a laboratory equipped to measure things and creatures only dimly known outside academic halls. On the lower level of a building cut into a hillside are some oak barrels and a tiny but scientifically sterile bottling room. (Medical people will recognize the air filter from hospital and laboratory applications.) The crusher and press are state-of-the-art types in keeping with the rest of the enterprise.

The production of this winery focuses on sweet white wines, especially Riesling. It includes dry Riesling, Chardonnay, and Gewürztraminer, and tiny lots of Cabernet Sauvignon and Pinot Noir. One other product of the house is an unfermented varietal grape juice.

Thomas Fogarty Winery is a handsome redwood structure overlooking most of the Bay Area from a perch some 2,000 feet above the urban sprawl. Tom Fogarty is a physician and noted inventor, among other things. His long-time interest in wine culminated in 1981 with this winery set among vines planted several years earlier.

The winery's interior is divided into two primary spaces. The fermentation room holds stainless steel tanks and cooperage. The other, larger area accommodates French oak barrels topped with coalescing wines. Crush-pad hardware outside includes, beside the stemmer-crusher, stainless steel settling tanks and a Bucher press.

Estate-grown Chardonnay heads the roster. There is also Gewürztraminer from a local Portola Valley vineyard, Pinot Noir, and a tiny amount of Cabernet Sauvignon. The winery is open by appointment on the first Saturday of each month for tours, tasting, and, weather permitting, a panorama stretching from the Stanford University campus below to the distant spires of San Francisco.

Frick Winery, one of the new breed of downtown wineries that have sprung up in California since the 1970s, is located in a one-time sash mill in Santa Cruz.

Proprietor William Frick started his winery in the more rural precincts of Bonny Doon in 1977 but moved soon after to his more spacious present quarters. Two wooden buildings face each other across a courtyard; the open space is used for crushing. The buildings house fermentors, French oak barrels, and other gear.

Pinot Noir is the specialty of the winery. Also on the roster are Chardonnay, Petite Sirah, and Zinfandel, as well as Cafe Red and White.

Obester Winery was founded by Paul and Sandy Obester in 1977 in the viticulturally unpromising environs of Half Moon Bay.

It has some instant history. Sandy Obester is the granddaughter of John Gemello, founder of the Gemello Winery in Mountain View (page 104). John was not only the inspiration, but also, at 95, the overseer of the construction and equipping of a winery that was, thus, three generations old at its birth.

The winery proper is located in an old pole barn with corrugated sheet-metal roof and siding. Set in a narrow draw in hills behind town, the one-time small box factory now houses a conventionally up-to-date small cellar with stainless steel fermentors, oak barrels, and the other familiar pieces of winemaking equipment. The tasting room is in a separate building with a picture window looking across a particularly fine coastal meadowland. The wood covering the walls once was meant to be fashioned into boxes by the former user.

The emphasis is on Riesling from Monterey grapes and Sauvignon Blanc from Mendocino. Obester also has limited lots of Cabernet Sauvignon.

Ridge Vineyards started as a weekend winery for three couples in 1959. It has long since grown past that stage, and become one of the largest of the Santa Cruz Mountain wineries. At this point there is enough Ridge to fill the original cellar and a much larger second building. Or, as its former proprietors put it, Ridge is about the size of a large chateau in Bordeaux. It was purchased by a Japanese corporation in 1986.

Ridge's two locations, almost a mile apart, are both spectacular. The name comes from the fact that the winery does indeed sit on a ridge due west of Cupertino. The topmost vineyard yields views out to the Pacific Ocean and down into San Francisco Bay.

Visitors are welcomed Saturdays at the rustic original winery, now a bottling and case storage building. It is hidden in a little fold 100 yards or so off Montebello Road. Drivers need to watch mailbox numbers carefully for the cue to angle left into a drive that, from the road, appears to go nowhere.

When the weather is reasonably good, tasting and talking go on outdoors, at one edge of a small patch of vines, but there is indoor space for gloomy days.

From time to time the hosts are moved to cart visitors up to the producing winery, a handsome old frame building that covers a sizable cellar dug into the stone hillside. The equipment there is modern, but the building goes back to before the turn of the century, when it housed the Montebello Winery.

The labels on Ridge Wines are among the most informative of any in California. The dominant wines are Cabernet Sauvignon and Zinfandel, supplemented by Petite Sirah and a small amount of Chardonnay.

Roudon-Smith Vineyards moved into its current home in the Scotts Valley district of Santa Cruz County in 1978 after being launched in 1972 on a nearby property. Like several other wineries of its era, it began as a cross between a hobby and a business, and grew.

The wood-sided structure, owned by Robert Roudon and James Smith, is best described as prim. Indeed, it would look at home somewhere in New England. But it is cut into a side slope above a fine meadow and is hedged all around by conifer forests that leave no doubt about its California location.

The well-equipped and tidily kept winery has stainless steel fermentors and other processing gear outside, barrels for fermenting and aging on the lower level, and an upper story for storage of cased goods and relaxed Saturday tastings. The roster of wines is led by Chardonnay and Zinfandel. Also on the list are Gewürztraminer, Pinot Blanc, Riesling, white Zinfandel, Cabernet Sauvignon, Pinot Noir, and Petite Sirah.

Since Bean Creek Road was underdesigned even for the Model T, the atmosphere is almost certain to be tranquil for those who make appointments to visit. Less intrepid souls will enjoy the tasting room in Soquel.

Sherrill Cellars, one of many husband-wife partnerships in this part of the wine country, moved into its current Palo Alto quarters in 1979 after several years of operating under the post office at Woodside.

The roof of the new building peeks out of trees from the downhill side of Skyline Drive some miles to the south of the original location. The two-story, woodframe, redwood-sided winery came into being in the old-fashioned American way. Nathaniel and Jan Sherrill threw a fine winery-raising party patterned after a midwestern barn raising as far as the work went, but with a distinctly different flavor to the refreshments served the friends and neighbors who raised up the roof beams. The sturdy result of their handiwork is so small that tours are generally conducted from one spot; tast-

Chardonnay

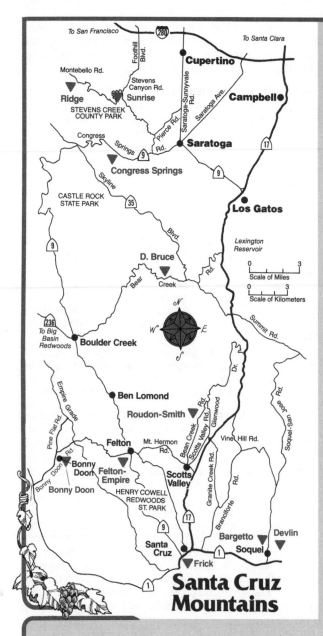

Santa Cruz Mountains

Devlin Wine Cellars. From State 1, Park Ave. exit, E to end of Park Ave. extension (P.O. Box 728, Soquel, CA 95073) Tel (408) 476-7288. By appt. only.

Felton-Empire Vineyards. From downtown Felton, .25 mi. W on Felton-Empire Rd. (P.O. Box A2, Felton, CA 95018) Tel (408) 335-3939. Sa-Su 11-3. GT/Ta.

Thomas Fogarty Winery. E side of Skyline Blvd., 2.7 mi. N of Alpine Rd. (5937 Alpine Rd., Portola Valley, CA 94025) Tel (415) 851-1946. GT/Ta by appt. only. (Outside map area).

Frick Winery. From State 1 in Santa Cruz, S 3 blocks on River St., W on Potrero to winery (17 Fresno St., San Francisco, CA 94133) Tel (408) 426-8623. F-Sa 12-6 June 15-Sept. 15 or by appt. IT.

Obester Winery. At 12341 San Mateo Rd. (State 92) 2 mi. E of State 1, or 6 mi. W of I-280 (Rt. 1, Box 2Q, Half Moon Bay, CA 94019) Tel (415) 726-9463. M-Th 12-5, Sa-Su 10-5. Ta. GT by appt. (Outside map area).

Ridge Vineyards. From jct. of I-280 & Foothill Expwy., 3.1 mi. S on Foothill Blvd./Stevens Canyon Rd., 4.4 mi W to 17100 Montebello Rd. (P.O. Box AI, Cupertino, CA 95015) Tel (408) 867-3233. Sa 11-3. Ta.

Roudon-Smith Vineyards. From Scotts Valley, 2 mi. N on Bean Creek Rd. (2364 Bean Creek Rd., Santa Cruz, CA 95066) Tel (408) 438-1244. Sa by appt. GT/Ta. Tasting room: From State 1, Soquel exit, right on Main St. to 2571. W-Su 12-6.

Sherrill Cellars. From jct. of State 84 and State 35 W of Woodside, 7.7 mi. S on State 35/Skyline Blvd. to 1185 (P.O. Box 1608, Palo Alto, CA 94302) Tel (415) 851-1932. Sa 1-5 by appt. (Outside map area).

Sunrise Winery. From jct. I-280 & Foothill Expwy. 3.1 mi. S on Foothill Blvd./Stevens Canyon Rd., .6 W on Montebello Rd. to winery (13100 Montebello Rd., Cupertino, CA 95014) Tel (408) 741-1310. F-Su 11-3 Ta.

Wineries Not on Map— Restricted or No Visitor Facilities

Ahlgren Vineyard. (P.O. Box M, Boulder Creek, CA 95006) Tel (408) 338-6071.

Cook-Ellis Winery. (2900 Buzzard Lagoon Rd., Corralitos, CA 95076) No phone.

Crescini Wines. (P.O. Box 216, Soquel, CA 95073) Tel (408) 462-1466.

Cronin Vineyards. (11 Old La Honda Rd., Woodside, CA 94062) Tel (415) 851-1452.

Grover Gulch Winery. (7880 Glen Haven Rd., Soquel, CA 95073) Tel (408) 475-0568.

McHenry Vineyard. (330 11th St., Davis, CA 95616) Tel (916) 756-3202.

Mount Eden Vineyards. (22020 Mt. Eden Rd., Saratoga, CA 95070) Tel (408) 867-5832.

Page Mill Winery. (13686 Page Mill Rd., Los Altos Hills, CA 94022) Tel (415) 948-0958.

Santa Cruz Mountain Vineyard. (2300 Jarvis Rd., Santa Cruz, CA 95065) Tel (408) 426-6209.

Silver Mountain Vineyard. (P.O. Box 1695, Los Gatos, CA 95031) Tel (408) 353-2278.

P. & M. Staiger. (1300 Hopkins Gulch Rd., Boulder Creek, CA 95006) Tel (408) 338-4346.

Walker Wines. (P.O. Box F-1, Felton, CA 95018) Tel (408) 335-2591.

Woodside Vineyards. (340 Kings Mountain Rd., Woodside, CA 94062) Tel (415) 851-7475.

Bargetto Winery. From State 1, Soquel exit, E on S. Main St. to Soquel Dr., then .25 mi. N on N. Main St. (3535 N. Main St., Soquel, CA 95037) Tel (408) 475-2258. Daily 10-5. IT/Ta.

Bonny Doon Vineyard. From State 1, 8 mi. N of Santa Cruz, NE 3.6 mi. on Bonny Doon Rd./Pine Flat Rd. to winery (10 Pine Flat Rd., Bonny Doon, CA 95060) Tel (408) 425-3625. Picnic. Tu-Su 12-5:30 Jun 15-Sep, Sa-Su 12-5:30 Oct-Jun 14. IT/Ta. GT by appt.

David Bruce Winery. From State 17, Bear Creek Rd. exit, 2 mi. W (21439 Bear Creek Rd., Los Gatos, CA 95030) Tel (408) 354-4214. Sa 11-4 by appt. Ta.

Congress Springs Vineyards. From Saratoga, 3.5 mi. W on State 9 to private drive at 4.09 mi. marker (23600 Congress Springs Rd., Saratoga, CA 95070) Tel (408) 867-1409. F 1-5, Sa-Su 11-5. GT.

KEY: GT (guided tour); IT (informal tour); Ta (tasting).

ing proceeds in an upper-story tasting room or on the airy deck. In fall and spring visits are by invitation only, other times are by appointment.

The roster of wines is mostly red: Cabernet Sauvignon, Petite Sirah, and Zinfandel from vineyards ranging southward as far as San Luis Obispo.

Sunrise Winery is notable on one hand as California's only wine-producing movie set. But if producers and photographers favor the authentic look of the 1880s landmark, a long stone building tucked among oaks on Montebello Ridge, wine lovers appreciate the history in those old stone walls even more. Wines made there by the Picchetti family were known worldwide for half a century or more.

Ronald and Rolayne Stortz leased the Picchetti Ranch from its trustees in 1983 and moved their winery operation there from Felton, where they'd begun making wine in 1976. The tasting room offers a clear glimpse of California's past, along with Chardonnay, Pinot Blanc, Riesling, Pinot Noir, and Cabernet Sauvignon; in short supply is the estate Zinfandel, from three acres of nineteenth-century vines.

More Wineries. Connoisseurs of California wine will recognize some prestigious names on this long list and will see some new ones. They are grouped here for a variety of reasons that make each almost as hard to get into as Harvard. In most cases, the main reason is lack of size. For those wine lovers willing to work patiently for an invitation, the addresses are noted with the regional map.

A man named Martin Ray managed to create, from 1943 on, vast interest in a tiny winery high in the hills west of Saratoga. Ray died in 1975 shortly after his property had been divided into two parts.

Son, Peter Martin Ray, operated the property as Martin Ray Winery for many years. Its twin, Mount Eden Vineyards, is operated by a consortium of vineyard owners who used to sell their grapes to Ray.

Martin Ray Winery had suspended operations in 1986 and is currently producing no wine. Its neighbor is too small to accept visitors other than established friends and true seekers, by appointment.

These wineries helped inspire a whole school of similar enterprises, most of them operated as second careers on evenings and weekends as changes of pace from regular jobs.

Ahlgren Vineyard is a tiny, family-owned winery founded in 1976 under the home of the Dexter Ahlgren family. The aim is to learn which grape varieties fare best in the complex microclimates around Boulder Creek.

Cook-Ellis Winery, hidden away in Corralitos on Buzzard Lagoon Road, accepts visitors reluctantly but has picnic facilities for those who persevere successfully. William J. Ellis founded the winery in 1981.

Crescini Wines in Soquel was a new start in 1980. A husband and wife partnership makes Sauvignon Blanc, Cabernet Sauvignon, and Merlot from Napa and Monterey grapes. By appointment, visitors may taste bottled wines and barrel samples with the owners.

Cronin Vineyards, in Woodside, uses some local grapes as well as imports from Napa, Sonoma, and Monterey. Owner Duane Cronin's list of wines includes Chardonnay, Cabernet Sauvignon, Merlot, and Pinot Noir.

Devlin Wine Cellars, the Santa Cruz winery of Chuck Devlin, has made small lots of Cabernet, Chardonnay, and Zinfandel from a broad range of coast counties' vineyards since 1978.

Grover Gulch Winery of Soquel, a 1979 partnership of Dennis Bassano and Reinhold Banek, makes Zinfandel and other reds from old vineyards near Gilroy and Paso Robles.

McHenry Vineyard is a wee operation in the vicinity of Bonny Doon, owned and operated by the McHenry family of Davis. Their four-acre vineyard, managed by Linda McHenry, supplies fruit for miniscule amounts of Chardonnay and Pinot Noir (red and rosé), produced by Henry McHenry. They made their first wines in 1980.

Page Mill Winery, founded in 1976 in Los Altos Hills beneath the home of the owning Richard Stark family, makes small lots of red and white varietals from selected vineyards. Mailing list customers are invited to biannual tastings; call the winery for details.

Santa Cruz Mountain Vineyard, in the hills above Santa Cruz, was founded in 1975 by Ken Burnap primarily to explore the possibilities of Pinot Noir, with excursions into Chardonnay, Merlot, and Cabernet Sauvignon.

Silver Mountain Vineyard, west of Los Gatos, is owned by Jerold O'Brien, who makes only Chardonnay and Zinfandel. His first crush was 1979.

P. & M. Staiger (1973), another family winery housed under its owners' residence, is tiny and inaccessible on its mountaintop above Boulder Creek. Its vineyard is planted to Cabernet Sauvignon and Chardonnay.

Walker Wines, in Los Altos Hills, is the property of the Russell Walker family. The label was founded in 1979 and covers tiny lots of Chardonnay, Petite Sirah, and other varietals, mostly from San Luis Obispo grapes.

Finally, in this alphabetic listing, comes Woodside Vineyards, property of Bob and Polly Mullen, who use their small winery to make—among other wines—a Cabernet Sauvignon from the last few vines of the legendary LaQuesta estate of Dr. E. H. Rixford. LaQuesta Cabernet Sauvignons were much treasured in pre-Prohibition California.

Other Than Wineries

Entirely in keeping with the wooded nature of this part of the world are two fine redwood parks with both picnic and camping facilities.

Big Basin Redwoods State Park is the larger of the two. On a loop road off State Highway 9, it is slightly more distant from the wineries than its running mate, but not far enough to disqualify it as a respite, or refuge.

The other is Henry Cowell Redwoods State Park, which straddles State 9 on the south side of Felton. It has several fine picnic grounds accessible from the highway. Its campground is reached via Graham Hill Road from Felton.

In addition to the parks, one other important diversion is the Roaring Camp & Big Trees Steam Railroad, a narrow-gauge line that was built for loggers but now amuses small fry and impresses their elders with some superior forest scenery. The railroad was once tied into a system that hauled logs and lumber to the coast, and brought supplies and equipment back up to the logging crews. When logging declined early in this century, excursion trains began hauling day-trippers from Santa Cruz to the redwoods and back. Part of the excursion track was recommissioned in 1986, and, although it won't provide viable transportation to the wineries, it does hold out promise of enjoying local wines with a picnic in the big trees, without the responsibility of driving afterward.

For information about the summer schedule (June-September) write to the railroad at P.O. Box 338, Felton, CA 95018.

From Boulder Creek down to Felton, State 9 is fairly regularly lined with visitor accommodations ranging from rustic cabins to fancy motels.

Santa Cruz Convention and Visitors Bureau, P.O. Box 921, Santa Cruz, CA 95061, will provide lists of accommodations in the county. See the Santa Clara Valley section for addresses of chambers of commerce in Los Gatos and Saratoga.

Wineries away from this core area can suggest parks and accommodations near them.

Plotting a Route

State Highway 9 forms a properly pastoral loop into the heart of the Santa Cruz Mountains from State Highway 17, the freeway connecting San Jose and Santa Cruz. One end of the loop is at Los Gatos, the other at Santa Cruz. Its offshoots easily transport visitors to wineries from Scotts Valley north to Saratoga.

Interstate Highway 280, a freeway, and State Highway 35, a curving hilly two-laner, are the main north-south routes to most of the cellars from Saratoga north. State Highway 1 is the route for cellars from Santa Cruz south through Soquel.

For anyone driving from San Francisco, I-280 is the fast way while State 1, more affectionately called Coast One, is a low-key route between the city and Santa Cruz. Another possibility is State 1 to Half Moon Bay, State Highway 89 east to State 35, then the latter road south to the neighborhood of Saratoga, where it intersects with State 9.

South Santa Clara

Time was when South Santa Clara was all of a piece, vinously speaking. Its wineries offered good, sound jug wines from local vines, and almost nothing else. That day is done.

Increasing urbanization, a wine boom that placed strong emphasis on varietal wines, vintage dates, bot-

tles with corks, and new blood in the region's community of winemakers all combined to broaden the spectrum of wines from Gilroy and Morgan Hill until it included high-priced varietals along with solid values in jugs.

If some new styles have joined the old ones, the countryside remains quietly appealing for winery visitors to seek out. U.S. Highway 101 cuts a straight swath through it, giving a hint of the character, but the nature of the region reveals itself more truly from byways close to the hills.

West of U.S. 101, beyond the tract homes, the district called Hecker Pass is made of vine-filled bottomlands, grassy hills, oak knolls, cactus farms, wandering creeks and reservoirs, the beginnings of conifer forests just below the namesake pass, and a nest of small, distinctly casual wineries.

Rapidly growing Gilroy is the focal point for touring. It has revitalized its downtown since being bypassed by the freeway. What used to be a tedious stretch of stoplighted highway now has become a stylish shopping street. Still, in season, a heavy, sweet aroma of drying fruit hangs in the quiet air, even in the middle of town, for this is prune and apricot as much as grape country, and the dehydrators perfume the district for week after warm summer week. Gilroy's other aroma comes later in the year, when the town is beyond any shadow of a doubt the Garlic Capital of the World.

The Wineries

Most of the south county's wineries are several miles west of U.S. 101, especially in the Hecker Pass district. However, Morgan Hill has a fair share of the roster close to the freeway on either side.

Fortino Winery is one of several establishments in the region in which a new proprietor shifted the production of a one-time jug winery over to vintage-dated varietals.

Ernest Fortino bought the old Cassa Brothers winery in 1970 and has been upgrading the property ever since, although without modernizing it very much. A Willmes press bought for the harvest of 1978 is one concession to contemporary winemaking. An automatic bottling line is another. Otherwise, Fortino is the sort of man who believes that the old ways are best.

His fermentors, in a building to the rear of the stucco-covered main cellar, are open-topped redwood. In the main cellar he ages his wines—nearly all of them reds—in redwood and good-sized oak tanks. Time is his favorite filter.

Fortino's list of wines includes Carignan (spelled here without the final "e"), Charbono, Cabernet Sauvignon, Petit Syrah, and Zinfandel, plus rosés and a Sylvaner. All are on hand in a spacious tasting room and gift shop at the front end of the winery. So are occasional limited bottlings of white wines from black grapes. A deli was added in 1986 to further abet picnics.

Emilio Guglielmo Winery, a mile east of U.S. 101 at Morgan Hill, recommends itself to visitors for several reasons.

Botrytis cinerea, the noble mold

Since 1969, extra-sweet wines patterned after French Sauternes and German Beerenauslese and Trockenbeerenauslese have become more and more a part of California winemaking. Most are simply called "late-harvest;" a few have more fanciful names. A great majority come from White (or Johannisberg) Riesling grapes, as do their German counterparts. Some come from Sauvignon Blanc or Semillon (or a blend of the two), the two grape varieties used in making Sauternes. An occasional example is made from Chenin Blanc, the grape variety of another French sweet wine called Coteaux du Layon, or from Gewürztraminer.

Most of California's concentratedly sweet wines come from low-lying vineyards near rivers, where cool fogs can linger well into a morning. Particularly consistent areas include Sonoma's Russian River Valley, especially the section called Alexander Valley; the Napa Valley near Napa Creek between Rutherford and Yountville; and Monterey County along the Salinas River course from Greenfield northward. No district can deliver such wines every year.

The secret of making all of these wines lies with a mold called *Botrytis cinerea,* more commonly called the noble mold in the world of wine. And the secret of Botrytis lies with the weather.

It confers its curious benefits only when a cool, damp spell is followed by a warmer, drier one at about the time normal grapes might be harvested. Once it attacks ripe berries, it nibbles delicately at the skins until only a membrane is left. The job is so refined that water can evaporate, but larger molecules cannot. The result is unusual concentrations of sugar and flavor components in the grapes.

Whereas grapes for dry white table wines are harvested at about 21 to 23 degrees Brix (a winemaster's yardstick of measuring sugar content and roughly equal to percentage of sugar), those thoroughly attacked by Botrytis weigh in at 28° to 30° B, even, rarely, up to 37° B.

When crushed, the grapes do not separate into free-running juice and solids, as is normally the case, but instead become a homely mush. (Typical fresh grapes yield about 140 to 160 gallons of wine per ton. Heavily botrytised grapes may yield as little as 60 or 70 gallons.) This is clarified with great difficulty. (As one winemaker put it, filtering botrytised must is a little bit like trying to pump corn syrup through a brick wall.) Then the juice is fermented, again with great difficulty. (Sugar inhibits the formation of alcohol above certain concentrations. Winemakers say a fermentation is complete when it uses up all of the fermentable sugars, or when it is deliberately stopped by chilling. Winemakers hardly ever say a late-harvest fermentation is complete, only that it dwindles to no visible progress after a period of several weeks, or even months.)

We can explain the wines in terms of technical balance. Typical, slightly sweet table wines (Chenin Blancs, for example) have about 12 to 13 percent alcohol and 1 to 2 percent of unfermented grape sugar (residual sugar, or RS, in the trade). Partially botrytised wines have about 10 or 11 percent alcohol and 4 to 8 percent RS. Thoroughly botrytised wines have 8 or 9 percent alcohol and anywhere from 10 to 25 percent RS.

The numbers do away with sweet mystery and other poetic thoughts. Habitués ignore them and enjoy these rarities for what they are—nectar.

Most directly to the point, the owning family has taken pains to make its tasting room and picnic area inviting. Inside, the tasting room is quiet and cool. The focal point is a serving bar fashioned entirely from tank staves, but there is ample space to step back between tastes. Outside, vines trellised along one side of the building allow the picnic area to be as sunny and warm as a winter day can get, or as cool as a summer day can be. Umbrellas add shade in hot weather.

An appointment to tour the winery can be worth the effort because of its unusual aspects. Foremost of these is a double file of stainless steel fermentors patterned after a type developed in Australia. The tank floors, instead of sloping in one direction, are conical so that grape solids empty automatically through doors at the very bottom of the cone. At the other end of tradition, the Guglielmos keep a sizable collection of oak oval casks that predate Prohibition. Some are in a cellar beneath the residence—the original winery. The rest of the casks are in the main aging cellars along with steel and redwood tanks and a growing collection of oak barrels.

The Emilio Guglielmo label was new in the 1970s, though the winery dates back to 1933. It reflects a shift from jug generics to vintage-dated varietals. (The jugs are still available under the original Emile's label.) The list includes Semillon, Sylvaner, and Riesling in whites, a Grignolino Rosé; and Barbera, Cabernet Sauvignon, Ruby Cabernet, and Zinfandel among reds.

One added reason to visit is the availability of small lots of selected older wines, sold only at the winery.

Hecker Pass Winery belongs to Mario and Frances Fortino, who launched their small cellar in 1972, but did not open it for tours until their first wines were ready for tasting in 1974.

Mario Fortino came to the United States from Italy in 1959 and worked for other cellars in the Santa Clara

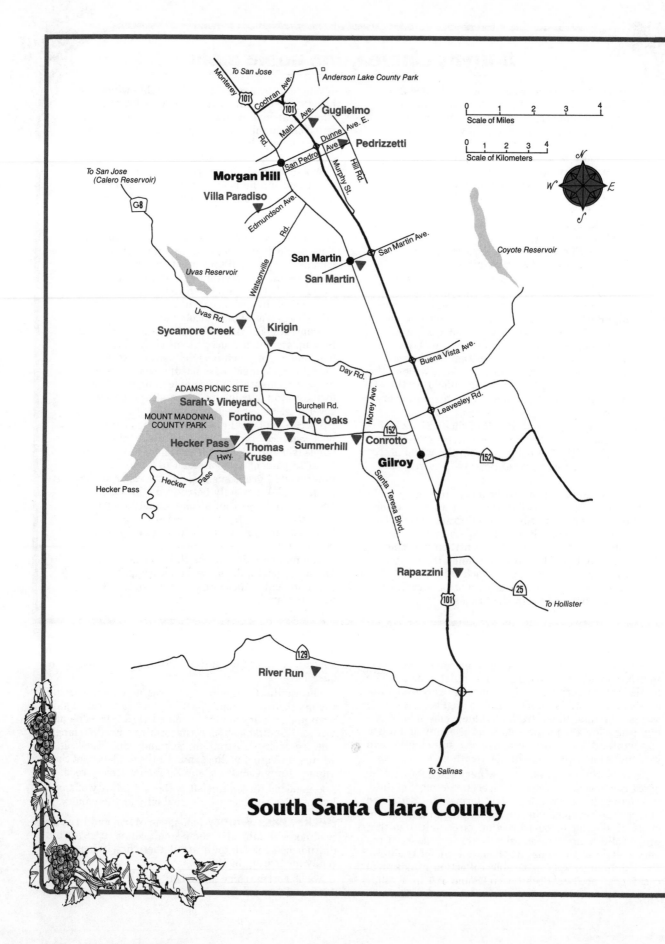

To San Jose

Monterey

101

Cochran Ave.

Anderson Lake County Park

101

Ave.

Main

Guglielmo

Dunne

Ave. E.

Rd.

Ave.

Pedrizzetti

San Pedro

Hill Rd.

Murphy St.

Morgan Hill

To San Jose
(Calero Reservoir)

G8

Villa Paradiso

Edmundson Ave.

Rd.

San Martin Ave.

San Martin

San Martin

Coyote Reservoir

Watsonville

Uvas Reservoir

Uvas Rd.

Sycamore Creek

Kirigin

Day Rd.

Buena Vista Ave.

ADAMS PICNIC SITE

Sarah's Vineyard

Burchell Rd.

Morey Ave.

Leavesley Rd.

MOUNT MADONNA
COUNTY PARK

Fortino

Live Oaks

Hecker Pass

Hwy.

**Thomas
Kruse**

Summerhill

152

Conrotto

152

Gilroy

152

Pass

Hecker

Santa Teresa Blvd.

Hecker Pass

Rapazzini

25

To Hollister

101

To Salinas

129

River Run

South Santa Clara County

Scale of Miles
0 1 2 3 4

Scale of Kilometers
0 1 2 3 4

N
W E
S

Conrotto Winery. S side of State 152, 1.5 mi. W of Monterey Rd. (1690 Hecker Pass Hwy., Gilroy, CA 95020) Tel (408) 842-3053. Sa-Su 11-5. Ta.

Fortino Winery. N side of State 152, 5.2 mi. W of Monterey Rd. (4525 Hecker Pass Hwy., Gilroy, CA 95020) Tel (408) 842-3305. Daily 9-6. GT/Ta.

Emilio Guglielmo Winery. From Monterey Rd. in Morgan Hill, E on Main Ave. 1.5 mi. (1480 E. Main Ave., Morgan Hill, CA 95037) Tel (408) 779-2145. Picnic. Daily 9-6. Ta. GT by appt.

Hecker Pass Winery. N side of State 152, 5.4 mi. W of Monterey Rd. (4605 Hecker Pass Hwy., Gilroy, CA 95020) Tel (408) 842-8755. Picnic. Daily 10-5. Ta.

Kirigin Cellars. From State 152, N 2.5 mi. on Watsonville Rd. (11550 Watsonville Rd., Gilroy, CA 95020) Tel (408) 847-8827. Picnic (groups must reserve). Daily 9-6. GT/Ta.

Thomas Kruse Winery. S side of State 152, 5 mi. W of Monterey Rd. (4390 Hecker Pass Hwy., Gilroy, CA 95020) Tel (408) 842-7016. Picnic. Daily 12-5 or by appt. IT/Ta.

Live Oaks Winery. N side of State 152, 4 mi. W of Monterey Rd. (3875 Hecker Pass Hwy., Gilroy, CA 95020) Tel (408) 842-2401. Daily 8-5. Ta.

Pedrizzetti Winery. From U.S. 101, Dunne Ave. exit, E to Murphy St., S to San Pedro Ave., then E .8 mi. to winery (1645 San Pedro Ave., Morgan Hill, CA 95037) Tel (408) 779-7389. Picnic. Daily 9:30–5:30. Ta. GT by appt.

Rapazzini Winery. E side of U.S. 101, 3 mi. S of Gilroy (4350 Monterey Hwy., Gilroy, CA 95020) Tel (408) 842-5649. Daily 9-6. IT/Ta.

River Run Vintners. From U.S. 101, NW 5.5 mi. on State 129, then SW .2 mi. toward Aromas on Rogge Ln./Carpentaria Rd. (65 Rogge Ln., Watsonville, CA 95076) Tel (408) 726-3112. GT/Ta by appt. only.

San Martin Winery. E side Monterey Rd., .1 mi. S of San Martin Ave. (1300 Depot, San Martin, CA 95046) Tel (408) 683-4000. Daily 10-5. Ta. GT (only groups by appt.).

Sarah's Vineyard. N side of State 152, 4.1 mi. W of Monterey Rd. (4005 Hecker Pass Hwy., Gilroy, CA 95020) Tel (408) 842-4278. GT by appt.

Summerhill Vineyards. S side of State 152, 4 mi. W of Monterey Rd. (3920 Hecker Pass Hwy., Gilroy, CA 95020) Tel (408) 842-3032. Daily 10-6. Ta.

Sycamore Creek Vineyards. From State 152, N 3.3 mi. on Watsonville Rd., W .1 mi. on Uvas Rd. to winery (12775 Uvas Rd., Morgan Hill, CA 95037) Tel (408) 779-4738. Sa-Su 12-5 or by appt. GT/Ta.

Villa Paradiso Vineyards. From Monterey Rd. in Morgan Hill, SW 2 mi. on Edmundson Ave. (P.O. Box 1133, Morgan Hill, CA 95037) Tel (408) 778-1555. Picnic. Sa-Su 11-5. Ta.

Wineries Not on Map— Restricted or No Visitor Facilities

Peter & Harry Giretti Winery. (Bus. off.: 791-5th St., Gilroy, CA 95020) Tel (408) 842-3857.

Ronald Lamb Winery. (17785 Casa Ln., Morgan Hill, CA 95037) Tel (408) 779-4268.

Key: GT (guided tour); IT (informal tour); Ta (tasting).

region—full-time until he founded his own winery, part-time until the business was well established. Some outgrowths of his earlier employment show up in the working winery. The basket presses and redwood fermenting tanks at the rear of the small stucco building are typical of old-line Gilroy, but inside the building the proprietor has a temperature-controlled stainless steel fermenting tank for his whites, sophisticated pumps, and other equipment to suggest he learned a great deal while he was getting ready to launch his own venture. The aging cellar has redwood tanks and oak barrels.

The table wines, most of them vintage-dated and labeled as "Estate Bottled," include Carignane, Petite Sirah, and Zinfandel, among others. There are also generics and dessert wines on the list. The tasting room overlooks the vineyard and picnic area.

Kirigin Cellars makes good use of one of the oldest properties in the Hecker Pass district but is one of its newer wineries.

Nikola Kirigin Chargin bought the one-time Bonesio vineyards and winery in 1976, and forthwith gutted the time-weary main cellar. The building now houses three rows of temperature-controlled stainless steel fermentors and racks of oak barrels in place of the old redwood tanks that once filled it. The cellar also holds modern filters and bottling equipment, all visible on the leisurely tour.

Even the exterior of the cellar got a face-lift, with buff stucco walls replacing the old barn-red, board-and-batten ones.

The proprietor, fifth generation of a Croatian winemaking family, had university training in his homeland and experience in other California wineries to lead him toward modern equipment and techniques.

The results are on hand for tasting in a pleasant building next to the cellar, and at another tasting room on Monterey Road in Morgan Hill. The roster includes Chardonnay, Malvasia, Opol Rosé, Cabernet Sauvignon, Pinot Noir, and a dessert specialty called Vino de Mocca.

In front of Kirigin Chargin's residence—originally the home of a local cattle baron named Henry Miller—a pine-shaded picnic ground can accommodate as many as 30 people.

Thomas Kruse Winery, across the Hecker Pass Highway (State Highway 152) from the end of County Road G8, more or less started the revolution that is changing this region from a country jug producer to a source of vintage-dated varietals.

A Chicagoan until wine caught his interest, Kruse acquired the property in 1971 and forthwith set about doing things differently from his neighbors of that time. He has not changed since. He ferments all his wines in oak barrels or small plastic tubs, sticks to varietals, and insists on bone-dry wine as his style.

The list is uncommon, too. It includes a white sparkling wine, a Carignane, a dry rosé from Cabernet Sauvignon, Sauvignon Blanc, Pinot Noir, Grignolino, and Gilroy Red, which carries a *pasta con pesto* recipe on its back label.

The winery is housed in classic wooden barns—two of them, about a hundred yards apart. Kruse spent sev-

It all begins with vines in the sun

A grape starts out in spring all acid and no sugar. As it ripens its acid level declines and its sugar level rises.

The winemaker's task is to harvest the grapes when the ratio of sugar to acid is right. The desired ratio differs from one class of wine to another. Port and other dessert types come from grapes with higher sugar and lower acid than grapes used for red table wines. Champagne, on the other hand, calls for unusually low sugar and very high acid.

In the end it comes down to the interactions of climate and grape variety. There is a "right" climate for each variety—or, more precisely, a right range of climate. California has richly diverse and complicated climate patterns. Furthermore, vineyardists in the state grow 130 varieties of *Vitis vinifera* in one amount and another.

After a long study, researchers at the University of California at Davis defined five general climate zones based on heat summation, the total number of degree-days above 50° F between (and including) April 1 and October 31. The measuring stick for degree-day calculations is mean temperature. For example, if the mean temperature was 70° F for 5 consecutive days, the summation would be $70 - 50 = 20 \times 5 = 100$ degree-days.

The five general climate zones are:

Region I (2,500 degree-days or fewer). Occurs in Anderson Valley, Carneros, Felton, and Gonzales, as examples. The university recommends table wine grapes as best suited to the region, especially such varieties as Chardonnay, Pinot Noir, and Riesling.

Region II (2,501–3,000 degree-days). Occurs in Glen Ellen, Hollister, Oakville, and Greenfield, as examples. The university recommends table wine grapes for this region also, especially Cabernet and Sauvignon Blanc. In both this region and Region I, in fact, it recommends nearly all the grapes used in familiar varietal table wines.

Region III (3,001–3,500 degree-days). Occurs in Cloverdale, Livermore, Calistoga, Paso Robles, and Ukiah, as examples. This begins to be the margin between purely table wine country and dessert wine country. The recommended table wine varieties include Barbera, Ruby Cabernet, Sauvignon Blanc, and Semillon. The university gives qualified recommendations for many others, depending on specific local conditions. It also recommends a good many of the familiar muscats and some sherry and port grapes, again depending on precisely measured local climate factors.

Region IV (3,501–4,000 degree-days). Occurs in Guasti, Livingston, Lodi, and Modesto, as examples. The balance goes over to dessert wine grapes. Nearly every Muscat, Sherry, and Port grape earns a university recommendation in this region. Among table wine grapes, Emerald Riesling, French Colombard, Barbera, and Ruby Cabernet get clear recommendations. As the presence of Emerald Riesling and Ruby Cabernet indicates, this is a region for which many of the UC Davis hybrid varieties are bred. (See "Grapes of the future," page 165.) As the national demand for table wine rises and the university program progresses, this region is turning more and more toward making table wine.

Region V (4,001 degree-days or more). Occurs in most of the southern San Joaquin Valley, from Madera to Bakersfield, and much of the Cucamonga district. All of the Sherry and Port grape varieties carry university recommendations in this region. It probably will always produce a great part of California's dessert wines, but the hybrids and a few other varieties, coupled with advances in vine-training techniques, make table wines a possibility in the warmest of these vineyards.

Harvest Time

eral years rehabilitating a weather-weakened main building, but never violated its appearance inside or out. The tasting room, in a back corner, is all old wood, a serene nook in keeping with the informal atmosphere.

Live Oaks Winery advertises itself best of the several cellars along State 152. A platoon of signs on the north side of the road invites visitors to turn and drive along beside an eclectic lot of frame buildings until the drive dips downhill and ends alongside a yellow-painted, board-and-batten winery.

In all its casual and good-humored aspects, this winery typifies what the Hecker Pass used to be in its entirety: a source of modestly priced, unpretentious, everyday wine made in and offered from an appropriate kind of cellar.

The tasting room appears to have been inserted into the hillside; it was founder Eduardo Scagliotti's original aging cellar. Richard and Barbara Blocher own the winery now.

The Live Oaks label, which has been around since 1912, appears on Chenin Blanc, Colombard, Gewürztraminer, Chardonnay, Riesling, rosés of Zinfandel and Grenache, and a well-aged Burgundy.

Pedrizzetti Winery has been a pillar of the south Santa Clara wine community since before Prohibition, and the Pedrizzetti family ranks with the state's most venerable wine clans. They welcome visitors to a newish tasting room, with tours of the historic winery by appointment.

The winery's history goes back to 1946 with the Pedrizzetti family, having begun in 1923 when Camillo Colombano first made wine on the property. Inside the rectangular cellar, two rooms full of well-seasoned redwood tanks are much as they have been from the beginning. However, the rest of the property has gone modern. Outside, two rows of stainless steel fermentors flank a processing deck with a new continuous press. Another row of stainless steel tanks snugs against an outside wall, and still more stainless tanks fill the white wine aging cellar inside.

The office and tasting room are in a small building at the rear of a courtyard on the opposite side of the winery from the fermenting area. The roster of wines is mostly varietal and vintage-dated. Included are Chardonnay, Chenin Blanc, and Petite Sirah. Also on the list are both reds and whites from Zinfandel and Barbera.

Rapazzini Winery was housed in this new building in 1982, but the business goes back to 1962.

Jon Rapazzini had to rebuild after fire destroyed the original premises in 1980. The new winery, on exactly the same highwayside spot as the old one, is a sizable prefabricated metal building; the new tasting room is a stone building attached to the front of the working cellar. Both parts of the replacement are more handsome than the 75-year-old, stucco-covered original structure.

A window at one end of the tasting bar gives a clear view of the entire working winery. The Rapazzinis open for tasting all of a wide range of wines from vintage varietals to fruit and specialty wines.

River Run Vintners is not, technically speaking, located in South Santa Clara. The winery of Kristine Arneson is near Aromas in that skinny, scenic tail of Santa Cruz County that separates Santa Clara and Monterey counties. Technicality aside, the wineries around Gilroy are River Run's nearest neighbors.

The place is simplicity itself. In a barn set back from Rogge Lane in the owners' apple orchard, the cellar is equipped with a basket press, a trio of open-topped redwood fermentors, and a double row of neatly stacked American oak barrels. Temperature-controlled fermentors, added in 1982 to make Riesling wines, update the equipment without disturbing the harmony. Tasting goes on across a card table next to the aging wines.

The River Run roster is dominated by Zinfandel, made in two or more styles each vintage, and Riesling. Chardonnay and Cabernet Sauvignon round out the list of varietals.

San Martin Winery is at once one of the Central Coast's oldest and most modern cellars. The Mission-style main cellar dates from 1906, when it was founded by local growers as a cooperative winery. Following Prohibition, the winery produced Port-type and fruit wines in addition to table wines, under the ownership of the Felice family. The present owners, Somerset Vintage Cellars, acquired San Martin in 1977.

Somerset renovated and re-equipped the formerly archaic cellars from end to end. The old redwood fermentors were replaced by temperature-controlled stainless steel tanks, now located outdoors beside large stainless steel dejuicers and computerized presses. An ongoing cooperage acquisition program has introduced French oak tanks and puncheons, and new American and French oak aging barrels. White wines are stored in a large new refrigerated cellar.

San Martin makes life easy for people who like to taste its wines near the source, but asks potential cellar visitors to work a bit harder. Although the large tasting room on Monterey Road is just across the railroad tracks from the winery, tours of the facility are offered to groups only, and only by appointment.

Wines which may be sampled in the tasting room include a wide range of vintage-dated varietals, non-vintage varietals and generics, all bottled under the Domain San Martin label. The vintage varietals include Sauvignon Blanc, Riesling, Chardonnay, Cabernet Sauvignon, and Zinfandel.

The group tours conclude with private tastings in a romantic room in the oldest and finest building on the property, an ivy-covered brick structure once full of redwood tanks but now used primarily for bottling.

Sarah's Vineyard is one of the new-era Hecker Pass wineries concentrating on varietals aged in French oak rather than on jug generics aged in venerable redwood tanks.

The tiny, well-equipped, neat-as-a-pin winery is around on the back side of a steep knoll from the entry and parking area. To get from the car to the natural wood cellar, one strolls around the knoll between blocks of vines and with an escort of geese. In the words of winemaker and co-owner Marilyn Otteman, the purpose is to "get the city off your back" before settling down to talk wine. The rest of a visit is similarly designed to lower blood pressure rather than raise it.

The price of a bottle of wine may include a rose, a bit of fresh fruit from the family orchard, or even a goose egg or two.

Principal wines on the list are Chardonnay and Merlot. There is a bit of late-harvest Riesling.

Summerhill Vineyards is a new start in one of the old-timer wineries in the Hecker Pass district.

Hilton (Red) Johnson, Debra Dodd, and partners have begun the long task of modernizing the old Bertero Winery, which opened in 1917 and had not seen much change during its long career. Soon after their 1980 purchase of the property, the new owners fitted stainless steel fermentors, a small collection of American oak barrels, and a new bottling line in among the ancient redwood tanks and oak casks. Visitors may check the progress before or after tasting in a handsome pavilion set among vines about halfway between the highway and the several winery buildings.

The list of wines is a long one, encompassing Cabernet Sauvignon, Zinfandel, and other varietals in bottles, generics in jugs, and a number of fruit wines.

Sycamore Creek Vineyards joined the ranks of South Santa Clara wineries in 1976. Its proprietors, Terry and Mary Kaye Parks, had acquired the old Marchetti winery and vineyards earlier, and could think of no better use of the old property than to resume making wine.

The producing winery is a classic wooden barn cut into a gentle slope and neatly refitted to modern standards. Crushing and pressing take place on a concrete pad on the uphill side of the steep-roofed white building. Just inside, on a sort of mezzanine, is the bottling department. Below it, at the downhill grade level, is a fermenting and aging cellar full of neatly stacked barrels and a trio of small oak tanks.

Tasting takes place on the upper level of a second barn just far enough from the first to give even better views across rolling vineyards. The roster of wines is anchored by estate-bottled Carignane and Zinfandel from old vines. Chardonnay, Gewürztraminer, Riesling, Gamay Rosé, and Cabernet Sauvignon also are produced.

Villa Paradiso Vineyards houses itself in an impressive hulk of a building, one with concrete walls imposing enough to summon up thoughts of a fortress.

However, there is nothing formidable about the welcome. All comers on weekends get a leisurely look through the cellars. Proprietors Hank and Judy Bogardus made Zinfandel and Petite Syrah from their debut vintage in 1981. Those wines followed a lot of Zinfandel from an earlier vintage. The proprietors offer easygoing tasting, and visitors are invited to spread a blanket under a shade tree and picnic if they wish.

Visitors who were here in earlier times will recognize the property as having been the Richert and Sons Winery before the Bogarduses took over and named it half for the accompanying Italianate villa and half for its location in what is locally known as Paradise Valley.

More Wineries. Several more cellars are located in the district, but are too limited in guest facilities to be readily visited.

Conrotto Winery, an old-timer dedicated to making house wines for the restaurant trade, in addition to varietal wines, has a tasting room but offers no tours. The Peter & Harry Giretti Winery is another local fixture, selling jug wines to a long-established clientele from an old cellar in Gilroy. Ronald Lamb Winery at Morgan Hill makes tiny lots of several varietals including Chardonnay, Cabernet Sauvignon, and Petite Sirah. Lack of size prohibits public visits. De Santis is a tiny winery in Gilroy.

Other Than Wineries

Several pleasing and temptingly diverse parks line the hills on either side of southern Santa Clara County.

Dry and parched as the east hills appear from U.S. 101, they hide a string of reservoirs, each developed for recreation.

The most highly developed of the lot, Anderson Lake County Park, is in the first range of hills east of Morgan Hill. Cochran Road goes directly to the main area. Though primarily designed for boaters, the park has a large picnic area. At the southern tip of the same lake is a second, smaller picnic area, this one reached via East Dunne Avenue.

Henry W. Coe State Park lies directly east of Anderson Lake on an extension of East Dunne Avenue. The distance from downtown Morgan Hill is 14 miles. A one-time working ranch, the park has its headquarters in old ranch buildings at an elevation of 2,600 feet. These buildings attract almost as many watercolorists as the park's rolling, grassy hills, except in late April and early May when the wildflowers capture every eye. There is a small day-use fee for picnic sites. The park also has a few campsites.

Farther south, Coyote Lake County Park offers picnickers another choice. Again, a cooling reservoir is the attraction. Access is from Gilroy via Leavesley Road.

Over in the west hills, Mt. Madonna County Park has its main entrance at the summit of Hecker Pass. Like Henry W. Coe State Park, this park has been built out of a one-time working ranch. Cattleman Henry Miller owned it and left some formal gardens for posterity. Also, the park has a herd of albino deer as a special attraction. Roads meander through oak forests at the higher elevations. At the foot of the hills, next to a creek and pond, picnic sites nestle in the shade of oaks and other trees. The entrance to this area is from State 152 just before it starts climbing. There is a day-use fee.

Finally, a small county park called Adams Picnic Site sits next to County Road G8 opposite the end of Burchell Road.

Plotting a Route

U.S. Highway 101 brings traffic into southern Santa Clara County from both north and south. State Highway 152, called the Hecker Pass Highway west of U.S. 101 and the Pacheco Pass Highway east of it, handles the cross traffic.

U.S. 101 is a divided highway through Santa Clara

County. The freeway is flat and straight, but close enough to hills to be pleasant driving.

The Pacheco Pass Highway, winding and scenic, carries a great amount of truck traffic in and out of the San Joaquin Valley, and also serves as a link in a much-used route to Yosemite National Park. It is hardly ever lonely. The Hecker Pass Highway to Watsonville does not climb so high or serve so many purposes, but does offer some fine panoramas of coast hills.

Not many local roads supplement the major highways. County Road G8 pokes and dawdles through fine hill country between Gilroy and San Jose. Where G8 starts into the hills north of Gilroy, Watsonville Road eases northeast toward Morgan Hill through a pretty countryside.

Monterey County

In the mid-1970s Monterey County exploded into prominence as a vineyard district. Between 1963 and 1973, vineyard acreage shot from a few hundred to more than 30,000. Today, there are nearly 33,000 acres planted to grapes.

Much of the early acreage is concentrated in the Salinas Valley between the towns of Gonzales and King City. Most of the more recent plantings stretch south from King City almost to the San Luis Obispo County line. One tiny patch is across the west hills in Carmel Valley.

Except for a couple of spots, vines do not come close to U.S. Highway 101 between Gonzales and King City. The rich, thick soils at the bottom of the valley still hold the more traditional crops of this part of the world: strawberries, peppers, and all sorts of leafy vegetables (above all, lettuce). The vines are up on steeply photogenic alluvial fans at each side of this long, broad furrow in the Coast Ranges, more easily seen from local roads than the highway.

In spite of all its vineyards, Monterey remains relatively modest as a district for vinous touring. Only a handful of wineries have formal visitor policies, and they are widely scattered in a valley that is as much as 10 miles wide and well more than 100 miles long. This curious state of affairs owes itself to the fact that vineyards in Monterey County originally were a response to urban pressure farther north in Santa Clara and Alameda counties; so, great volumes of Monterey grapes belong to or are bought by Paul Masson, Mirassou,

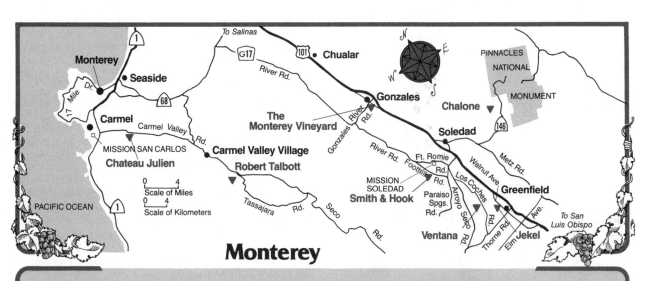

Monterey

Chalone Vineyard. From Soledad, State 146 10 mi. E to Stonewall Canyon Rd., NW .3 mi. to winery road (Mail: 655 Sutter St., San Francisco, CA 94102) Tel (415) 546-7755 GT/Ta by appt. only.

Chateau Julien. From State 1, SE 5.1 mi. on Carmel Valley Rd. to winery at 8940 (P.O. Box 221775, Carmel, CA 93922) Tel (408) 624-2600. M-F 8:30-5 by appt. GT/Ta.

Durney Vineyard. Directions to winery with appt. (P.O. Box 222016, Carmel, CA 93922) Tel (408) 625-5433. By appt. only. (Not on map).

Jekel Vineyard. From U.S. 101, Walnut Ave. exit, W 1 mi. (P.O. Box 336, Greenfield, CA 93927) Tel (408) 674-5524. Daily 10-5. GT/Ta.

Monterey Peninsula Winery. (Mail: 467 Shasta Ave., Sand City, CA 93955) Tel (408) 394-2999. Tasting room on Cannery Row at 786 Wave St., Monterey. Daily 10-6. Ta. (Outside map area).

The Monterey Vineyard. From U.S. 101, Alta St. exit, N .5 mi. to winery (800 S. Alta St., Gonzales, CA 93926) Tel (408) 675-2481. Daily 10-5. GT/Ta.

Morgan Winery. From U.S. 101 at Salinas, John St. exit W .7, S .3 on Abbott, E 1 blk. on Chamberlain, S ½ blk on Brunken to winery at 526E (19301 Creekside Circle, Salinas, CA 93908) Tel (408) 455-1382. Ta by appt. only. (Outside map area).

Smith & Hook Winery. From U.S. 101, Arroyo Seco Rd. exit, W on Arroyo Seco Rd./Paraiso Springs Rd. to Foothill Rd., then N 1.8 mi. to winery at 37700 (Drawer C, Soledad, CA 93960) Tel (408) 678-2132. Daily 10-4. GT/Ta.

Robert Talbott Vineyard & Winery. Directions to winery with appt. (P.O. Box 267, Carmel Valley, CA 93924) Tel (408) 375-0505. GT/Ta by appt. only.

Ventana Vineyards. From U.S. 101, Arroyo Seco Rd. exit, W then S on Arroyo Seco Rd. to Las Coches Rd., then SE on Las Coches 3 mi. to winery (Mail and tasting at Jct of State 68 and Canyon Del Rey, 2999 Monterey-Salinas Hwy., Monterey, CA 93940) Tel (408) 372-7415. Daily 12-5. Ta. GT of winery by appt.

KEY: GT (guided tour); IT (informal tour); Ta (tasting).

Wente Bros., and other firms with long histories and most of their winemaking capacities in the more northerly counties.

The Wineries

The Monterey Vineyard and its colossal sibling, Taylor California Cellars, loom up right next to the freeway and to each other. Except for them, a trip to Monterey County wineries requires taking local roads for anything from a quick detour to a genuine pilgrimage.

Chalone Vineyard occupies a special niche in Monterey in every sense of the term. It is in an aerie of its own, and both vineyard and winery are the oldest in the county.

The vineyards roll across limestone slopes high above the east side of the Salinas Valley floor. The topmost rows almost reach the foot of a striking geologic curiosity, the Pinnacles. (An abstraction of the near-vertical basalt outcrop decorates Chalone's labels. Another representation of it is set in tile in the bottling room walls.) The next nearest vineyards are miles west and hundreds of feet lower.

The oldest Chalone vines go back to 1919, planted then by a man named Bill Silvear, who put his grapes on the site of a still-older vineyard. After Silvear died in 1957, the vines endured ups and downs until 1965, when more than 100 wine buffs formed Gavilan Vineyards, Inc., and bought the property. In 1969 the company metamorphosed into Chalone, Inc., which is now a public corporation and also runs Acacia Winery (page 98), Carmenet Vineyard (page 35), and Edna Valley Vineyards (page 128). The chairman is Chalone proprietor, Dick Graff.

Monterey Bay Aquarium

First, the proprietors put the old vines right. Then, beginning in 1972, they began to expand their plantings. The original plot approached 30 acres. Current acreage is a bit more than 170.

Interim owners between Silvear and Gavilan Vineyards had built a tiny winery. The white-walled, oak-shaded original served through 1974. Now dwarfed by a new cellar upslope, it holds bottled wines.

Scaled to hold the expanded vineyard's full production, the handsome newer building cuts into its hillside so that crusher, press, and red wine fermenting tanks adjoin the high side. The upper floor holds cased goods, lab, and bottling room. Underneath are extensive caves filled with fat French barrels from Burgundy, used to ferment the whites and age all of the wines.

Getting up to see the place requires an appointment and considerable effort, especially when rains soften unpaved roads between Stonewall Canyon Road and the winery, but diligent admirers of California wine make the trip gladly.

The shy-yielding vineyards produce a predominantly Burgundian list of wines: Pinot Noir, Pinot Blanc, and Chardonnay, plus Chenin Blanc.

Chateau Julien is a Carmel wine estate in the old world manner. No expense was spared by Great American Wineries, Inc., to capture the feeling of a rural French chateau in the fractured Carmel Valley landscape. The largess extended to the winery itself, where visitors can see such rare hardware as a Demoisy crusher, a computer-driven Europress, and a Schenk-Kapitan milipore filter, along with Limousin, Allier, and Nevers oak barrels. First crush was 1983.

The wines, produced from purchased grapes, include Chardonnay, Sauvignon Blanc (in two styles), and Merlot. Dry and cream Sherries are produced from an old Solera (sherry yeast culture). Visitors are required to tour before tasting, a small price to pay for the chance to scrutinize a textbook-perfect winery.

Durney Vineyard stands in the same sort of lonely splendor as Chalone, but on the other side of the county, on the seaward side of the Santa Lucia Mountains.

William and Dorothy Durney's vineyards and winery occupy one of a mere handful of reasonable slopes in some seriously steep hill country a few miles east of Carmel Valley Village.

For dedicated students of California wine, a visit well repays the effort of assembling the required group, arranging an appointment, and making the trek up Cachagua Road to a genuine estate winery. Founded in 1977, the cellar occupies a handsomely renovated hay barn and a newer second building. Crusher and press are just outside the rear wall of the original, and stainless steel fermentors fill most of the interior. The newer building is the oak aging cellar.

Vineyards run across a series of gentle hills and dips on the downhill, north side of the winery. The roster of wines made from their grapes includes Chardonnay, Chenin Blanc, Riesling, Cabernet Sauvignon, and Gamay Beaujolais.

Jekel Vineyard lies just northwest of the main business district of Greenfield.

The winery is housed in a classically red, barn-shaped building, but this is mostly illusion. A steel building with eight inches of insulation sandwiched between its inner and outer skins, the Jekel winery is modern to the minute. A fermenting room full of stainless steel tanks is directly behind the front wall. Just outside stand a big crusher rigged to handle machine-harvested grapes and a horizontal basket press. Alongside the fermenting room is a cellarful of oak barrels. Adjacent to it is a sterile bottling room, and so it goes.

A comfortable visitor facility is but a few paces from any of these elements in the compact winery; so, tours are effortless. Because mechanical pickers work in Jekel-owned vineyards right around the winery, it is a particularly good place to see them in action during harvest.

Wines from those vines include Chardonnay, Pinot Blanc, Riesling, and Cabernet Sauvignon.

The owning Jekel brothers, William and August, planted the vineyards in 1972 and built the winery in 1978.

Monterey Peninsula Winery has evolved from
picturesque but unwieldy beginnings into a model of efficiency. In its original quarters, a fine stone building near Monterey's airport, dim light and stone walls made a romantic impression. But the mazelike cellars were difficult to negotiate with any precision, so the owners up and moved the entire operation in 1986. The new winery is a tilt-up industrial building in Sand City, north of Monterey.

Both sides of the large space are lined with a mix of wooden and stainless steel tanks. The rest of the building is occupied by oak barrels, American for the red wines and French for the whites. All the fruit is purchased from Monterey County vineyards except for Zinfandel, which comes from Amador County.

Founders Deryck Nuckton and Roy Thomas remain general partners. In addition to Zinfandel, the primary wines are Chardonnay, Pinot Blanc, Cabernet Sauvignon, and Merlot.

The Monterey Vineyard winery building looms up
alongside U.S. 101 on the south side of Gonzales. In a region with very few large buildings, it would seem huge except for the tempering influence of extensive landscaping undertaken by the current owners, Joseph E. Seagram & Sons, Inc.

The architectural style is a remarkable mixture of early and late California. Arches, towers, and red-tile roofs are the main distinguishing marks of the early corner containing the tasting room. Diagonal steel end walls and buttressed concrete side walls provide the modern counterpoint.

Visitors work their way through the whole building on a carefully engineered route that takes them past crushers and presses, into a large fermenting hall, through aging cellars full of large and small oak cooperage, and, finally, the tasting room.

Close attention to the gear will show any number of unusual details, most of which were designed by founding winemaker Dr. Richard Peterson. One example is a system of closed conveyors for moving pomace and lees (solid residues) out of the fermentors and into

presses or filters. Another is a metal pallet for barrels in the small wood aging cellar. Most of these details bask in warm light from rows of towering stained-glass windows in the two side walls.

The tasting room has available vintage-dated Chardonnay, Chenin Blanc, Sauvignon Blanc, Gewürztraminer, Pinot Noir, and Zinfandel, plus generics. When nature agrees, there is a botrytised Sauvignon Blanc. A fine collection of Ansel Adams photographs provides another reason to visit.

The original scheme for The Monterey Vineyard, under another ownership, was a grand one. After the company was purchased by the Coca Cola Company, that notion was abandoned in favor of keeping The Monterey Vineyard a small, prestigious label to complement its Napa Valley running mate, Sterling Vineyards (page 94).

Morgan Winery keeps its two identities separate.
Chardonnay and Pinot Noir, the Burgundian varietals, are bottled under the Morgan imprimatur, whereas the Bordeaux varietals, Sauvignon Blanc and Cabernet Sauvignon, are labeled St. Vrain.

Both labels issue from leased space in industrial Salinas. The first wines were produced in 1982. The Morgan family plans to have their own winery built by the 1989 vintage.

In the meantime, tours are by appointment only. Visitors will see a bare-bones example of the typical California winery in its larval stage: one big room with glycol-jacketed tanks on one side and French oak barrels everywhere else, some used for Chardonnay fermentation, most used for aging.

Smith & Hook Winery, one of the area's newest
wineries, looks as though it is one of the oldest. It gets its name and its fine old buildings from horse ranchers who were the previous occupants of a dramatic hillside site west of Soledad. Nicolaus Hahn owns the winery.

The winery occupies the old stable, a long, low, board-and-batten building painted pale blue and refitted to its new purpose in time for the vintage of 1979. Old tack hangers still line one wall of the laboratory, but all traces of horse have been cleared out of the stalls, now two barrel aging cellars at opposite ends of the building. Open-topped redwood fermentors out back look across vineyards divided by original corral fences judged too handsome to be removed when the property was planted to vines.

Smith & Hook makes only one wine, Cabernet Sauvignon, from grapes grown on the more tractable parts of a steep property cut in places by apprentice canyons.

Ventana Vineyards opened its winery doors in 1978,
using grapes from a substantial vineyard planted some years earlier by owner J. Douglas Meador.

The winery building is a well weathered, gap-sided, leaky-roofed barn that stands as a considerable testimonial to a local climate so temperate it can be allowed to pass through unchanged. In striking contrast, the stainless steel fermentors, French oak barrels, and other equipment are modern to the minute. (The bottling line and bottled wines are pampered in a well-insulated prefabricated metal building next to the old barn.)

The roster of wines is headed by Chardonnay, and includes Riesling, Chenin Blanc, Sauvignon Blanc, Gewürztraminer, Pinot Noir, and Cabernet Sauvignon. When harvest-season weather encourages it, there also is a botrytised Sauvignon Blanc. If the name, Ventana Vineyards, seems familiar from other labels, it is because Meador sells grapes to a number of wineries, some of which identify the source on their label. Ventana operates a tasting room in Monterey. Winery tours are by appointment only.

More Wineries. As Monterey gathers speed as a wine district, it has begun to acquire its share of tiny cellars. Carmel Bay Wine Company is perhaps the tiniest. Owned by stockbroker Fred Crummey, it is located in a one-time airplane hangar at the Monterey Peninsula airport. Zampatti's Champagne Cellar, another very small firm, sells to a local trade from its location in Carmel Valley Village.

Robert Talbott Vineyard & Winery is a little viticultural jewel set into the Carmel Valley hills off Tassajara Road. Visits are difficult to arrange but are worth the effort for a glimpse of a model California wine estate.

Other Than Wineries

In addition to its vineyards and wineries, Monterey County has varied attractions, natural and otherwise.

The pure article is Pinnacles National Monument, an imposing array of columnar basalt and caves left over from one of the more explosively formative moments of the local landscape. The monument is high in the Gavilan Mountains, which form the east side of the valley.

Much the greater development—including the visitor center and campgrounds—is on the east side of the monument, accessible via State Highway 25 from Hollister or King City. You can see a fair sampler of the lunar landscape, however, by driving to the end of State Highway 146 from Soledad.

Incidentally, the fogs and breezes that cool the valley floor do not penetrate to the Pinnacles in summer, when it becomes downright hot. Fog is cheap in Monterey, however, and a drive to the coast is the standard therapy for too much vineyard dust. In numerous winery tasting rooms along Cannery Row, the day's tours gain a leisurely perspective.

Cannery Row also offers an attraction spectacular enough to draw visitors from all over the world. The Monterey Bay Aquarium redefines the aquarium concept. It is nothing more or less than a slice of Monterey Bay under glass; flora, fauna, old tin cans and all have been surrounded by plexiglass and beamed up to a modern concrete hall just yards from their former habitat. The centerpiece is a kelp forest in a towering tank that is battered by an artificial surge timed to the real one outside; it can be viewed at several levels. Another tank provides a crab's-eye view of a rotting pier, with myriad creatures demonstrating that life among the pilings has its share of pathos and intrigue. Nor will shark fans be disappointed.

Advance tickets are available, and recommended. For information write to the Monterey Bay Aquarium at 886 Cannery Row, Monterey, CA 93940.

Two of California's 21 Franciscan missions are in the vineyarded reaches of the Salinas Valley. They are at Soledad and west of King City.

Soledad Mission—Mission Nuestra Señora de la Soledad, to give it its full name—has one mostly melted adobe wall surviving from the original complex. (A chapel of newer style flanks it.) In its forlorn way the old wall tells the history of the region. Soledad was essentially a desolate, lonely failure. Very little would grow for the missionaries in this place of scarce rainfall, and grapes were no exception. The padres had no idea that the Salinas River was full of water because none showed on the surface.

West of U.S. 101, visitors can reach the mission via Paraiso Springs and Fort Romie roads.

You can get a far truer look at how life went in the mission days at Mission San Antonio de Padua, located in a high valley west of the main Salinas River Valley, approximately at the latitude of King City. Jolon Road leads to it from U.S. 101 at King City.

Within, the nearly complete building has restorations or replicas of a great deal of working mission gear. Included is the old wine cellar, a structure guaranteed to gladden the hearts of all who drink wine from newer, more manageable fermentors and aging cellars.

Picnickers in search of a table in the Salinas Valley have only one choice in the neighborhood of the wineries. A few tables flank the chapel grounds at Mission Soledad. A municipal park at King City is the next nearest opportunity.

Plotting a Route

Monterey County is long on its north-south axis and slender on its east-west one. More important, two lofty ranges of coast hills—the Gavilans on the east and the Santa Lucias on the west—trend northwest to southeast.

The coast side of the county has two-lane State Highway 1, and the Salinas River valley has freeway U.S. Highway 101 to transport people along the long axis. The trouble for wine fanciers is that the wineries string themselves out east and west at about midcounty. Local roads tying them together get into and over the hills as best they can, but expressways they are not.

State Highway 68 from Salinas to Monterey links coast and valley, and passes near two wineries in the process. It is a fairly level two-laner for most of the distance. This is the shortest route (via County Road G20) from Salinas to the Carmel Valley wineries.

Arroyo Seco-Carmel Valley Road (County Road G16) is the other, more southerly cross route. It is sometimes two lanes, sometimes a lane and a half, high, winding, and mostly glorious from Greenfield to Carmel.

State Highway 46 (Stonewall Canyon Road) echoes on the east what Carmel Valley Road does on the west. Like its counterpart, it's best undertaken with a full gas tank.

River Road, Foothill Boulevard, and Fort Romie Road are the most useful local roads for getting to several of the wineries. River Road also is an alternative to U.S. 101 for those who would rather look at flowers.

San Benito County

San Benito County is a considerable curiosity within the larger curiosity of a region that has its wineries in one place and its vineyards in another. Three small-to-tiny wineries with no more than 200 acres among them do accept visitors, though their size and remoteness limits the welcomes a great deal.

Except for Hollister and San Juan Bautista on its northern boundary, this is a sparsely settled county.

The Wineries

All of the visitable wineries in the county are in the Cienega district, along the west side of the San Benito River valley, in the shadow of the Gavilan Mountains.

Calera Wine Company is a dramatic place built on the stillborn frame of a huge limekiln in the Gavilan Mountains. Its name (Spanish for "limekiln") was chosen when the winery began operations in 1975.

In March 1982, the seven levels of the working winery were completed on a steep site above Cienega Road. From every level the view is spectacular: down an oak-clad slope to a small pond, then out across a low range of hills, a higher one, and, finally, on clear days, to the distance-hazed Diablo Range.

There was a functional reason for choosing the property. Proprietor Josh Jensen's winery is arranged so that gravity will do much of the work once grapes arrive on the premises. They come in at the top, level with the crusher. Stainless steel fermentors are one step down, the press another. Then come holding tanks, barrel cellars, and, at the bottom, the bottling and case storage.

The wines are Pinot Noir from winery-owned grapes and from a vineyard in Santa Barbara, Zinfandel from several sources, and, beginning with the 1986 harvest, estate-grown Chardonnay.

Cygnet Cellars occupies a modest prefabricated metal building on an oak-studded, grassy site just off Cienega Road. Within, the small cellar is conservatively equipped with basket press, small crusher, and American oak barrels. An unusual note is 500-gallon fermentors made of fiberglass.

Cygnet is directed by two partners, James Johnson and C. Robert Lane. Their principal wine is a late-harvest Zinfandel. They also produce small lots of Pinot St. George, Petite Sirah, and Carignane.

Enz Vineyards is tucked away toward the top of Limekiln Canyon in a spot so peaceful and agreeable that it looks like the setting for a Disney movie, or maybe an episode from the nostalgic days of *The Waltons*.

This is almost an anachronism: a small winery run along the lines of a family farm. In the midst of the vineyards—the oldest blocks date back to 1895—are the family home, a white barn converted to an aging cellar, fermentors and crusher set on an open pad, and, well upslope, a metal building that serves as both barrel and bottle aging cellar.

San Benito

Calera Wine Company. From Hollister, State 25 (San Benito St./Nash Rd.) to Cienega Rd., S on Cienega 11 mi. to private lane (11300 Cienega Rd., Hollister, CA 95023) Tel (408) 637-9170. GT by appt. only.

Cygnet Cellars. From Hollister, State 25 (San Benito St./Nash Rd.) to Cienega Rd., S on Cienega 11.2 mi. to winery drive (11736 Cienega Rd., Hollister, CA 95023) Tel (408) 733-4276. By appt. only.

Enz Vineyards. From Hollister, State 25 (San Benito St./Nash Rd.) to Cienega Rd., S on Cienega 16 mi. to Limekiln Rd., then W on Limekiln to winery (1781 Limekiln Rd., Hollister, CA 95023) Tel (408) 637-3956. GT/Ta by appt. only.

KEY: GT (guided tour); IT (informal tour); Ta (tasting).

The roster of wines is relatively short, focused on Pinot St. George and Zinfandel, and on an aperitif called Limekiln in tribute to a former use of the property.

Other Than Wineries

The agreeable old mission village and stagecoach stop of San Juan Bautista is a gateway to the winery district, and the most notable change of pace from touring cellars. Mission San Juan Bautista and San Juan Bautista State Historic Park are on the original plaza.

Plotting a Route

Since all of San Benito's visitable wineries flank Cienega Road, the only question is where to pick it up.

From downtown Hollister, San Benito Street runs west to its end. A left turn onto Nash Road leads in two blocks to the head end of Cienega Road.

Those coming from the west via State Highway 156 can turn south short of Hollister at Union Road (marked by a round-backed hill planted to grape vines), which joins Cienega Road about five miles later.

Central Coast South

New territories for the vine

Mission Santa Barbara

Even by California's swift standards, the coastal valleys of San Luis Obispo and Santa Barbara counties have emerged as vineyard districts with unusual speed.

When wine began to boom in the early 1970s, San Luis Obispo was puttering along with a handful of wineries making small lots of rustic red from a few patches of Zinfandel. Santa Barbara, virtually without grapes, had one local winery. In spring 1987, San Luis Obispo County had 20 cellars and nearly 6,000 acres in vineyard. In Santa Barbara County the counts were 20 cellars and 9,253 acres of vines. More wineries and more vineyards were in the works in both counties.

Though district boundaries still are blurred in many spots, the region has at least five U.S. viticultural areas within it, with more to emerge. One is the old wine area of San Luis Obispo County near Paso Robles, now much enlarged. The second, lying south of San Luis Obispo city, is called Edna Valley. Santa Barbara County has a fully tourable district centered on Solvang and called the Santa Ynez Valley. Adjacent on the north is the Santa Maria district, which has substantial vineyards and is also beginning to have wineries of substance.

Before the vines came, these districts had much to appeal to visitors. San Luis Obispo is an agreeable university and mission town close to Hearst Castle and ocean beaches at Pismo and Avila. Solvang is a well-developed gateway to beautiful ranching country in the Santa Ynez Valley and is another mission site.

Paso Robles

The northern part of San Luis Obispo County has a bit of vinous history in the forms of three old wineries near Templeton and a great deal of new development both east and west of Paso Robles.

In addition to being a useful road, U.S. Highway 101 marks the dividing line between two very different terrains. To the west is steep, thickly wooded hill country. To the east, only a few oaks poke up out of gentle, grassy hills. Most of the vines are out with the grasses. Most of the cellars are up in the woodsy hills.

This is a bigger territory than it appears at first glance. A good many miles separate the wineries east of

U.S. 101 from one another. On the west side, distances are less, but no road goes in a straight line for more than a few hundred feet at a time, and some are spurs.

The Wineries

As the combination of old and new promises, there is variety to be found among the several cellars in this sprawling district.

Arciero Winery is a grand mission-style structure on a landscaped knoll among some 400 acres of vines. Despite the crowning bell tower, the roof looks lower than it actually is because the interior floors are 17 feet below ground level. A self-guided tour takes in four cave-like chambers holding stainless steel tanks and various denominations of French oak cooperage.

The owners are two of four Arciero brothers, who immigrated from Italy in the 1940s. Frank Arciero, Sr., did some time as a race-car driver, which explains a brace of retired Indy 500 cars displayed in the visitors' center, a separate building below the winery.

Wines poured there include Chardonnay, Chenin Blanc, Sauvignon Blanc, Cabernet Sauvignon, Petite Sirah, red and white Zinfandels and a small quantity of Muscat Canelli, available only at the winery. A deli and a rose garden help to make the Arciero grounds an inviting picnic spot.

Caparone Vineyard is owned by a specialist of two sorts. Owner-winemaker M. David Caparone makes only red wines and only from Central Coast grapes. But he also is an experimental grower of Nebbiolo and Brunello. As his young vineyard has matured, varietal wines from these two Italian grapes have joined the roster, though in very small lots.

Caparone's winery is a no-nonsense, chocolate brown, prefabricated metal building kept in impeccable order. Stainless steel fermentors fill one end. Racks of American oak barrels take up most of the rest of the space, save for an aisle given over to bottled wines and a small lab. In harvest season the proprietor rolls a small crusher and horizontal basket press onto a concrete pad outside the main cellar door to get new wines started.

Caparone is not only the owner-winemaker, but also the whole staff, and a jazz trombonist on the side. Visitors may taste from barrels with him whenever he does not have an out-of-town gig.

Cross Canyon Vineyards and winery are situated on a long sideslope directly above a remote stretch of Ranchita Canyon Road, well east of the old mission village of San Miguel.

The operation was founded as Ranchita Oaks Winery in 1979 by Ronald Bergstrom, who housed its modest workings in a neatly maintained prefabricated metal building in the midst of equally neat vineyards. In 1985 the winemaking and vineyard management were assumed by Jerry and Micaela Barnhill; at the same time, Ranchita Oaks' second label became its primary one.

Cross Canyon Vineyards produces Cabernet Sauvignon, Petite Sirah (the particular specialty), and Zinfandel, all from the estate vines.

Eberle Winery is a handsome cedar structure with a shake roof, containing the usual stainless steel fermentors and, in a separate aging area, about 300 French oak barrels. W. Gary Eberle, one of the founders of Estrella River Winery, began making his own wines in 1979 and built the winery in 1982. The estate vineyard, planted in limestone-rich soil, supplies fruit for Chardonnay, Muscat Canelli, and Cabernet Sauvignon.

The tasting room is easily the district's most stylish. Gray carpet with maroon borders, oak wainscoting, and a large fireplace give it the air of a modern home, except that broad windows in an interior wall overlook the working winery below.

Estrella River Winery became a landmark on the road between Paso Robles and Shandon as soon as the building went up in 1977.

It had to be, given the size of the stucco-walled main cellar, its lofty observation tower, and its location at the high point of some 700 acres of rolling vineyards. The founder, Clifford R. Giacobine, manages the winery.

The observation tower looks north to the Gavilan Mountains and west to the Santa Lucia Mountains. Below the open-air tower, a closed-in gallery gives close views of the stemmer-crusher and adjoining continuous press.

Inside the main walls, an open platform looks first across a spacious fermenting room full of stainless steel tanks, then into an aging cellar full of oak upright tanks and barrels, the latter piled high on metal pallets. At the foot of stairs leading down from the platform, a large window looks into a modern, sterile bottling room.

Estrella River offers varietal table wines from its own grapes, including Zinfandel, Chardonnay, Sauvignon Blanc, and Muscat Canelli among whites; Cabernet Sauvignon and Syrah among reds; and a Blanc de Blancs sparkling wine.

Martin Brothers Winery perches amid its own young vines near the top of an eye-pleasing slope east of Paso Robles.

The owners have wrought a remarkable rejuvenation of a faded one-time dairy ranch. Their main cellar occupies the old barn, a jaunty board-and-batten structure painted pale gray. Its natural wood-finished interior is trim enough to satisfy a sea captain. Three stainless steel fermentors march in a row beneath the roof peak. Racks of French oak barrels fill the two wings so tightly that the proprietors do not offer guided tours for lack of room.

The Martin family does, however, welcome visitors in a tasting room at the corner of Highway 46 East and Buena Vista Drive.

The Martins make small lots of four wines: Sauvignon Blanc, Chenin Blanc, Chardonnay, Nebbiolo, and Zinfandel. The winery crushed its first grapes in 1981 and planted its first vines the same year.

Mastantuono Winery is the centerpiece of the Pat and Leona Mastan family's self-sufficient ranch in the Adelaide district west of Paso Robles. The Mastans started Buck Creek Ranch from scratch in 1977, seizing

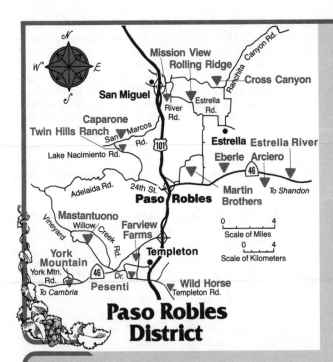

Paso Robles District

Farview Farm Vineyard. From U.S. 101, W 1.5 mi. on State 46 to Bethel Rd., S .25 mi. to drive (Rt. 2, Box 40, Bethel Rd., Templeton, CA 93465) Tel (805) 434-1133. GT/Ta by appt.

Martin Brothers Winery. From U.S. 101, State 46-East exit, 1 mi. E to Buena Vista Rd., 1.1 mi. N to 4230 (P.O. Box 2599, Paso Robles, CA 93447) Tel (805) 238-2520. Daily 10-5. IT/Ta.

Mastantuono Winery. Winery: From U.S. 101 N of Templeton, SW 4.4 mi. on State 46, NW .8 on Vineyard Dr., N 3 mi. on Willow Creek Rd. (101½ Willow Creek Rd., Paso Robles, CA 93446) Tel (805) 238-0676, 238-1078. GT by appt. Tasting room: From U.S. 101 at Templeton, W 3.1 mi. on Vineyard Dr. at Hwy. 46 intersection. Daily 10-5 Nov-Apr, 10:30-6 May-Oct.

Mission View Vineyards and Winery. From San Miguel, .9 mi. E on 14th St./River Rd./Estrella Rd. to winery (4040 Estrella Rd., San Miguel, CA 93451) Tel (805) 467-3104. Daily 11-5. GT/Ta.

Pesenti Winery. From U.S. 101, Vineyard Dr. exit, W 2.5 mi. to winery (2900 Vineyard Dr., Templeton, CA 93465) Tel (805) 434-1030. M-Sa 8-5:30, Su 9-5:30. IT/Ta.

Rolling Ridge Winery. From San Miguel, 1.7 mi. E on 14th St./River Rd./Estrella Rd., N .4 mi. on Magdelina Dr. to winery (P.O. Box 250, Magdelina Dr., San Miguel, CA 93451) Tel (805) 467-3130. GT/Ta by appt.

Twin Hills Ranch Winery. From U.S. 101 at Paso Robles, exit State 46-East, W 4 mi. on 24th St./Lake Nacimiento Rd. to winery (2025 Lake Nacimiento Rd., Paso Robles, CA 93446) Tel (805) 238-9148. Picnic. Daily 11-5. Ta.

Wild Horse Winery & Vineyards. From U.S. 101 at Templeton, E .7 mi. on Vineyard Dr., S 2.1 mi. on Templeton Rd. to 85B (P.O. Box 638, Templeton, CA 93465) Tel (805) 434-2541. GT/Ta by appt.

York Mountain Winery. From U.S. 101, State 46-West exit, 9 mi. W, then N .4 mi. on York Mountain Rd. (Rt. 2, Box 191, Templeton, CA 93465) Tel (805) 238-3925. Daily 10-5. Ta. GT by appt.

Wineries Not on Map— Restricted or No Visitor Facilities

Watson Vineyards. (Adelaida Rd., Star Route, Paso Robles, CA 93446) Tel (805) 238-6091.

Arciero Winery. From U.S. 101 at Paso Robles, E 4.8 mi. on State 46 to winery (Hwy. 46 & Jardine Rd., Paso Robles, CA 93447) Tel (805) 239-2562. Picnic. Daily 10-5. IT/Ta.

Caparone Vineyard. From U.S. 101, San Marcos Rd. exit, 3 mi. W to winery (2280 San Marcos Rd., Paso Robles, CA 93446) Tel (805) 467-3827. Daily 11-5. GT/Ta.

Cross Canyon Vineyards. From San Miguel, 7 mi. E on Cross Canyon Rd. to intersection with Ranchita Canyon Rd. (Estrella Rt., San Miguel, CA 93451) Tel (805) 467-3422. Sa-Su by appt. only. IT/Ta.

Eberle Winery. From U.S. 101 at Paso Robles, E 3.2 mi. on State 46 to winery (P.O. Box 2459, Paso Robles, CA 93447) Tel (805) 238-9607. Picnic. Daily 10-5. IT/Ta.

Estrella River Winery. From U.S. 101 at Paso Robles, 6.5 mi. E on State 46 (P.O. Box 96, Paso Robles, CA 93447) Tel (805) 238-6300. Picnic. Daily 10-5. GT/IT/Ta.

Key: GT (guided tour); IT (informal tour); Ta (tasting).

---

15 acres of limestone soil from their various grazing animals a year later to plant a vineyard.

The winery, like their house, is a white stucco, cross-timbered structure in a vaguely Tudor style. It's an interesting example of a specialized winery because only their red wines are produced there; visits require an appointment made well in advance.

No appointment is needed to taste the wines, however. The Mastans' white wine production facility at the corner of Highway 46 West and Vineyard Drive includes a tasting room. There, visitors may sample the unfined, unfiltered Zinfandels for which Pat Mastan is noted, in addition to Chardonnay, Muscat Canelli, and Cabernet Sauvignon. A sweet Orange Muscat is produced in miniscule quantity and can be bought only on site.

Mission View Vineyards and Winery is aptly
named. The prospect from its hilltop perch features

the venerable Mission San Miguel. The alpine-style redwood winery, with its blue tile roof like a piece of fallen sky, was designed by owners Terry and Catherine Peterson and built in time for the 1984 vintage.

The upper-level tasting room offers two views of its own. One looks out over the vineyard, which supplies all the fruit for Mission View wines. An interior balcony looks into the fermentation room. Tours are self-guided when the family is busy, but as things ease up the owners may show visitors around personally. The roster includes Chardonnay, Sauvignon Blanc, Muscat Canelli, Cabernet Sauvignon, and Zinfandel.

Pesenti Winery, old as it is, was long known as the youngest winery in Templeton. Founder Frank Pesenti opened the doors in 1934 as a home for grapes from vineyards he had planted earlier, and his cellar stayed the youngest kid on the block until Mastantuono (see page 125) came along in 1978.

The winery reached its present size in 1947, and continues almost unchanged in the second and third generation hands of its founding family. Tours are at staff convenience only because the white-walled cellars and their rows of venerable redwood and oak tanks do not lend themselves to casual wandering. However, the spacious tasting room is open to all comers.

The Pesenti label features Zinfandel and includes a wide range of other varietals.

Rolling Ridge Winery sits in the oak-studded, broken high country above the Salinas River near San Miguel. The wood-sided metal pole barn, surrounded by 40 acres of vines, looks over a lower ridge toward Mission San Miguel and its sleepy civic namesake. The operation began its life in a different location several miles south, before owner Alan West moved it here in 1983. An appointment is required to see both the view and the winery, which produces Chardonnay, Cabernet Franc, Petite Sirah, and Zinfandel, all French-oak aged.

Twin Hills Ranch Winery sits, as might be guessed, between a pair of hills northwest of Paso Robles. The first vintage was in 1980. The vineyards and large, metal-sided winery are well off the road and are not open to the public.

However, the copper-roofed tasting room across the road offers picnic spots in a shady arbor, along with the full range of estate-grown wines: Sauvignon Blanc, Chardonnay, Chenin Blanc, white Zinfandel, a somewhat heartier Zinfandel rosé, and red Zinfandel. Proprietor John Lockshaw also makes a red table wine called Festival, which is primarily Zinfandel.

York Mountain Winery is the westernmost cellar around Templeton, and is several scores of feet higher in the hills than its neighbors.

Andrew York established the winery in 1882 to use his surplus grapes. The property went two more generations in York family hands, until 1970, when a veteran winemaker named Max Goldman bought it.

Goldman's original intention was to turn the onetime Zinfandel winery into a *méthode champenoise* sparkling wine house. The first cuvées were made from the vintage of 1981, a tribute to patient endurance. Meanwhile, Zinfandel and other table wines have been, and continue to be, the staples. The founder and his family have replanted the first 10 acres of York's old vineyard, and are making small lots of Chardonnay, Pinot Noir, and Cabernet Sauvignon from them. The Goldmans also buy grapes in the district to round out the line, which includes Merlot Port.

The winery, wearing a properly aged air, may be toured by appointment, though its racks of old redwood tanks and oak barrels can be seen from the entry door. The brick-walled tasting room makes a comfortable stop in any season with its big fireplace and miscellaneous memorabilia of earlier days.

More Wineries. Several more wineries are just getting into stride in the district.

Farview Farm Vineyard is also an established label belonging to the proprietors of a vineyard of the same name. Construction of a winery on the property at the intersection of State 46-West and Bethel Road was completed in 1986. Chardonnay, Merlot and Zinfandel comprise the all-estate roster.

Watson Vineyards, on Adelaida Road west of Paso Robles, produced a tiny first vintage of Riesling in 1981. Chardonnay and Pinot Noir joined the roster in 1982. The winery is not open for tours, tasting, or sales.

Wild Horse Winery & Vineyards was known as Santa Lucia Winery until 1987, when owner Ken Volk promoted his second label to primary status. The tiny winery produces Chardonnay and Cabernet Sauvignon from the young estate vineyard, and Riesling, Merlot, and Pinot Noir from purchased grapes.

Two other small wineries operate in the district. El Paso de Robles Winery is a near neighbor of Mastantuono, west of Templeton. Tobias Winery is southwest of Paso Robles.

Other Than Wineries

This is not an easy part of the world for picnickers or for families needing to offer small children a respite from tasting rooms and winery tours.

A county picnic park is located on the east side of U.S. 101 at Templeton. The big recreational park in the region is Nacimiento Reservoir, several miles into the hills west of Paso Robles.

Templeton Corners, a cafe in Templeton owned by Brenda Black, serves as a central tasting room for those wineries in the Paso Robles district lacking their own facilities. There is a modest tasting fee.

Accommodations and restaurants are plentiful at Paso Robles. A listing may be obtained from the Paso Robles Chamber of Commerce, P.O. Box 457, Paso Robles, CA 93447.

Plotting a Route

Major routes in the region are simplicity itself; U.S. Highway 101 traverses it north and south. State Highway 46 crosses the territory east to west, with a slight jog. However, the roads to many of the wineries are narrow, ill-marked, and winding. Several do not connect to other roads, requiring at least some backtracking. The map on page 126 shows the useful ones.

Edna Valley

As wine districts go, Edna Valley blossomed overnight. It remains small in vineyard acreage but has five wineries nestled into superbly scenic coastal hill country a few miles south of the city of San Luis Obispo.

Chamisal Vineyard, the smallest winery of the four, occupies a tall stucco box of a building at one end of a long, rolling vineyard. The property of the Norman Goss family, Chamisal made its first wines in 1981, though the vines go back several years more than that.

As in the case of many small wineries, the lack of size makes a visit instructive. The crusher and an old-fashioned basket press sit on a small pad between the winery and a mobile home. Inside, stainless steel fermentors and French oak barrels share a single room, so the whole process can be seen step by step.

These are Chardonnay specialists. The vineyards are dominated by a particularly venerable clone of that variety.

Corbett Canyon Vineyards was the Lawrence Winery until 1984, when Glenmore Distillers bought the operation and expanded it considerably. There are no vineyards on the 100-acre property south of Edna, only the old Lawrence family house (now offices) and three winery buildings. The brick main winery con-

tains stainless steel fermentors and French and American oak barrels, some for fermentation and the rest for aging wines. A separate aging cellar is also brick. Production and bottling facilities occupy an aluminum-sided structure. Yet another facility was being constructed in 1987 to produce the company's Shadow Creek sparkling wines, previously made under contract in Sonoma County.

Wines available in the main cellar's tasting room (and also at a tasting room in nearby Shell Beach) include Sauvignon Blanc, Chardonnay, Chenin Blanc, Gewürztraminer, Muscat Canelli, red and white Zinfandels, Cabernet Sauvignon, and some generics.

Edna Valley Vineyard is an unusual joint venture by the owners of the local Paragon Vineyards on the one hand and the California winery group called Chalone, Inc., on the other.

The Chalone influence is easily visible to anyone who has visited there. The stucco-covered cellars at Edna Valley are architectural and technical copies of those at Chalone. The state-of-the-art upper level has inside it a laboratory, modern bottling line, and space to store bottled wines. Outside at the rear are the crusher, press, and red wine fermentors. In the ultratraditional underground cellars are three purposefully damp galleries filled with French oak barrels. Here the white wines ferment and both whites and reds age in conditions imitating those in the great underground cellars at Beaune, in France's Burgundy.

As the Burgundian connection promises, the primary wines are Chardonnay and Pinot Noir, the latter made both as a red and a *vin gris* (a pale wine somewhere between blanc de noir and rosé in color, and made dry). Cabernet Sauvignon was added in 1986. A visit will reward the studious with both tastes of the wines and explanations of the techniques behind them.

Maison Deutz applies three centuries of French Champagne experience to limestone-grown California grapes, in a stylish facility within sight of the Pacific ocean. The joint venture of Wine World, Inc., and the Deutz firm of Ay, France, was founded in 1983, although its inaugural sparkling wine wasn't released until 1986.

Deutz president and Chef de Caves André Lallier planted the vineyard and set up the cellars; he supervises operations personally. In addition to vast experience, Lallier brought with him a fascinating piece of equipment, the wooden Coquard basket press that is now the centerpiece of an enclosed crush pad at the rear of the winery. Hand-picked grapes are emptied into it from lug boxes holding 30 pounds each. The grapes are subjected to gentle, steady pneumatic pressing, and only the initial portion of free-run juice goes into the temperature-controlled tanks for fermentation. Further processes are as meticulous.

A look at the press, main cellar, and disgorging room is worth the effort needed to secure the necessary appointment. The single wine is Brut Cuvée.

Saucelito Canyon Vineyard can be reached only by four-wheel drive during dry months, and not at all during winter rains. Since there is no electricity at the remote property, owners Bill and Nancy Greenough

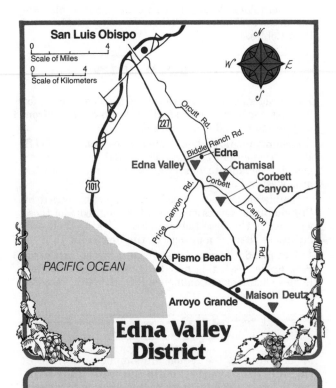

Edna Valley District

Chamisal Vineyard. From State 227, E on Biddle Ranch Rd. to Orcutt Rd., then 2 mi. SE (7525 Orcutt Rd., San Luis Obispo, CA 93401) Tel (805) 544-3576. Picnic. W-Su 11-5. GT/IT/Ta.

Corbett Canyon Vineyards. Winery: From San Luis Obispo, S 6.6 mi. on State 227, SE 1.3 mi. on Corbett Canyon Rd. to 2195. (P.O. Box 3159, San Luis Obispo, CA 93403) Tel (805) 544-5800. M-F 1 & 3, Sa-Su 11, 1, & 3. GT/Ta. Tasting: From U.S. 101, Shell Beach Rd. exit, S 1.3 mi. to 353. Daily 11-6 May-Sept, Daily 11-5 Oct-Apr.

Edna Valley Vineyard. From State 227, .3 mi. E on Biddle Ranch Rd. (2585 Biddle Ranch Rd., San Luis Obispo, CA 93401) Tel (805) 544-9594. Tu-Sa 10-4. GT/IT/Ta.

Maison Deutz. 2.3 mi. S of Arroyo Grande on E side of U.S. 101 (453 Deutz Dr., Arroyo Grande, CA 93420) Tel (805) 481-1763. GT/Ta by appt. Fee.

Saucelito Canyon Vineyard. Directions to winery with appt. (1600 Saucelito Creek Rd., Arroyo Grande, CA 93420) Tel (805) 489-8762/543-2111. GT/Ta by appt. (Outside map area).

Key: GT (guided tour); IT (informal tour); Ta (tasting).

make their wines the old-fashioned way. They welcome groups of five or more by appointment.

The 15-acre vineyard was first planted in 1880 by Henry Ditmas. The Greenoughs bought the ranch from Ditmas' grandchildren in 1974, and built their wooden, tin-roofed winery in 1982. All wines are estate grown: red and white Zinfandels, from the original rootstock, and Cabernet Sauvignon.

Other Than Wineries

Edna Valley proper is mostly ranches. It has no parks or other diversions aside from its wineries. However, it is at the center of an attractive vacation area. The San Luis Obispo mission is only a few miles north. Also within easy distance are Hearst Castle at San Simeon and ocean parks at Avila and Pismo beaches.

Of particular interest to students of viticulture are the area's pelagic limestone deposits, more precious than gold to winegrowers. Masses of it were embedded along this coast 100 million years ago after forming in the equatorial Pacific. As limestone is deemed a perfect medium for wine grapes, the larger deposits are easy to spot, being defined by vineyards.

Plotting a Route

State Highway 227 runs east of U.S. Highway 101, from San Luis Obispo on the north to Arroyo Grande on the south. (At the San Luis Obispo end, it crosses Higuera, the main street, under the name of Broad Street.)

Three wineries are on a neat rectangle east of State 227. From the north, it is best to follow State 227 about 2 miles south of the San Luis Obispo Airport to Biddle Ranch Road. From there, the sequence of Biddle Ranch Road, Orcutt Road, Tiffany Ranch Road, and Corbett Canyon Road passes each of the wineries, ending up on State 227 again. This avoids making an uphill left turn from State 227 onto Corbett Canyon Road in the middle of a blind curve. Drivers coming from the south can take the loop in either direction with equal safety.

Santa Barbara County

Having started well behind San Luis Obispo in numbers of wineries and acres of vines, Santa Barbara had evened the score on both counts by 1987.

The focal point, well-known to vacationers in this part of the world, is the town of Solvang, where a thick layer of Danish all but hides old traces of Franciscan missionary times and a more recent era of cowboys.

Vineyards and wineries alike hide in beautiful, rolling hill country on either side of U.S. Highway 101 from Buellton north to Santa Maria, but are not so far off the freeway as to make visiting difficult. Quite the opposite, a well-articulated web of secondary roads allows easy access to the wineries at a very small price in extra miles.

In time, this sprawling area is likely to become two distinct wine districts called Santa Ynez Valley and Santa Maria Valley. For now, the two blend rather easily into one district for touring.

The Wineries

All but one of the county's cellars have been founded since 1970, most since 1978. If history is lacking, variety is not, and more wineries are in the planning stage.

Au Bon Climat is the label of Clendenen-Tolmach Vintners, which occupies a former dairy building in the midst of Los Alamos Vineyards. Partners Jim Clendenen and Adam Tolmach don't own the vineyard, but their winery lease includes first choice of selected vine blocks each harvest. Their inaugural vintage was 1982.

The wines are handmade by methods the partners observed in rustic French cellars. For example, they don't crush their grapes. Instead, the Chardonnay is gently pressed, and the juice is fermented in toasted Burgundian barrels. Pinot Noir bunches are fermented whole, after being trodden lightly underfoot (sterile boots are worn), and the wine is then aged in Burgundian cooperage.

Only these two varietals are produced. Because the winery is strictly a two-man show, visits are by appointment only.

Austin Cellars occupies a no-nonsense metal shed in the rolling hill country near Los Alamos. Owner and winemaker Anthony Austin represents the fourth generation of an Alexander Valley winegrowing family. Seeking greener vineyards, perhaps with a bit of limestone in the soil, he ventured south to found his own winery in 1983.

There are no visitor facilities at the Austin ranch proper, but there is a tasting room in Los Olivos where visitors may taste Chardonnay, Sauvignon Blanc, Riesling, a rare example of Cabernet Franc Blanc, and Pinot Noir. Grapes are purchased from established local vineyards. In propitious years, Austin takes the trouble to turn out botrytised Riesling and Sauvignon Blanc (see the special feature, *Botrytis cinerea,* the noble mold," on page 113).

Ballard Canyon Winery sits in the shade of a fine old oak tree partway up a long, gentle, vine-clad slope.

A small winery, it has stainless steel fermentors, office, and lab in a prefabricated metal building, and French oak barrels in a wood-frame lean-to attached to the rear. Tours are informal and can be quick. Tasting, on the other hand, tends to be leisurely. In fair weather, the proprietors prefer to present their wines on a deck beneath the same oak that shades the winery buildings.

The owning Gene Hallock family made the first Ballard Canyon wines in 1978. The roster includes regular and botrytised Riesling, Chardonnay, Muscat Canelli, and white and red Cabernet Sauvignons.

Brander Winery is an established specialist in the region. It offers only estate wines from grapes native to France. Sauvignon Blanc and Chardonnay dominate a small production. There are tiny lots of Cabernet Sauvignon, Cabernet Franc, and Merlot.

Owner-winemaker C. Frederic Brander has been making wine in the area since 1976. His own cellar dates from 1981.

The brown-painted winery, visible from State Highway 154 but approachable only via Refugio Road, is an ingenious adaptation of a pole barn. Tall and steep-roofed, it has a small open-walled crushing and fermenting area at one end. The aging cellar full of French oak barrels and bottled wines uses a far larger proportion of the space, in part because Brander is a proponent of starting fermentations in tanks, then moving quickly to barrels for the major part of that process. His reasons for doing so take up a fair part of the tour.

Byron Winery is set like a knotty-pine jewel at the mouth of Tepusquet Canyon near Santa Maria. Visitors view it initially over 6 acres of Chardonnay vines planted along a pond (a duck pond, in season). Byron Ken Brown, who acquired his practical experience during a 10-year stint as founding winemaker at Zaca Mesa Winery, runs the winery built by several partners in 1984.

The structure dutifully recalls the classic California barn, but with cleaner, more modern lines. The tasting room, also knotty pine, gives way to a barrel room packed with French oak cooperage. Behind that is stainless steel territory, with the crush pad out back. Tours, tasting, and sales are offered daily.

The Byron roster includes Sauvignon Blanc, Chardonnay (in both stainless steel and wood-fermented styles), Pinot Noir, and Cabernet Sauvignon. A proprietary Blanc de Noir blends Gamay and Riesling. Picnic enthusiasts will appreciate the wide, grassy area by the edge of the canyon, overlooking Tepusquet Creek, which runs year 'round.

J. Carey Cellars looks like one of the oldest wineries in the region because it is housed in a 50-year-old barn painted exactly the correct shade of red. In fact, the first winemaking was in 1978.

The much-refurbished original barn holds stainless steel fermentors and oak upright tanks. An expansion at the rear holds French oak barrels for final aging of the wines. Tasting goes on in an informal corner of the fermentation cellar directly inside the door. Picnic tables are around at the other end of the building, next to the crushing area.

The winery and adjoining vineyard were founded by a trio of Dr. J.s, all physicians, not NBA forwards: Dr. James Carey, Sr., and his sons, Dr. James, Jr., and Dr. Joseph. Brooks and Kate Firestone acquired the winery in 1986 and continue to make varietal wines largely from the 25-acre estate vineyard.

Firestone Vineyard's winery building soars dramatically above the southernmost ridgeline of the mesa called Zaca. Rooflines set at varying angles to one another give the place a bold, sculptured quality. Beneath those roofs the architectural drama continues. The highest peak gives the fermenting room an almost cathedral atmosphere, where the lowest eave swoops so close to earth that barrels can be stacked only two high along the downhill wall, and then only because the floor drops a level to make a separate gallery.

Well-trained tour guides explain winemaking from beginning to end, starting with vineyards that surround the cellars, and ending with tasting in a wood-walled room in which an upper set of windows looks out to nearby hills, while a lower set gives views into the cool darkness of a wood-aging cellar.

Founded in 1974, Firestone is the largest winery in the Santa Ynez Valley and likely to remain so for some time to come. A partnership of the Leonard Firestone family and Suntory International Ltd., the firm offers estate-grown varietal wines, including Chardonnay, Gewürztraminer, Sauvignon Blanc, Riesling, Cabernet Sauvignon, Pinot Noir, and Merlot.

The Gainey Vineyard offers visitors the equivalent of several UC Davis crash courses in the ways and means of wine production. The Daniel Gainey family, who also breed Arabian horses on the 2,000-acre Santa Ynez Valley ranch, eschewed compromise in designing their dream winery and equipping it with the world's most sophisticated hardware. They made their first wines from the vintage of 1984.

Visitors follow the wine from bud-break to bottle, beginning in a demonstration vineyard that offers side-by-side comparison of the ranch's six grape varieties and the various methods employed in growing them. Back in the well-lit and immaculate winery, such marvels as computerized temperature-controlled fermentation are shown and explained.

After all that, the wines may be appraised with heightened understanding in a comfortable tasting room furnished with French antiques by Robin Gainey. Current offerings include Chardonnay, Sauvignon Blanc, Riesling, and Cabernet Sauvignon.

Houtz Vineyards demonstrates what can happen when innocent, well-meaning people start looking for a place to live in wine country.

David and Margaret Houtz moved to their little farm near Los Olivos in the late 1970s. Before they knew it, the mysterious wine bug had bitten them, and in 1981 they found themselves planting 16 acres of vines. Three years later they opened a winery.

The Houtz winery is a typical California redwood barn. An undivided interior space contains four stainless steel tanks on one side and stacked French oak barrels on the other. In 1986 a new cellar was built into the hillside for energy-efficient barrel aging.

Estate-grown wines include Chardonnay, Sauvignon Blanc, and Cabernet Sauvignon. There is also Chenin Blanc (blended with Chardonnay) from a neighboring vineyard. Margaret Houtz' rose garden amplifies the appeal of an already picturesque picnic spot that, like the tasting room, is open to all comers on weekends; weekday use requires advance notice.

Rancho Sisquoc hides away about as well as a winery can. It is deep in the Sisquoc River canyon, two miles beyond public roads and about halfway between the town of Los Olivos and the village of Sisquoc.

Most California vineyard properties are known as ranches. This one puts the rest in the shade, not because of its 211 acres of vines, but because of the other 38,000 acres, mostly used for grazing cattle.

The winery building is quietly unobtrusive, hidden among older work buildings and dwellings at ranch headquarters, as the vines are hidden in rangeland. Still, even as a miniature cog in a giant wheel, the cellars are pleasing to visit.

The first crusher is nailed to one wall of the cozy tasting room. It is a baseball bat, too short and light to do the work now, but not by much.

Behind the tasting room, with its front wall of local river rock, lies the small barrel-aging cellar. Fermentors, presses, and other working gear are in the other wing of an L-shaped, board-and-batten building.

Behind the winery is a pleasant picnic lawn. All around it, the ranchhouse grounds come close to being an unofficial arboretum, with oaks, peppers, palms, peaches, avocados, pecans, and pines growing in harmonious confusion.

Although the ranch goes back beyond the turn of the century, the first major block of vines dates from only 1970. Owner James Flood of San Francisco bonded the winery just in time for the harvest of 1977.

The list of wines includes Franken Riesling, Johannisberg Riesling, and Cabernet Sauvignon, among other varietals.

Ross Keller Winery like several other relatively new wineries, began in three bays in one of those rent-to-fit warehouses that have sprung up through the state during the past decade. In 1982 owners Howard and Jacqueline Tanner moved to a new winery on 20 acres in Nipomo; a separate storage warehouse was added the following year.

Wines, from grapes purchased locally, include Chardonnay, Riesling, red and white Zinfandel, and Pinot Noir, and Cabernet Sauvignon.

Not incidentally, the name translates from German as Horse Cellar, and is a nod to the proprietors' principal occupation—racing harness horses.

Sanford Winery combines elements of the newest and oldest in Santa Ynez Valley viticulture. As a partner in the Sanford ·& Benedict Vineyards (see page 133), Richard Sanford planted the valley's first modern-day vineyards in 1971. A decade later, he and his wife, Thekla, began producing their own wines in a Buellton industrial space, purchasing grapes from established South Coast vineyards.

The Sanfords bought their 738-acre Rancho El Jabali in 1982, renovated an old house on the property for themselves, and began constructing an adobe winery and planting vines. The year 1986 saw the completion of their winery and a separate tasting room, and fermentation of the first estate-grown wines.

The roster of Sanford varietals, labeled with colorful Sebastian Titus paintings of California wildflowers, includes Chardonnay, Sauvignon Blanc, Vin Gris (a Pinot Noir rosé), Merlot, and Pinot Noir.

Santa Barbara Winery occupies a one-time warehouse near the waterfront of the city for which it is named.

It is the old-timer in the county. Proprietor Pierre LaFond in 1962 bonded his first cellar. The business grew enough to require a move to the present premises

Field Crusher

in 1965. Continued growth has required several expansions since then.

Though the cellars are well apart from the others in the county, the vineyards are not. LaFond grows grapes for his varietal table wines along the lower reaches of the Santa Ynez River west of Buellton. The varietals include Chardonnay, Chenin Blanc, Cabernet Sauvignon, and Zinfandel. All may be tasted at the winery.

Santa Ynez Valley Winery is one of a considerable number of new California cellars housed in old dairy buildings. This bespeaks a trend toward more small wineries and fewer small dairies and saves the pouring of a great many new concrete floors. In this case it also causes a good deal of extra walking for winemakers and visitors alike.

Inside the plain walls at Santa Ynez, bottled wines are stored at one level in two separate rooms; wines aging in oak barrels and stainless steel tanks are at three other levels in two rooms; and the stainless steel fermentors are outdoors on still another level. If the floor plan is a bit unorthodox, the equipment is not, and tours are as instructive here as in other small wineries where the parts come in logical sequence.

Santa Ynez Valley Winery was founded in 1976 by a trio of partners, all residents of the region. Their vineyards—most of them at the winery, some a few miles away at Los Olivos—supply the grapes for a list including Chardonnay, Riesling, Sauvignon Blanc, and Merlot, along with late-harvest wines and a rare Gewürztraminer Port. These wines and the rest of the list may be sampled in a spacious tasting room.

The property, not incidentally, once held the forerunner of St. Mary's College, hence the signpost reading "Old College Ranch" at the head of the entry drive.

Vega Vineyards has its cellars in a classic red barn so close to U.S. 101 south of Buellton that drivers on the freeway sometimes can catch a fleeting whiff of newly fermenting wine during the harvest season.

The old barn and an 1853 adobe house next to it give the property an enduring air, but the winery is a recent development. Owners Bill and Jeri Mosby made their first wines on these premises in 1979, having started the business a year earlier in leased space.

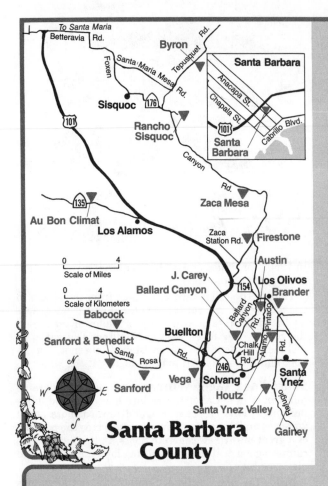

Santa Barbara County

Au Bon Climat. From U.S. 101 at Los Alamos, W 5.1 mi. on State 135 to winery at 2625 (Office: 1131 Nopal St., Santa Barbara, CA 93103) Tel (805) 344-3035. IT by appt.

Austin Cellars. Tasting room: From U.S. 101 N of Buellton, SE 2.7 mi. on State 154 to Los Olivos, S .1 on Grand Ave. (2923 Grand Ave., Los Olivos, CA 93441) Tel (805) 688-9665. Daily 10-4. Ta.

Babcock Winery. From U.S. 101 at Buellton, W 9.2 mi. on State 246 to winery (5175 Hwy. 246, Lompoc, CA 93436) Tel (805) 736-1455. Daily 11-4 or by appt. IT/Ta.

Ballard Canyon Winery. From downtown Solvang, 2.8 mi. N on Atterdag Rd./Chalk Hill Rd./Ballard Canyon Rd. (1825 Ballard Canyon Rd., Solvang, CA 93463) Tel (805) 688-7585. Daily 11-4. IT/Ta.

Brander Winery. From U.S. 101 N of Buellton, 3 mi. E on State 154 to Roblar Ave./Refugio Rd. intersection, NW .3 mi. on Refugio Rd. (P.O. Box 92, Los Olivos, CA 93441) Tel (805) 688-2455. M-F 11-4, Sa-Su 10-4. IT/Ta.

Byron Winery. From U.S. 101 at Santa Maria, E 7.3 mi. on Betteravia Rd./State 176, SE 4.2 mi. on Santa Maria Mesa Rd., N .4 on Tepusquet Rd. to winery (5230 Tepusquet Rd., Santa Maria, CA 93454) Tel (805) 937-7288. Picnic. Daily 10-4. IT/Ta.

J. Carey Cellars. From Solvang, 1 mi. E on State 246 to Alamo Pintado Rd., N 3 mi. (1711 Alamo Pintado Rd., Solvang, CA 93463) Tel (805) 688-8554. Picnic. Daily 10-4. IT/Ta.

Firestone Vineyard. From U.S. 101 N of Buellton, 2 mi. E on Zaca Station Rd. to 5017 (P.O. Box 244, Los Olivos, CA 93441) Tel (805) 688-3940. M-Sa 10-4. GT/Ta.

The Gainey Vineyard. From Solvang, E 5.2 mi. on State 246 to winery (3950 Hwy. 246, Santa Ynez, CA 93460) Tel (805) 688-0558. Daily 10-5. GT/Ta.

Houtz Vineyards. From U.S. 101 N of Buellton, SE 4.3 mi. on State 154, W .2 mi. on Roblar Ave., SW .3 on Ontiveros Rd. to winery (2670 Ontiveros Rd., Los Olivos, CA 93441) Tel (805) 688-8664. Picnic. Sa-Su 12-4 or by appt. IT/TA.

Rancho Sisquoc. From U.S. 101 N of Buellton, 2 mi. NE on Zaca Station Rd. to Foxen Canyon Rd., N 18 mi. to winery drive, then E 2 mi. (Rt. 1, Box 147, Foxen Canyon Rd., Santa Maria, CA 93454) Tel (805) 937-3616. Picnic. Daily 10-4. GT/Ta.

Ross Keller Winery. From U.S. 101, take Nipomo exit, S on frontage road to Southland Road, W to Orchard Ave. to winery drive (985 Orchard Ave., Nipomo, CA 93444) Tel (805) 929-3627. Daily 12-5. IT/Ta. (Outside map area).

Sanford & Benedict Vineyards. 9 mi. W of Buellton on Santa Rosa Rd. (5500 Santa Rosa Rd., Lompoc, CA 93463) Tel (805) 688-8314. GT/Ta by appt.

Sanford Winery. 4.8 mi. W of Buellton on Santa Rosa Rd. (7250 Santa Rosa Rd., Buellton, CA 93427) Tel (805) 688-3300. Picnic. M-Sa 11-4. Ta.

Santa Barbara Winery. From U.S. 101 at Santa Barbara, take Anacapa St. 1 blk. toward the ocean (202 Anacapa St., Santa Barbara, CA 93101) Tel (805) 963-3633. Daily 9:30-5. IT/Ta.

Santa Ynez Valley Winery. From Solvang, E 2 mi. on State 246 to Refugio Rd., S 1 mi. to winery drive (343 Refugio Rd., Santa Ynez, CA 93460) Tel (805) 688-8381. Daily 10-4. GT/Ta.

Vega Vineyards. From downtown Buellton, .7 mi. S on Santa Rosa Rd. (9496 Santa Rosa Rd., Buellton, CA 93427) Tel (805) 688-2415. Daily 10-4. IT/Ta. GT by appt.

Zaca Mesa Winery. From U.S. 101 N of Buellton, E 9 mi. on Zaca Station/Foxen Canyon Rds. to 6905 (P.O. Box 547, Los Olivos, CA 93441) Tel (805) 688-9339. Picnic. M-F 10-4, Sa-Su 10-5 May-Jul; daily 10-5 Jul-Oct; daily 10-4 Nov-Apr. GT/Ta.

Wineries Not on Map— Restricted or No Visitor Facilities

Douglas Vineyards. (P.O. Box 532, Los Olivos, CA 93441.)

Qupé. (P.O. Box 440, Los Olivos, CA 93441) Tel (805) 688-2477. By appt. only.

Key: GT (guided tour); IT (informal tour); Ta (tasting).

Visitors can have an informal look around a thoughtfully designed cellar as a prelude to tasting. The Mosbys used a little slope at the rear of the building to great mechanical advantage. Their bin dump sits directly above the grape hopper, which in turn looks down to the crusher. Similarly, the press sits over a conveyor that hauls pomace to a still lower spot. Inside, the winery is mostly stainless steel tanks because the primary production is Gewürztraminer and Riesling. A small collection of oak between fermentors and cased goods is for Chardonnay and Pinot Noir. All four wines are from winery-owned vineyards nearby.

Zaca Mesa Winery offers a complete look at a well-designed, flawlessly equipped cellar of the sort that draws bits and pieces from everywhere and still manages to look as native as the oak trees growing on grassy hills all around it.

Wine follows a wayward, international course through a prim, cedar-sided refinement of a classic California barn. It begins at the rear in a new, French-designed crusher that looks like cockle shells whirling around inside a metal sleeve, advances to an equally modern German press, or to American stainless steel fermentors located where the building's waist pinches in. It ages in French oak barrels or American oak tanks toward the front of the building before heading to the rear again for bottling on a German-made line, sometimes in Canadian glass. Visitors follow the same route, though more quickly.

Zaca Mesa nestles into a small hollow along the Foxen Canyon Road side of the mesa from which it takes its Spanish name.

Weathered wood on some inside walls reveals a 1981 expansion of the original cellar of 1978. One of the added parts is a spacious, high-ceilinged tasting hall in the rear wing. Available in it are Chardonnay, Riesling, Cabernet Sauvignon, Pinot Noir, and other varietals from wine-affiliated vineyards up on top of the mesa proper.

Tree-shaded picnic tables are located just outside the tasting room and up on a gentle slope behind the winery.

More Wineries. Santa Barbara County, like neighboring San Luis Obispo, is developing rapidly. Some of its existing wineries are changing course. New ones continue to appear.

Babcock Winery sits on 40 acres near Lompoc, in a cool area best suited to white grapes. Owners Mona and Bryan Babcock make Chardonnay, Sauvignon Blanc (both barrel-fermented), Riesling, and Gewürztraminer. They grow apples, too, a good reason for a fall visit.

Douglas Vineyards, formerly La Zaca, is the label of vineyard owner Douglas Kramer, who has his wines made in leased space, then returned to their home ranch for aging. There are no visitor facilities.

Qupé was founded by Bob Lindquist in 1982. The name is the Chumash Indian word for California's golden poppy. Lindquist has a passion for Syrah wine, and is one of its few producers in California.

Sanford & Benedict Vineyards made its first wines in 1976. Now under the direction of Michael Benedict, the winery, located on Santa Rosa Road between Buellton and Lompoc, continues with its original specialties: Chardonnay and Pinot Noir, plus Cabernet Sauvignon and a Riesling called La Purisima, all from the surrounding vineyards. Because of a small staff and the remote location, visitors must have appointments. The winery asks, to use its words, "serious inquiries only."

The California Central Coast Wine Growers Association maintains an up-to-date list of visitable wineries in Santa Barbara and San Luis Obispo counties. Copies may be ordered from the association, 3201 Skyway Dr., Suite 103, Santa Maria, CA 93455. There is a fee.

Other Than Wineries

This region, though new as a wine district, has been a major destination for tourists for years. Solvang alone draws as many as five million visitors annually with its Danish flavors.

The *Sunset Southern California Travel Guide* provides detailed information on this town, the missions of Santa Ynez and La Purisima, and ocean-shore parks and resorts at Santa Barbara and Gaviota.

For picnickers, the closest parks to wineries are Santa Rosa County Park, on Santa Rosa Road west of Buellton, and Los Alamos County Park, on the west outskirts of Los Alamos town. The biggest, most versatile park in the region is some miles east of Santa Ynez via State Highway 154. It is Lake Cachuma County Park, which has swimming and boating as well as picnic grounds.

Accommodations and restaurants are abundant in and around Solvang, Buellton, and Santa Maria. For lists, write to the Solvang Chamber of Commerce, P.O. Box 465, Solvang, CA 93463, or to the Santa Maria Chamber of Commerce, P.O. Box 377, Santa Maria, CA 93456.

Plotting a Route

U.S. Highway 101 neatly divides the vineyarded reaches of northern Santa Barbara County into western and eastern sectors. It is a freeway for the whole of its run through the winemaking district, though rolling hill country keeps it from being monotonously straight and out of touch with the countryside.

When speed is required, the freeway can be used in getting from one winery to another. However, local roads east of the freeway are bucolic, but straight and uncrowded enough to add very little time and very few miles to a tour, while improving the scenery and the feeling of being in the country.

As the map on page 132 shows, most of the county's wineries can be reached on a single loop with its ends at Buellton and Santa Maria.

From Santa Ynez, Refugio Road connects with State Highway 154 at Los Olivos; from Los Olivos, Foxen Canyon Road rambles north to a junction with State Highway 176. The latter rejoins U.S. 101 at Santa Maria. Getting to all the wineries on or east of U.S. 101 involves a minimum of backtracking. Only two cellars are any distance west of the freeway.

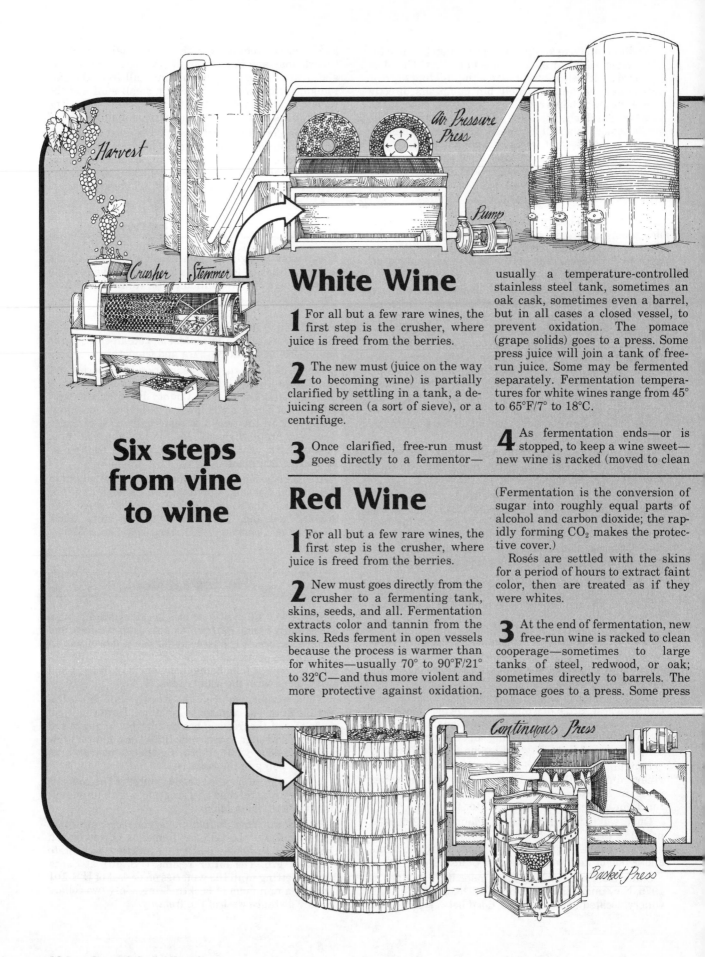

Harvest

Crusher *Stemmer*

Air Pressure Press

Pump

Six steps from vine to wine

White Wine

1 For all but a few rare wines, the first step is the crusher, where juice is freed from the berries.

2 The new must (juice on the way to becoming wine) is partially clarified by settling in a tank, a de-juicing screen (a sort of sieve), or a centrifuge.

3 Once clarified, free-run must goes directly to a fermentor—

usually a temperature-controlled stainless steel tank, sometimes an oak cask, sometimes even a barrel, but in all cases a closed vessel, to prevent oxidation. The pomace (grape solids) goes to a press. Some press juice will join a tank of free-run juice. Some may be fermented separately. Fermentation temperatures for white wines range from 45° to 65°F/7° to 18°C.

4 As fermentation ends—or is stopped, to keep a wine sweet—new wine is racked (moved to clean

Red Wine

1 For all but a few rare wines, the first step is the crusher, where juice is freed from the berries.

2 New must goes directly from the crusher to a fermenting tank, skins, seeds, and all. Fermentation extracts color and tannin from the skins. Reds ferment in open vessels because the process is warmer than for whites—usually 70° to 90°F/21° to 32°C—and thus more violent and more protective against oxidation.

(Fermentation is the conversion of sugar into roughly equal parts of alcohol and carbon dioxide; the rapidly forming CO_2 makes the protective cover.)

Rosés are settled with the skins for a period of hours to extract faint color, then are treated as if they were whites.

3 At the end of fermentation, new free-run wine is racked to clean cooperage—sometimes to large tanks of steel, redwood, or oak; sometimes directly to barrels. The pomace goes to a press. Some press

Continuous Press

Basket Press

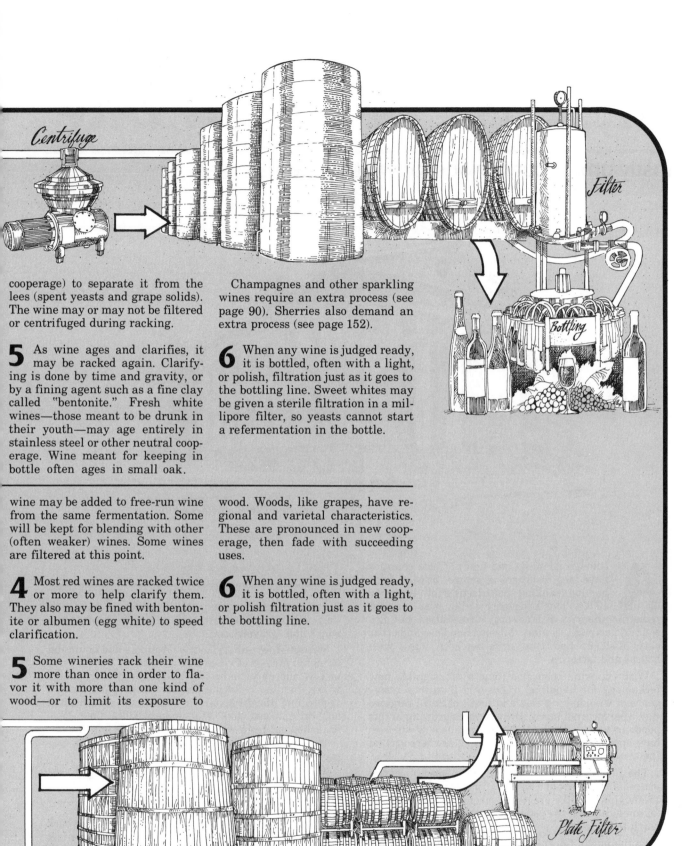

Centrifuge

Filter

Bottling

Pump

Plate Filter

cooperage) to separate it from the lees (spent yeasts and grape solids). The wine may or may not be filtered or centrifuged during racking.

5 As wine ages and clarifies, it may be racked again. Clarifying is done by time and gravity, or by a fining agent such as a fine clay called "bentonite." Fresh white wines—those meant to be drunk in their youth—may age entirely in stainless steel or other neutral cooperage. Wine meant for keeping in bottle often ages in small oak.

Champagnes and other sparkling wines require an extra process (see page 90). Sherries also demand an extra process (see page 152).

6 When any wine is judged ready, it is bottled, often with a light, or polish, filtration just as it goes to the bottling line. Sweet whites may be given a sterile filtration in a millipore filter, so yeasts cannot start a refermentation in the bottle.

---

wine may be added to free-run wine from the same fermentation. Some will be kept for blending with other (often weaker) wines. Some wines are filtered at this point.

4 Most red wines are racked twice or more to help clarify them. They also may be fined with bentonite or albumen (egg white) to speed clarification.

5 Some wineries rack their wine more than once in order to flavor it with more than one kind of wood—or to limit its exposure to

wood. Woods, like grapes, have regional and varietal characteristics. These are pronounced in new cooperage, then fade with succeeding uses.

6 When any wine is judged ready, it is bottled, often with a light, or polish filtration just as it goes to the bottling line.

The East & North Bay

Mostly urban, but famous for white wines

1852
Benicia State Capitol

Although Alameda and Contra Costa counties have long traditions as sources of wine, both had long sinking spells lasting into the early 1970s. The Livermore Valley was the last remaining district with not only a reputation, but also a sizable acreage, in vines. Mission San Jose and other early districts had long since replaced vines with houses and factories.

With the wine boom has come a considerable new technology for handling grapes and a curious resurgence of winemaking east and north of San Francisco Bay. There are not many new vineyards growing in this populous part of the world, but numerous new wineries have sprung up to use grapes grown elsewhere around the state.

The Livermore Valley, with its open spaces, continues to look the part of a wine district, as it has since the 1880s. However, the greater number of East Bay wineries are located on the populous bay shore from Fremont north to Berkeley.

To the north, Contra Costa County and neighboring Solano County make a tidy loop drive that touches pretty vineyard country as well as wineries.

The wine bug has even bitten in Marin County, where two established wineries were preparing to welcome several fledglings in the spring of 1987.

The Livermore Valley

Say "Livermore" to students of California wine, and they will make the automatic associations of "white wine" and "gravelly soil."

Pioneer vineyardists Charles Wetmore and Louis Mel brought cuttings of vines from Chateau d'Yquem early in Livermore's wine history and made Sauternes-like wines from the resulting grapes. The original Carl H. Wente and the first James Concannon concentrated on white wines, too. Winemakers since then have branched out from white wines but never left them.

The entire county of Alameda produces much less than 1 percent of the state's wine each year.

The Wineries

The pioneer names of Concannon and Wente reach back to Livermore's earliest days of winegrowing, the last two names from that era. In recent years several other, smaller wineries have joined them.

Concannon Vineyard for almost a hundred years has proved conclusively that the Irish can make wine if given a reasonable climate to do it in.

As with any Irish enterprise, there is a fine story about how Concannon got started. In the 1880s the then Archbishop of San Francisco, Joseph S. Alemany, was a bit short of sacramental wine. His solution was to suggest to James Concannon, printer and stamp maker, that he should buy a vineyard and make wines. Concannon had a flexible enough mind to make the professional jump easily.

While the printing talent has lapsed in all subsequent Concannons, some of the family remain active in management of the cellars in which four generations of them have grown up.

For the most part, the cellars appear unhurried and informal. The oldest part of the building dates from the early years of the winery. Subsequent additions have been made out of need for space rather than from any desire to add frills. Some sections of wall are brick; others are clapboard. A fair proportion is made of corrugated iron to match the roof. Inside, old oak upright tanks and oval casks from the founder's day run in orderly but crowded rows.

Appearances aside, the winery always has had an eye to the future. Not only does it keep abreast of research at UC Davis and other centers but also actively participates in the research itself. For example, Concannon has contributed a few acres from its small vineyards to serve as test plots for grape varieties not commonly grown in Livermore and for experimental combinations of rootstocks with fruiting varieties.

White wines under the Concannon label include Chenin Blanc, Sauvignon Blanc, and Livermore Riesling. Among the reds are Cabernet Sauvignon, Petite Sirah (which the winery was the first to offer as a California varietal), and Zinfandel. From time to time the owners offer special lots of Sauvignon Blanc, Cabernet Sauvignon, and Petite Sirah in limited bottlings.

The Concannon tasting room is as easygoing as the rest of the property. A large room lined with rough-sawn redwood, it has a small tasting bar at one side, and some picnic foods and gifts along the other two walls. The bottling room is where the fourth wall might be. On special occasions the regular bar is supplemented with extra tables. Across a small parking lot from the tasting room door, picnic tables under shading trees look out across winery-owned vineyards.

Fenestra Winery has operated under numerous identities, in several different places, since Lanny and Fran Replogle began making wine together in the mid-1960s. Their first commercial vintage was 1976; they came to their current site, a centenarian ghost winery that they lease from the Catholic Church, in 1980.

George True originally built the compact brick, stone, and wood winery in 1889, but it fell idle in the wake of Prohibition. The return to its original function had to wait until the Replogles excavated considerable evidence of the structure's long misuse as a barn.

Historical restoration was not their primary concern. Fenestra is a working cellar, although its past and the rustic setting impart plenty of natural romance. The lower story, a brick chamber built into the hillside, has just enough room amid massed cooperage for a make-shift foul-weather tasting room; tasters migrate out to the crush pad under clear skies.

The roster includes Chardonnay, Riesling, white Zinfandel, Cabernet Sauvignon, and Merlot, all from North Coast vineyards.

Livermore Valley Cellars is by miles the smallest established winery in the district.

The property of Chris Lagiss, it occupies a small prefabricated metal building at the rear of the family home. Both buildings are surrounded by the winery's 34-acre vineyard.

Tours do not take much time here. Stainless steel fermentors run along one wall of the winery, barrels along the other, and cased goods or new bottles pretty much fill the middle. The press is out back.

Tasting, on the other hand, may last awhile. The tasting counter is set up next to a three-car parking area and beneath an overhanging roof outside the small building in which Lagiss stores wines available for sale. Trees cast more shade and flowers grow around the perimeter. Hand-lettered signs carry quotes from wine sage Maynard Amerine, advice from the proprietor, and current prices of a roster of white wines grown on the property. Chardonnay, Grey Riesling, and Sauvignon Blanc are the mainstays.

Stony Ridge Winery was a label without a permanent home in spring 1987. Wines were being custom-crushed at an East Bay winery pending the scheduled 1988 completion of a winery by owners Dominic and Monica Scotto, members of a local wine family.

The label began in a building constructed as the Ruby Hill Winery in 1887. Founder John Crellin placed the fine, stone building into a gentle hillside with vineyards sloping away from its skirts. Ernest Ferrario bought it from the Crellin family in 1921 and held on through a little bit of thick and a lot of thin until 1973, when he sold it to the Southern Pacific Land Company. The old property was doomed when a computer company bought it for offices in 1980; the firm lasted only long enough to rip out Crellin's original vineyards. The Scottos purchased the label and some equipment in 1985.

Wente Bros. is the oldest wine business and owns the two newest working wineries in the Livermore Valley, one of those temporal paradoxes that typify vinous California.

The first Wente in Livermore was Carl H. Wente, who arrived in 1883, a year or so ahead of James Concannon. The two men were close in age. Subsequent generations of the two families have grown up within a stone's throw of each other. But there is no stone throwing; they get along so well that it was a long-standing tradition for the oldest child to take charge of both broods when the parents went somewhere together.

The Wentes, on the opposite side of Tesla Road from Concannon and a few hundred yards east, retained their original cellar until 1966. By then the old wood frame building had become a small part of the winery and had to yield to a more efficient structure. With the original building's dismantling, all of Wente took on a modern appearance. There have been subsequent additions to the concrete cellars; the age of the ivy on various walls helps to peg the different construction dates.

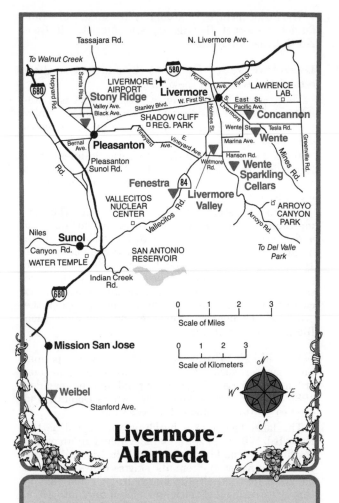

Livermore- Alameda

Concannon Vineyard. From Livermore flagpole, S 2 mi. on Livermore Ave./Tesla Rd. (4590 Tesla Rd., Livermore, CA 94550) Tel (415) 447-3760. Picnic. M-Sa 10-5, Su 12-5. GT/Ta.

Fenestra Winery. N side of Vallecitos Rd./State 84 3.8 mi. SW of Livermore (83 E. Vallecitos Rd., Livermore, CA 94550) Tel (415) 447-5246. By appt. only.

Livermore Valley Cellars. From Vallecitos Rd., S .5 mi. on Wetmore Rd. to winery drive (1508 Wetmore Rd., Livermore, CA 94550) Tel (415) 447-1751. Daily 11-5. GT/IT/Ta.

Stony Ridge Winery. Tasting room on Main St. in Pleasanton, just W of St. John St. (818 Main St., Pleasanton, CA 94566) Tel (415) 484-4870. M-F 11-6, Sa-Su 11-5, Ta.

Weibel Champagne Vineyards. From Mission San Jose, S 1 mi. on State 238, E on Stanford Ave. .5 mi. to winery at 1250 (P.O. Box 3398, Mission San Jose, CA 94539) Tel (415) 656-2340. Picnic. GT: M-F 10-3. Ta: daily 10-5.

Wente Bros. From Livermore flagpole, S 2.5 mi. on Livermore Ave./Tesla Rd. (5565 Tesla Rd., Livermore, CA 94550) Tel (415) 447-3603. GT: M-Sa 10, 11, 1, 2, 3, Su 11, 2, 3. Ta: M-Sa 9-4:30, Su 11-4:30.

Wente Bros. Sparkling Wine Cellars. From I-580, Portola Ave. exit, SE .5 mi., E on North L St. through Livermore, S 3 mi. on Arroyo Rd. to winery (5050 Arroyo Rd., Livermore, CA 94550) Tel (415) 447-3694. Restaurant (447-3696). Daily 11-6:30. GT/Ta.

Key: GT (guided tour); IT (informal tour); Ta (tasting).

Beginning in the late 1970s, a new sparkling wine facility began to take shape just a few miles away on Arroyo Road. Built atop extensive sandstone aging caves on a knoll overlooking gardens and rolling vineyards, the sparkling wine cellar has its own visitor center and an elegant upscale restaurant, opened in 1986.

Few wineries offer visitors a clearer picture than Wente does of how still and sparkling wines are made from start to finish. Guides on daily tours of both facilities explain the fine points. Following the tours, the wines produced at each facility are available for tasting in the respective hospitality centers.

Among the still wines, the Sauvignon Blanc, Semillon, and Grey Riesling now being made by the fourth generation of Wentes have traditions going back to the earliest days of Livermore.

Other Than Wineries

Reliably warm and sunny, the Livermore Valley has spawned several picnic parks.

The handiest of the lot is Shadow Cliffs Regional Park, nestled into the old arroyo bed alongside Stanley Drive between Livermore and Pleasanton. It has tree-shaded picnic sites, some playground gear, and a bit of water to splash in. Stanley Drive, not incidentally, has a bike path connecting the two towns.

Del Valle Regional Park, another part of the fine East Bay Regional Parks system, hides away in beautiful rolling hills southeast of Concannon and Wente. The park encompasses much of a reservoir lake's shoreline. It has abundant picnic sites in the shade of oaks, as well as swimming beaches and a boat launch. The park entrance is a bit more than 7 miles south of Tesla Road by way of Mines and Del Valle roads.

A lower-key park is Arroyo Canyon, on the road that passes the old Cresta Blanca winery and the Wente Bros. sparkling wine facility.

At Sunol, the San Francisco Water District maintains picnic tables and other comforts around its water temple. The entrance is at the intersection of State 21 and State 84, just at the head of Niles Canyon.

Pleasanton's main street has an early American flavor about it still, in spite of the town's being ringed with contemporary housing tracts.

The Alameda County Fair, held in early summer at Pleasanton, demonstrates that a good many cows remain in the area—and also encompasses winemaking.

For information on restaurants and overnight accommodations, write to the Livermore Chamber of Commerce, P.O. Box 671, Livermore, CA 94550.

Plotting a Route

The Livermore Valley is crisscrossed by a pair of freeways. Interstate Highway 580 goes east-west; Interstate Highway 680 runs north-south. One or the other will get a visitor into the region from almost anywhere.

I-580 turns toward Livermore from the San Francisco Bay basin at Hayward and connects with Interstate Highway 5 in the San Joaquin Valley. Heading east, the first real vista is the Livermore Valley, which springs into full view at the crest of a long upgrade. A second and much larger panorama is the San Joaquin Valley from the top of Altamont Pass east of Livermore.

I-680 courses for most of its length in the shelter of the East Bay hills. The route begins at its junction with Interstate Highway 80 and ends at its intersection with U.S. Highway 101 at San Jose, so it is useful to visitors from the Sacramento Valley or the South Bay.

For the traveler heading up to Livermore from the south end of San Francisco Bay, State Highway 84, through Niles Canyon, offers a low-speed alternate.

South Alameda

Alameda County's southwest corner was a flourishing vineyard district before Prohibition and remained a fairly sizable one through the years before World War II. But by 1965, the roster of surviving wineries and vineyards had dwindled to one, and there it remains.

Weibel Champagne Vineyards leans east into a steep and photogenic line of hills and looks west out over baylands at Warm Springs. Look from Weibel toward the hills and time has changed nothing: except for vine rows, the hand of humanity shows but little. Look the other way and the story is different: westward, beyond a tract of houses, lies a vast automobile assembly plant. It is the south end of an industrial-residential chain that runs unbroken to Oakland and beyond.

Being caught on the boundary between the worlds causes certain difficulties for the Weibels, but they go on in good humor at a winery that once belonged to Governor Leland Stanford.

Some of the buildings still would be recognizable to Stanford if he could stop by today, but the originals of 1869 have been supplemented since the Swiss family Weibel acquired the site in 1940. The winery is several hundred yards off State Highway 238. The access road, bordered on one side by eucalyptus trees and on the other by olive trees, runs alongside the vineyard until it comes to the small adobe-style building which houses Weibel's tasting room. Just north of it, a long, low, red brick building houses all of the champagne-making and most of the stored still wines aging in bottles. Uphill from these are two rows of stainless steel aging tanks, the outdoor sherry soleras, and the original winery building. A good deal of the redwood and oak cooperage inside holds Weibel table wines, most of them made at a new-in-1973 Weibel winery near Ukiah, in Mendocino County (see page 67), and transported to Mission San Jose for aging and bottling. Some wine is still made at Mission San Jose.

Selected wines from an extensive roster are available for tasting. There are several arbor-shaded picnic tables alongside the tasting room.

North Alameda

There is no growing of grapes in Berkeley or Emeryville, but the industrialized east shore of San Francisco Bay is right in the center of other places where grapes grow abundantly and well: Napa and Sonoma are not far north; Livermore is across the hills to the east; Santa Clara, Monterey, and San Luis Obispo stretch away to the south. Once freeways, field crushers, and other technical solutions had come into being, no great difficulties stood in the way of making wine downtown.

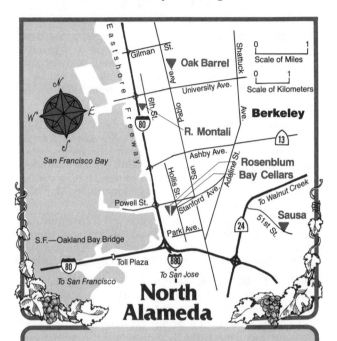

Bay Cellars. From I-80, E .4 mi. on Powell St., S 1 blk. on Hollis St. W on Stanford Ave. to winery at end of street (1401 Stanford Ave., Emeryville, CA 94608) Tel (415) 526-0469. By appt. only.

R. Montali Winery. From I-80, E .5 mi. on University Ave., S 1 blk. on 6th St., W 4 blks. on Addison St. to winery (600 Addison St. at Aquatic Park, Berkeley, CA 94710) Tel (415) 540-6152. Daily 12-6. Ta. GT by appt.

Oak Barrel. From I-80, E on University Ave., N on San Pablo Ave. (1443 San Pablo Ave., Berkeley, CA 94702) Tel (415) 849-0400. M-Sa 10-6:30.

Rosenblum Cellars. From I-80, E .4 mi. on Powell St., S 1 blk. on Hollis St., W on Stanford Ave. to winery at end of street (1401 Stanford Ave., Emeryville, CA 94608) Tel (415) 653-2355. By appt. only.

Sausa Winery. From State 24, SE 1 mi. on 51st St. to winery. (426 - 51st St., Oakland, CA 94609) Tel (415) 655-5262. GT/Ta by appt.

Wineries Not on Map— Restricted or No Visitor Facilities

Fretter Wine Cellars, Inc. (805 Camelia St., Berkeley, CA 94710) Tel (415) 525-3232. By invitation only.

Piedmont Cellars. (429 Linda Ave., Piedmont, CA 94611) Tel (415) 654-3617. No visitors.

Key: GT (guided tour); IT (informal tour); Ta (tasting).

And, lo, an urban wine country grew up in the East Bay, in one-time bakeries, warehouses, and other converted structures.

Most visitors come to this densely populated district to see a specific winery. None come for bucolic charm.

The Wineries

Like many another downtown business group, the East Bay wineries can be difficult to notice at first glance. The added fact that several are too small to court any visitors except customers buying wine means that the district is of real interest mainly to serious bibbers.

R. Montali Winery is a plain operation in a magnificent urban setting. The views across San Francisco Bay from the winery site near Berkeley's Aquatic Park rival any wine country landscapes, while the large metal building is strictly functional. Ralph Montali founded the winery in 1982. The current owners, a corporation headed by Hubert von Wulffen and including Montali, have run the winery since 1986.

Grapes are purchased in Sonoma and Napa counties. The roster includes Chardonnay, Sauvignon Blanc, Pinot Blanc, and Cabernet Sauvignon. The tasting room, a trailer near the winery, is open by appointment.

Oak Barrel, an enterprise located on University Avenue in Berkeley, is both a winery and a supplier of home-winemaking equipment.

There is no tour of a working winery here, but visitors can buy everything they need to start one of their own, along with wine by the barrel or bottle to tide them over while they get started. Proprietor John Bank has a private tasting room that more or less doubles as a clubhouse for some of the area's home winemakers.

More Wineries. Despite an obvious lack of vineyard acreage, the East Bay has hosted a modest winery boom in recent years. The new urban winery is characterized by altruistic motives (wine for wine's sake) and ebullient team effort (friends do much of the work). Most will accommodate visitors by appointment.

Bay Cellars typifies the new wave of urban East Bay wineries. Owners Richard and Carol Rotblatt operate in an Emeryville industrial space, with the whole North Coast at their fingertips. The specialty is Pinot Noir from Carneros district grapes. Chardonnay, Cabernet Sauvignon, and Merlot are also produced, in small quantities. The first crush was in 1982.

Fretter Wine Cellars was bonded in 1977 by Travis Fretter and his father, William, at the family home in Berkeley. Serial vintages of the Fretters' Chardonnay, Pinot Noir, and Merlot present vinous portraits of several fine vineyards. Visits are by invitation only.

Piedmont Cellars was founded by an electronics engineer as a labor of love in 1981. Tiny lots of Chardonnay and Cabernet Sauvignon are produced from selected vineyards. There are no tours or tasting.

Rosenblum Cellars occupies an unlovely but quite efficient industrial space in Emeryville, to which grapes from established North Coast vineyards are brought to make Zinfandel and several other varietals. Small lots of sparkling wine also are produced by Kent

and Kathy Rosenblum, who founded the winery in 1978 with several partners. Visits are by appointment.

Sausa Winery has the distinction of being the only bonded wine producer in Oakland's residential Rockridge neighborhood. Partners Laurence Sausa and Michael McKracken began making varietal wines in Sausa's house in 1984. Gradually the emphasis has shifted toward fruit and berry wines, fermented in a dozen small stainless steel tanks in a former art studio.

Other Than Wineries

Set in the midst of the populous East Bay, these cellars are handy to every sort of diversion from the Oakland A's to an afternoon at the movies, a tour of the Oakland Museum, or picnics in any of dozens of parks. The *Sunset Northern California Travel Guide* provides detailed discussions of the possibilities.

Berkeley Marina, at the foot of University Avenue, provides the handiest picnic sites.

Plotting a Route

Interstate highways 580 and 880 connect to Interstate 80—the Eastshore freeway—at Emeryville. All three of the North Alameda wineries are less than a mile from the freeways. Those visitors who want to try public transportation can take BART and Alameda-Contra Costa Transit coaches.

Contra Costa County

Contra Costa County contained a single producing winery in the spring of 1987. Although it is surrounded by less urbanization than its counterparts in bayside Alameda, it is hardly rural.

Conrad Viano Winery, on one edge of Martinez, has much of the air of a country winery. The family home has a rear corner of the basement set aside for tasting and retail sales. Three other smallish buildings of painted concrete block are behind that and slightly downhill; they are the winery and storage buildings.

Beyond, on the upslope, several acres of vineyard look back at the clustered structures (and at several neighboring residences).

There is not enough gear on hand to call for a guided tour. The tasting room is worth a visit, however. The Vianos have under their well-designed label Chardonnay, Sauvignon Blanc, Zinfandel rosé, Cabernet Sauvignon, Gamay, and Zinfandel (which they prize). Among appetizer and dessert types are Muscatel, Port, and Sherry.

The family bought the vineyard in 1920, founded the winery in 1946, and had to build a bigger cellar in 1967 and an addition in 1971. The third generation of Vianos is at work today.

There is a picnic lawn under a small grove of almonds next to the winery for those who would tarry over a bird and a bottle.

Solano County

No self-respecting geographer would identify Solano County as part of the East Bay. However, Solano County faces Contra Costa County across the Sacramento River, the two neatly connected by a bridge at Martinez and a second upstream at Antioch. Between them, the two counties have enough wineries to make an enjoyable day of touring for those in search of either costly varietals or bargain jug wines.

The Wineries

A short roster of wineries stretches out from Benicia on the west to Fairfield on the east and manages to provide some genuine variety for visitors along the way.

Cadenasso Winery is a traditional stop for wine-bibbers who travel regularly between the San Francisco Bay area and the Sacramento Valley. The one-story, tan-colored winery with its red roof is visible to motorists on I-80 just as they approach the Abernathy Road exit ramp on the west side of Fairfield. The winery contains an eclectic collection of oak ovals and small redwood uprights. The wines can be tasted and purchased in a tidy tasting room.

The tasting room used to occupy the cellar beneath Frank and Joan Cadenasso's home, but the winery outgrew it in 1987. The move to new quarters nearby ended more than 60 years at the same location. Joan currently manages the winery, with son John as winemaker.

Cadenasso began in 1906 when father Giovanni Cadenasso planted vines north of Cordelia. It continued when he moved to Fairfield to plant vines across the street from the present winery. That vineyard became county hospital grounds after the senior Cadenasso sold the land and dismantled the winery as a sensible response to Prohibition.

Cadenasso wines, served for tasting with great pride but no pretense, include Chenin Blanc, Grey Riesling, Chablis, and Sauterne among whites; Rosé; Burgundy, and Cabernet Sauvignon among reds.

Chateau De Leu nestles into an archetypal landscape in California's Coast Ranges. The building looks out across 80 acres of vines and up to grassy hills forming the west side of Green Valley. Inside, the winery is every bit as classically Californian: stainless steel fermentors, tidy rows of French oak barrels, and a handsome tasting room finished in redwood. All this makes the building an especially agreeable surprise, for it is modeled on a half-timbered Alsatian country house.

In another tradition far more Californian than Alsatian, the owning Ben Volkhardt family crushed its first vintage in a half-built winery in 1981, then finished the building and the debut wines together during 1982.

The all-white roster includes Chardonnay, Sauvignon Blanc, and a Chenin Blanc-based white table wine, all from the estate vineyard.

Wooden Valley Winery has an appealing informality about it. There are no tours. The tasting and sales room, one of four wood-frame buildings grouped around

Contra Costa-Solano

Cadenasso Winery. From I-80, Abernathy Rd. exit, N to winery at 4144. (P.O. Box 22, Fairfield, CA 94533) Tel (707) 425-5845. Daily 9–5, closed holidays. Ta. GT by appt.

Chateau De Leu. From I-80, Green Valley Rd. exit, NW on Green Valley Rd. 2 mi. to W. Mason Rd., then NW to winery at end of road (1635 W. Mason Rd., Suisun, CA 94585) Tel (707) 864-1517. Daily 11-4:30. GT/Ta.

Conrad Viano Winery. From I-680, W 1 mi. on State 4, N 1 mi. on Morello Ave. (150 Morello Av., Martinez, CA 94553) Tel (415) 228-6465. Picnic. Daily 9-12, 1-5. IT/Ta.

Wooden Valley Winery. From I-80, Suisun Valley Rd. exit, NW 4.5 mi. on Suisun Valley Rd. (4756 Suisun Valley Rd., Suisun, CA 94585) Tel (707) 864-0730. Tu-Su 9-5. Ta.

Key: GT (guided tour); IT (informal tour); Ta (tasting).

a sizable courtyard, is unmistakable. On weekends, especially, the court is full of parked automobiles and the tasting room full of local patrons exchanging empty jugs for full ones.

Proprietors Richard and Mario Lanza (no relation to the singer) offer several generic table wines in bottles and jugs and a broad spectrum of varietal wines in bottles only. A complete list of appetizer and dessert wines also can be sampled.

The tasting game

The names of wines do little to explain how they will taste. Colombard and Pinot Blanc do not sound much alike. Pinot Blanc and Pinot Noir sound more alike. But when you get down to cases, the wines of the first pair taste more like each other than do the wines of the latter pair.

Most wineries run tasting rooms to help overcome the semantics of the business. The hosts will help organize a sequence of wines so each sample will show off to its best advantage. Dry whites are served first, followed by rosés, reds, sweet wines, appetizers, then dessert wines. Sparkling wines come last.

Newcomers usually find it useful to explore at least one candidate from each of the five classes (see the chart on page 105). Experienced tasters sometimes organize a day in the wine country just to taste one class or even one variety.

All "tasting" amounts to is making a considered judgment about whether or not a wine pleases the drinker. This is a purely personal exercise but is most rewarding if it includes some basic tests by which professionals make their decisions.

Sight. The appearance of a wine reveals something of its character. The liquid should be clear to brilliantly clear. Young table wines should not have brownish tints (whites range from pale gold to straw yellow, reds from crimson to ruby or slightly purplish, rosés from pink orange to pink). Most dessert wines will have a brownish tint and some may even be deep amber, depending on type.

Smell. Young table wines should have a fresh, fruity quality of aroma. The many types add a wide range of subtle variations. The fruitiness may be overlaid with bouquet. (Aroma is the smell of grapes; bouquet the smell of fermentation and aging.) But one seldom encounters bouquet when drinking new wines at the winery. Appetizer and dessert wines have little aroma but substantial bouquet.

Taste. In fact, taste is simply sweet, sour, bitter, and salty. Most "taste" is an extension of smell. Some qualities can be perceived only after the wine is on the taster's palate: acidity (liveliness versus flatness), astringency (young red wines will have a tannic puckeriness in most types except mellow ones), and weight or body (light versus rich).

One further note. "Dry" describes the absence of sugar, nothing else. Dry wines are sometimes thought to be sour because acidity and tannin are more evident.

Other Than Wineries

Solano County offers no great abundance of picnic parks or other recreational diversions close to its wineries.

One exception, directly next to the Cadenasso Winery on West Texas Street, is Alan Witt Park, a spacious collection of playgrounds and picnic lawns.

Back on the Contra Costa side of the river, the tiny, waterside town of Port Costa offers another kind of diversion altogether.

Once a teeming Sacramento River town, Port Costa declined in the 1930s but later revived itself with an antique collection of shops and restaurants. The village is just off State Highway 4, near Martinez.

Plotting a Route

Interstate highways 80 and 680 form a "T" that gets to the heart of the region from any direction.

I-680 has some agreeable moments as it slips along the flat from Cordelia down to the Sacramento River at Suisun, where the U.S. Navy's mothball fleet provides a wistful vista. But the freeways are mainly the means to get from point A to point B in a hurry.

The joys of driving in this part of the world belong with Suisun Valley Road, Wooden Valley Road, State Highway 121 from Cordelia to Lake Berryessa (and on across into the Napa Valley if time does not weigh heavily), and whatever connecting roads seem promising on the spot.

The Suisun and Wooden valleys, both small, look fine in all seasons. They even smell good early in March when their abundant orchards bloom a fragrant cloud of white and pink above carpets of indelibly yellow mustard and beneath canopies of blue sky.

These are old roads, narrow and curving. Summer drivers bustle along in hopes of finding some cooler place; but in late winter or early spring when the weather is balmy, some of them tend to grow forgetful of their goals. On such days the wheels of progress grind as slowly as those of justice, but the views are fine.

Marin County

Considering Marin County's image as a mecca for connoisseurs of the good things in life, it is not surprising that wineries are beginning to emerge there. The Marin wine boom is appropriately laid back. There were only two established cellars in the spring of 1987. More are in the works, however. Marin's equal access to urban resources plus the vineyards of Sonoma, Napa, and Mendocino counties makes it likely that the southern border of North Coast Wine Country will creep steadily toward the Golden Gate through the 1990s.

The Wineries

Marin's two existing wineries establish its viticultural poles. One is a small vineyard estate that has been in the same family for 150 years; the other operates in leased industrial space, purchasing all its grapes. Both approaches work, although future wineries probably will tend more toward the latter than the former, for one simple reason: although the weather and terrain in Marin are quite suitable for vineyards, the real-estate climate is decidedly not.

Kalin Cellars takes its name from an old Marin County Indian word meaning "ocean." It began in 1977 as a combined hobby and research station for microbiology professor Terry Leighton and his wife, Frances, a research associate in Terry's department at UC Berkeley. Within a short time it became a commercial winery, too.

Kalin occupies a cavernous leased bay in a Novato industrial park. There is nothing especially winerylike about the exterior, but the cool, dim interior has the air of a classic Burgundy cave. Several different types of oak are represented in the barrel stacks that take up most of the room. Some of the wines are fermented in barrels; others ferment in several tall vats, which are set into a raised deck to allow easy access for cap punching and other high-level operations.

The Leightons buy grapes from carefully selected, older vineyards, which they generally designate on the labels. The roster includes Chardonnay, Sauvignon Blanc, Semillon, Pinot Noir, and Cabernet Sauvignon.

Pacheco Ranch Winery is twice unique: once for its past, as the only surviving chunk of a land grant awarded to Ignacio Pacheco by the Mexican government in 1834, and again today, as the only winery estate in Marin County.

Pacheco's great-great-grandson, Herb Rowland, is the current proprietor. Frances Rowland, Herb's mother and Ignacio's great-granddaughter, resides in the classic Victorian house built by Ignacio's son. A recent marriage in the family has added a veteran Sonoma County winemaker to the clan, too, which holds considerable promise for the historic property's future.

The winery occupies a former carriage house that was built concurrently with the Rowland home. The ground level contains oak uprights and smaller French oak cooperage for wine aging. Upstairs are a lab, more barrels, and a genteel tasting room that also serves as the ranch's historical museum.

In addition to Marin County's only estate-grown Cabernet Sauvignon, the winery makes Chardonnay from Sonoma County grapes. Students of wine and history alike will want to make an appointment to visit this unique property.

Other Than Wineries

New Albion was what Sir Francis Drake called Marin County. The famous mariner is thought to have landed there about 1582, after sailing past the Golden Gate in heavy fog. Drake's Bay, the shallow lagoon and estuary that he mistakenly believed to be San Francisco Bay, is now part of one of California's finest park systems.

Point Reyes National Seashore is the largest in an unbroken series of state and national parks running the whole length of the Marin coastline, from the Marin Headlands to the mouth of Tomales Bay. The visual feast in between includes Mt. Tamalpais, Muir Woods, and Stinson Beach.

Plotting a Route

Access to the Marin coast is from State Highway 1. Driving north from San Francisco, take the Highway 1–Stinson Beach exit off of U.S. 101. From the north, leave U.S. 101 at the Sir Francis Drake Boulevard exit, and navigate due west. Sections of the coast highway are subject to closure during winter months due to rockslides and flooding. Expect heavy traffic during summer months and on weekends throughout the year.

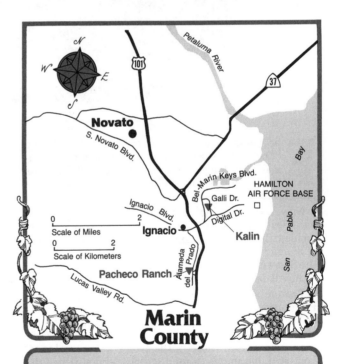

Kalin Cellars. From U.S. 101, Ignacio Blvd. exit, NE .3 mi. on Bel-Marin Keys Blvd., E 1 blk. on Digital Dr., N .2 mi. on Galli Dr. to winery (61 Galli Dr., Ste. F & G, Novato, CA 94947) Tel (415) 883-3543. By appt. only.

Pacheco Ranch Winery. From U.S. 101, N 1 mi. on Alameda del Prado to winery (5495 Redwood Hwy., Ignacio, CA 94947) Tel (415) 883-5583. By appt., groups only. GT/Ta.

Key: GT (guided tour); IT (informal tour); Ta (tasting).

The Mother Lode & Lodi

Two adjoining districts are worlds apart

Lodi Brick Barns

For years, when a wine industry official said "Lodi," the word encompassed most of the northern San Joaquin County, Sacramento and its surroundings, and several bits and pieces of the Mother Lode.

Now Lodi pretty much means Lodi. Vineyards and wineries in the Mother Lode country have established an identity of their own under the general district name of Sierra Foothills. A whole new district is emerging in the Sacramento Delta west of Lodi, and the Sacramento Valley is becoming a separate area.

The old shorthand was forgivable. From the end of Prohibition until the early 1970s, the dozen or so wineries right around Lodi outnumbered all the others two to one. Several of them individually made more wine each year than did all those in the fringe areas combined. Lodi still dominates in total gallons, and still has the biggest wineries, but the Mother Lode now has more than twice as many cellars to visit.

The Mother Lode

The Mother Lode is that California region where local grape growers are most likely to say of themselves, "We don't have to be crazy, but it helps."

Theirs is an altogether different weather from that of the San Joaquin Valley floor below. Spring frosts are but one major aspect of a climate that makes grapes a dubious crop for investment. Indeed, one scientist at the University of California at Davis says that a Sierra Nevada foothill winegrower will harvest, over the long haul, approximately 25 percent of what he or she might expect in easier climes.

People learned this soon after 1849, when local winemaking sprang up to help satisfy the thirsts of Gold Rush miners. The rigorous climate has been a damper on would-be vineyardists since; vineyard acreage in the Mother Lode never has been large.

Still, despite the chancy economics, Zinfandel from this region has enjoyed fame in every era of California winemaking. Vines have persisted in this region against all odds, and now they are perhaps at their zenith. Not only are vineyard acreages and the roster of regional wineries at their peaks, but cellars in many other counties are making Sierra foothills Zinfandels in competition with stay-at-home bottlings. A single statistic tells the tale: Of 6,468 tons of Mother Lode grapes crushed by California wineries in 1986, 4,778 were Zinfandel.

Even if wines from this region were less well received by connoisseurs, the Mother Lode would be worth a vinous visit. Its hills compose and recompose themselves into beautiful scenes. The whole region is full of appealing memorabilia from 1849 and full of people who keep some of that gaudy spirit. Not least, an easy friendliness pervades the small, mostly family-owned wineries.

The El Dorado district runs from Placerville south to the Amador County line, where the Shenandoah Valley vineyard district begins. Combining the two into a single tour is not only easy, but sensible.

The wineries in Calaveras and Tuolumne counties are farther south, in Mark Twain country. They should be part of a separate tour. The entire township of Columbia has been preserved as a State Historical Park and looks much as it did when Twain was reporting for its newspaper. The nearby cabin where Twain wrote "The Celebrated Jumping Frog of Calaveras County" and other classic tales is also an historic landmark.

The Wineries

Most of El Dorado County's wineries are small, family-owned cellars in wooded hill country south and east of Placerville. Amador County's viticultural focus is the Shenandoah Valley appellation in the hill country east of Plymouth. Several wineries are farther south, in the vicinity of the Calaveras-Tuolumne county line; appropriately, Nevada County's only commercial winery is located in the county seat.

Amador Foothill Winery is part of the new wave of Sierra foothill wineries by age and design. Owner Ben Zeitman built the winery in time for the harvest of 1980 and designed it to be the world's most energy-efficient metal building. Zeitman, ex-NASA scientist, made the plans with a little help from old colleagues who had impeccable credentials in the subject. His wife, enologist Katie Quinn, shares winemaking responsibilities.

Gleaming white, the passive solar structure stairsteps down a steep north slope otherwise covered in vines. Crusher, basket presses, and an off-season picnic-tasting table occupy a concrete pad at one end of the upper level. Great views are all around. Stainless steel fermentors for whites and redwood ones for reds are just inside well-insulated walls. The cooler lower level has oak uprights, barrels, and bottled wines alongside a huge bin of rocks cooled by night air. Warm daytime air establishes a convection flow as it exits through a long vent at the peak of a soaring roof.

Wines produced in this scientifically precise environment include Sauvignon Blanc, white Zinfandel, Cabernet Sauvignon, and Zinfandel, the last from nearby vineyards including one believed to date to the 1860s.

Amador Winery, founded in 1966, is a tasting room and small cellar housed in a building alongside State 49 in the village of Amador City. To taste here is to tour. The list of wines is basically generic.

Argonaut Winery is near the village of Ione, a shade down the Sierra Nevada slopes from most of the other Mother Lode cellars.

Perhaps the smallest of the regional lot, it belongs to six partners who otherwise work in the aerospace industry. One of the partners lives at the winery site,

but weekends are the only time visitors are allowed to have a look at the small cellar and its collection of oak casks. An appointment is required.

In accordance with local tradition, the all-red list of wines is led by Zinfandel.

Baldinelli Vineyards makes its wines alongside and in a spruce, prefabricated metal building perched atop a knoll looking down onto Shenandoah Road.

This is an instructive example of a modern small winery. The press is an up-to-the-minute model of the horizontal basket type. The row of stainless steel fermentors alongside the cellar building has some exposed tanks and some covered with insulating foam. Inside, the cooperage is a mixture of French and American oak barrels.

Founding partner Ed Baldinelli's first crush was 1979. The roster of wines, all from an adjoining vineyard managed by partner John Miller, includes Sauvignon Blanc, Cabernet Sauvignon, and Zinfandel (white and red).

Black Sheep Vintners joined the El Dorado fold in 1984, supplanting Chispa Cellars in an old barn at the end of Main Street in Murphys. Dave and Janis Olson conduct tasting informally among their French oak barrels, wherein ages Cabernet Sauvignon and Zinfandel from local grapes. In their spare time, the Olsons both moonlight at a larger winery nearby, where their inaugural 1984 wines were crushed.

Boeger Winery is, like a great many other California wineries, both old and new. Here, however, the contrast is easier to see than it is almost anywhere else.

The current winery went up in 1973, a tidy concrete block structure with stainless steel fermentors, a Willmes press and other processing gear out back, and racks of oak barrels and puncheons within.

A few yards downstream, along a creek that bisects the property, is an old stone building that originally was the Fossati-Lombardo winery in the 1870s, but now houses the tasting room. The upper floor held a hand-cranked crusher that now sits in the tasting room. Two chutes above the tasting bar are used to drop newly crushed fruit into open fermentors.

In good weather, visitors can picnic just above the creek in a spot between the two buildings and consider how winemaking has changed.

The list of Boeger varietal wines includes Chardonnay, Chenin Blanc, Riesling, Semillon, and Sauvignon Blanc in whites. Cabernet Sauvignon and Merlot are the reds. There are two blush wines and a pair of generics called Hangtown Gold and Hangtown Red after Placerville's original name. The wines come from four patches of grapes, one in the pocket valley that holds the winery, the other three nearby.

Incidentally, owners Greg and Susan Boeger also grow pears and apples on the home ranch.

D'Agostini Winery is the genuinely durable cellar in this lofty region. The first vines on the site east of Plymouth belonged to a Swiss named Adam Uhlinger, who planted them in 1856. For a good many years Uhlinger made wine under his own label. The D'Agostini family bought the vines and the winery in 1911. They sold to the current owner, Armagan Ozdiker, in 1984.

Uhlinger built for the long haul. He laid stone walls and strung heavy beams. The D'Agostinis kept his handiwork intact, though the winery prospered substantially and required a series of additions. They also kept several of the oak casks that were coopered on the site by a neighbor of Uhlinger. In his turn, Ozdiker has discreetly introduced state-of-the-art equipment, including refrigerated fermentors for white wines.

The buildings, old and new, are set at the foot of a gentle, vine-clad slope. Beyond the 125 acres of vineyard are hills wooded more thickly than is common in California wine districts.

Tours start with the fermentors and end with a new tasting room. Zinfandel still heads the list of wines.

El Dorado Vineyard is the sole representative of viticulture on Apple Hill, a regional ranch market with the air of a festival, off Highway 50 at Camino, north of Placerville. Proprietor John Mirande and his family grow apples as well as grapes; their bakery and pie shop is next door to the winery.

El Dorado was founded in 1976 by Earl Maguire. Mirande joined Maguire as partner in 1980 and became sole owner in 1986. The winery's front end presents a rustic appearance, carried into the tasting room by pecky cedar paneling and a large fireplace. The business end of the 150- by 42-foot building is divided between stainless steel and plastic fermenting vats, and American oak barrels in racks.

Mirande produces Chardonnay, Cabernet Sauvignon, and Merlot from his own grapes and purchases local fruit for his Zinfandel. Forty-Niner Red and Gold are proprietary blends.

Fitzpatrick Winery once shared a slope below Fairplay Road with a nursery called Famine's End. Founded in 1980 as FBF Winery, it began in makeshift quarters behind the main nursery building but by 1987 had moved two miles up the road to be reborn as one of the state's more impressive wine properties.

Fitzpatrick Lodge is modeled after classic mountain lodges of the 1930s. It was hand-built by owners Brian and Diane Fitzpatrick (with only an occasional helper) from individually peeled and fitted logs. The building incorporates the Fitzpatrick home, a 5-room inn, a commercial kitchen, the winery tasting room, and subterranean wine aging space. The more noisome aspects of winemaking are addressed on an outdoor crush-fermentation pad some distance from the lodge.

The roster includes Chardonnay, Sauvignon Blanc, Cabernet Sauvignon, and Zinfandel (white and red).

Gerwer Winery is set among oaks beside Stony Creek, at the base of a vine-covered slope so steep that there is a 10°F difference from the bottom to the crest on warm days.

Vernon and Marcia Gerwer left the dairy business in Sacramento to found their winery in 1981. The woodframe and concrete-block building extends into the hillside, keeping bottled wine and stacks of French and American oak barrels cool at the back of the cellar. Stainless steel tanks and processing gear are up front,

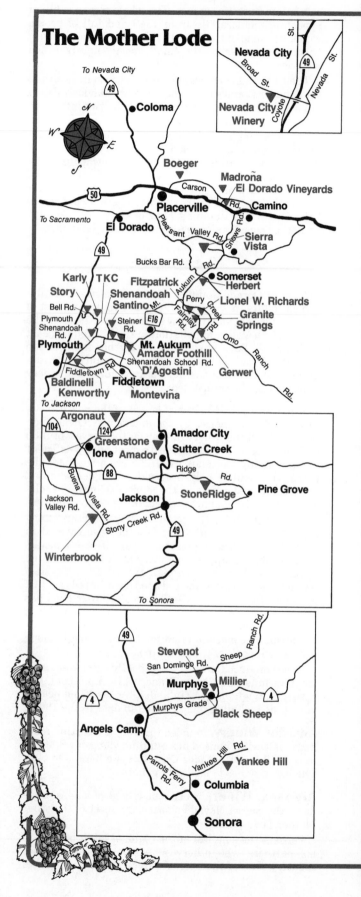

Amador Foothill Winery. From Plymouth, NE 5 mi. on E-16/Shenandoah Rd., N 1.1 mi. on Steiner Rd. (12500 Steiner Rd., Plymouth, CA 95669) Tel (209) 245-6307. Picnic. Sa-Su 12-5. IT/Ta.

Amador Winery. On State 49 in Amador City (Hwy. 49 and Water St., Amador City, CA 95601) Tel (209) 267-5320. Daily 10-6. Ta.

Argonaut Winery. Directions given with appt. (13675 Mt. Echo Dr., Ione, CA 95640) Tel (209) 274-4106 or 274-2882. GT/Ta by appt.

Baldinelli Vineyards. From Plymouth, NE 3.5 mi. on E-16/Shenandoah Rd., W .1 mi. on Dickson Rd. (10801 Dickson Rd., Plymouth, CA 95669) Tel (209) 245-3398. Sa-Su 11-4 or by appt. IT/Ta.

Black Sheep Vintners. From State 4, W .5 mi. on Main Street to winery at intersection of Murphys Grade Rd. and Main St. (P.O. Box 1851, Murphys, CA 95247) Tel (209) 728-2157. Sa-Su 12-5. IT/Ta.

Boeger Winery. From U.S. 50, Schnell School Rd. exit N .25 mi., E .3 mi. on Carson Rd. to winery (1709 Carson Rd., Placerville, CA 95667) Tel (916) 622-8094. Picnic. Daily 10-5. IT/Ta.

D'Agostini Winery. From Plymouth, NE 8 mi. on E-16/Shenandoah Rd. (14430 Shenandoah Rd., Plymouth, CA 95669) Tel (209) 245-6612. Daily 10-5. IT/Ta.

El Dorado Vineyard. From U.S. 50, 5.7 mi. N of Placerville, Camino exit to winery (3551 Carson Rd., Camino, CA 95709) Tel (916) 622-7689. Daily 9-5 Sep-Dec, Sa-Su 11-4 Jan-Aug, or by appt. Ta.

Fitzpatrick Winery. From E-16/Mt. Aukum Rd., E 2 mi. on Fairplay Rd. (7740 Fairplay Rd., Somerset, CA 95684) Tel (916) 626-1988. Picnic. Sa-Su 11-5, W-F by appt. IT/Ta.

Gerwer Winery. From E-16/Mt. Aukum Rd., E 3.5 mi. on Fairplay Rd. to Stoney Creek Rd., left on Stoney Creek to winery (8221 Stoney Creek Rd., Somerset, CA 95684) Tel (209) 245-3467. Picnic. Sa-Su 11-5. GT/Ta.

Granite Springs Winery. From E-16/Mt. Aukum Rd., E 1.5 mi. on Fairplay Rd. to pvt. drive (6060 Granite Springs Rd., Somerset, CA 95684) Tel (209) 245-6395. Sa-Su 11-5 or by appt. GT/Ta.

Greenstone Winery. On State 88, 3 mi. W of intersection with State 124 (P.O. Box 1164, Ione, CA 95640) Tel (209) 274-2238 or 274-4182. Picnic. W-Su 10-4 summers, F-Su 10-4 rest of year. IT/Ta.

Herbert Vineyards. Directions with appt. (P.O. Box 438, Somerset, CA 95684) Tel (916) 626-0548. GT/Ta by appt.

Karly Winery. From Plymouth, NE 4 mi. on E-16/Shenandoah, N .25 mi. on Bell Rd. to winery drive (11076 Bell Rd., Plymouth, CA 95669) Tel (209) 245-3922. M-F by appt, Sa-Su 12-5. Ta. GT by appt.

Kenworthy Vineyards. From Plymouth, NE 1.7 mi. on E-16/Shenandoah Rd. (10120 Shenandoah Rd., Plymouth, CA 95669) Tel (209) 245-3198. Sa-Su 11-5; M-F by appt. Ta. GT by appt.

Madroña Vineyards. From U.S. 50, 5 mi. E of Placerville, take Carson Rd. exit, W .25 mi. on Carson Rd. to High Hill Rd., N .75 mi. on High Hill Rd. (through High Hill Ranch) to winery (P.O. Box 454, Camino, CA 95709) Tel (916) 644-5948 or 644-1154. Sa 10-5, Su 1-5 or by appt. IT/Ta.

Millier Winery. From State 4 at Murphys, N 1 blk. on School St. to 99 (P.O. Box 1554, Murphys, CA 95247) Tel (209) 728-1100. By appt. GT/Ta.

Monteviña Wines. From Plymouth, NE 2 mi. on E-16/Shenandoah Rd., E 1 mi. on Shenandoah School Rd. (20680 Shenandoah School Rd., Plymouth, CA 95669) Tel (209) 245-6942. Picnic. Sa-Su 11-4. GT/Ta.

Nevada City Winery. From State 49 at Nevada City, Broad St. exit W 1 blk., S 1 blk. on N. Pine St., W 1 blk. on Spring St. (321 Spring St., Nevada City, CA 95959) Tel (916) 265-9463. Daily 12-5. IT/Ta.

L. W. Richards Winery. From E-16/Mt. Aukum Rd. S of Somerset, S .1 mi. on Fairplay Rd., E 2.4 mi. on Perry Creek Rd. (7360 Perry Creek Rd., Somerset, CA 95684) Tel (209) 245-4054 or (916) 443-1905. Picnic. Sa-Su 11-5, or by appt. Ta. GT by appt.

Santino Winery. From Plymouth, E 5 mi. on E-16/Shenandoah Rd., NE 1 mi. on Steiner Rd. (12225 Steiner Rd., Plymouth, CA 95669) Tel (209) 245-6979. Picnic. Daily 12-5. Ta. GT by appt.

Shenandoah Vineyards. From Plymouth, E 5 mi. on E-16/Shenandoah Rd., NE 1 mi. on Steiner Rd. (12300 Steiner Rd., Plymouth, CA 95669) Tel (209) 245-4455. Daily 11-5. IT/Ta.

Sierra Vista Winery. From U.S. 50, Missouri Flat Rd./Diamond Springs exit, S on Missouri Flat Rd. to end of rd., E 10 mi. on Pleasant Valley Rd., W 2 mi. on Leisure Ln. to winery drive at end of road (4560 Cabernet Ln., Placerville, CA 95667) Tel (916) 622-7221. Sa-Su 11-5 or by appt. IT/Ta.

Stevenot Winery. From Murphys, N 2.5 mi. on Sheep Ranch Rd., W .25 mi. on San Domingo Rd. to winery (2690 San Domingo Rd., Murphys, CA 95247) Tel (209) 728-3436. Picnic. Daily 10-5. GT/Ta.

StoneRidge Winery. From State 49, S of Sutter Creek, E 2.3 mi. on Ridge Rd. (13862 Ridge Rd., Sutter Creek, CA 95685) Tel (209) 223-1761. Sa-Su 12-4 or by appt. IT/Ta.

Story Vineyard. From Plymouth, NE 4 mi. on E-16/Shenandoah Rd., N 1.5 mi. on Bell Rd. (10525 Bell Rd., Plymouth, CA 95669) Tel (209) 245-6208. Picnic. Sa-Sun 11-5 or by appt. Ta. GT by appt.

TKC Vineyards. From Plymouth, NE 4 mi. on E-16/Shenandoah Rd., N .1 mi. on Bell Rd. W .25 mi. on Valley Dr. (11001 Valley Dr., Plymouth, CA 95669) Tel (619) 446-3166. By appt. only.

Winterbrook Vineyards. From Ione, SW 2 mi. on State 124, SE 4 mi. on Buena Vista Rd. to winery gate (4851 Buena Vista Rd., Ione, CA 95640) Tel (209) 274-4627. Picnic. Sa-Su 11-5 or by appt. IT/Ta. GT by appt.

Yankee Hill Winery. From Columbia State Historic Park, E .75 mi. on Yankee Hill Rd. to winery (P.O. Box 163, Columbia, CA 95310) Tel (209) 532-3015 or (209) 533-2417. Picnic. W-Su 10-5. IT/Ta.

Key: GT (guided tour); IT (informal tour); Ta (tasting).

close to the outdoor crush pad. The tasting room is in a separate, smaller building nearby.

The wines are made from estate-grown grapes, supplemented with fruit purchased locally. They include Chardonnay, Sauvignon Blanc (blended with Semillon), Ruby Cabernet, Cabernet Sauvignon, and Petite Sirah. Most of the Gerwers' 20 picnic tables are set in the shade.

Granite Springs Winery

nestles into an idyllic fold in gentle hills south of Somerset. Owners Les and Lynne Russell did their own construction work on a sturdy, barnlike winery building cut into a rocky slope overlooking vineyards and two ponds. An overhanging roof shelters crusher and press. Inside, stainless steel fermentors line one wall of a single, large room. Upright oak tanks and oak barrels take much of the remaining space. A cable spool is the tasting table.

The Russells first crushed here in 1981 after making wine elsewhere in 1980. The roster includes Sauvignon Blanc, Chenin Blanc, Cabernet Sauvignon, Petite Sirah, and Zinfandel (white and red). Their first Ports were released in 1987.

Greenstone Winery

calls its location, well downslope from Amador's other cellars, the gateway to the Mother Lode.

The building makes a dramatic gate. Set amid vines and well back from State Highway 88, it has the sort of high, steep-pitched roof and tall gables that bring to mind prosperous farmhouses in Brittany. Greenstone earned its name when a plywood skin tacked on just in time for the debut harvest of 1981 was later covered with a distinctly green local stone, quarried from a site next to winery-owned vines across the highway.

Owned by two couples who like company, the winery is designed to welcome visitors to the point of having an entry road and parking area sized for recreational vehicles. An oak-shaded picnic area flanks the winery and tasting room.

As a winery, Greenstone still is growing into its generous building. A small crusher and basket press occupy a roofed-over deck at one end. Inside is plenty of room to add to a row of four stainless steel fermentors and two short stacks of American oak barrels. Partner Stan Van Spanje is the winemaker and partner Durward Fowler manages the vineyard.

The roster embraces a full range of varietals, including several variations on Zinfandel, from rosé to Port.

Herbert Vineyards

exemplifies the viticultural homestead that was common in the Gold Rush country around the turn of the century. Frank and Beverly Herbert began planting vines on their 50-acre property in 1974, living in a trailer while building their redwood ranch-style house among the oaks and cedars. They sold their grapes to an established winery nearby, which is where they made the first Herbert Vineyards wines in 1980. Most of their grapes still go to that winery, and they still make their wines there: a type of working relationship that's as old as the hills.

The spectacular vineyard averages 2,400 feet elevation on several faces of a sandy loam hillside. Zinfandel and Sauvignon Blanc are the varieties planted, and those are the varietals the Herberts make. By appointment, visitors may stroll to the top of the vineyard and, perhaps, taste the Herberts' wines in their home.

Karly Winery

occupies a small, well-made building next to the residence of winemaker-partner Lawrence (Buck) Cobb. Exactly which building comes into view depends on the speed of the trip. The original board-and-batten barn of 1980 was replaced in 1985 by a permanent winery with a tasting room that is open to the public on weekends and by appointment otherwise.

The property is a pleasure to see. The winery is set well back from Bell Road amid the vines, next to a small lake. Grassy, oak-dotted hills frame the picture.

Karly's short list of wines comes partly from local grapes and partly from Santa Barbara County. The locals are Sauvignon Blanc, Petite Sirah, and Zinfandel (white and red); Chardonnay is the import. Cobb, a one-time U.S. Air Force fighter pilot, ferments his red wines in stainless steel and ages them in French and American oak. He ferments his whites in French oak puncheons.

Kenworthy Vineyards

is a modern, well-built structure nested inside the faithfully preserved, irreplaceable old white barn pictured on the label. The tasting room annex was added in 1986.

The cellar belongs to long-time home winemakers John and Patricia Kenworthy, whose first commercial vintage here was 1980. The roster is Chardonnay, Cabernet Sauvignon, and Zinfandel, some from the Kenworthy's own grapes, some from other growers in the Sierra foothills.

Although an affable clutter of old farm implements and odds and bits of equipment surrounds the building, the interior is neat as a pin. A small fermenting room with stainless steel tanks is in an attached shed at the rear. Inside the main building is an aging cellar full of American oak barrels. The setting is a quiet delight of gently rolling vines, oak-dotted meadows, and a pond.

Madroña Vineyards

is, by a narrow margin at 3,000 feet elevation, the highest wine estate in California. As is the local habit, owners Richard and Leslie Bush did much of the construction work on a gracefully proportioned wood-sided winery cut into a long slope and shaded by a small grove of conifers. In the California tradition, construction ran right through the first crush, 1980.

The vineyard was planted in 1973, around a gigantic madrona tree that gave the property its name. The winery is open for tasting on weekends and for touring by appointment. The Madroña label covers several estate-grown varietals including Chardonnay, Cabernet Sauvignon, and Zinfandel.

Millier Winery

is considered a tiny cellar in a region noted for small ones. Steve and Liz Millier produce Sauvignon Blanc, Chenin Blanc, Cabernet Sauvignon, and Zinfandel beneath their house. First crush was 1983.

Monteviña Wines

retained until recently its long-held title of largest winery in Amador County, although it would rank among only the medium-to-small wineries in Napa or Sonoma County.

Owner W. H. Fields and then-partner Cary Gott founded Monteviña in 1973. In 1981, having outgrown the original prefabricated steel building, the owners added a handsome second building with arched windows and other Spanish touches. The original cellar still has the modern crushers, presses, and stainless steel fermentors, and still has European oak barrels stacked more than head-high in close rows. The second building, to the rear of the original, has more space for barrel aging, a bottling line, and the offices. Having grown to this size, Monteviña in 1982 established the first program of formal tours and tastings in the region. A handsome tasting room is nested inside the new barrel-aging cellar. Two wisteria-shaded picnic patios are available outside.

Monteviña is an estate winery by the classical definition. All its wines come from 160 acres of vines owned by its proprietors, including one 85-year-old block. The emphasis is on Zinfandel in a variety of styles ranging from a light-hearted one made by carbonic maceration to a heavyweight meant for long aging. (To explain carbonic maceration in detail is beyond the scope of this book, but essentially it means fermenting whole grapes in clusters rather than crushed grapes separated from their stems. The idea is to achieve red wines ready for instant drinking.) Also in the roster of varietal wines are Sauvignon Blanc, Barbera, and red and white Cabernet Sauvignon. Port joined the roster in 1978.

Nevada City Winery takes up where the Gold Rush left off. A century ago the local foundry bought hard-won gold dust from the Forty-Niners and processed it into a valuable commodity. Today Nevada County's only winery, located between the old foundry and the American Victorian Museum on Spring Street, does virtually the same thing with the fruit of local wine-growers' labors.

The winery occupies the old foundry garage, a weathered tin-sided structure that was gutted and insulated in time for the 1980 crush. A tasting room on the open mezzanine, added in 1982, overlooks the first-floor fermentation area and massed cooperage of French and American oak. Upstairs are more barrels, along with case goods. Crushing and pressing occur out back.

The varietal roster represents virtually all of Nevada County's growers, whose combined acreage barely exceeded 200 in 1987. There is Chardonnay, dry and sweet Riesling, dry and sweet Sauvignon Blanc, Gewürztraminer, Cabernet Sauvignon, Zinfandel, Pinot Noir, Petite Sirah, and a blush wine called Alpenglow. Charbono is bottled here under its French name, Douce Noir.

L. W. Richards Winery is one stop on the tour that children will enjoy as much as their parents. The Richards family keeps kites and other toys on hand, and they pour apple juice (the current vintage, of course) for youngsters to taste while racing remote-controlled boats on the pond.

Adults will find a handsome wooden winery in the Pennsylvania Dutch style, containing an informal tasting room, stacked French and American oak barrels, and case storage. The winery was built in 1986. A substantial addition was being constructed in 1987 for the Richards' fermentation tanks and processing gear, currently housed at another winery.

The roster of wines, most from a 9-acre vineyard planted in 1981, includes Chardonnay, Chenin Blanc, white Zinfandel, Cabernet Sauvignon, and Merlot. The winery is open to the public on weekends, but an appointment is required for midweek visits.

Santino Winery is the only one in the Mother Lode built in a Spanish California style. Adobe blocks and red-tile roof make it an uncommon sight in a part of the state not trod by Franciscan missionaries, whose architectural legacy is common in the coastal districts.

Architecture aside, this winery is instructive for having modern equipment in compact space, allowing visitors to grasp readily the sequence of winemaking steps. A short, fairly straight line runs from outdoor crusher, press, and stainless steel fermentors, through an aging cellar full of French oak, to the bottling line. A sparsely furnished but friendly tasting room is at the opposite end of the winery from the crushing and fermenting area. Just outside the tasting room, two picnic tables for visitors are set in the shade of an overhang.

Owner Nancy Santino's primary focus is Zinfandel, in several styles. The Santino label also covers Sauvignon Blanc, Riesling, Barbera, and Cabernet Sauvignon.

Shenandoah Vineyards occupies a lofty knoll overlooking the Shenandoah Valley. The property of Leon and Shirley Sobon since 1977, the ranch belonged for many years to a prominent local family named Steiner, which directly explains the outward appearance of the place. "Stein" in German means "stone," and Mr. Steiner took his name very seriously indeed. All of the house walls and one wall of what now is the winery are made of rock carted up from the nearby Cosumnes River and mortared in place by the former owners. The stonework has enough landmark status locally that old-timers come now and again to see that the new proprietors have not damaged the Steiner legacy.

The Sobons have not, though they more than tripled the size of the winery building in 1978 by adding two concrete-block levels behind and below the original, and enlarged it further in 1981, then again in 1984 and 1986. It is now the largest winery in Amador County.

The expanded winery is tidy and well equipped. A tasting room, open daily, offers samples of Sauvignon Blanc, Cabernet Sauvignon, and Zinfandel. Dessert

Wine Barrels

wines include rare examples of Black and Orange Muscat, Ports, and Sherry from the Mission grape.

Sierra Vista Winery is aptly named. Owners John and Barbara MacCready can see the Crystal Range of the high Sierra whenever they look up from winery work. The long driveway, part paved and part gravel, is a bona-fide county road called Cabernet Lane.

Founded in 1977 as a tiny rustic operation, Sierra Vista has evolved through several phases. The wines were initially fermented in one-time dairy tanks; now, there is a battery of temperature-controlled stainless steel fermentors. The tiny original cellar was replaced in 1980 by a 40- by 50-foot winery, which the MacCreadys built out of Ponderosa pines milled from the property. The impressive collection of cooperage inside is divided between French and American oak.

The steady roster includes Chardonnay, Sauvignon Blanc, Cabernet Sauvignon, and Zinfandel (the last two in rosé and red). There is a small quantity of Syrah, and an occasional late-harvest Semillon from a small plot of that variety near the winery. The wines are either estate-produced or from grapes purchased within 5 miles of the winery. The tasting room is open on weekends or during the week by appointment.

Stevenot Winery may have as romantic a site as a winery can have in California. The road to it runs up to a ridge above Murphys' main street, passes Mercer Caverns, then plunges down a tree-clad slope to the bottom of a deep gorge. There owner Barden Stevenot's vineyards begin right next to the road. His cellar is hidden away behind them, beneath a looming outcrop of rock.

Except for being housed in a notably picturesque hay barn, the winery proper is a typically well-equipped, modern California cellar. Visitors are encouraged to have leisurely looks at the working gear, which includes horizontal basket press, stainless steel fermentors, and French oak barrels.

The tasting room is located across a small clearing on the lower level of a wood-frame, unpainted house that ought to be in movies, preferably ones about the Last Frontier. In it visitors may sample Chardonnay, Sauvignon Blanc, Chenin Blanc, Muscat, Cabernet Sauvignon, and Zinfandel (white and red), mostly from Calaveras grapes. Of special interest is an array of photographs taken by local photographers. The collection captures the visual impact of the winery and its locale.

StoneRidge Winery is a thinking person's small cellar, designed into its site—or sites—to ease the burdens of moving both grapes and wine.

The crushing, fermenting, and pressing go on in a small shed at the high side of a hilly property. There, grapes feed into a crusher set on a platform that pivots to fill any of three open-topped redwood fermentors. On a lower level is a stainless steel tank used for the first racking. It ties into an underground line that allows new wine to flow by gravity to an aging cellar beneath the residence of proprietors Gary and Loretta Porteous.

The Porteouses salvaged several ancient oak casks and puncheons from a one-time miners' boarding house that had made wine for its clientele in the gaudy days of the Gold Rush. These are the majority of the oak

cooperage, though they are supplemented by newer French and American barrels.

Production focuses on Zinfandel from an old vineyard nearby and Ruby Cabernet from the home property.

The winery is small enough that the tasting room consists of a barrel set on end in the aging cellar. It is also small enough that an appointment is required to visit it. The Porteouses have no plan for their winery to grow much in the next few years.

Story Vineyard concentrates on Zinfandel, in the best tradition of this region, but also makes a white wine from Mission grapes as a limited-production specialty.

This is an instructive small winery. Founded by the late Eugene Story and continued by his family, the yellow brick building on Bell Road is flanked by a 50-year-old vineyard. Between the first row of vines and the main door, crusher and press occupy a concrete pad. Inside, a row of temperature-controlled, stainless steel fermentors runs along one wall while racks of American oak barrels take up most of the rest of the space. A small bottling line is at the rear. Thus, the cellars allow the process of winemaking to be seen from beginning to end without moving a step, though for clear looks at some of the details it is advisable to stroll a few feet.

Story founded the business in 1973 as Cosumnes River Vineyard and completed the cellar in 1974. He changed the name to Story in 1979 after finding that almost nobody but locals could pronounce Cosumnes.

TKC Vineyards is a looming presence from either Bell or Shenandoah Road in spite of its being buried almost to its roof in a small knoll. A pair of substantial doors flanked by retaining walls makes an impressive, highly visible facade. In time, the winery will be capped by the residence of proprietors Harold and Monica Nuffer; for now, they commute from China Lake.

TKC made its first Zinfandel in 1981. The owners plan to continue as specialists in that variety. The name combines the initials of three Nuffer children.

Winterbrook Vineyards occupies a redwood barn, dating from 1860, in the oak-dotted pastureland of the Jackson Valley. The tasting room is paneled with the barn's original siding, replaced during the winery conversion in 1984. Bob and Joan Roberts make Chardonnay and Cabernet Sauvignon from the estate vineyard, planted in 1980.

Yankee Hill Winery, a mile east of Columbia State Historic Park, is the property of the Ron Erickson family. It originally was Columbia Cellars, built by another owner in 1972.

The Ericksons offer vintage-dated Zinfandel, Grenache, and several generic table and sparkling wines under the original Columbia label. They also offer picnicking under an arbor alongside a small wood-sided building that serves both as tasting room and cellar.

Other Than Wineries

The Mother Lode, like several other California wine districts, gains considerable appeal from having a romantic nineteenth-century history. Unlike the others, the early appeal was only slightly vinous. The real story in these parts was gold.

Though large-scale mining lies in the distant past, the countryside still shows a good many signs of the time: headframes of old mines, washes from sluicing operations, and, not least, towns with some uncommon architecture dating back to an era of easy spending.

Sonora, the Tuolumne County seat, makes an ideal touring headquarters. Over $40 million in gold came out of the hills within two miles of the stately old town. That still shows in the Victorian glow of a Gold Rush metropolis that is not only well preserved, but thriving.

North on Highway 49 is Angels Camp, the Argonaut crossroads of Calaveras County that hosts the annual Jumping Frog Jubilee. Virtually every town of substance has a museum, each with its own tales to tell.

The landmarks are too many, in too many different places, to be covered here. An engaging guide is the *Sunset* book, *Gold Rush Country*.

Plotting a Route

One U.S. highway and a plethora of state highways ascend from the San Joaquin Valley floor to intersect with State Highway 49, the Mother Lode's north-south artery. The fastest way up is U.S. Highway 50 from Sacramento to meet State 49 at Placerville.

Of the slower state routes, State Highway 88 from Lodi to Jackson is ranked at the head of the list for scenic beauty by more than a few connoisseurs. Almost as attractive is State Highway 16 from Sacramento to Plymouth. The latter road has the further advantage of arriving in the heart of the most vinous part of the Mother Lode.

Within the region, winery visitors can make a tidy and efficient loop by using U.S. 50, State 49, and Amador County Road E16 (which becomes Pleasant Valley Road in El Dorado County). Nearly all the wineries in Amador and El Dorado counties are on these routes or are very close to them. The Calaveras and Tuolumne wineries are near State 49 some miles south of the loop.

Lodi, town & country

Lodi is a genuine Central Valley agricultural center. Most of its 40,000 people live in tidily kept, tree-shaded residential districts around the main shopping area. Vineyards and other farmlands come right up to the edge of town.

Local farmland is, by force of geography, compact. Lodi nestles within the angles formed by the meeting of the Sacramento and San Joaquin rivers. To the east, the Sierra Nevada foothills form the third leg of a triangular boundary. Though other crops grow here, grapes predominate. The town long has been a table grape center, a brandy capital, and a natural source of sherry types. In more recent times, new grape varieties produced by the University of California at Davis have helped refocus local production toward table wines. (See "Grapes of the future," page 165.)

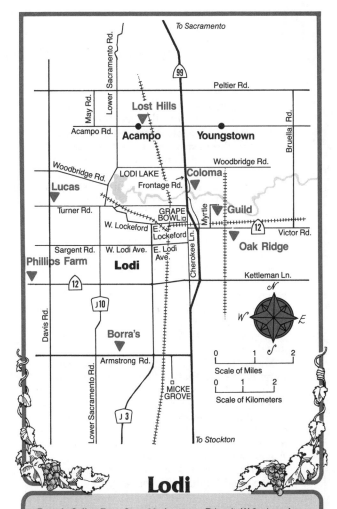

Lodi

Borra's Cellar. From State 99, Armstrong Rd. exit, W 2 mi. on Armstrong Rd. (1301 E. Armstrong Rd., Lodi, CA 95242) Tel (209) 368-5082. By appt. only.

Coloma Cellars. From State 99, east side of frontage road, N of State 12 (P.O. Box 1300, Lodi, CA 95241) Tel (209) 368-7822. Daily 10-5. Ta.

Guild Wineries & Distilleries. From State 99, E .5 mi. on State 12-East to Myrtle Ave., N .5 mi. to winery (One Winemaster's Way, Lodi, CA 95240) Tel (209) 368-5151.

Lost Hills Winery. From State 99, W 1 mi. on Acampo Rd. (3125 E. Orange Ave., Acampo, CA 95220) Tel (209) 369-2746. Daily 9-5. Ta.

The Lucas Winery. From State 99, Turner Rd. exit W 3.5 mi., N .1 mi. on N. Davis Rd. to winery (18196 N. Davis Rd., Lodi, CA 95242) Tel (209) 368-2006. Picnic. GT/Ta by appt.

Oak Ridge Vineyards. From State 99, E 1 mi. on State 12-E (6100 E. Hwy. 12, Lodi, CA 95240) Tel (209) 369-4768. Picnic. Daily 9-5. Ta. GT by appt.

Phillips Farms Vineyards. From State 99, W 6.9 mi. on State 12-West (4580 West Hwy. 12, Lodi, CA 95242) Tel (209) 368-7384. Picnic. Daily 9–5. Ta. GT by appt.

Key: GT (guided tour); IT (informal tour); Ta (tasting).

The Wineries

For one reason or another, Lodi has been—and still is—a traditional home for wineries owned by cooperatives of grape growers. Two of its visitable cellars are

Sherry: Variations on the theme

As a word, "sherry" is not a great deal more precise than, say, "nuts." Both cover a vast ground (and they go well together).

The most noticeable difference from one Sherry to the next is in degree of sweetness. Some relatively dry ones are intended as appetizer drinks. Others, very sweet, come under the dessert category. In California the appetizer Sherries for the most part are labeled "dry" or "cocktail." The dessert types mostly go forth as "Cream Sherry."

Sherry begins being Sherry when the winemaker adds a bit of brandy to a newly fermented dry white wine. The purpose is to stabilize the wine so it will not turn to vinegar when it is exposed to oxidation, the next step.

After this initial step, California winemakers produce their various Sherries in several ways, adding still more distinctions of flavor than sweetness.

Many "bake" it, though the word suggests more heat than they in fact apply. The usual limits are 120° to 140° F (49° to 60° C) for 45 to 120 days. Air space is left in the barrel or tank. Heat and air together produce the darkened color and characteristic flavor. Sweeter Sherries are made by blending in a certain amount of Angelica or a similar wine after the base Sherry has been baked. The wine may or may not be aged further after baking.

A variant method is the long aging of partly filled barrels without the unusual warmth. In this instance, oxygen and wood form the flavor.

A radically different method involves cultivating a specific yeast as a film floating atop aging Sherry in a partially filled barrel or tank. The yeast, "flor," produces a distinctive flavor of its own. The yeast, oxidation, and the wood of the barrels all come together to form the characteristic flavors of this type of Sherry. In the case of flor Sherries, the initial addition of brandy is very slight and is augmented at the end of the aging period.

In California several wineries use a variant method developed at the University of California. It is called "submerged yeast culture," an unromantic but accurate designation. Instead of a film of yeast being allowed to form and then work very slowly, a yeast is introduced into the wine and episodically agitated so it is present throughout the wine. The method, faster than film flor, produces a characteristic yeast flavor but without the wood flavor associated with film flors.

Whichever of these methods it uses, a winery may establish a "solera." Solera indicates only that a barrel is never emptied of all its wine. Rather, a certain fraction is removed for bottling, then a newer wine is added to the remaining part to keep the flor viable.

---

co-ops. Probably because so many of its growers have a piece of the co-op action, Lodi has lacked small, family-owned cellars in recent years. But that may be balancing out. Two of its visitable cellars are indeed family-owned and small. One of them, a new winery owned by an old Lodi family, may presage a revival.

Borra's Cellar is one of three recently established small family-owned wineries in Lodi. It may be the only one in California with an aging cellar that can be entered through a good, old-fashioned storm cellar door, the kind that angles up against a wall to cover the stairs beneath.

An appointment is required to get through that door to see neatly stacked rows of American oak barrels, or to have a look at the tasting room and bottling line in the upper story of what used to be a family residence but now is a winery from top to bottom. Proprietors Stephen and Beverly Borra can be talked into strolling out beyond an equipment shed to show the crusher, press, and fermentors. The latter include both open-topped redwood and stainless steel tanks. The family vineyard stretches away beyond them. The Borra's Cellar label is used mostly for Barbera and Zinfandel from those vines.

Coloma Cellars operates from an adobe-faced building on the State 99 frontage road just north of Lodi.

Visitors to the small aging cellar find a variety of table, dessert, and specialty wines available for tasting. There are no tours of the cellar or of the adjacent building where grape concentrate is produced for home winemakers. The owning company, California Cellar Masters, has several tasting rooms elsewhere in the state.

The label, incidentally, originated in the Gold Rush town of Coloma.

Guild Wineries & Distilleries, largest producer of wine and grape spirits among California's cooperatives and one of the state's farthest-flung associations of vineyardists, has its ancestral home and much of its presence in or near Lodi.

For visitors, the action is all at Central Cellars just off Victor Road (State Highway 12) on the east side of town.

A modern, spacious, and cool tasting room is in front of the main aging cellar. Some of Guild's visitors limit their explorations to this oasis, especially when the summer sun heats Lodi into the 100° F (38° C) range, or when winter rain pelts the countryside. However, the hosts willingly conduct tours in the worst of weather as well as the best.

Visible in the big cellars during the tours are concrete storage tanks of great capacity and steel tanks of still greater volume, a complete Charmat champagne cellar, a huge bottling room that clanks and rattles at a furious enough pace to satisfy the Sorcerer's Apprentice, and, not least, the cased goods warehouse. There is an immense amount of wine at Guild, and the people there have worked out ingenious arrangements for dealing with it. For example, a sunken lane goes straight through the middle of the warehouse. It is just wide enough to accommodate flatbed truck and trailer rigs and just deep enough for forklifts to drive right on and off the flatbeds to load them.

No grapes are crushed at these premises; crushing occurs at other Guild locations in Lodi, Fresno, and Bakersfield. However, the firm maintains a display vineyard adjacent to the winemaster's house. In this vineyard the proprietors have planted three or four of each of the wine grape varieties recommended for California. Nowhere else can visitors see with so few steps how varied is the vine.

Back in the tasting room, Guild offers a full line of table, appetizer, dessert, and sparkling wines. Most are bottled under the affiliated Cresta Blanca (see Mendocino chapter) and Cribari (see Fresno in San Joaquin chapter) labels.

Lost Hills Winery, known until 1986 as Barengo Vineyards, looms up alongside Acampo Road in an expansive and rather graceful brick building that dates back to 1868.

It became the Barengo winery in 1944 when Dino Barengo bought it to establish his own business. The property now belongs to Verdugo Vineyards, Inc., after two brief interim ownerships during which the winery was modernized and its capacity more than doubled from Barengo's day.

After years of being a tantalizing presence beyond the tasting room window, the winery is open to tour. The crushers and fermenting tanks sit in open air behind the old still house. Inside the brick-walled, wood-beamed main cellar, visitors can look through the long series of cellars, some filled with stainless steel storage tanks, others with an agreeable mixture of redwood and oak cooperage ranging in size from 50,000-gallon tanks down to 50-gallon barrels.

Across from the tasting room door, under a row of trees, several picnic tables are available on a first-come, first-served basis.

The Lucas Winery is Lodi's smallest cellar.

David Lucas makes wine mostly for local customers, having started in 1978. Much of it he sells each autumn to a mailing list. What is left he sells at the cellar door, first-come, first-served, between Thanksgiving and Christmas. Home winemakers are welcome in harvest time, when David and Tamara Lucas sell grapes from their 30-acre Zinfandel vineyard. Visitors with appointments are welcome year-round.

The crusher and press are housed in an old-fashioned redwood barn during the off-season and are pulled out in the open air during harvest. Stainless steel fer-

mentors occupy a roofed area behind the barn. Two small, tidily kept wood-frame buildings between the barn and the proprietor's residence hold a tasting room and several small racks of barrels full of aging Zinfandel, from vines that are over 65 years old.

Oak Ridge Vineyards is a new name for the well-known East Side Winery, which for many years was known by its labels as Royal Host or Conti Royale. Its tasting room is inside a retired 50,000-gallon redwood wine tank.

The vessel, tailored to its new purpose with a large door and interior varnishing, still gives a clear impression of how it feels to be inside a wine tank. It creates the sensory illusion of being bigger inside than outside.

The main winery buildings stretch southward from the roadside tasting room. As is often the case with cellars built in the 1930s, the architecture does not conform to romantic notions of a winery. Still, at Oak Ridge, the scenic deficiencies are only external. The interiors are full of handsome cooperage.

After tasting a substantial list of varietal table wines, visitors can retire to shaded picnic tables.

Phillips Farms Vineyards produced its first wines in 1984, a mere five generations after the Phillips family began growing grapes. Michael Phillips is the winemaker. His brother Dave, and his parents, Don and Jeanne, are partners.

The winery occupies an old wooden barn behind the Phillips Farms produce stand (the family grows 69 different fruits and vegetables in addition to grapes). Crushing equipment and stainless steel fermentors are outside, beneath an overhang. The temperature-controlled interior holds French and American oak barrels full of aging wine.

Michael Phillips is among a growing number of California winemakers working with the Symphony grape (see Tremont Vineyards, page 156). He also makes French Colombard, Chardonnay, Cabernet Sauvignon, Pinot Noir, and Carignane from vines planted in 1929 by his great-grandfather. Semirée Blanc is a proprietary blend of Sauvignon Blanc and Semillon.

More Wineries. In the course of poking around Lodi, one is bound to encounter other wineries. Most are marked by the tall towers that house their column stills. (Lodi is a center for beverage brandy as well as for the production of dessert wines.)

One of the most architecturally striking wineries in the district is on Woodbridge Road at Bruella. Once the Cherokee Co-op, later Montcalm, still later Filice, it now belongs to Robert Mondavi. Two or three other Lodi wineries are purely in the bulk trade and not open to visit. These include Woodbridge Vineyard Association and Community Winery (United Vintners) in the northwest quarter of town, and Liberty Winery in the northeast quarter.

Other Than Wineries

The year-round attractions of the wineries are supplemented by an annual Lodi Grape Festival. It takes place all over town on a weekend in mid-September, usually the one following Labor Day. Several wineries hold open house during the festival just as they do all year.

Most of the festivities are in the Grape Bowl, a fairground near State 99 northeast of Lodi. Wineries mount exhibits, and the local wine growers' association sponsors daily wine tasting in the midst of general farm displays and the most widely advertised feature of the festival, the grape mosaics.

The mosaics are what their name suggests—pictures or designs wrought by placing grapes one at a time on wire mesh. Panel sizes range up to 5 by 10 feet. Club women spend hours plucking thousands of grapes and poking them into words and pictures that follow a pre-announced theme. (A typical motif is "early California.") Grapes come in a wider range of colors than many people would suspect. The mosaics are as much a lesson in grape physiology as they are folk art.

The main event is an hours-long parade with bands, floats, and drill teams. It assembles on the west side of town, winds through the business district, and finishes up two or three miles later under the summer sun at the Grape Bowl.

Lodi has two recreational parks. Lake Lodi Park, on Turner Road a mile west of State 99, rings the municipal lake, a diverted part of the Mokelumne River. Trees shade the shore and picnic tables. The park has rental boats and swimming beaches.

Micke Grove, south of town in a large stand of valley oaks, has a small zoo, gardens, and fine picnic sites. It is west of State 99 on Armstrong Road.

For a listing of restaurants and accommodations in the area, write to Lodi District Chamber of Commerce, P.O. Box 386, Lodi, CA 95241.

Plotting a Route

The town of Lodi straddles State Highway 99, the quick route from almost any of the other Central Valley towns north or south.

For visitors coming from the San Francisco Bay region, the freeway route is Interstate Highway 580 through Livermore to Tracy, then north along the connector Interstate Highway 205 to Interstate Highway 5. To change from I-5 to State 99, you can continue on State Highway 120 to Manteca, or make a brief descent onto one local road. Lathrop does the job as well as any, connecting with I-5 about 4 miles north of its junction with I-205.

Another speedy but fairly scenic route between the San Francisco Bay area and Lodi combines Interstate Highway 80 as far east as Fairfield, then the two-lane State Highway 12 from Fairfield to Lodi.

A slower, still more scenic variation of the I-80–State 12 route between the Bay region and Lodi stays closer to the Sacramento River delta for a longer time. This route requires getting to the Contra Costa County town of Martinez by whatever means, then working east to Antioch on State Highway 4, and from there to Rio Vista along the levee road, State Highway 160. At the Rio Vista Bridge, change to State 12 for the last leg.

Within the neighborhood of Lodi, getting around requires little effort. West of State 99, Turner, Woodbridge, and Acampo roads serve well for east-west travel. The main north-south roads other than the freeway are De Vries and Lower Sacramento.

East of the freeway, things spread out a bit more, but the same east-west roads continue, with the important addition of Victor Road. The north-south roads are Kennefick and Bruella.

Within these grids the terrain is flat, given over mainly to vineyards, but with occasional surprises such as a line of olive or palm trees, or an old dry river course with its bottom full of vineyards and an occasional home garden.

Sacramento & West

For years Sacramento had the odd winery or two hidden away in back corners but was mainly notable for being the state capital. The city proper still has its same handful of wineries, but its suburbs have sprouted almost twice as many.

Much of the interest is some miles to the southwest, near the Sacramento River delta town of Clarksburg, where a fairly large winery has some substantial vineyard acreage to go with it. Nearby Davis, home of the University of California's Department of Viticulture and Enology, has visitable cellars, as do the towns of Winters and Woodland.

The Wineries

The range in size and character among Sacramento area wineries is as great as in far more crowded districts.

Belle Creek Ranch is a working ranch first and a winery second. J. P. Bowman's chickens lay their eggs precisely on the Paradise City limits. The winery is so small that Bowman talks in gallons rather than cases of wine, but it is well worth seeing as an example of the kind of efficiency winery that was part of many an early California homestead.

Bowman ferments his wines in food-grade plastic vats in the top of a two-story concrete-block building. He bottles them shortly after fermentation and keeps them cool on the lower level. No sulfur dioxide is used; clarity is achieved by racking, rather than by filtering or fining. Bowman even keeps his own yeast culture on ice between vintages. The winery pulls its weight another way, too: Once a year, Bowman's cattle feast on pomace (pressed grape skins).

The short, red roster consists of Cabernet Sauvignon and Zinfandel, the latter from Amador County grapes.

Caché Cellars belongs to a growing tradition in California, that of the winery housed in a former dairy.

In this case the architecture, to borrow a line from Duke Ellington, "ain't much to look at, ain't nothin' to see." But the winery within transcends both the building's exterior and the plain fields around it in the flats west of Davis.

Sacramento County

Belle Creek Ranch. From Chico, take Skyway to Pearson St. exit, E on Pearson .25 mi. to Foster Rd., S on Foster 1.5 mi. to Belle Creek Ln., E on Belle Creek to ranch (576 Belle Creek Ln., Paradise, CA 95969) Tel (916) 877-4124. By appt. only. GT/Ta. (Outside map area)

Caché Cellars. From I-80 W of Davis, Pedrick Rd. exit, N 2.3 mi. on Pedrick Rd. to winery drive (Route 2, Box 2780, Davis, CA 95616) Tel (916) 756-6068. Picnic. Sa-Su 11-4 or by appt. GT/Ta.

R & J Cook Winery. From Clarksburg, SE 2.8 mi. on Netherlands Rd. to winery (P.O. Box 227, Clarksburg, CA 95612) Tel (916) 775-1234. Picnic. M-F 9-4 or by appt. GT/Ta.

Frasinetti Winery. From State 99, Florin Rd. exit E to Frasinetti Rd., then S .5 mi. (7395 Frasinetti Rd., Sacramento, CA 95828) Tel (916) 383-2444. Restaurant. M-F 9-9, Sa 11-9, Su 11-5. IT/Ta.

Gibson Wine Company. From State 99, E 1.5 mi. on Elk Grove Blvd., S .2 mi. to end of Kent St. (9750 Kent St., Elk Grove, CA 95624) Tel (916) 685-9594. GT/Ta by appt.

Orleans Hill Vinicultural Corporation. From I-80 W of Davis, State 113 exit N 13 mi., W 5.8 mi. on State 16, N 2 mi. on Rd. 94B, W 1 mi. on Rd. 19 to winery drive (P.O. Box 1254, Woodland, CA 95695) Tel (916) 661-6538. By appt. only.

Paradise Vintners. From Chico, take Skyway to Pearson Rd., E on Pearson Rd. to Clark Rd., N 1 blk. on Clark to Nunnely, E on Nunnely 2 mi. to winery (1656 Nunnely Rd., Paradise, CA 95969) Tel (916) 872-WINE. Daily 1-7 or by appt. IT/Ta. (Outside map area)

Satiety Winery. From I-80 at Davis, N 8 mi. on State 113 to winery (P.O. Box 1056 Davis, CA 95616) Tel (916) 661-0680. Picnic. Daily 1-5. GT/Ta.

Tremont Vineyards. Accessible from westbound I-80 only, 3.6 mi. W of Davis, take Olmo Lane exit, E .4 mi. on frontage road, N .5 mi. on levee rd. to winery (9163 Olmo Lane, Davis, CA 95616) Tel (916) 753-0508. Picnic. GT/Ta by appt.

Winters Winery. From I-505, State 128 exit, W .3 mi. to Main St., S .7 mi. to winery (15 Main St., Winters, CA 95694) Tel (916) 795-3201. Daily 10-5. Ta. GT by appt.

Wineries Not on Map— Restricted or No Visitor Facilities

Bogle Vineyards. (Route 1, Box 276, Clarksburg, CA 95612) Tel (916) 744-1139. By appt. only.

Harbor Winery. (7576 Pocket Rd., Sacramento, CA 95831). By written appt. only.

Renaissance Vineyard & Winery. (Renaissance, CA 95962) Tel (916) 692-2222. By appt. only.

Schumacher Cellars. (721 Barcelona Ave., Davis, CA 95616) Tel (916) 758-1052. GT/Ta by appt.

Key: GT (guided tour); IT (informal tour); Ta (tasting).

Owner-winemaker Charles Lowe chose the inexpensive building and site so there would be more money left to fill it with stainless steel fermentors and a varied collection of American and French oak barrels, and to fill them with wines from grapes purchased across much of the state. The list, to give some idea, includes Chardonnay from Monterey, Sauvignon Blanc from San Luis Obispo, Pinot Noir from Sonoma, and North Coast Cabernet Sauvignon. The first crush was in 1979, and a new tasting room was opened in 1985.

R & J Cook Winery is the great pioneer in the Sacramento River delta country around Clarksburg.

The winery is typical of modern small cellars in California: a big horizontal basket press, stainless steel fermenting and storage tanks inside and out, and French and American oak barrels for final aging. Neither is the part concrete-block, part wood-frame lean-to cellar building any sort of surprise. A ranch house with Tudor touches is somewhat unusual, but the real surprise is vines growing right to the dry edge of delta levees. The view from a tree-shaded, levee-top picnic area—across water but down to vines—is not easy to find anywhere else in the world. Owners Roger and Joanne Cook are pleased to explain why the deep, sandy soil here is an ideal environment for wine grapes.

The roster of white wines from their vines includes Sauvignon Blanc and several renditions of Chenin Blanc. Reds include Cabernet Sauvignon, Merlot (white and red), and Petite Sirah.

Frasinetti Winery dates back to 1897, a long career by local standards. Founder James Frasinetti died in 1965 at the age of 91. His sons and grandsons forge on.

After the original building burned to the ground in 1924, it was replaced by a utilitarian collection of corrugated iron structures. During the early 1970s, the family added warm-hued stucco faces to the main cellar and bottling building, made a handsome tasting room, and otherwise turned the property into a peaceable, even serene, island at the end of a busy industrial street running alongside the Southern Pacific line.

A restaurant was built into the winery's old east cellar in 1985. Eating and sipping take place among nineteenth-century redwood vats.

Gibson Wine Company is best known as a pioneer in the making and marketing of fruit and berry wines, including one from kiwi, but the firm also makes a range of table, dessert, and sparkling wines.

The substantial winery was founded in 1943 by Robert Gibson and has been continued since 1960 by a grower cooperative. The wines may be sampled by appointment at the Gibson tasting room a mile south of the winery, next to State 99 at Grant Line Road.

Orleans Hill Vinicultural Corporation, temporarily housed in a rented part of the old Woodland Olive Products processing plant, is one of those tiny wineries that tempt home winemakers to make the jump, in this case for a particularly good reason.

Owners James and Carol Lapsley are the staff, having graduated to the bonded ranks in 1980 after a decade as home winemakers. (Prudently, they keep other jobs. James organizes wine courses at UC Davis extension.) A small crusher and an ingenious, home-built hydraulic press are the main pieces of processing gear. American oak barrels serve both as fermentors and aging vessels for Lodi and Amador Zinfandel made in a range of styles from white to red.

The name comes from a long-ago vineyard of Arpad Haraszthy (see the Buena Vista entry, page 35) near the village of Esparto. The vineyard's name came, in turn, from a grape variety called Orleans, which allegedly has some flavor kinships with Riesling, and which the Lapsleys hope to see replanted for their use.

Paradise Vintners is notable for producing 42 different varietal wines, most of them from owner Wilson Bruce's 250-acre vineyard in the red foothills east of Chico. The mineral-rich volcanic ash that colors the soil also has a noticeable effect on the grapes that grow in it. The red wines are inky, almost black, and reds and whites alike are intensely flavored.

Doubly so in this case, because Bruce dislikes the taste of oak in wine. "Fouls it up," he declares, so the wines pass from fermentation to bottling without the tempering influence of wood. The only barrels in the barn-style winery are metal ones, used for racking the wines in lieu of fining or filtering. Bruce's dedication to purity extends even to fermentation. No sulfur dioxide is used; the must is fermented by naturally occurring yeast stains.

He easily sells every drop he can make, right at the winery. The wines aren't available anywhere else. The roster includes all the usual varietals, plus offbeat ones such as Scarlet and Ruby Red. There is also a rare example of Mission, California's original wine grape, first planted two centuries ago by the Jesuit brethren of Junipero Serra. Paradise is open seven days a week.

Tremont Vineyards is unique in the wine world. Proprietor Paul Olmo produces his wines exclusively from grape varieties hybridized by his father, the renowned UC Davis viticulturist, Dr. Harold Olmo. (See "Grapes of the future," page 165.)

The grapes are Symphony (a cross between Grenache and Muscat of Alexandria), Flora (Gewürztraminer and Semillon), Centurion (Carignane and a Cabernet-type), Carnelian (Grenache and a Cabernet-type), and Carmine (Cabernet Sauvignon and Merlot). Tasting these varietals for the first time is roughly equivalent to being on the scene in ancient times when early winemakers were discovering some of the wine grapes we know today.

With that in mind, the winery itself is an anticlimax. The two-story wooden structure sits on flat land between Davis and Dixon, near Putah Creek. Inside, barrel racks line three walls. The rest of the first story is taken up by plastic fermentation bins and a walk-in refrigerator, used for temperature control during fermentation and for cold storage during the rest of the year. The upper floor is a residence.

Winters Winery occupies a fine brick building that did time in the Gaslight Era as the dining room of the Winters Opera House.

Owner David Storm has installed within these walls a typical small, modern winery in which he makes a broad range of wines from a remarkably local assemblage of vineyards. Notable in the roster is a Petite Sirah from century-old vines at Orleans Hill (see Orleans Hill Vinicultural Corporation, left). There are also varietals from Napa and Amador counties, including Pinot Noir, Petite Sirah, and Zinfandel. There is, alas, no Port under the jug label, Storm Cellars.

More Wineries. Five small wineries in the Sacramento district round out the roster.

Bogle Vineyards is a much smaller neighbor of R & J Cook near Clarksburg. A producer of Chenin Blanc, Petite Sirah, and a proprietary rosé called Merritt Island Rosé after the Delta vineyard location, the family-owned winery is open only by appointment.

Harbor Winery is the property of a professor of literature named Charles Myers, who makes small lots of table wines from Napa and Amador grapes, and a dessert wine from Mission grapes grown in Amador. The cellar, in a riverfront building at the edge of the city, has been active since 1972 but is not open to tour.

Renaissance Vineyard & Winery is a striking three-tier building set into a mountainside amid 300 acres of steeply contoured vineyard. Its first wines, produced under the auspices of former Schloss-Volrads winemaster Karl Werner, were scheduled for release in late

Unraveling the mystery of Zinfandel

The only place on Earth where Zinfandel grows in any quantity is California, but like most Californians it originated somewhere else. Exactly where is a mystery that may never be solved.

For nearly a century it was thought that Colonel Agostin Haraszthy introduced Zinfandel along with the Old World grape varieties he imported by sea. More recent information suggests that Zinfandel may have arrived as part of an overland horticultural shipment from New England. In any case, we know that it emerged in Sonoma County about the same time that California became a state, having shed its previous identity along the way.

Zinfandel is now the most widely planted grape in California. It is also the most versatile. Its long ripening curve, intense flavor, and deep skin pigment make it suitable for everything from rosé to Port; there is even sparkling Zinfandel. Those wines, however, are only sideshows to the main attraction: red Zinfandel table wine, the object of fascination and desire for California wine lovers everywhere.

Generally described as a spicy, robust wine, Zinfandel reflects differences in vintage and growing conditions with bold strokes of aroma and flavor. Such a protean nature is a thorn in the side of wine marketing personnel, who have long since run out of adjectives, but Zinfandel lovers find it only adds to the fun.

The way for a novice to become familiar with the range of Zinfandel characteristics is to taste as many Zinfandels as possible from a single vintage. It is helpful to compare several at a sitting, tasting "blind" to start with and only revealing each wine's identity after forming an impression of it. (No need to finish the bottles—leftover Zinfandel is good for several days.)

Pay close attention to appellation and other seemingly minor details (side and back labels often are troves of information). Attentive tasters will quickly begin to associate the geographic factors that produced a Zinfandel with the way it smells and tastes.

Part of the fun is trying to identify all the fruit and spice flavors. Zinfandels from the red, volcanic slopes of Howell and Spring mountains, for example, sometimes have a distinct black pepper component, while those from the Mother Lode's granite hills often show cherry-like flavors. Within a given area, younger vines may tend to yield spicy, raspberrylike tartness; wines made from older vines frequently lean more toward the richness of blackberries.

Having discovered favorite wineries and vineyards by tasting, the next step is going to visit them. Zinfandel specialists are an extremely hospitable lot. After all, to them Zinfandel is more than just a grape or a wine—it's a way of life.

1987, at which time the winery will be open for appointment-only visits.

Satiety Winery (rhymes with "society") was founded in 1983 by UC Davis professor Sterling Chaykin and his wife, Elaine. The 25- by 100-foot Dutch barn produces three proprietary table wines: White Perfection (Colombard and Chenin Blanc with "a suspicion of Orange Muscat"), Caressed (the white wine "caressed" by Cabernet Sauvignon), and Serenity (95 percent Cabernet Sauvignon). There is tasting daily.

Schumacher Cellars is operated by owners John and Lorraine Schumacher (and most of their neighbors) in the former garage of their Davis home. The first vintage was 1984. Among several varietals is a Petite Sirah from Yolo County vines planted in 1904. Visits are by appointment only.

Other Than Wineries

Though the Department of Viticulture and Enology at UC Davis is not open to the public, it deserves a bow from any appreciator of California wine who whistles past on I-80 or cruises by on State Highway 128 on the opposite side of the campus. The campus, 14 miles west of the state capital, is a pretty place to while away an hour or two in the midst of a great many trees and even more bicycles.

It would stretch matters to say that all California's technical progress in winemaking is owed to the academicians at Davis, but the school had a lot to do with creating the spirit of enlightened inquiry that marks professional vintaging in the state.

Sacramento and its environs are barely an hour's drive from the San Francisco Bay Area, but those with time to spare should consider stepping back into history by traveling up the Sacramento River on an excursion boat. Stay overnight in a bed-and-breakfast inn, and rent a car to tour the wineries before floating back downstream to San Francisco.

Plotting a Route

At the hub of Interstate Highway 5, Interstate Highway 80, U.S. Highway 50, and State Highway 99, Sacramento is not hard to find.

Most of the district's wineries are fairly close to one or another of these freeways. The exceptions, at Clarksburg and Paradise, also are in the only part of the district that could be called scenic. State Highway 160 cuts west from I-5 at Sacramento and passes through Clarksburg on its way to a junction with State Highway 12 at Rio Vista. Paradise is reached via state Highway 70 north from Sacramento, continuing north on State Highway 191 just north of Oroville.

San Joaquin Valley

California's biggest vineyard of them all

California barn

The San Joaquin Valley is not Wine Country in the compact sense of the North Coast counties, where wineries may be as thick on the ground as six per square mile. But this huge and implausibly diverse agricultural empire is Wine Country on a scale the coastal regions cannot match. Its 38 wineries produce something like 70 percent of the state's annual volume of wine. Fresno County alone sends 700,000 tons of grapes to wineries in a good year, compared to 320,000 for all 14 coast counties combined.

Not unexpectedly, this vineyard of the giants requires its visitors to wear seven-league boots. Some 200 miles of State Highway 99 separate Modesto on the north from Bakersfield on the south. In all that space, only 16 cellars had visitor facilities in the spring of 1987. What is more, the area's distance from other major population centers matters to all people except valley residents. Modesto is 95 miles southeast of San Francisco; Bakersfield 111 miles north of Los Angeles. For these reasons most winery visits come as diversions, either during travels between coast and mountains, or on north-south vacation trips.

The handful of survivors from the family-farm era of winemaking lend spice to visits, but in the main the tourable wineries fit the size of this great valley.

In business terms, the San Joaquin is one huge district because the large wineries draw grapes from the length and breadth of the valley. For visitors, though, the region divides into at least three focal points: Modesto, Fresno, and Bakersfield.

Modesto & surroundings

Modesto and the wine business did not get together until the 1930s, but the two have prospered mutually since then. The city's population doubled between 1950 and 1960 and has doubled again. The total now surpasses 141,000. The production of wine has grown faster than that.

Modesto is well equipped to handle visitors in large numbers. A gateway to Yosemite National Park, it has a substantial selection of motels and restaurants, most of them ranged along McHenry Boulevard and Yosemite Avenue.

The Wineries

No great distance separates Lodi from Modesto, but in those few miles the pattern of winery ownership changes markedly. Lodi is a capital of grower cooperatives. Modesto does not have a single one.

E & J Gallo is far and away the dominant winery among the 10 that ring Modesto. Some establishments that seem small next to Gallo have impressive size when measured against the average cellar of other districts. A set of genuinely small premises still give the region a diverse character.

Six wineries welcome visitors in one way or another. Bella Napoli Winery and Delicato Vineyards are on or near State Highway 99. Cadlolo and Franzia are east of 99, on State 120.

Bella Napoli Winery evokes an era that seems to be passing in the San Joaquin Valley. The winery, a separate structure at the rear of the family home, is in every respect a small, old-fashioned country enterprise.

Because of this, proprietor Lucas Hat cannot encourage a tourist trade in the usual sense. There are no tours or tastings, only the agreeably uncomplicated opportunity to stand in the courtyard amid whitewashed farm buildings and buy a supply of country red or white in bottle or jug.

Lucas is the second generation of Hats—the family name is Neapolitan—to make Vine Flow table wines for sale to a mainly local trade.

The wines come from a 60-acre vineyard surrounding the house and winery. Hat takes only a small part of his crop for his own use. The rest he sells to a larger winery.

Cadlolo Winery, in the town of Escalon, presents a fresh face to the world. The main building of concrete and red brick looks almost new beneath its coat of pale cream paint. Almost the only signs of age are an old-style evaporative cooler on the roof and a mature tree shading the front wall. But the building dates from 1913 when L. Sciaroni launched a winery on the site. Charles Cadlolo held the reins from 1937 until 1955. His sons, Raymond and Theodore, maintained the business until 1980. The current owner of these still-small cellars is Dorothy Walton.

The owners' pride in the premises is evident in more than the freshly painted appearance of the main building. The crusher alongside one wall has a well-scrubbed air. The interior of the winery is just as tidy.

Not-quite-formal tours (sometimes interrupted for a bit of work on the part of the guide) start at the crusher and go all the way through to the bottling department. Tasting is in a casual room just to one side of the main cellar, within sniffing range of its aromatic redwood tanks full of wine. On hand for sampling are several generic table wines and an equal number of appetizer and dessert wines.

Crystal Valley Cellars had one foot in Modesto and one in the Napa Valley in early 1987. Proprietor Mitch Cosentino, who founded the winery in 1981, purchased property on the St. Helena Highway, south of Oakville, in 1986. His intention is to make a reality of the winery depicted in a sketch on his 1984 Crystal Valley Cellars Chardonnay label.

In the meantime, the small metal-frame winery near Modesto houses stainless steel fermentation tanks, about 250 Limousin and Nevers oak barrels, and a wine library. The tasting room is fitted with a long white-topped bar, the better to display subtle variations in color from wine to wine.

Grapes are purchased from established North Coast vineyards. The roster includes Chardonnay, Sauvignon Blanc, Merlot, and Cabernet Sauvignon under the Crystal Valley label; under the proprietary Cosentino label, the same varietals are designated The Novelist, The Poet, and so on. Robin's Glow is a proprietary sparkling wine made from Chardonnay and Pinot Noir.

Delicato Vineyards occupies a considerable plot of ground just alongside the southbound lanes of State 99, on a frontage road near Manteca.

Signs give ample warning before the freeway exit leads onto what is nearly a private lane. The winery has on each flank a residence of one or another branch of the owning family, the Indelicatos. (Given the family name, the proprietors must have taken great delight in naming the place. He who doubts the authenticity of the reverse twist has only to read the names on the mailboxes on either side of the winery.)

Delicato has grown greatly over the past 15 years. At one time an informal tour could cover all the ground within a small, iron-sheathed winery building in a few minutes. Now guided tours, launched from a modern textured-block tasting room, take in impressive arrays of outdoor stainless steel fermentors and storage tanks—almost 22 million gallons worth—and such esoteric contrivances as rotary vacuum filters. The immaculately clean original cellar, full of redwood tanks, is on the route as is a much enlarged bottling line. This tour is the most complete and informative of any offered by a sizable producing winery in the district. The wide range of Delicato wines includes varietal and generic table wines, and appetizer, dessert, and sparkling wines.

Franzia Winery is on State 120 east of Ripon. An attractively designed and furnished tasting room sits in the midst of a decorative block of vines next to the highway. The several large buildings of the winery proper stand farther back, amid larger blocks of vines.

Giuseppe Franzia, having emigrated from Genoa, started his family in the California wine business in 1906. After the untimely intervention of Prohibition necessitated a second start in 1933, Giuseppe and his five sons built the enterprise up to an annual production of 15 million gallons by the time the family sold to a corporate owner in 1971. The new proprietors have kept the winery growing.

The company offers tours of its vast, mechanically efficient plant only by appointment. Appointments are generally limited to groups.

The tasting room, however, is open to all visitors. Franzia wines include a broad spectrum of generic and varietal table wines, several sparkling wines, and Vermouth.

A tree-shaded picnic ground on lawns adjacent to the tasting room is open to casual drop-in visitors when it has not been reserved for groups. It's a good place to enjoy a deli lunch with an impromptu blind tasting.

More Wineries. Visitors to Modesto are likely to notice other wineries on the landscape.

By far the largest winery in Modesto (and one of the largest in the world) is E & J Gallo. At present, it is not open to visitors. Alas for that, because the Gallos have come from small and perfectly ordinary beginnings to a dazzlingly complex center for making wine under the most rational of conditions with the most efficient of equipment. Nothing is left to wayward chance. The Gallos even have their own bottle manufactory on the premises, yielding glass made to their own patented formula.

Gallo's made-on-the-spot bottles receive a complete range of varietal and generic table wines, sparkling wines, and appetizer, dessert, and flavored types made from grapes grown the length and breadth of the state. The firm owns huge vineyard acreages in Modesto, Livingston, and the Sierra foothills, buys still more grapes on contract, and also buys the entire wine production of grower cooperatives in the Central Valley, Sonoma, and Napa.

Even though there is no admittance, serious students of California wine owe themselves a drive past the

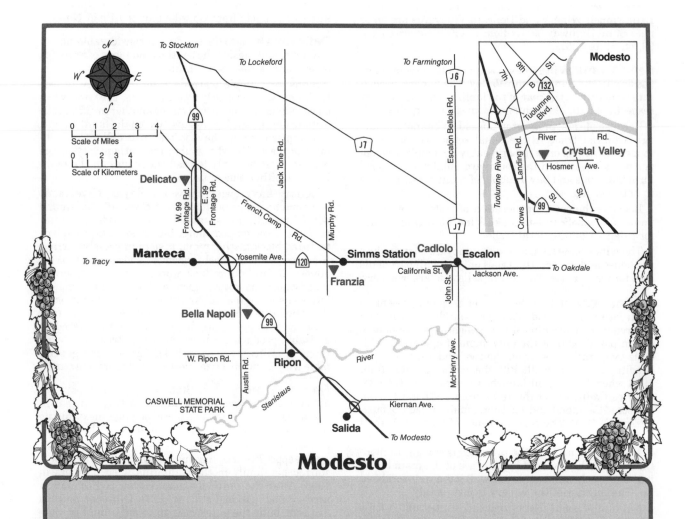

Modesto

Bella Napoli. From State 99, Austin Rd. exit, S on Austin .5 mi. (21128 S. Austin Rd., Manteca, CA 95336) Tel (209) 599-3885. Daily 9-5.

Cadlolo Winery. From State 120 at W side of Escalon, S on McHenry Ave. across RR tracks, W on California St. 100 yards to winery (1124 California St., Escalon, CA 95320) Tel (209) 838-2457. M-Sa 8-5. IT/Ta.

Crystal Valley Cellars. (dba Cosentino Wine Co.) From State 99, Tuolumne Blvd. exit, E 2 blks on B St., S 3 blks on 9th St., W ¼ mi. on Hosmer to winery (417 Hosmer, Modesto, CA 95351) Tel (209) 577-0556. M-F 10-4. IT/Ta.

Delicato Vineyards. From State 99, French Camp Rd. exit, S .5 mi. on westside frontage rd. (12001 Hwy. 99, Manteca, CA 95336) Tel (209) 239-1215. Daily 9-5:30. Ta. GT daily at 10, 2 & 4, or by appt.

Franzia Winery. From St 99, E 4.5 mi. on State 120 (17000 E. Hwy. 120, Ripon, CA 95366) Tel (209) 599-4111. Picnic. Daily 10-5. Ta. GT by appt., groups only.

Key: GT (guided tour); IT (informal tour); Ta (tasting).

headquarters and winery on Fairbanks Avenue in the southeast quarter of Modesto. There is no crushing at this facility: that goes on at other Gallo wineries west of Livingston and in Fresno.

Another sizable winery in the district that bottles wine but does not have visitor facilities is JFJ Bronco. At its Ceres location, the winery makes a wide range of varietal and generic table wines.

A. & L. Pirrone Vineyards operates a substantial, durable bulk winery alongside State 99 at the town of Salida. It has been a family cellar since 1936; the vineyards date from 1923.

Finally, observant travelers will notice that quite a few other wineries, large and small, are regular features of the landscape up and down the San Joaquin Valley. Some of them look abandoned, and have been for some time. Most, however, manage to operate regularly despite the frequent changes of ownership which reflect these uncertain times for viticulture in the valley.

Other Than Wineries

Unlikely as it may seem, Modesto is in the midst of a great deal of water. The Tuolumne and Stanislaus Rivers join the San Joaquin just west of town. Just to the east, folds in the hills harbor three major reservoirs with recreational developments.

These reservoirs, along with Yosemite National Park, draw a great many vacationers through the Modesto district. But for casual visitors, they are too far away to combine with winery visits.

Caswell State Park solves that problem. It extends along 4 miles of the Stanislaus River west of Salida. The river, shallow here, has a number of swimming holes. Picnic sites under spreading oaks are 10 to 15 degrees cooler than are nearby farm fields. To get to the park, exit west from State 99 on Austin Road 2 miles south of Manteca. The park is about 5 miles west of the freeway.

Each of the major towns in the district has a tree-shaded municipal park for quick picnics or a lazy afternoon nap.

For a list of overnight accommodations, write to the Modesto Chamber of Commerce, P.O. Box 844, Modesto, CA 95353.

Plotting a Route

Most of the wineries open to visit in the Modesto area are either on the freeway, State 99, or the two-lane road, State 120. These two roads form an awkward, toppling "T." State Highway 108, another two-laner, runs from State 120 at Escalon into Modesto, the third leg of a triangle that can turn a tour of all six wineries in the region into a tidy loop for anyone starting and finishing in Modesto.

On the San Joaquin Valley floor, these and all other roads are flat, with few or no curves.

The visual interests are subtleties on a vast canvas. A shift from row crop to orchard is gross change, es-

pecially when February and March light the orchards with blossom. Random single oaks or small clusters of them in the fields produce eerie perspectives on a misty day. There is a prodigious number of unpainted, decaying small barns to consider in this era of large-scale agriculture. Residential architecture ranges from a rare brick colonial to a profusion of wooden cottages.

To get into the region from the San Francisco Bay area, use Interstate Highway 580 to Tracy, Interstate Highway 5 to its junction with State 120, then the state route to get to or across State 99.

From Los Angeles, I-5 intersects both State Highway 132 into Modesto and State 120.

Fresno

The highest point in Fresno is the twenty-second floor of the county office building. Look out from that floor on a typical heat-hazy day in summer, and no hill of stature will appear in view. Fresno is flat.

The city has grown big enough to have traffic jams and other nonagricultural qualities. (In the last census, its 285,000 population was enough to rank it eighth largest among California cities, sixty-fourth largest in the nation.)

Yet it manages to have charms. The main street of Fresno's original business district, fading a few years ago, has been turned into a spacious shopping mall with fountains, many trees (and shaded sitting places), and 20 specially commissioned sculptures. Nearby, a big convention center of unusual architecture is the stage for attractions both home-grown and imported.

To the north of the original city center, West Shaw Avenue has become a long, often architecturally distinctive, sequence of shopping centers and office buildings.

The central city may have begun to acquire a certain urbanity in this era of large-scale and mechanized farming (everybody in the Central Valley calls it "agribusiness" these days), but Fresno is, nonetheless, a farm center. The talk in the coffee shops has to do with one crop or another.

Among those crops, grapes figure most prominently. Fresno and neighboring counties north and south produce enough raisins for the Western Hemisphere and enough table grapes for much of the United States. In recent years the district's share of wine production has slipped below its old level of 50 percent of all California wine, but only because other districts have added vineyards more rapidly than Fresno has.

Traditionally the production has leaned toward Sherries, Ports, Muscats, and other sweet dessert wines. The long, sunny summers favor sugar-laden grapes with their ancestral roots in Portuguese or Spanish soils. Here, as in Lodi and Modesto, specially developed warm-climate grapes for table wines are replacing other varieties or supplementing them.

Reading the founding dates of wineries, an innocent visitor might assume that winemaking did not get going in Fresno until 1936 or so, as in the case of Modesto. Blame Prohibition for creating yet another false impression. A man named Lee Eisen planted the first vineyard in the district in 1873. (Three rail-sitters of the day volunteered to eat the entire crop, which they might have done the first year but never thereafter.) Grapes have flourished in Fresno from Eisen's time on, and a good many have gone into wine since 1876.

The Wineries

The Fresno district covers an awesome number of square miles from Madera on the northwest to Cutler on the southeast. Within that vast expanse, fewer than a dozen wineries welcome visitors. But sparse as the numbers might be, the wineries are of such diverse character as to make a complete sampler of everything from giant to miniature, from generalist to specialist, from ultramodern to entirely traditional.

Anderson Wine Cellars is a tidy model for small wineries everywhere in California. Amid 20 acres of vineyard purchased in 1977, Donald and Catherine Anderson built a handsome white stucco, Spanish-style building in time for the 1980 crush. Under the red shingle roof are a tasting room, lab, and hospitality room leading to a long, narrow cellar stocked with stainless steel fermentors, a pair of 2,500 French oak uprights, and a couple hundred small French oak barrels. The whole thing is 45 × 90 feet.

Estate grapes are supplemented with purchased fruit for a short varietal roster weighted toward whites: French Colombard, Chenin Blanc, Ruby Cabernet Blush, and Ruby Cabernet, a hybrid grape developed at UC Davis. The tasting room is kept open at regular hours during the summer, but visits are by appointment only during the rest of the year.

Bianchi Vineyards was one of the newer labels in the Fresno district in 1974, when the Bianchi family took over a 1930s winery and refitted it to the state of the art. It still is.

Just for the romance, owner Joseph Bianchi saved an old still tower fitted out to please the taste of a Henry VIII. New buildings were added for large-scale bottling, and storage. Otherwise the property has been made into a modern San Joaquin-style cellar, but not quite a typical one: Bianchi Vineyards operates with a patented process for both red and white wines that keeps grape skins and seeds out of contact with the juice during fermentation. Guides explain the details to groups that tour the winery. No provision is made for individual tours.

Individuals are welcome in the tasting room, however, to sample the roster of wines produced under a half-dozen labels in addition to the house brand. Wines labeled Bianchi Winery include Chardonnay, Sauvignon Blanc, Chenin Blanc, Cabernet Sauvignon, and Zinfandel.

Cribari Winery is located in the colorful complex of brick buildings originally built as the Roma Winery.

When John Cella was developing Roma in the post-Prohibition era, he meant to have a giant of a winery. The fact that the property is laid out on a grid of streets attests to his ambition. The winery is not the giant it once was because standards have changed, but it covers more ground than many newer places. It is also a good deal more colorful than most contemporaries.

Cribari is now owned by Guild Wineries & Distilleries (see the Lodi section, page 152).

The proprietors took a huge, brick-walled aging cellar, removed the tanks from it, and turned it into a reception and tasting hall for visitors. Fanciful flags and pennants hang from the lofty ceiling and on some of the tall walls. Hourly tours leave from this reception hall.

The tour route is along B Street to 4th, across to C, then back. Along the way it passes Cribari's huge crushers, dejuicers, and temperature-controlled stainless steel fermenting tanks. Finally, in the brandy distillery, the tour provides the only close-up look at column stills to be had in all California.

Available in the tasting room is the full line of Cribari table, sparkling, and dessert wines.

Ficklin Vineyards, out of Madera, is one of the smallest wineries in the Central Valley and is certainly the most single-minded.

The specialty is a Tinta Port made entirely from four selected Portuguese grape varieties. It is not only the speciality: it is nearly the sum of winery production. (The owners started making Emerald Riesling and Ruby Cabernet in the 1960s mainly for their own table, but this remains a casual part of the enterprise.)

The Ficklin family ranch dates back to 1911, when Walter Ficklin, Sr., arrived in the Fresno area and immediately launched into grapes and other fruit growing. Wine entered the picture in the early 1940s when Ficklin responded to a request by scientists at UC Davis to plant trial blocks of several Portuguese grape varieties that had shown promise in university tests.

David Ficklin, after studying at Davis, began as the winemaker and winery manager. He continues in those roles, assisted now by his son Peter, also a Davis graduate. The vineyardist is Steven Ficklin, son of the now-retired Walter Ficklin, Jr.

The winery was founded in 1946, and in 1948 the first wine was made from Tinta Cão, Tinta Madeira, Alvarelhão, Souzão, and Touriga grapes. The Alvarelhão grapes have since been abandoned.

The main cellar, small and low in a flat sea of vineyards west of State 99, is of adobe block fashioned on the site by the family. It is a substantial tribute to the traditional bent of the Ficklins. So is a handsome cellar full of fat oak barrels and puncheons. However, the family is only bent toward tradition, not bound by it. For example, they have done away with their original concrete fermentors in favor of more practical stainless steel tanks. And they have abandoned binning their bottled wines in favor of storing them in their case boxes to minimize handling.

The Ficklins sell their Tinta Port (along with small lots of Emerald Riesling and Ruby Cabernet) in a retail room next door to the cellar. Because the winery and ranch are owned and worked by the family, the Ficklins can offer tours by appointment only, when their days are not too full of jobs that need doing immediately.

A. Nonini Winery, on the west edge of Fresno, was founded in 1936 by A. (equally appropriate for Antonio

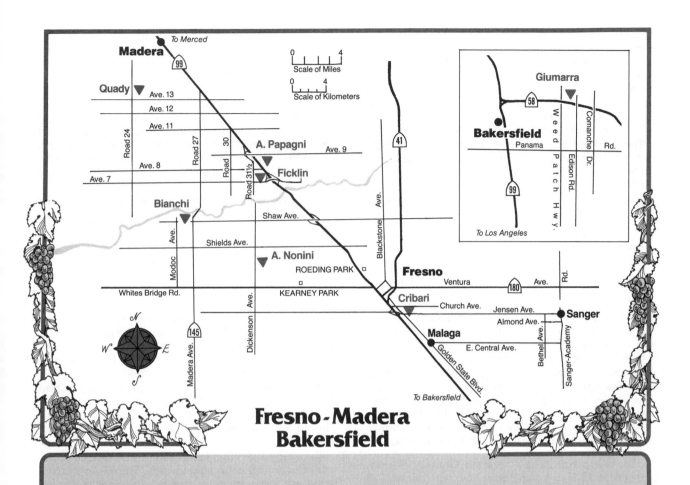

Fresno-Madera Bakersfield

Bianchi Vineyards. From State 99, W on Shaw Ave. to Modoc Ave., N on Modoc to winery (5806 N. Modoc Ave., Kerman, CA 93630) Tel (209) 846-7356. M-F 8-4. IT (except during crush)/Ta.

Cribari Winery. From State 99, Jensen Ave. exit northbound or Ventura Ave. exit southbound, take Golden State Blvd. to Church Ave., then E .25 mi. to winery (3223 E Church Ave., Fresno, CA 93714) Tel (209) 485-3080. Picnic. Daily 10-5. Ta. GT 10, 11, 1, 2, & 3.

Ficklin Vineyards. From State 99, Ave. 9 exit, W on Ave. 9 to Rd. 30, S on Rd. 30 to Ave. 7½, E to winery (30246 Ave. 7½, Madera, CA 93637) Tel (209) 674-4598. GT by appt.

Giumarra Vineyards. From State 99, State 58 exit, SE 6.5 mi. to Edison Rd. exit, N .25 mi. to Edison Hwy., W 100 yds. to winery entrance on right (P.O. Bin 1969, Bakersfield, CA 93303) Tel (805) 395-7000. F & Sa 9-4. Ta. GT by appt.

A. Nonini Winery. From State 99, McKinley Ave. exit, W 7.5 mi. to Dickenson Ave., then N .5 mi. to winery (2640 N. Dickenson Ave., Fresno, CA 93722) Tel (209) 275-1936. M-Sa 9-5. Ta. GT by appt.

Angelo Papagni Winery. From State 99, E on Ave. 9 to winery (31754 Ave. 9, Madera, CA 93638) Tel (209) 674-5652. GT/Ta by appt.

Quady Winery. From State 99, W on Ave. 12 to Rd. 24, N on Rd. 24 1.25 mi. to winery (13181 Road 24, Madera, CA 93637) Tel (209) 673-8068. M-F 8-5. GT/Ta. Sa, Su, & holidays GT/Ta by appt.

Outside Map Area

Anderson Wine Cellars. From State Hwy. 99, take Visalia exit, E 15 mi. on Hwy. 198 to Woodlake Hwy. (Hwy. 245), N 1.1 mi. to Avenue 306, W past canal to 1st rd. (20147 Avenue 306, Exeter, CA 93221) Tel (209) 592-4682. Picnic, playground. Daily (hours vary, call ahead). IT/Ta.

California Growers Winery. From State 99, Ave. 384 exit, E 15 mi. on Ave. 384 to winery at intersection of Ave. 384 and Rd. 128 (38558 Rd. 128, Cutler, CA 93615) Tel (209) 528-3033. M-F 8-5.

Key: GT (guided tour); IT (informal tour); Ta (tasting).

and wife Angiolina) Nonini, and since has passed to the hands of three sons, Geno, Gildo, and Reno. The third generation has now entered the family wine-making arena.

The Noninis grow their own grapes. Production is limited to table wines, including Grenache Rosé, Barbera, and Zinfandel as well as generics.

A tour of a tidy wood-frame cellar takes in every step from crushing to bottling, ending up in a fittingly informal tasting room housed in a cottage just in front of the cellar's front wall.

Along with Bella Napoli and Cadlolo, this is one of the last survivors of a once-abundant roster of family wineries catering to a local trade. This one has not lost a bit of flavor from the days when Basque shepherds would fill botas or buy barrels on the way from winter to summer pastures and back. It is still possible to buy Nonini wine in small barrels or fill your own.

Angelo Papagni Winery tucks into one-quarter of a freeway cloverleaf just south of Madera.

The buildings went up in 1973-75. Though the exterior walls are unornamented workaday warehouse metal, this is an impressive place. The Papagni crushing facility rivals the nearby freeway cloverleaf for size. Inside, stainless steel fermentors and aging tanks share space with an imposing collection of oak barrels.

The property was designed to make vintage-dated varietal table wines, including the rarely produced Alicante Bouschet and Charbono among reds, Chardonnay and Chenin Blanc among whites, and Moscato d'Angelo as a signature among the sparkling wines.

Quady Winery has joined Ficklin in Madera as a specialist in making fortified sweet wines, but the tack is somewhat different.

Where the older winery makes what might be called Wood Ports, Quady produces Vintage Ports. The differences between the two depend most on aging and blending. Wood Ports are blended from different vintages that have spent varying amounts of time aging in barrel. True Vintage Ports all come from a single vintage, and are bottled after approximately 2 years in barrel. Quady also produces wines from rare Muscat varieties.

Proprietor Andrew Quady offers looks at Port from the perspective of the vintage style in the handsome, wood-frame winery building behind the family residence. It was expanded considerably in 1985. Other Quady dessert wines are Essencia, made from Orange Muscat grapes, and Elysium, from Black Muscat.

More Wineries. The California Growers Winery, launched in 1936 as a cooperative and owned since 1973 by the Setrakian family, offers neither tours nor tasting in its large winery near Cutler, but it does sell wine at retail weekdays. The Growers and Setrakian labels cover varietal and generic table wines and brandy.

A good many more large wineries operate within this sprawling district. Included in the roster are these: California Products, E & J Gallo, Guild, Sierra, Vie-Del, and Viking in Fresno; Bisceglia (Canandaigua), Paul Masson, and Mission Bell (United Vintners) in Madera; Cella (United Vintners) and Mt. Tivy (The Christian Brothers) in Reedley; and Selma in Rio Vista. These wineries have no visitor accommodations of any sort. They do not even sell wines at retail prices.

Other Than Wineries

Fresno has two excellent parks and a mysterious underground grotto as diversions to winery tours. And photographers, both novice and advanced, will find good hunting in the sprawling ranch and vineyard country.

Roeding Park, 157 acres tucked between State 99 and State 99-Business and between Olive and Belmont avenues, is a tree-shaded, quiet respite from the valley sun. There are several areas for children, including a storyland, a zoo, an amusement arcade, a sizable pond with rental boats, and spacious picnic areas beneath tall rows of eucalyptus.

Kearney Park is 7 miles west of Fresno on Kearney Boulevard. It is a huge, county-operated picnic park on the grounds of the old M. Theo Kearney estate. Several large areas are set aside for group reservations. Interspersed between these are a great many small areas for first-come, first-served family use.

The underground grotto of Baldasare Forestiere is north of Fresno, two blocks west of State 99 on Shaw Avenue. Forestiere was a Sicilian possessing Herculean powers with a pick and a shovel. After digging for 38 years, he ended up with a maze of tunnels that runs beneath 7 acres of surface ground. The deepest rooms are 25 feet below ground and on summer afternoons are 20 degrees cooler than is the surface.

For information on accommodations and restaurants in the area, write to the Fresno Chamber of Commerce, 2331 Fresno Street, Fresno, CA 93721.

Plotting a Route

For people in the San Joaquin Valley, State Highway 99 is the obvious means of approaching Fresno-area wineries from either north or south. Anyone starting from the San Francisco Bay area can get across the coast ranges most efficiently on Interstate Highway 580, though State Highway 152, the Pacheco Pass Highway, is more scenic and only slightly slower.

In addition to being the basic approach route, State 99 is also a useful thread in getting from one winery to another since it makes a long, diagonal slice through the region that somewhat parallels the sequence of cellars.

Generally speaking, none of the roads leading to the wineries provides stunning scenery. The possible exceptions are those roads in the Reedley-Sanger district that get close to the course of the Kings River. These lead past changing terrain and brightened colors.

Bakersfield

Bakersfield is the urban anchor for the southern end of the San Joaquin Valley. Unlike Fresno and other valley cities, Bakersfield is as involved in drilling for oil as it is in growing crops. In fact, it is not at all uncommon to see the bobbing heads of pumps at wells between vine rows. The other instantly noticeable fact of local life is a general passion for country-and-western music.

The Wineries

It isn't easy for visitors to get a taste of wines or to see how the work gets done. Only one of its four wineries maintains a tasting room and offers tours (to groups and by appointment only).

Giumarra Vineyards was first opened to visitors in 1974, at the same time the family-owned winery released its first vintage-dated varietal wines from local vineyards.

The winery occupies the western end of a long line of buildings near Edison. The other structures are used for aspects of a diverse farming business, and there are

Grapes of the future

Winemaking technology has changed so rapidly since Repeal that we tend to forget that the vine itself is evolving, too. Advances in the vineyard may not be nearly as flashy as those in the computer-driven winery, but they are inexorable and, perhaps, of greater long-term significance.

New grape varieties issue regularly from the University of California at Davis, virtually all of them created by Professor of Viticulture, Emeritus Dr. Harold Olmo. Among the better-known wine grapes developed by Dr. Olmo are Ruby Cabernet and Emerald Riesling (popularized by Paul Masson Vineyards as Emerald Dry), although some of his more recent hybrids may one day eclipse them.

A new grape variety is made by genetically crossing two vines having complementary attributes. The basic notion is to capture as many positive traits as possible while eliminating undesirable characteristics. It is a game of chance to some extent. Grapevines are genetic melting pots, like people, and their progeny vary as much as human children do. Still, selective propagation makes steady refinement possible over a period of time.

The process begins in late spring when the grape flowers begin to open. Before they can self-pollinate, a flower cluster from one parent (male) is bagged and taken to a depollinized (female) parent, where a few quick shakes and a crumple of paper seal the bargain. With any luck at all, there will be a new kind of grapevine in the greenhouse by next spring. Years of testing and evaluation follow.

The viticulturist starts with a specific goal. Some genetic crosses are aimed at physically improving vines and their fruit, while others combine the sensory characteristics of different varieties.

Rubired was developed to correct poor color in certain red wine grapes grown in hot regions such as the San Joaquin Valley. As parents for *Rubired*, Dr. Olmo chose Alicante Ganzin (a French hybrid with brilliant red pigment) and Tinta Cão (a heat-loving Portuguese variety that ripens prodigously and is disease-resistant). *Rubired* was widely accepted, not for varietal bottling but as a base (along with its sibling,

Royalty) for sweet generics and flavored wines.

Flora is a highly aromatic new white grape made by crossing Gewürztraminer with Semillon. It has the perfume and crispness of the former, with the body and aging potential of the latter.

The name *Symphony* appears in the varietal rosters of several wineries in this book. To make this white grape, Dr. Olmo crossed the fragrant Muscat of Alexandria with Grenache. The result makes beguiling, ageworthy wine in several styles, from bone-dry to sweet.

As red wines inevitably come back into style, Dr. Olmo's three new red grapes may win hearts and palates, too. *Carmine* is a Bordeaux-style blend in a single crimson package: a cross between Cabernet Sauvignon and Merlot. *Carnelian* is a cross between a lighter Cabernet-type and Grenache. Its wine is full-bodied, with the kind of spicy, black-pepper flavors and aromas often associated with the Rioja wines of Spain. Yet another combination of a Cabernet-type with Grenache produced *Centurion*, which makes an intensely aromatic, flavorful wine.

New wine grape varieties aren't produced overnight. More than ten years pass between initial pollination and commercial availability. Even after its release to growers, the grape may take decades to win favor with winemakers and consumers. Or it may never be accepted at all.

Not all viticultural research is concerned with hybridizing new grapes. The established varieties are constantly being improved and refined, too. The Chardonnay we know in California is not quite the same as that grown in Meursault; our Chardonnay clones have been modified for warm-weather service. For that matter, the Chardonnay grown around San Luis Obispo may be a bit different from that grown in the Russian River Valley.

Wine drinkers in ancient Greek and Roman times would not have recognized our contemporary grape varieties, nor would we be familiar with theirs. It is quite possible that future imbibers may sip wines that would seem more alien to us than Zinfandel does to the French, while gazing out over vineyards full of grapes we've never imagined.

---

enough of them that it takes a couple of minutes to drive from the property entrance to the sculpted concrete building that houses the tasting room.

On the second floor, the tasting room allows visitors to watch work on the bottling line while they sample from a list that includes Chenin Blanc, Riesling, French Colombard, Cabernet Sauvignon, and Pinot Noir.

Groups can arrange for walking tours of the crushing area and aging cellars.

More Wineries. Three companies in the region make and move wine only in bulk. They are Delano Cooperative, a dessert wine cellar belonging to Guild Wineries & Distilleries (see page 152), and Sierra Wine Corp.

Southern California

New frontiers back where it all began

Garrett's Ghost...

T ime and the restless tide of population in Southern California have caused a whole series of shifts in vineyards of this oldest of California's winegrowing regions.

Father Junipero Serra planted the first vines at the mission in San Diego circa 1769. As early as 1831 Jean Louis Vignes planted the first commercial vineyard in what is now downtown Los Angeles. All traces of these and some other early districts are long gone. The one reminder of early times is a small room at Mission San Gabriel, kept more or less the way it was when the Franciscans were making wine in it.

For decades the greatest concentration of vineyards was in the Cucamonga district east of Los Angeles, between the San Bernardino County towns of Ontario and Fontana. However, as population pressures grew more severe with each passing year, this region too suffered a steadily tightening squeeze.

In searching for new land to plant, several vineyardists turned south to Temecula in Riverside County; others looked still farther south, to Escondido, only a few miles from the old mission in San Diego. To the north, Ventura County began to look promising.

Ventura County

In 1985 the California Agricultural Commission listed Ventura County as having exactly one acre of wine grapes. By 1987 that figure had more than doubled. Perhaps more telling is the steady proliferation of wineries in the county. In spring of 1987, the two established producers were about to be joined by four new ones, with others preparing in the wings.

Ventura County's diverse economy includes fishing, oil, poultry, livestock, and the military, but agriculture is the staple. The Oxnard Plain is a cornucopia of produce, and citrus orchards in the coastal valleys have been shipping oranges, grapefruit, and lemons across the country since the nineteenth century. There is even a Shangri-la: Ojai, which played the enchanted city in the original film version of *Lost Horizon*.

The Wineries

The winery movement in Ventura County is unique for two reasons. One is the conspicuous lack, as of 1987, of major corporate involvement. The other is the fact that both of the established wineries, and virtually all of the projected ones, have spun out of the Cellarmasters Club and other home winemakers' coalitions, which provide extraordinary moral and material support for their more ambitious members.

Daumé Winery is the flagship of a proud fleet of small wineries. John Daumé is its admiral. A one-time businessman who dropped out of corporate life to be his own boss, Daumé bought a Los Angeles wine shop in 1972 with the intention of supplying wine buffs with the equipment and moral support necessary to serious home winemaking. Early gatherings at the shop evolved into the Cellarmasters Club. As of 1987, more than a dozen Cellarmasters had founded commercial wineries in California, and that many more were giving the proposition serious thought.

Daumé, meanwhile, founded his own winery near Camarillo in 1982. Like most Cellarmasters operations, Daumé's is conducted in plain but functional leased quarters in an industrial park. He carefully selects the vineyards from which he purchases grapes, going so far as to specify the acceptable clones of each variety and other seemingly arcane details.

Students of wine will revel in Daumé's methodology, which combines time-honored Burgundian techniques with the technological resources available to modern Californians. One example is his use of a walk-in refrigerator to cool barrels of fermenting wine. That notion is almost as old as deep limestone caves, but its modern application amounts to tacit admission of Cellarmasters affiliation (see Leeward Winery, below).

Daumé produces Chardonnay, Sauvignon Blanc, Vin Gris (a Pinot Noir rosé), and his specialty, red Pinot Noir. Visits are by appointment only.

Leeward Winery is an especially good place for the novice to get a feel for winemaking. Unlike most winery owners, Chuck Brigham and Chuck Gardner encourage visitors to poke around the winery and examine the equipment, while they answer questions in as much detail as desired.

The winery is two blocks off the freeway in Ventura. It was built in time for the 1982 crush, after Brigham and Gardner had been making wine commercially for three years in Camarillo. There are two buildings. One contains the tasting room, offices, a well-equipped lab, and case storage. The other, larger building is the processing center. In addition to the crusher, press, and bottling line, it houses the winery's most remarkable feature: a room-size refrigerator designed to keep 150 barrels of fermenting wine at optimum temperature. This is not a new idea (Louis M. Martini did it first in the 1940s), but it amounts to an innovation in modern times.

Following the informal guided tour, Leeward wines are poured at a long bar in the tasting room, where there are also photo albums documenting the winery's development.

The Leeward roster includes Chardonnay (two or three separate wines each vintage), Merlot, and Cabernet Sauvignon. Coral is a proprietary rosé of Pinot Noir.

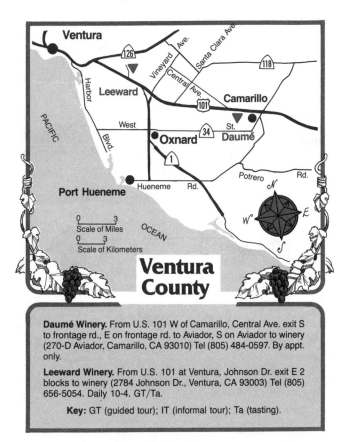

Ventura County

Daumé Winery. From U.S. 101 W of Camarillo, Central Ave. exit S to frontage rd., E on frontage rd. to Aviador, S on Aviador to winery (270-D Aviador, Camarillo, CA 93010) Tel (805) 484-0597. By appt. only.

Leeward Winery. From U.S. 101 at Ventura, Johnson Dr. exit E 2 blocks to winery (2784 Johnson Dr., Ventura, CA 93003) Tel (805) 656-5054. Daily 10-4. GT/Ta.

Key: GT (guided tour); IT (informal tour); Ta (tasting).

Other Than Wineries

Somehow, the California of a more tranquil age has been preserved in much of Ventura County. Its diversity of climates and landscapes, plus large areas of relatively sparse population, make it particularly rewarding for explorers and ramblers. Organized, goal-oriented tourists may find Ventura County frustrating, but happy wanderers will find a treasure trove of memorable experiences.

Among these are the heady brew of orange blossoms and moonlight on a warm Camarillo evening; an early-morning sighting, along the backroad to Ojai, of wild horses plunging down a cliff on a hairline path; a spring drive through the commercial flower farms on the Oxnard Plain, with fields of color rippling away from the road in tangy ocean breezes. The red-rock canyons on the dry side of the coast range make no apologies to Utah. The hot springs and waterfalls on the ocean side evoke Maui. The possibilities are endless.

There is one Ventura County resource that is worth a little planning and effort. Channel Islands National Park consists of half a dozen large islands a few miles offshore, which delineate the Santa Barbara Channel.

Santa Cruz Island, the largest of the group, is believed to be the site of California's earliest human habitation. Artifacts found there date back more than 18,000 years, still only a fraction the age of the Santa Cruz Island Fox, a species unique to that dot in the sea.

Los Angeles County

Ahern Winery. From State 118, Glenoaks Blvd. exit, NW 7 blks. to Arroyo Ave., SW ½ blk. to winery (715 Arroyo Ave., San Fernando, CA 91340) Tel (818) 365-3106. Daily by appt.

Donatoni Winery. From I-405, Imperial Hwy. exit W to La Cienega Blvd., N on La Cienega to winery near 106th St. (10604 S. La Cienega Blvd., Inglewood, CA 90304) Tel (213) 645-5445.

McLester Winery. From I-405, Imperial Hwy. exit W to La Cienega Blvd., N on La Cienega to winery between Lennox Blvd. and 106th St. (10670-D S. La Cienega Blvd., Inglewood, CA 90304) Tel (213) 641-9686. Sa 12-5, or by appt. GT/Ta.

Palos Verdes Winery. From I-405, Imperial Hwy. exit W to La Cienega Blvd., N on La Cienega to winery between Lennox Blvd. and 106th St. (10620-D S. La Cienega Blvd., Inglewood, CA 90304) Tel (213) 645-3273. Sa-Su 12-4 or by appt. GT/Ta. (Call ahead).

San Antonio Winery. From I-5, Main St. exit W 5 blks. to Lamar, S 2 blks. on Lamar to winery (737 Lamar St., Los Angeles, CA 90031) Tel (213) 223-1401. M-Th and Sa 8-7; F 8-8; Su 10-6. GT/Ta.

Key: GT (guided tour); IT (informal tour); Ta (tasting).

Strict protective regulations govern actual landings on the islands. Arrangements must be made with the National Park Service well in advance of a planned visit. However, excursion boats depart regularly from Channel Islands Harbor, Port Hueneme, and Ventura Harbor for day trips around the islands. Scuba divers can book passage on dive boats to explore the magnificent jade-green world on the underwater skirts of Anacapa Island.

For maps and information, write to the Ventura Visitors Bureau, 785 S. Seaward Avenue, Ventura, CA 93001, or to the Oxnard Visitors Bureau at 400 Esplanade Drive, Suite 100, Oxnard, CA 93030.

In addition, Los Padres National Forest (which occupies more than half of the county) offers hiking and camping. Contact the National Park Service for information.

Plotting a Route

The major route through Ventura County is U.S. 101. State Highway 126 runs inland from Montalvo, through Santa Paula and Fillmore, to intersect Interstate 5 just north of Valencia. Los Padres National Forest is reached via Route 33 from Ventura; to make a scenic loop, leave Route 33 at its intersection with Route 150, drive west through Ojai to Santa Paula, and return to the coast on State Highway 126.

State Highway 1, contiguous with U.S. 101 along the northern Ventura County coast, splits away at Oxnard to pick its own way south along a spectacular coastline.

Los Angeles

Early in the history of wine in California, a sizable vineyard grew where Union Station now stands. Times have moved so far that even the railroad station is now on its way to becoming a part of the local past.

The Wineries

San Antonio Winery has proved that large-volume wine production can work in urban Los Angeles, but as of 1987 the trend was clearly in the other direction, toward discreet, labor-intensive operations with all the frills inside the bottle.

Ahern Winery is easily the most technologically sophisticated winery in the San Fernando Valley. The fact that it's the only one doesn't diminish the impact of such gleaming marvels as a Gai Monoblock bottling line and Comen labeler, capable of filling, corking, and labeling nearly 1,500 bottles an hour. Jim Ahern also has a state of the art crusher, a Howard 1200 press, and a powerful glycol refrigeration system hooked up to several jacketed stainless steel fermenting tanks. He knows how to use it all, too.

Ahern began fooling around with home winemaking in 1972 and quickly became serious. He and his wife, Joyce, founded Ahern Winery in 1978. With grapes purchased from old, proven vineyards as far away as the Sierra foothills and as near as Paso Robles, the Aherns produce Chardonnay, Sauvignon Blanc, Cabernet Sauvignon, and Zinfandel. Visits are by appointment only.

Donatoni Winery anchors a trio of tiny wineries on an industrial stretch of La Cienega Boulevard, at the edge of Los Angeles International Airport. Former pilot Hank Donatoni and his wife, Judy, bonded their large air-conditioned space in 1979. The varietal roster is short and dry: Chardonnay and Cabernet Sauvignon.

McLester Winery tips off its location with a pair of proprietary wines called Runway Red and Runway White. The labels depict 747s landing between rows of grapevines. Cecil and Marcella Mattson-McLester founded the winery in 1980 and are currently producing Sauvignon Blanc, Merlot, Cabernet Sauvignon, and Zinfandel.

Palos Verdes Winery is the smallest member of the airport area winery group (see Donatoni and McLester). Owners Herb and Pat Harris began as home winemakers but discovered that it's easier to take grape deliveries in industrial space than at home. They welcome visitors on weekends only.

San Antonio Winery, with increasing ease, perseveres as a producing winery in spite of its downtown Los Angeles location. The development of field crushing means that the owning Riboli family can bring unfermented grape juice via road tanker from Santa Barbara, Monterey, or other Central Coast vineyards for fermenting in the industrial surrounds of Lamar Street.

The walk-through tour of the winery shows the new developments alongside bits and pieces of equipment from the old days, when they brought whole grapes in trucks from Cucamonga. The clearest evocation of the old era is a big stemmer-crusher, still anchored to its original spot in a room that has been transformed into an Italian restaurant. The clearest evocation of the new era is at the rear of the main cellar: a fermenting room full of stainless steel tanks.

In the tasting room, visitors can assess an extensive line of wines of all types, from varietal table wines to flavored dessert specialties. A picnic ground with space for 100 adjoins the main cellar.

Other Than Wineries

The San Fernando Mission, one of the best-preserved in Father Junipero Serra's entire chain, is open to the public daily. Many of the adobe rooms have been restored to what passed as opulence for their Spanish military occupants. There is a small admission fee. In west Los Angeles, the burgeoning artistic community of Venice is worth a visit as are several art museums.

Plotting a Route

The most useful freeways for getting around in Los Angeles are I-10 for east-west travel, and Interstates 5 (inland) and 405 (coast) on the north-south axis. A detailed street map is essential.

Temecula

The Temecula district started all in a rush as a winegrowing area when a real-estate development operation turned much of the southwest corner of Riverside County into Rancho California and simultaneously encouraged buyers to plant grapes on their parcels.

The first small plantings in 1968 quickly expanded to 2,000 acres. By 1987 the total approached 4,000 acres. The first winery, built in 1974, now has six neighbors, with more in the planning stages.

This is relentlessly hilly country. The section where the vines grow is a sort of catch basin for what little runoff water there is from a sparse annual rainfall. It also draws cool, moist sea breezes through a gap in the hills to the west. The combination makes the local climate as pleasant for people as it is for vines. The climate notwithstanding, Temecula has tended to business, rather than developing into a vacation retreat.

The Wineries

The short roster of young wineries offers a remarkable diversity of size and architectural style.

Callaway Vineyard & Winery started the new trend in winemaking south of the Tehachapi Mountains. It pioneered the shift toward small, estatelike wineries producing varietal table wines.

Occupying a series of rolling knolls east of Temecula, the winery and vineyards were founded by retired business executive Ely Callaway, who planted his first vines in 1969, built the first cellars in 1974, and sold his much-enlarged properties to Hiram Walker Resources, Ltd., the Canadian distillers, in 1981.

The present winery looms up from the top of a sharp rise above Rancho California Road. Its tall, white walls are unbroken by windows except on the west face, where the visitors' hall is a light and airy room. Around back, a short length of metal wall and another of concrete block reveal the original size of the building.

From custom-made crusher to continuous dejuicer and press, stainless steel fermentors, and centrifuge, this is a first-rate example of a modern California winery. Each hourly tour finishes with a sit-down tasting of selected wines.

Callaway's wines include Chardonnay (regular and late-harvest), Riesling (regular and late-harvest), Sauvignon Blanc, and Chenin Blanc (regular and late-harvest).

Picnickers may make use of a well-designed area behind the winery on a first-come, first-served basis, except when it has been reserved for a group.

Cilurzo Vineyard & Winery was launched in 1978, but the Cilurzo vineyard goes back to 1967. Its oldest block has the first commercial vines planted in Temecula.

The two-story cellar building is cut into one of the infinity of sandy hillocks that make up this part of Rancho California, its plywood hide painted almost the same hue. In the time-honored way of hillside wineries, grapes arrive at the uphill side for crushing, and new juice flows to fermentors below. A tidy cellar full of oak barrels nestles in an angle formed by two perpendicular rows of stainless steel fermentors. Amid stored cases of wine and bottling gear on the upper story is an affable, informal tasting room.

Hollywood lighting director Vincenzo Cilurzo and his wife Audrey started growing grapes almost on a whim, fell into home winemaking, and ended up taking winemaking courses at UC Davis. (The depth of their involvement can be measured not only in the winery but in the name of their daughter, Chenin.) The winery came as the inevitable final step.

The roster of Cilurzo wines includes Chardonnay, Chenin Blanc, Sauvignon Blanc, white Zinfandel, Cabernet Sauvignon, Petite Sirah, and Pinot Noir.

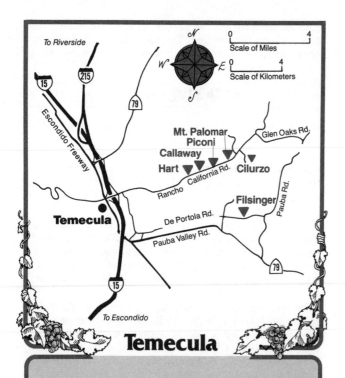

Temecula

Callaway Vineyard & Winery. From I-15, Rancho California Rd. exit, E 4 mi. (32720 Rancho California Rd., Temecula, CA 92390) Tel (714) 676-4001. Picnic. M-Su 10-5. GT/Ta.

Cilurzo Vineyard & Winery. From I-15, Rancho California Rd. exit, E 5.5 mi. to Calle Contento, S .25 mi. (41220 Calle Contento, Temecula, CA 92390) Tel (714) 676-5250. Picnic. Daily 9-5. GT/Ta.

Filsinger Vineyards & Winery. From I-15, State 79 exit, E 4.8 mi. to Anza Rd., N .5 mi. to De Portola Rd., then E 2.8 mi. (39050 De Portola Rd., Temecula, CA 92390) Tel (714) 676-4594. Picnic. Sa-Su 11-5, weekdays by appt. GT/Ta.

Hart Winery. From I-15, Rancho California Rd. exit, E 3.8 mi. (41300 Avenida Biona, Temecula, CA 92390) Tel (714) 676-6300. Picnic. Sa-Su 11-4, weekdays by appt. IT/Ta.

Mt. Palomar Winery. From I-15, Rancho California Rd. exit, E 5 mi. (33820 Rancho California Rd., Temecula, CA 92390) Tel (714) 676-5047. Picnic. Daily 9-5. GT/Ta.

Piconi Winery. From I-15, Rancho California Rd. exit, E 4.5 mi. (33410 Rancho California Rd., Temecula, CA 92390) Tel (714) 676-5400. By appt. only.

Key: GT (guided tour); IT (informal tour); Ta (tasting).

Filsinger Vineyards and Winery is not only family owned but also family built. Whenever they could spare time from their demanding regular jobs, Bill and Kathy Filsinger planted vineyards, built cellars, and made wine.

Moved by stories of earlier generations of family winemaking in Germany, they began with vines in 1974, first made wine in 1980, and opened for sales and visitors in 1981.

The white stucco, Spanish colonial-style building housing their tasting room and bottled wines has tile floors, a handsomely carved bar, Casablanca fans, and other refined details that make it one of the most pleasant places to visit in the district. The winery proper hides a hundred or so yards away behind a small knoll. A prefabricated metal building with a wood-frame extension, it is not the architectural equal of its companion structure but remains an instructive example of what a small, modern winery should be. The proprietors do not press visitors to look through it, but they and their winemaker are glad to show it off to those who ask.

The wines are Emerald Riesling, Chardonnay, Sauvignon Blanc, Gamay Beaujolais, and Petite Sirah.

Hart Winery is a small winery by the modest standards of a district full of small wineries and is almost a one-person cellar. The boxy, brown, plywood-covered cellar perches on a shelf cut into a typical Temecula sandy knoll directly next to the one Callaway Vineyard & Winery is on. In contrast to the neighboring winery, to step through the front door here is to see all there is of equipment.

Owner-winemaker Travis Hart welcomes visitors when he has wine to sell. When he has none, he posts a "sold out" notice on his roadside sign and, like as not, spends the day elsewhere at more fruitful tasks.

The list from the first vintage, 1980, included Chardonnay, Sauvignon Blanc, Semillon, Cabernet Blanc, Cabernet Sauvignon, and Merlot.

Mt. Palomar Winery announces itself by means of a loudly painted, upright redwood wine tank perched on a grassy slope above Rancho California Road. The winery proper hides on the reverse slope.

The property of John Poole, Mt. Palomar is set efficiently into a side slope, much as old cellars were in turn-of-the-century Napa or Sonoma. The stemmer-crusher feeds grapes down into a galley containing stainless steel fermentors and a pneumatic Europress. This is where the new ends: the fermentors feed new wine into a cave full of venerable oak oval casks and new French barrels. (Outdoors is a sun-baked solera for Sherry types.)

Tours cover all of these points, as well as a small bottling line, ending up in the tasting and sales room. The owner has thoughtfully added a small deli to the tasting room in compensation for the remoteness of his site. Picnic tables in a grove of trees are available to first-comers.

The Mt. Palomar wines available for tasting include Chardonnay, Chenin Blanc, Sauvignon Blanc, Riesling (regular and late-harvest), Cabernet Sauvignon, Gamay Beaujolais, and—rare bird—a dessert Cabernet Sauvignon made after the fashion of Ruby Port.

More Wineries. In the early 1980s, several established small cellars comprised what was to have been the vanguard of an eagerly anticipated viticultural new wave in the Temecula district. By 1985 the initial surge had subsided; rather than swelling, the ranks had thinned. In 1987, however, there were new indications (in the form of winery bond applications and construction permits) that a regional boom was again imminent.

Piconi Winery is almost an old-timer by now. It was completed in time for the 1982 crush by Dr. John Piconi, formerly a partner in the Cilurzo & Piconi Winery (now Cilurzo Vineyards & Winery). Piconi had been making his own wine in other quarters for several years before embarking on construction of his own facility. Visitors are welcome by appointment.

Plotting a Route

Nothing could be simpler than organizing a day of winery touring in Temecula. Rancho California Road exits east from Interstate Highway 15 at the town of Temecula about midway between Riverside and San Diego. All but one of the region's visitable wineries lie along that road within six miles of the freeway. The lone exception is found on a parallel road three miles to the south.

San Diego County

Escondido is the agricultural heart of San Diego County. A dramatically hilly countryside between sea on one side and desert on the other, it gets enough water to grow avocados, citrus, and some grapes.

Once highly respected for its wines, the district dwindled almost to extinction as a vineyard after Prohibition but is now making a modest comeback.

Not quite large enough to call for a pilgrimage, it is close enough to San Diego to make a pleasant day trip. It also can be visited in combination with Temecula, some 27 miles to the north via Interstate Highway 15.

The Wineries

San Diego County has two old-timers and three relative newcomers.

Bernardo Winery, one of the old-timers, is a surprising place in almost every respect. Tucked into a narrow draw behind a classy country club development, the property looks a bit like a main street movie set from an old western. More than merely looking the part, the place is actually a village of shops, of which the winery is one.

Visitors can buy indoor plants, worked silver, antique mirrors, and heaven knows what else in addition to wine.

Winery and tasting room sit on the uphill side of the main street, at its intersection with a side road. Both are wooden buildings, welcoming and more than faintly time-worn. Tours of the cellars are informal, offering an instructive look at a working example of a basket press and at other equipment not often in use these days.

Some long-aged dessert wines lead the roster.

Ferrara Winery dates from the same era as Bernardo and has a similar cellar full of old upright redwood tanks and some kindred wines. It also has the warm, familial air that makes visitors feel notably welcome.

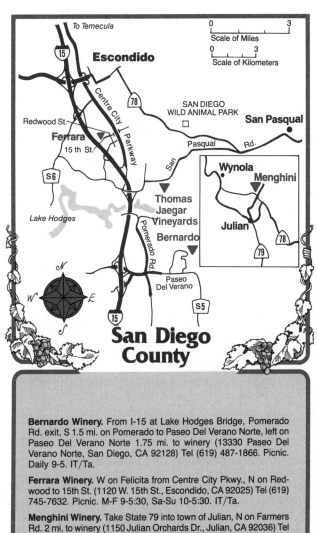

Bernardo Winery. From I-15 at Lake Hodges Bridge, Pomerado Rd. exit, S 1.5 mi. on Pomerado to Paseo Del Verano Norte, left on Paseo Del Verano Norte 1.75 mi. to winery (13330 Paseo Del Verano Norte, San Diego, CA 92128) Tel (619) 487-1866. Picnic. Daily 9-5. IT/Ta.

Ferrara Winery. W on Felicita from Centre City Pkwy., N on Redwood to 15th St. (1120 W. 15th St., Escondido, CA 92025) Tel (619) 745-7632. Picnic. M-F 9-5:30, Sa-Su 10-5:30. IT/Ta.

Menghini Winery. Take State 79 into town of Julian, N on Farmers Rd. 2 mi. to winery (1150 Julian Orchards Dr., Julian, CA 92036) Tel (619) 765-2072. Picnic. F-Sa-Su 10-4, M-Th by appt. IT/Ta.

Thomas Jaegar Vineyards. From I-15, 3 mi. S of Escondido, Via Rancho Pkwy. exit, NE 1 mi. to San Pasqual Rd., then E (13455 San Pasqual Rd., Escondido, CA 92025) Tel (619) 741-0855. Picnic. Daily 11–5. Ta. Sa–Su or by appt. GT.

Key: GT (guided tour); IT (informal tour); Ta (tasting).

It differs in singleness of purpose. No galaxy of shops surrounds the winery, which hides away at the end of a quiet residential street not far from the downtown.

Ferrara also differs from Bernardo in having a few surprisingly contemporary touches, not the least of which is an elegant stainless steel stemmer-crusher.

A small patch of vines marks the property. The winery is tucked in behind the family home and can be seen only from two doorways—one leading to the fermentors, the other to the aging cellar. Tasting is conducted in a comfortable building between house and cellar.

Menghini Winery is tucked among apple orchards in the high country east of Escondido. Julian is an apple community first and last, but grapes have been making modest inroads since 1982, when Michael and Tony Menghini made a winery out of a stucco apple-packing shed dating from the 1940s. They removed a couple of joists to make room for big stainless steel fermentors, and filled the rest of the space with processing equipment and French oak barrels.

The 4,500-foot elevation balances the roster in favor of white varietals. The Menghinis produce Chardonnay, Sauvignon Blanc, Riesling, Muscat Canelli, Chenin Blanc, a rosé of Gamay, and Cabernet Sauvignon. Tasting is conducted in the cellar, among the tanks. The picnic area overlooks a landscape that strongly evokes the Gold Rush country; in fact, gold miners beat Johnny Appleseed to Julian by decades.

Thomas Jaegar Vineyards is a new kid in town, different from its old neighbors in every way.

Located on the road leading to the San Diego Zoo's Wild Animal Park, the winery is a plain, fabricated steel building set atop a knoll at one corner of its vineyards. The property dates from 1976.

The vines, within an agricultural preserve, are the source of San Diego County's only estate-bottled, vintage-dated, varietal table wines. At informal weekend open houses, the winery staff explains the modern, well-equipped cellars and offers tasting from a roster that includes Chenin Blanc (dry and off-dry), Sauvignon Blanc, Muscat Canelli, and Gamay. The proprietors also have an arbor-shaded picnic area.

Plotting a Route

Local vinous geography is almost as simple as at Temecula. Three of the wineries are accessible via three consecutive exits from Interstate Highway 15. None is more than a mile off the freeway.

Getting to Julian takes a little more driving, but it's not difficult. From Escondido, take State Highway 78 roughly 35 miles to its intersection with State Highway 79; bear south 7 miles to Julian.

For information on accommodations write to the Escondido Visitors & Information Bureau, 720 North Broadway, Escondido, CA 92025. The San Diego Convention and Visitors Bureau, Suite 824, 1200 Third Avenue, San Diego, CA 92101, offers county information.

Cucamonga

A wide, relatively unpopulated strip separates Ontario from Fontana. Within it lies nearly all of the present-day Cucamonga wine district.

Cucamonga hardly exists as a specific place; it is an intersection of Archibald Avenue and Foothill Boulevard, or a post office. The more general description of the area these days would be Pomona Valley. But wine goes back to the 1830s in Cucamonga, and that will be the name of the wine district for as long as its vines endure.

Whatever its name, this is a curious countryside. The San Gabriel Mountains rise sharply on the north, effec-

tively forming a wall on that side of the valley. At the foot of these mountains, a gently sloping and remarkably even alluvial fan runs more than a mile before it flattens out and becomes true valley floor. To the south, a less imposing range of hills called the Jurupas marks the limit for grapevines.

Industry and population press in from both east and west. In the late 1960s, San Bernardino County had 23,000 acres in bearing vines. By 1987 the figure had dwindled to 3,500, the owners of many of these acres allowing vines to die by inches while they await a day of higher land prices.

Still, 3,500 is a considerable acreage, and the history of the vine in this district is long and strong. Furthermore, just because vines are in trouble does not mean wineries are. In these times of fast, efficient transport, grapes are being brought from elsewhere to keep wineries active hereabouts.

The Wineries

It has been a habit among Cucamonga proprietors to play the part of the traditional country winery, selling much—sometimes all—of their production at the cellar door. The custom continues, even though some of the larger cellars have had to build extra doors in favorable locations to make supply and demand come out right.

Get down to business, and there are four full-fledged producing wineries to visit in the Cucamonga district.

J. Filippi Vintage Company, on the edge of Fontana and at the end of a row of industrial concerns, encourages visitors to limit their inspection of the premises to the tasting room, which is comfortably airy.

The working winery has grown right through the walls of its original building in a series of additions, with the result that there is no easy path to follow through it. The earliest walls date from 1934. The most recent additions—a row of foam-insulated stainless steel storage and fermenting tanks—stand outside of all the walls. Persistent visitors may have a look inside, where the working equipment is mostly modern.

On hand for tasting are a number of table, sparkling, and dessert wines. The varietal table wines are produced elsewhere. The generic types are made here, as are several dessert wines, including a specialty called Marsovo (marsala with a trace of egg in it). The labels are Joseph Filippi and Chateau Filippi.

The winery and adjacent family homes are surrounded by an expansive vineyard, all well trained, much of it planted since the mid-1960s. It makes a startling contrast to the dead and abandoned vines across Etiwanda Avenue and elsewhere in the immediate neighborhood.

The Filippi family maintains tasting rooms at other locations in Southern California. They will send a list of addresses on request.

Galleano Winery, after years of shy withdrawal from public attention, opened a tasting room in the early 1970s and now offers tours as well.

Founded by Domenic Galleano in 1933, the property is a perfect evocation of the sort of small, family enterprise that once dotted this whole countryside. The main cellar has tidy rows of ancient redwood tanks, plus some oak. Crusher and presses also go back to an earlier day.

The tasting room is housed in a modest wood-frame building at the rear of a courtyard formed by the main cellar on one side and the family residence on the other. Within, visitors may taste the pride of the house, a local Zinfandel, usually with one of the Galleanos as host. The roster of wines includes other varietals, generics, and some dessert wines. Galleano wines are sold nowhere else.

Opici Winery has a tasting room open to the public. Tucked away at the end of a street next to a platoon of Alta Loma tract homes, the square, flat-roofed, cream-colored building offers a surprising range of wines made in facilities located elsewhere in the district and state.

This is headquarters for the company, which sells most of its wine along the Atlantic seaboard, limiting the home audience to this one outlet. The opportunity to taste and buy at the source is congenial.

Thomas Vineyards, in Cucamonga, is housed in the oldest winery building still standing and in use in California. At least part of the adobe structure dates from 1839, when Governor Juan Batista Alvarado of Mexico deeded the property to a winegrower named Tiburcio Tapia. (The east end of the building dates from only 1969, but is a faithful restoration of the original, which was washed away in a flood.) The owners are the Joseph A. Filippi family.

The wines, labeled Thomas Vineyard and Old Rancho, are available for tasting and sale only on the premises. Visitors are free to wander through an aging cellar full of fine old oak ovals, and out back, where there is a modest collection of old winemaking equipment.

Other Than Wineries

The most notable tourist attraction other than wineries in this region is the annual Los Angeles County Fair. It runs during the last two weeks of September, the right time for a companion look at the new vintage in progress. The grounds are located north of Interstate Highway 10 in Pomona.

A number of motels and restaurants can be found in the area. For specific information write to the Greater Los Angeles Visitors and Convention Bureau, 515 S. Figueroa, 11th Floor, Los Angeles, CA 90071.

Plotting a Route

The towns of Ontario and Upland run into one another so smoothly that the change is imperceptible to all but devoted readers of roadside signs. Together, the communities straddle every major east-west road between Los Angeles and the state line. For visitors to wineries, the most useful of these are Interstate Highway 10 (the San Bernardino Freeway) and Foothill Boulevard, a moderately fast four-lane commercial road that once was part of the much-sung-about Route 66.

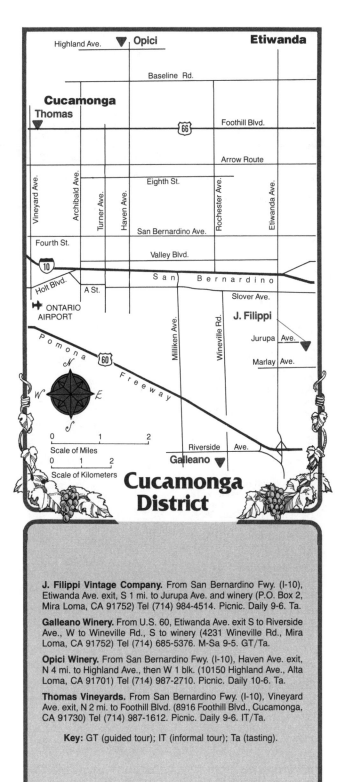

Cucamonga District

J. Filippi Vintage Company. From San Bernardino Fwy. (I-10), Etiwanda Ave. exit, S 1 mi. to Jurupa Ave. and winery (P.O. Box 2, Mira Loma, CA 91752) Tel (714) 984-4514. Picnic. Daily 9-6. Ta.

Galleano Winery. From U.S. 60, Etiwanda Ave. exit S to Riverside Ave., W to Wineville Rd., S to winery (4231 Wineville Rd., Mira Loma, CA 91752) Tel (714) 685-5376. M-Sa 9-5. GT/Ta.

Opici Winery. From San Bernardino Fwy. (I-10), Haven Ave. exit, N 4 mi. to Highland Ave., then W 1 blk. (10150 Highland Ave., Alta Loma, CA 91701) Tel (714) 987-2710. Picnic. Daily 10-6. Ta.

Thomas Vineyards. From San Bernardino Fwy. (I-10), Vineyard Ave. exit, N 2 mi. to Foothill Blvd. (8916 Foothill Blvd., Cucamonga, CA 91730) Tel (714) 987-1612. Picnic. Daily 9-6. IT/Ta.

Key: GT (guided tour); IT (informal tour); Ta (tasting).

The whole district is divided into a tidy gridwork by local roads. The most useful of the north-south arteries are Vineyard, Archibald, and Etiwanda avenues.

Index